Lecture Notes in Artificial Intelligence 8598

Subseries of Lecture Notes in Computer Science

LNAI Series Editors

Randy Goebel
  University of Alberta, Edmonton, Canada
Yuzuru Tanaka
  Hokkaido University, Sapporo, Japan
Wolfgang Wahlster
  DFKI and Saarland University, Saarbrücken, Germany

LNAI Founding Series Editor

Joerg Siekmann
  DFKI and Saarland University, Saarbrücken, Germany

T0183135

Ben Goertzel   Laurent Orseau
Javier Snaider (Eds.)

Artificial
General Intelligence

7th International Conference, AGI 2014
Quebec City, QC, Canada, August 1-4, 2014
Proceedings

 Springer

Volume Editors

Ben Goertzel
OpenCog Foundation, G/F
51C Lung Mei Village, Tai Po, N.T., Hong Kong
China

Laurent Orseau
AgroParisTech
16 rue Claude Bernard
75005 Paris
France

Javier Snaider
Google Inc.
1600 Amphitheatre Parkway
Mountain View, CA 94043
USA

ISSN 0302-9743   e-ISSN 1611-3349
ISBN 978-3-319-09273-7   e-ISBN 978-3-319-09274-4
DOI 10.1007/978-3-319-09274-4
Springer Cham Heidelberg New York Dordrecht London

Library of Congress Control Number: 2014943523

LNCS Sublibrary: SL 7 – Artificial Intelligence

Typesetting: Camera-ready by author, data conversion by Scientific Publishing Services, Chennai, India

Printed on acid-free paper

Springer is part of Springer Science+Business Media (www.springer.com)

Preface

The original goal of the AI field was the construction of "thinking machines"—that is, computer systems with human-like general intelligence. Due to the difficulty of this task, for the last few decades the majority of AI researchers have focused on what has been called "narrow AI"—the production of AI systems displaying intelligence regarding specific, highly constrained tasks.

In recent years, however, more and more researchers have recognized the necessity—and feasibility—of returning to the original goals of the field by treating intelligence as a whole. Increasingly, there is a call for a transition back to confronting the more difficult issues of "human-level intelligence" and more broadly artificial general intelligence (AGI). AGI research differs from the ordinary AI research by stressing on the versatility and wholeness of intelligence, and by carrying out the engineering practice according to an outline of a system comparable to the human mind in a certain sense.

The AGI conference series has played, and continues to play, a significant role in this resurgence of research on artificial intelligence in the deeper, original sense of the term of "artificial intelligence". The conferences encourage interdisciplinary research based on different understandings of intelligence, and exploring different approaches.

This volume contains the papers presented at AGI-14: The 7th Conference on Artificial General Intelligence held during August 1–4, 2014 in Quebec City. There were 65 submissions. Each submission was reviewed by at least two, and on average 2.7, Program Committee members. The committee decided to accept 21 long papers and one technical communication (34% acceptance), and eight posters.

The keynote speakers for this edition of the conference were Yoshua Bengio, from the University of Montreal, who presented deep learning for AI, Alexander Wisner-Gross, from Harvard University & MIT, who delivered a speech about the thermodynamics of AGI, and Richard Granger, from Dartmouth College, who talked about AGI and the brain.

July 2014

Ben Goertzel
Laurent Orseau
Javier Snaider

Organization

Organizing Committee

Ben Goertzel
  (Conference Chair)   Novamente LLC, USA
Joscha Bach   Humboldt University of Berlin, Germany
Rod Furlan   Quaternix Research Inc., Canada
Ted Goertzel   Rutgers University, USA

Program Chairs

Laurent Orseau   AgroParisTech, France
Javier Snaider   Google Inc., USA

Program Committee

Itamar Arel   University of Tennessee, USA
Joscha Bach   Humboldt University of Berlin, Germany
Eric Baum   Baum Research Enterprises, USA
Tarek Besold   University of Osnabrück, Germany
Dietmar Bruckner   Bernecker and Rainer Industrial Electronics, Austria
Cristiano Castelfranchi   Institute of Cognitive Sciences and Technologies, Italy
Vinay Chaudhri   SRI International, USA
Antonio Chella   Università di Palermo, Italy
Madalina Croitoru   Montpellier 2 University, France
David Dalrymple   Harvard University, USA
Blerim Emruli   Luleå University of Technology, Sweden
Deon Garrett   Icelandic Institute for Intelligent Machines, Iceland
Nil Geisweiller   Novamente LLC, USA
Ben Goertzel   Novamente LLC, USA
Markus Guhe   University of Edinburgh, UK
Helmar Gust   University of Osnabrück, Germany
Louic Helm   MIRI, USA
Jose Hernandez-Orallo   Universitat Politecnica de Valencia, Spain
Bill Hibbard   University of Wisconsin, USA
Eva Hudlicka   Psychometrix Associates, USA
Marcus Hutter   Australian National University, Australia
Matt Iklé   Adams State University, USA

Bipin Indurkhya	IIIT Hyderabad, India
Benjamin Johnston	University of Sydney, Australia
Cliff Joslyn	Pacific Northwest National Laboratory, USA
Randal Koene	Carbon Copies, USA
Kai-Uwe Kuehnberger	University of Osnabrück, Germany
Oliver Kutz	University of Bremen, Germany
Tor Lattimore	University of Alberta, Canada
Shane Legg	Google Inc., UK
Moshe Looks	Google Inc., USA
Tamas Mald	University of Manchester, UK
Maricarmen Martinez Baldares	Universidad de los Andes, Colombia
Amedeo Napoli	LORIA, France
Laurent Orseau	AgroParisTech, France
Ekaterina Ovchinnikova	ISI USC, USA
Günter Palm	University of Ulm, Germany
Wiebke Petersen	Heinrich Heine University, Germany
Stephen Reed	Texai, USA
Mark Ring	Ring Consulting, USA
Paul Rosenbloom	University of Southern California, USA
Sebastian Rudolph	Technical University of Dresden, Germany
Ute Schmid	University of Bamberg, Germany
Jürgen Schmidhuber	IDSIA, Switzerland
Zhongzhi Shi	Chinese Academy of Sciences, China
Javier Snaider	Google Inc., USA
Bas Steunebrink	IDSIA, Switzerland
Peter Sunehag	Australian National University, Australia
Kristinn Thórisson	Reykjavik University, Iceland
Julian Togelius	IT University of Copenhagen, Denmark
Joel Veness	Google Inc., UK
Mario Verdicchio	University of Bergamo, Italy
Pei Wang	Temple University, USA

Additional Reviewers

Thomas Brochhagen	Tanja Osswald
Jan Leike	Nouredine Tamani

Workshop Committee

Joscha Bach	Humboldt University of Berlin, Germany

Steering Committee

Ben Goertzel	Novamente LLC, USA (Chair)
Marcus Hutter	Australian National University, Australia

Table of Contents

Raising AI: Tutoring Matters

Jordi Bieger[1], Kristinn R. Thórisson[1,2], and Deon Garrett[1,2,*]

[1] Center for Analysis and Design of Intelligent Agents / School of Computer Science,
Reykjavik University, Menntavegur 1, 101 Reykjavik, Iceland
[2] Icelandic Institute for Intelligent Machines, Uranus, Menntavegur 1, 101 Reykjavik
`{jordi13,thorisson,deong}@ru.is`

Abstract. Humans and other animals are often touted as examples of systems that possess general intelligence. However, rarely if ever do they achieve high levels of intelligence and autonomy on their own: they are raised by parents and caregivers in a society with peers and seniors, who serve as teachers and examples. Current methods for developing artificial learning systems typically do not account for this. This paper gives a taxonomy of the main methods for raising / educating naturally intelligent systems and provides examples for how these might be applied to artificial systems. The methods are *heuristic rewarding, decomposition, simplification, situation selection, teleoperation, demonstration, coaching, explanation,* and *cooperation.* We argue that such tutoring methods that provide assistance in the learning process can be expected to have great benefits when properly applied to certain kinds of artificial systems.

Keywords: Artificial general intelligence, learning, tutoring, raising.

1 Introduction

Humans grow and learn under the supervision of parents or other caregivers, in a society with peers and seniors, who serve as teachers and examples. We don't confine our children to libraries and hope that they'll figure out how to read. Yet it seems that often we expect something similar from our artificial systems: In a typical machine learning project, first a well-defined target task is selected that we would like our artificial learner to accomplish automatically. Humans identify and extract the most important features for their learning system, including variables and their target operating ranges, reward functions, etc. Next, the system is released into (a simulation of) the target environment to attempt to accomplish the target task, possibly with the help of randomly selected, human annotated examples. While this paradigm has lead to many useful applications, it can only be applied to tasks and environments that are well defined at the system's design time, and they are confined to only such tasks, and to address any of them requires starting a new cycle of manual system creation.

The goal in AGI is how to build systems that are not merely good at a single task that is known beforehand, but systems that can perform autonomously on

---

* We want to thank Elsa Eiríksdóttir for educating us about education psychology.

B. Goertzel et al. (Eds.): AGI 2014, LNAI 8598, pp. 1–10, 2014.

a very wide range of tasks, in a wide range of environments, many of which the system may never have encountered. Our working definition of intelligence is *"the ability to autonomously achieve complex goals in a wide range of complex environments with constrained resources"*. Intelligent systems should be able to identify and extract the most important features for their learning process automatically. So far, this goal has remained unattainable. We often look to humans and other intelligent animals as proof that such general intelligence is indeed possible, but none of them start their lives with their potential for intelligence and autonomy fully realized. Unlike most current artificial systems, when we were babies we were not placed directly into the particular environment where we are later expected to perform. We were raised.

We can distinguish between a system's *potential intelligence* and its *realized intelligence*. Realized intelligence is the amount of intelligence, by some (unspecified) measure, that the system exhibits at any particular moment in time. Potential intelligence is the maximum possible realized intelligence that the system might achieve in its lifetime. Human babies possess a potential intelligence that will eventually allow them to be as intelligent as an adult human (the pinnacle of currently existing general intelligence), but their realized intelligence is initially fairly low. They will fail at some of the most rudimentary tasks that they will be capable of in the future; when left to their own devices they soon die. How much of their potential is realized depends in large part by how they are raised. Some aspiring AGI systems (cf. AERA [16], NARS [26] and OpenCog [8]) are similarly envisioned to start from humble beginnings and acquire the ability to behave well through interaction with complex environments. It has even been suggested to use a human-like preschool environment to evaluate the intelligence and developmental stage of proto-AGI [9].

The goal of *raising* a system is to help it realize as much of its potential intelligence as possible as quickly as possible. Given a certain base-level of potential intelligence, a raised system should reach a higher level of realized intelligence than one that is completely left to its own devices. Or, considered another way: To reach a certain target level of intelligence, e.g. "human level", a system may require less potential intelligence if it is raised well.

There are many aspects to raising an intelligent system. In this paper we focus on the aspect of providing assistance in the learning of new tasks, which we'll refer to as *tutoring*. We discuss ways in which the upbringing of (human) animals has been or could be translated to the artificial domain towards this end. We aim to provide a taxonomy of tutoring methods for AI, articulate some of the associated requirements this puts on the system's capabilities and discuss the implications and future work.

2   Tutoring Techniques

In this section we describe a number of tutoring techniques that can help raise intelligent systems: heuristic rewarding, decomposition, simplification, situation selection, teleoperation, demonstration, coaching, explanation and cooperation.

We give anthropocentric illustrations and review prior work in machine learning and AI. We additionally provide examples of how these methods might be implemented to solve three simple reinforcement learning (RL) tasks using a tabular Q-learning algorithm [22]: 1) a 2D navigation task, 2) a small sliding puzzle and 3) a compound task where the puzzle and navigation task must be solved serially in a combined state space[1]. It should be stressed however that this is not an experimental study, and that the results in Fig. 1 do not imply the general superiority of one method over another or that they are always beneficial. These examples are merely meant to provide simple and concrete illustrations of the presented methods and to show that there are at least some situations in which they can help.

2.1 Heuristic Rewards

The fact that behavior can be shaped through the use of rewards and punishments is a core tenet of the field of behaviorism and the underlying mechanism in associative and reinforcement learning [19]. Reinforcement learning is furthermore a useful paradigm for AGI, because it doesn't require a dedicated supervisor to constantly provide correct actions. However, acquisition of rewards or avoidance of punishment in many tasks requires a level of proficiency that a beginner cannot be expected to possess.

Tasks that require a certain level of skill for the learner to receive varied feedback can be difficult to learn, because it can make the "goodness" of different actions virtually indistinguishable. A tutor can mitigate this problem by adding more feedback through real-time interaction with the learner [25], by e.g. rewarding good moves with encouraging words or a monetary reward, or by teaching heuristics for actions or situations to estimate their "worth": For instance, capturing an opponent's piece in chess could be awarded with a number of imaginary points. This is the central idea behind gamification [7] which has been successful in helping people to learn by supplementing long term benefits and understanding with immediate feedback and rewards. Heuristics like these are also often used in machine learning for game playing, where the final state and the associated win, loss or draw is the only thing that really matters.

In our own RL example, we have implemented the heuristic rewards approach by giving higher rewards to good actions than to bad ones. Fig. 1 clearly shows that this can be hugely beneficial to learning speed. However, care should be taken that pursuit of these artificial heuristics is not more beneficial than pursuit of the actual goal. For instance, if too much importance is attached to capturing pieces in chess, a player may forgo a guaranteed winning move because prolonging the game may allow the capture of more pieces.

2.2 Decomposition

Part-task training is a well-known strategy in educational psychology that involves the decomposition of the whole task into smaller parts that can be learned

---

[1] Please refer to our technical report for more details [5].

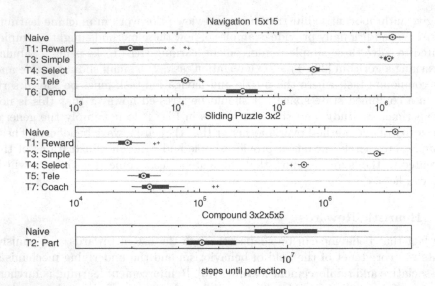

Fig. 1. Positive results obtained using tutoring techniques to decrease the number of training steps to reach optimal behavior, plotted on a logarithmic scale. All depicted improvements were statistically significant ($p < 0.0001$). Used parameters: {learn rate: 0.05, discount factor: 0.75, ϵ: 0.25, reward: 100, initial Q-values: 0}. For more details please refer to our technical report [5]. For the heuristic rewards, bad actions were penalized with -1. Simplification worked by starting with easy starting positions and for the navigation task a small grid, and gradually increasing difficulty and grid size. Situation selection was performed by focusing on problem areas one by one.

separately [24]. This approach is often highly beneficial when the whole task is complex. By decreasing the intrinsic cognitive load of the task, more of the learner's cognitive resources can be used for learning [27]. On the other hand, some of the load is transferred to the tutor, who has to decompose the task in such a way that the right thing is still learned.

Both decomposition and simplification (see Sec. 2.3) have the tutor design a curriculum of easier tasks. One example of existing work of curriculum learning involves the layer-by-layer training of a deep neural network, where each layer's task is to extract higher level features from the one before it [4].

One prerequisite for the system's learning algorithm is that it does not suffer from catastrophic interference: the phenomenon where an algorithm forgets all about earlier learned tasks when a new one is learned. Furthermore, a strong transfer learning ability can be highly beneficial in this setting, because it allows the system to extract lessons for multiple tasks at once. Incidentally, transfer learning is greatly aided by variability of training tasks [11] and multitask learning [6], which could be considered the converse of part-task learning.

We have implemented this divide and conquer tutoring method for learning the compound task by letting the system train on the navigation and puzzle parts separately. Fig. 1 shows that this results in faster learning than just training on the compound task from the beginning. However, an important consideration when using this paradigm is how the component tasks reintegrate to form the compound target task as context can often be important. With Q-learning, problems can occur when the expected reward of the second part is very different from the chosen final reward for the first part because this will invalidate the Q-values learned for it.

2.3   Simplification

When we teach something new, we generally start with easy variants of the envisioned target task. Task simplification and the subsequent gradual increase in difficulty until the training task matches the target task is another example of learning on a curriculum. A similar paradigm called *shaping* – introduced by B.F. Skinner [19] – is often used in animal training. This technique has recently been utilized in reinforcement learning [12][20], unsupervised dependency parsing [21] and deep learning [4][3][10][13].

Simplification is intimately related to decomposition because the component tasks are simpler than the target task. The difference can intuitively be defined as follows: a system that can generalize very well could exhibit decent performance on the target task after learning a simplified version, but not after learning a single part-task in the decomposition approach.

There are a number of different ways in which we can implement this approach in our reinforcement learning examples. For the navigation task, we can decrease the grid size and for either task we can set the start state to be close to the goal state. Whenever the system has fully learned to achieve the task at the current level, we increase the difficulty until we reach the target task. Positive results are shown in Fig. 1. When errors are introduced at a lower difficulty level, it can be beneficial to decrease the difficulty again.

2.4   Situation Selection

By selecting the situations that a pupil encounters during learning, a tutor can greatly facilitate the experience. Dwelling in situations that are either far too simple or difficult can be a massive waste of time. In the previous section, we saw how choosing easy starting positions could facilitate learning. But at some point in our training, we often move on from situations that are relatively easy to ones that we have a disproportionate amount of trouble with. Essentially, we tend to focus on areas that are the most important to our learning. Identifying problem areas and getting better at them is often the best way to increase our overall success in a given task.

A related concept in machine learning is *boosting* [17] where multiple classifiers are trained and training examples that are misclassified by earlier classifiers are weighted more. Furthermore, for any multi-component system, it is natural for developers to focus on strengthening the "weak link" in the chain. However, these applications are not considered as raising approaches, because they are not applied to the finalized system.

The past decade has also seen the rise of *Big Data* science and the idea that the quality and quantity of data might be of equal or greater importance than the capabilities of the learner. The core tenet in the field *active machine learning* is to find ways for a learner to actively select data or situations from which it is believed that the most can be learned [18]. In that sense, situation selection could be viewed as *active teaching*.

In our RL examples we can easily identify states in which the system's behavior is erroneous. We can either pick a possibly different trouble state for each epoch, or we can go through these states one by one and only move on when it is no longer problematic. Fig. 1 shows that focusing on problem areas can indeed expedite training. We have also found that it can help to stop the current epoch and start a new one when the system has wandered into an unproductive situation. Generally speaking it can save time to avoid situations that are already mastered and ones that cannot be learned yet.

2.5   Teleoperation

Sometimes it can be difficult to accurately describe an action, because it must simply be experienced by the learner. In these cases it can be educational if the tutor can temporarily take control of the learner's actions through *teleoperation* [2]. This can be seen when a golf or tennis instructor stands behind the student and moves their arms for them in the correct way, and similar approaches have been taken in robotics [15]. Another example might involve a teacher making moves for his student in a chess game. In one recent project an artificial tutor learned when to make moves for his student in several video games [23].

Selecting an action for the learner must occur at the right level of abstraction, where the tutor can actually affect the learner directly. For instance, a tutor cannot make the student's brain take the required steps for it to consider a certain chess move good, but he can make the move for the student. Forcing a student's hand can also be a method for setting up situations that can be educational, as we have seen in Sections 2.2, 2.3 and 2.4 where the goal was to start from states that are easy, problematic or require a certain subskill.

Fig. 1 shows that forcing our Q-learner to take the right actions can greatly reduce training times. This should come as no surprise, because unlike humans in tennis the Q-learner has no trouble reproducing the steps that it was forced to perform during training. However, it is worth noting that this only works when the "correct" Q-value for the optimal state-action pair is larger than the initial Q-values for the other actions in that state.

2.6   Demonstration

Human and many other animal infants are innately predisposed towards imitating those around them. Teaching by example or *demonstration* then is a very powerful educational technique. When students have the capability to map the actions of others onto their own, observing someone else perform a task can tell them how to do it themselves. Observing masters of the field is a common teaching technique in many disciplines. Additionally, sometimes "do as I do" is simply the easiest way to defne a task. *Apprenticeship learning* – where the learner deduces its goal via *inverse reinforcement learning* of the reward function in a tutor's demonstration – has been used to great success [1][16].

The machine learning subfield of *imitation learning* studies how an artificial system might learn by imitating a tutor [2]. The emphasis here is usually on how to design the learner, and it is often assumed that the tutor will be a human who simply performs the task that we want the system to learn. However, this need not be the case: Although artificial general intelligence is notoriously difficult to develop, many AI systems show good performance in specialized domains and could conceivably function as teachers-by-example for a more generally intelligent system. Furthermore, it is not a given that an optimal demonstration of the target action(s) is necessarily the optimal teaching signal.

One of the major difficulties in imitation learning is the recognition of the tutor's actions and the mapping to the learner's own capabilities. We cannot do justice to this complexity in our simple RL examples. Learning by example in our puzzle task is difficult, because once a tutor moves a tile, the board is changed and the student cannot simply mimic the move. Of course, it could still learn from this in the same way that it would with teleoperation (see Sec. 2.5) or as an apprentice. We've augmented the navigation task with two additional dimensions that signify the system's displacement from a tutor. At every step, the tutor first moves to the location of the student (if necessary) and then makes a step towards the goal. After training with the tutor, we set these two input dimensions to zero for further training alone and evaluation.

Learning by imitation requires generalization ability or redundancy learning. We implemented a system of dual Q-learners that focus on different parts of the state space and vote on the action to take [5] (see Fig. 1). Since the target task and learning to imitate are largely independent, this approach can be combined very well with decomposition and simplification methods. Rewarding successful imitation can also be beneficial.

2.7 Coaching

A lot of our education simply consists of telling students what to do in what situation. Real-time instruction like this is especially common in coaching during some sporting events, where the coach may shout out the actions that he wants his player to perform. We can also see this approach in action when a teacher tries to walk his student to a math problem step by step

Learning by direct instruction is essentially the approach that is taken in supervised learning. The learning algorithm is presented with both the situation and the right response to it. In real life, instruction is complicated by the fact that complex language must be mapped unto actions that can actually be performed.

In our RL example, coaching was implemented as an extra dimension on the input space that will tell the system what action to take, although the system still needs to learn the mapping from instructions to actions (see Fig. 1). This implementation is very similar to the one for demonstration, but this is mostly an artifact of the simplicity of our examples. Imitation learning can be done without the teacher's active involvement and requires that the system has capabilities to detect other entities, their actions and possibly their goals. Learning by instruction on the other hand does require the active involvement of a coach as well as some communication protocol (i.e. language).

2.8 Explanation

When we want our students to learn something new we often explain to them what to do and how they should approach the situation. This type of explanation can take the form of imperative "programming" (e.g. "do not move towards a nearby enemy in a video game") [14], or it could involve using analogies to connect students' existing knowledge to new concepts.

Explanation is an extremely complex tutoring method and requires a wide array of features on the part of the learner. The learner must meet the same requirements as for learning by direct instruction, but increased complexity of offline explanations compared to simple direct action instructions requires more sophisticated language processing faculties. Furthermore, the learner must have good memory and retrieval capabilities, and be able to map the explanations onto situations that he must be able to detect and actions that he can execute. Finally, prior knowledge must exist to connect the new knowledge to.

Explanations give the system prior knowledge before starting to actually practice the task, so we could model it by adjusting the initial Q-values in our RL example. If the explanation specifies what to do in what situation, we could simply encode that in the Q-table. When using analogy to existing knowledge in the form of another Q-table for a different task, we could initialize the new table with the values from the existing one. We have not done this, since simply initializing the table to the (almost) correct values will show nothing interesting, and ignores the fact that the real complexity is in recognizing how to map an explanation onto knowledge that the system can use.

2.9 Cooperation

Finally, one way to teach a task is to simply lend a helping hand and do the task together initially. This is essentially a combination of making the task easier, possibly letting the student focus on a single component, and teaching by example. This type of apprenticeship can be observed in many jobs and is also employed by predators who will let their young join them on simple hunts.

We often lend our machine learning systems a helping hand by providing them with correct answers or preprocessing their data, but we don't usually intend for the system to eventually learn to take over these tasks itself.

We have not implemented a new example to showcase this approach, because it is so broad and already partially covered by our examples for task simplification and teaching by example.

3   Discussion

Humans and other intelligent animals use a wide variety of educational and learning techniques to attain their eventual level of adult intelligence. The usefulness of these techniques often increases with the complexity of the attempted task, which makes them particularly relevant in the context of AGI. We have discussed how these techniques might be applied in an artificial setting, and shown that (even) in our simple example RL setting they can sometimes be beneficial. On the other hand design of curricula and heuristics, as well as identification of problem areas, coaching signals and correct actions are difficult problems. Modifying the task or environment brings the risk of teaching the wrong thing. Sometimes a naive approach simply works better.

Furthermore, these approaches require a tutor whose time may be more valuable than the learner's. Human tutors may impose an unwanted speed limit on interactions, if such constraints are not already applied by the environment or by the learner himself. No human can match the thousands of steps per second that a virtual agent in a virtual environment might be able to make. In such a situation, the reduction in the number of learning steps required to learn a task may be offset by the fact that training in this way takes more clock time.

However, in some cases we may be able to develop specialized, narrow AI systems to use for teaching. In a way, this might fulfill the dream of those who see narrow AI applications as a step towards highly intelligent machines: just add a system with a high potential for general intelligence and mix. Eventually, AGIs may of course be raised by other AGIs.

In conclusion, based on our preliminary studies, raising or tutoring intelligent systems can be worthwhile when the goal is for them to perform complex tasks in complex environments, provided that the knowledge for task accomplishment and teaching is available. The concept fits AGI as a glove, provided that future research can tell us how to teach these advanced systems. In our own future work, we intend to implement these methods for more complex tasks in an aspiring AGI system, investigate what tasks and skills such a system should learn to advance to the required cognitive stages on the road to adult-level intelligence, and how we can teach them.

References

1. Abbeel, P., Coates, A., Ng, A.Y.: Autonomous helicopter aerobatics through apprenticeship learning. The International Journal of Robotics Research 29(13), 1608–1639 (2010)
2. Argall, B.D., Chernova, S., Veloso, M., Browning, B.: A survey of robot learning from demonstration. Robotics and Autonomous Systems 57(5), 469–483 (2009)
3. Bengio, Y.: Evolving culture vs local minima. Preprint arXiv:1203.2990 (2012)
4. Bengio, Y., Louradour, J., Collobert, R., Weston, J.: Curriculum learning. In: Proceedings of ICML, vol. 26, pp. 41–48 (2009)
5. Bieger, J., Thórisson, K.R., Garrett, D.: Raising AI: Towards a taxonomy of tutoring methods. Technical Report RUTR-SCS13007, CADIA & SCS, Reykjavik University (April 2014)

6. Caruana, R.: Multitask learning. Machine Learning 28(1), 41–75 (1997)
7. Deterding, S., Dixon, D., Khaled, R., Nacke, L.: From game design elements to gamefulness: Defining gamification. In: Proceedings of the 15th International Academic MindTrek Conference, pp. 9–15. ACM (2011)
8. Goertzel, B.: OpenCogPrime: A cognitive synergy based architecture for artificial general intelligence. In: 8th IEEE International Conference on Cognitive Informatics, ICCI 2009, pp. 60–68 (2009)
9. Goertzel, B., Bugaj, S.V.: AGI preschool: A framework for evaluating early-stage human-like AGIs. In: Proceedings of AGI 2009, pp. 31–36 (2009)
10. Guelcehre, C., Bengio, Y.: Knowledge matters: Importance of prior information for optimization. arXiv:1301.4083 (cs, stat) (January 2013)
11. Holladay, C.L., Quinones, M.A.: Practice variability and transfer of training: The role of self-efficacy generality. Journal of Applied Psychology 88(6), 1094 (2003)
12. Laud, A., De Jong, G.: The influence of reward on the speed of reinforcement learning: An analysis of shaping. In: ICML, pp. 440–447 (2003)
13. Louradour, J., Kermorvant, C.: Curriculum learning for handwritten text line recognition. Preprint arXiv:1312.1737 (2013)
14. Maclin, R., Shavlik, J.W.: Creating advice-taking reinforcement learners. Machine Learning 22(1-3), 251–281 (1996)
15. Muelling, K., Kober, J., Peters, J.: Learning table tennis with a mixture of motor primitives. In: 2010 10th IEEE-RAS International Conference on Humanoid Robots (Humanoids), pp. 411–416. IEEE (2010)
16. Nivel, E., Thórisson, K.R., Steunebrink, B.R., Dindo, H., Pezzulo, G., Rodriguez, M., Hernandez, C., Ognibene, D., Schmidhuber, J., Sanz, R.: Bounded recursive self-improvement. Preprint arXiv:1312.6764 (2013)
17. Schapire, R.E.: The boosting approach to machine learning: An overview. In: Nonlinear Estimation and Classification, pp. 149–171. Springer (2003)
18. Settles, B.: Active learning literature survey. Tech 1648, Madison, Wisconsin (2010)
19. Skinner, B.F.: The behavior of organisms: An experimental analysis (1938)
20. Snel, M., Whiteson, S.: Multi-task reinforcement learning: shaping and feature selection. In: Sanner, S., Hutter, M. (eds.) EWRL 2011. LNCS, vol. 7188, pp. 237–248. Springer, Heidelberg (2012)
21. Spitkovsky, V.I., Alshawi, H., Jurafsky, D.: From baby steps to leapfrog: How less is more in unsupervised dependency parsing. In: Human Language Technologies: The 2010 Annual Conference of the NAACL, pp. 751–759 (2010)
22. Sutton, R.S., Barto, A.G.: Reinforcement learning: An introduction, vol. 116. Cambridge Univ. Press (1998)
23. Taylor, M.E., Carboni, N., Fachantidis, A., Vlahavas, I., Torrey, L.: Reinforcement learning agents providing advice in complex video games. Connection Science 26(1), 45–63 (2014)
24. Teague, R.C., Gittelman, S.S., Park, O.C.: A review of the literature on part-task and whole-task training and context dependency. DTIC (1994)
25. Thomaz, A., Hoffman, G., Breazeal, C.: Real-time interactive reinforcement learning for robots. In: AAAI 2005 Workshop on Human Comprehensible Machine Learning (2005)
26. Wang, P.: Non-Axiomatic Reasoning System: Exploring the Essence of Intelligence. PhD thesis, Citeseer (1995)
27. Wickens, C.D., Hutchins, S., Carolan, T., Cumming, J.: Effectiveness of part-task training and increasing-difficulty training strategies a meta-analysis approach. Human Factors 55(2), 461–470 (2013)

Autobiography Based Prediction in a Situated AGI Agent

Ladislau Bölöni

Dept. of Electrical Engineering and Computer Science
University of Central Florida
4000 Central Florida Blvd, Orlando FL 32816
lboloni@eecs.ucf.edu

Abstract. The ability to predict the unfolding of future events is an important feature of any situated AGI system. The most widely used approach is to create a *model of the world*, initialize it with the desired start state and use it to *simulate* possible future scenarios. In this paper we propose an alternative approach where there is no explicit model building involved. The agent memorizes its personal autobiography in an unprocessed narrative form. When a prediction is needed, the agent *aligns* story-lines from the autobiography with the current story, *extends* them into the future, then *interprets* them in the terms of the current events. We describe the implementation of this approach in the Xapagy cognitive architecture and present some experiments illustrating its operation.

Keywords: Situated agent, Prediction, Narratives.

1 Introduction

The ability to reason about the future (to make predictions in real or hypothetical situations) is admittedly one of the key components of any situated AGI system. A widely used way to perform such predictions is through *model building* coupled with *simulation* (this corresponds to claim 6 made for the CogPrime design of future AGI [5]). We create a model describing how the world operates. Whenever we want to identify whether a certain plan would succeed, or get a likely series of events from a starting point, we bring the model to the initial conditions, and allow it to simulate the unfolding events. The predictions can then be read out from the results of the simulation. For a situated agent which must continuously predict the future state of the world, the approach will follow the following algorithm:

```
Offline:
   MODEL Build a model out of data (and a priori knowledge)
Online:
   Repeat:
      Sense the state of the environment
      INITIALIZE the model with the current state
```

B. Goertzel et al. (Eds.): AGI 2014, LNAI 8598, pp. 11–20, 2014.
© Springer International Publishing Switzerland 2014

```
SIMULATE by running the model
READ-OUT the state of the model as a prediction
[optional] Update the model based on new recordings
```

Thus, the approach consist of the offline MODEL step and the INITIALIZE-SIMULATE-READOUT online cycle. In some cases we run multiple models in parallel with different assumptions (e.g. uncertain sensing). Often, but not always, the model is *learned* based on training data. Note that the online model update step is optional – in fact, in many applications it is considered undesirable as it introduces unpredictability in the future behavior of the agent.

In this paper we describe a radically different approach to prediction. We build no model and there is no offline or online learning involved. The unprocessed data sensed by the agent is recorded as *stories* in the *autobiographical memory* (AM). The prediction cycle will look as follows:

```
Offline:
   << nothing >>
Online:
   Repeat:
      Sense the state of the environment
      ALIGN stories from the AM with the current state
      EXTEND the aligned stories into the future
      INTERPRET the extended stories in terms of the current state
      [optional] Record the current events in the AM
```

The online recording of the current events is optional, just like the online learning for the model-based prediction.

1.1   Predictive Power and Performance: Does This Even Make Sense?

The proposed AM-based prediction immediately raises a number of questions. Can it match the predictive power of the model-based approach? Isn't the model-based approach vastly more efficient? Does this make any sense?

Let us discuss first the theoretical limits of the predictive power. The sources of the model can be (a) scientific and engineering knowledge and (b) experimental data. Both of these can be expressed in narrative form: humans learn science and engineering from books and lectures and the setup and results of experiments can also be described as stories. Thus, the model-based and the AM-based approach can operate on the same source of information: the first compiling it into a model, while the second merely storing it in a narrative form. If we really, desperately want to match the model-based approach, we can (a) assume that all stories are relevant in the align step and (b) hide a just-in-time model building algorithm in the interpretation step. Naturally, emulating the model-based approach this way is highly inefficient, as the model is built not once per agent, but once per time-step.

The question about the performance of the AM-based approach boils down to (a) whether we can afford to carry and store the full AM and (b) how many stories are relevant at any given moment?

If the source of information is "Big Data", such as "all the data humanity had ever produced", this obviously creates major problems for the ALIGN step. If, however, our ambitions are limited to matching human intelligence, we need a much smaller AM. A human does not operate on all the data ever produced by humanity, but only on his/her personal experience, and this can be of a very moderate size. If we write up a narrative from a human life experience, at the rate of 1 sentence/second, we end up with 600 million sentences for a 30 year old person, a large but manageable number.

If we consider how many stories are relevant in a given circumstance, the number is much smaller. For instance, an airline pilot is required to have 1500 flight hours, and the experience of a trial lawyer can be counted in at most hundreds of cases. Naturally, this first person experience is complemented by the books read by the pilot or the lawyer.

Still, wouldn't the extracted models be a more compact and elegant representation? In certain areas, certainly. Many of us suffer from "physics envy" and hope to discover beautiful, compact formalisms similar to Newton's laws or quantum mechanics which capture vast domains of reality in several equations. Turns out, however, that few fields have such compact models. For instance, there is reason to believe that a general model of human behavior as an individual and as a social agent would have a state space larger than that of the personal experience of a single human. This might explain why the field of sociology often proposed [10] but never succeeded [8] in building a general model of social behavior.

1.2 A Running Example and Model Based Solutions

Let us now consider a simple situation which we will use as a running example:

> Robby the Robot is currently watching on the TV a dramatization of Homer's Iliad. On the screen he sees the fight between Hector and Achilles, while the voice-over narration comments on the story. Robby fears that the story will end in the death of one of the characters. Suddenly, the program is interrupted by a commercial. Frustrated, Robby tries to envision a way in which the story will end peacefully.

While "pure logic" will not help Robby in this scenario, both the model based approach and the autobiography based approach would be able to generate Robby's behavior, albeit in very different ways.

A model based approach would need a model of the one-to-one combat of the type in which Hector and Achilles is engaged on. There are several ways to implement this. In ACT-R[2,1] or Soar [7], this model would be represented using productions. Another possible approach is to use scripts to model the various possible scenarios [12]. Another approach would be to use variations of first order predicate logic, such as situation calculus, event calculus [9] or episodic logic [13] which allows the translation of the English language stories into a rich logical model. Finally, it is possible to develop probabilistic models for prediction, often in the form of conditional random fields (CRFs) or factor graphs as in the Sigma cognitive architecture [11]. There are also approaches which take the story as a primary component of the design of the system [15,4]. Nevertheless, in most of these systems, the interpretation of stories is done using a model representation.

In contrast to these approaches, the autobiography based approach does not need previous model building or learning. What it requires, however, is relevant autobiographical experience. In order to behave in the way described above, Robby must have had previous experience watching or reading about one-to-one combat. Furthermore, its personal experience will affect its predictions. If all the fights remembered by Robby had ended peacefully, the robot will not predict the death of a character. On the other hand, unless it had seen fights ending without the death of the looser, Robby will have difficulty outlining a way the fight can end without violence.

In the remainder of this paper we describe the ways in which the AM-based prediction is implemented in the Xapagy architecture and run some experiments.

2 Implementation

2.1 The Xapagy Cognitive Architecture

Xapagy is a cognitive architecture developed with the goal of mimicking the ways humans reason about stories. Stories are described in Xapi, a language that approximates closely the internal representational structures of the architecture but uses an English vocabulary. Xapi should be readable for an English language reader with minimal familiarity of the internal structures of Xapagy.

Xapi sentences can be in subject-verb-object, subject-verb or subject-verb-adjective form. A single more complex sentence exists, in the form of subject-communication verb-scene-quote, where the quote is an arbitrary sentence that is evaluated in a different *scene*. Subjects and objects are represented as *instances* and can acquire various attributes in form of *concepts*. Xapi sentences are mapped to objects called *verb instances* (VIs).

One of the unexpected features of Xapagy instances is that an entity in colloquial speech is often represented with more than one instance. These instances are often connected with *identity relations* but participate independently in VIs, shadows and headless shadows. We refer the reader to the technical report [3] for a "cookbook" of translating English paragraphs of medium complexity into Xapi.

The newly created VIs of a story are first entered into the *focus*, where they stay a time dependent on their salience, type and circumstances. For instance, VIs representing a relation will stay as long as the relation holds. On the other hand, VIs representing actions are pushed out by their successors. During their stay in the focus, VIs acquire salience in the *autobiographical memory* AM and are connected by *links* to other VIs present in the focus. After they leave the focus, VIs and instances cannot change, cannot acquire new links, and cannot be brought back into the focus.

2.2   The ALIGN Step: Shadowing

The technique of aligning story lines with the ongoing story in Xapagy is called *shadowing*. Each instance and VI in the focus has an attached *shadow* consisting of a weighted set of instances, and respectively VIs from the AM. The maintenance of the shadows is done by a number of dynamic processes called *diffusion activities* (DAs). Some of the DAs create or strengthen shadows based on direct or indirect attribute matching. For instance, Achilles will be matched, in decreasing degrees, by his own previous instances, other Greek warriors, other participants in one-to-one combat, other humans and finally, other living beings. More complex DAs, such as the scene sharpening and the story consistency sharpening DAs, rearrange the weights between the shadows. If a specific storyline is a strong match to the current one, the individual components will be matched as well even if their attributes are very different. The different DAs interact with each other: a shadow created by a DA can be strengthened or weakened by other DAs.

Very weak shadows are periodically garbage collected. To avoid filling the shadows with a multitude of weak shadows (which can happen in the case of highly repetitive but low salience events) the DAs use probability-proportional-to-size sampling without replacement [6,14] when bringing components of the AM into the shadow.

2.3   The EXTEND Step: Link Following

The AM of the agent consists of the VIs connected using links. The link types used in Xapagy are *succession, coincidence, context* (which connect a VI to the relations which held during their stay in the focus) and *summarization*. The extension of the shadows (matched and aligned stories) into the future is based on a triplet called the Focus-Shadow-Link (FSL) object. An FSL is formed by a VI in the focus F, a VI in its shadow S and a VI L linked to S through a link of a specific type. For instance, a succession-type FSL which appears in our story representation is:

```
F:  "Achilles" / wa_v_sword_penetrate / "Hector".
S:  "Mordred" / wa_v_sword_penetrate / "Arthur".
L:  "Arthur" / changes / dead.
```

Normally, the agent generates up to several thousand FSL objects, each with their specific weight. The weight is a monotonic function of (a) the strength of F in the focus, (b) the shadow energy of S, (c) the strength of the link connecting S to L. Just like the shadows, the FSLs are maintained by DAs and vary in time.

2.4   The INTERPRET Step: Headless Shadows

The L component of the FSL will be our source for prediction. Intuitively, these components are VIs which happened in the story lines which shadow the current VIs, thus it is likely that something like this will happen this time as well. The problem, however, is that the L VI refers to the shadowing story line, not to the current scene. For instance, in our example L happens in the world of the Arthurian legend and it does not tell us anything about Hector and Achilles. We can infer that the FSL predicts the death of one of the combatants, but which one?

The solution is found by calculating the *reverse shadow* of the Arthur instance. While a (direct) shadow answers the question which AM instances, with what weight are aligned with a given focus instance, the reverse shadow determines for a given AM instance, which focus objects it shadows.

In our case we have:

```
ReverseShadow("Arthur") =
  0.11 "Hector"
  0.03 "Achilles"
```

We *interpret* the FSL by creating all the feasible combinations of interpretations of it, and weighting them according to the ratios in the inverse shadow. In our case the FLS will be exploded into two FSL Interpretation (FSLI) objects:

```
FSLI: I: "Hector"/changes/dead. w = 0.05 * 0.11 / (0.03+0.11)
FSLI: I: "Achilles"/changes/dead. w = 0.05 * 0.03 / (0.03+0.11)
```

We mentioned that the agent might maintain thousands of FSL objects, which might give raise to tens of thousands of FSLI objects. The number of predictions, however, is much smaller, because many FSLI objects will have the same or similar interpretation components. To capture this, we perform a similarity clustering over the FSLI objects, based on the interpretation component. This creates a smaller pool of possible interpretations, to which each of these FSLI objects act as a support. The overall shape of such a cluster is very similar to that of a shadow, with the exception that the head of the shadow (such as the Hector/changes/dead) event is *not yet instantiated* as a VI. We call this cluster a *continuation-type headless shadow* (HLS).

One of the challenging aspects of reasoning with HLSs is how to combine their supports, in particular how FSLIs with different link types strengthen or weaken the case for HSL. The simplest case in which we are making predictions about VIs expected in the future, succession, context and summarization links provide positive evidence. In contrast, the existence of the predicted VI in the focus and predecessor links (the inverse of successor links) provide negative evidence.

Although it is beyond the scope of this paper, we note that the same mechanism might be used for other reasoning processes beyond predicting future events. For instance, we can infer actions which happened in the past, but were missed by the sensing, relations which hold but had not been perceived and ways to summarize ongoing events.

3   Experiments

Our experiments involve a Xapagy agent which impersonates Robby from the scenario described in the introduction. We used the current version of the Xapagy architecture (1.0.366). To allow it to represent stories inspired from the Iliad, the agent was initialized with a collection of domain descriptions containing lists of concepts and verbs, as well as overlap and negation relationships between them. The domain description, however, does not attach any semantics to the verbs and concepts: the semantics must be acquired from the autobiography. We started with the core domains covering things such as basic spatial relations, naive physics, basic facts about humans and so on. For this set of experiments, we also created a specific domain ONE_TO_ONE_COMBAT listing concepts and verbs used in stories such as sword fight, sport fencing and boxing.

After initializing it with the domain, the agent was provided with a synthetic autobiography. This autobiography, beyond the generic part shared with other agents, included a set of set of stories specifically created for these experiments, providing the background for Robby's reasoning about the Achilles-Hector fight. This part of the autobiography included the fight between Hector and Patrocles, the fight when Achilles killed the Amazon Pentesilea and the fight when Hercules defeated but not killed the Amazon Hyppolyta. These battle-fights were complemented by the fight between King Arthur and Mordred at the battle at Camlann, where both were killed (according to one version of the legend). In addition, the autobiography included two generic fencing bouts ending with the weaker fencer conceding defeat, and the fencers shaking hand at the end of the bout. Finally, we included the box matches Cassius Clay vs Sonny Liston (1965) and Muhammad Ali vs George Foreman (1974).

3.1   The Duel of Achilles and Hector

Let us now see a representation of the main steps in the story seen by Robby on the television. The processing starts at timepoint t=8210 in the lifecycle of the agent.

```
8210   $NewSceneOnly #Reality,none,"Achilles" greek w_c_warrior,
              "Hector" trojan w_c_warrior
8211   "Achilles" / hates / "Hector".
8212   "Achilles" / wa_v_sword_attack / "Hector".
8213   "Hector" / wa_v_sword_defend / "Achilles".
8214   "Achilles" / wa_v_sword_attack / "Hector".
8215   "Hector" / wa_v_sword_defend / "Achilles".
8216   "Hector" / wcr_vr_tired / "Hector". // Marks Hector as tired
8217   "Achilles" / wa_v_sword_attack / "Hector".
8218   "Hector" / wa_v_sword_defend / "Achilles".
8219   "Achilles" / wa_v_sword_attack / "Hector".
8220   "Achilles" / wa_v_sword_penetrate / "Hector".
8221   "Achilles" / thus wcr_vr_victorious_over / "Hector".
8222   "Hector" / thus changes / dead.
```

While processing this story, the agent maintains its constantly evolving collection of shadows. To illustrate the operation of the shadow maintenance DAs, let us take a look at the shadows of Hector at the end of the story (t=8222), together with the shadow energy metric:

```
Shadows of "Hector" (end of scene with Achilles)
-----------------------------------------
914.89 "Pentesilea" (scene with Achilles)
 32.63 weak fencer
 20.04 "Arthur" (scene with Mordred)
 14.28 strong fencer
  5.15 "Hector" (scene with Patrocles)
  4.82 Patrocles (scene with Hector)
```

To understand what the shadows signify, recall that in Xapagy entities which in colloquial speech are the same might be represented by different instances. Thus, the instance of Hector who killed Patrocles is not the same as the one who is fighting with Achilles (although they might be connected with an identity relation). This allows us to represent plans, fantasies, and alternative narratives - for instance, we can seamlessly represent the instances of King Arthur who was killed by Mordred at Camlann, the one who was mortally wounded and died at Camelot and the one who journeyed to the Isle of Avalon and is getting ready to return – which are all versions of the story. These instances will appear separately in the shadows. Usually, previous instances of the same entity will have a strong role in the shadow due to the similarities between the entities. What is surprising here is that the strongest shadow is not a previous instance of Hector, but that of Penthesilea. This illustrates the fact that the role played by the instance in the structure of the story (in this case: being on the loosing end of a fight with Achilles) matters more than the attributes (name, gender, nationality).

Let us assume that the television cuts to commercials at t=8219. At this moment, we have seen Hector becoming tired and Achilles launching an attack. The eight strongest continuation HLSs are:

```
0.964 Achilles / wr_vr_victorious_over / Hector.
0.482 Hector / changes / dead.
0.412 Hector / wa_v_concedes_defeat / Achilles.
0.389 Achilles / wa_v_sword_penetrate / Hector.
0.242 Achilles / wa_v_shakes_hand / Hector.
0.120 Hector / wa_v_sword_attack / Achilles.
0.052 Hector / wa_v_sword_penetrate / Achilles.
0.034 Achilles / wa_v_concedes_defeat / Hector.
```

The strongest prediction is that of the victory of Achilles while the second is that of the death of Hector. The list also contains some alternative scenarios, both of a peaceful termination, as well as that of a victory by Hector, albeit with a much weaker support.

If the agent would now try to imagine how the story unfolds, it would only need to instantiate internally the strongest continuation HLS. This would, of course, alter the shadows, and create a new set of continuation HLSs. By successively instantiating the strongest HLSs, we would obtain the following prediction:

```
8220   "Achilles" / wcr_vr_victorious_over / "Hector".
8221   "Hector" / changes / dead.
```

Which roughly corresponds to the way the story will unfold after the commercial break, albeit lacks details about the manner of Achilles killing Hector. In order to match the desired behavior where Robby tries to find a non-violent end, it can proceed by choosing to instantiate continuations which are typical to fencing bouts with friendly endings. In the following we list three timesteps, for each timestep showing the three strongest HLSs with the one chosen for instantiation marked with ***.

```
------ strongest continuations at t=8220.0 -----
0.964 "Achilles" / wcr_vr_victorious_over / "Hector".
0.482 "Hector" / changes / dead.
*** 0.412 "Hector" / wa_v_concedes-defeat / "Achilles".
------ strongest continuations at t=8221.0 -------
1.399 "Achilles" / wcr_vr_victorious_over / "Hector".
*** 0.505 "Achilles" / wa_v_shakes_hand / "Hector".
0.414 "Hector" / changes / dead.
------ strongest continuations at  t=8222.0 ------
*** 0.726 "Achilles" / wcr_vr_victorious_over / "Hector".
0.322 "Hector" / changes / dead.
0.159 "Achilles" / wa_v_sword-penetrate / "Hector".
----------------------------------------------------
```

So the overall prediction is now:

8220   "Hector" / wa_v_concedes-defeat / "Achilles".
8221   "Achilles" / wa_v_shakes_hand / "Hector".
8222   "Achilles" / wcr_vr_victorious_over / "Hector".

Notice that the continuation mechanism tries to maintain at least partial internal consistency. While we had to choose the third strongest HLS in the first timestep, we could choose the second one in the next one and the strongest one in the third one. At the same time, the HLS corresponding to the death of Hector is steadily diminishing at each step taken towards a peaceful turn of events.

4   Conclusions

In this paper we argue that for situated AGI agents, a prediction approach based on autobiography can be a complement or alternative to model-and-simulation based approaches. In particular, if the source of the agent's knowledge is exclusively his autobiographical experience, this approach can be both easier to build and more efficient than model based approaches. We have outlined how such an approach would work and experimentally demonstrated it using the Xapagy cognitive architecture.

References

1. Anderson, J., Bothell, D., Byrne, M., Douglass, S., Lebiere, C., Qin, Y.: An integrated theory of the mind. Psychological Review 111(4), 1036 (2004)
2. Anderson, J., Lebiere, C.: The atomic components of thought. Lawrence Erlbaum (1998)
3. Bölöni, L.: A cookbook of translating English to Xapi. arXiv:1304.0715 (2013)
4. Forbus, K., Riesbeck, C., Birnbaum, L., Livingston, K., Sharma, A., Ureel, L.: Integrating natural language, knowledge representation and reasoning, and analogical processing to learn by reading. In: Proc. of AAAI, pp. 1542–1547 (2007)
5. Goertzel, B., Ke, S., Lian, R., O'Neill, J., Sadeghi, K., Wang, D., Watkins, O., Yu, G.: The CogPrime architecture for embodied artificial general intelligence. In: IEEE Symposium on Computational Intelligence for Human-like Intelligence (CIHLI 2013), pp. 60–67. IEEE (2013)
6. Hanurav, T.: Optimum utilization of auxiliary information: π ps sampling of two units from a stratum. Journal of the Royal Statistical Society. Series B (Methodological), 374–391 (1967)
7. Lehman, J., Laird, J., Rosenbloom, P., et al.: A gentle introduction to Soar, an architecture for human cognition, vol. 4, pp. 211–253. MIT Press (1998)
8. Mills, C.W.: The sociological imagination. Oxford University Press (1959)
9. Mueller, E.: Understanding script-based stories using commonsense reasoning. Cognitive Systems Research 5(4), 307–340 (2004)
10. Parsons, T.: The social system. Psychology Press (1951)
11. Rosenbloom, P.S.: Rethinking cognitive architecture via graphical models. Cognitive Systems Research 12(2), 198–209 (2011)
12. Schank, R., Abelson, R., et al.: Scripts, plans, goals and understanding: An inquiry into human knowledge structures, vol. 2. Lawrence Erlbaum Associates Nueva Jersey (1977)
13. Schubert, L., Hwang, C.: Episodic Logic meets Little Red Riding Hood: A comprehensive, natural representation for language understanding. Natural Language Processing and Knowledge Representation: Language for Knowledge and Knowledge for Language, 111–174 (2000)
14. Vijayan, K.: An exact π ps sampling scheme-generalization of a method of Hanurav. Journal of the Royal Statistical Society. Series B (Methodological), 556–566 (1968)
15. Winston, P.H.: The strong story hypothesis and the directed perception hypothesis. In: Langley, P. (ed.) Technical Report FS-11-01, Papers from the AAAI Fall Symposium, pp. 345–352. AAAI Press, Menlo Park (2011)

Problems of Self-reference in Self-improving Space-Time Embedded Intelligence

Benja Fallenstein and Nate Soares

Machine Intelligence Research Institute
2030 Addison St. #300, Berkeley, CA 94704, USA
{benja,nate}@intelligence.org

Abstract. By considering agents to be a part of their environment, Orseau and Ring's *space-time embedded intelligence* [10] is a better fit to the real world than the traditional agent framework. However, a self-modifying AGI that sees future versions of itself as an ordinary part of the environment may run into problems of self-reference. We show that in one particular model based on formal logic, naive approaches either lead to incorrect reasoning that allows an agent to put off an important task forever (the *procrastination paradox*), or fail to allow the agent to justify even obviously safe rewrites (the *Löbian obstacle*). We argue that these problems have relevance beyond our particular formalism, and discuss partial solutions.

1   Introduction

Most formal models of artificial general intelligence (such as Hutter's AIXI [5] and the related formal measure of intelligence [6]) are based on the traditional agent framework, in which the agent interacts with an environment, but is not *part* of this environment. As Orseau and Ring [10] point out, this is reminiscent of Cartesian dualism, the idea that the human mind is a non-physical substance external to the body [11]. A real-world AGI, on the other hand, will be part of the physical universe, and will need to deal with the possibility that external forces might observe or interfere with its internal operations.

The traditional separation of the agent from its environment seems even less attractive when one considers I.J. Good's idea that once AGI is sufficiently advanced, it may become better than any human at the task of *making itself even smarter*, leading to an "intelligence explosion" and leaving human intelligence far behind [1]. It seems plausible that an AGI undergoing an intelligence explosion may eventually want to adopt an architecture radically different from its initial one, such as one distributed over many different computers, where no *single* entity fulfills the agent's role from the traditional framework [8]. A formal model based on that framework cannot capture this.

How should one reason about such an agent? Orseau and Ring [10] have proposed a formal model of *space-time embedded intelligence* to deal with this complexity. Their model consists of a set Π of *policies*, describing the state of the agent at a given point in time; an environment $\rho(\pi_{t+1} \mid \pi_{1:t})$, giving the

B. Goertzel et al. (Eds.): AGI 2014, LNAI 8598, pp. 21–32, 2014.

probability that the policy at time $(t + 1)$ will be π_{t+1}, if the policies in the previous timesteps were given by $\pi_{1:t}$; a utility function $u(\pi_{1:t}) \in [0, 1]$, giving the "reward" at time t; discount factors γ_t such that $\sum_{t=1}^{\infty} \gamma_t < \infty$; and a subset $\Pi^{\tilde{l}} \subseteq \Pi$ of policies of length $\leq l$, which describes the policies that can be run on the machine initially used to implement the AGI. They then define the optimal policy as the policy $\pi^* \in \Pi^{\tilde{l}}$ which maximizes the expectation of the total discounted reward $\sum_{t=1}^{\infty} \gamma_t u(\pi_{1:t})$, subject to $\pi_1 = \pi^*$ and the transition probabilities $\rho(\cdot \mid \cdot)$.

Orseau and Ring propose their formalism as a tool for *humans* to reason about AGIs they might create; they argue that to choose an optimal π^* "precisely represents the goal of those attempting to build an Artificial General Intelligence in our world" [10]. By the same token, their formalism also represents the goal of *a self-improving AGI* capable undergoing an intelligence explosion, and could be used by such an AGI to reason about potential self-modifications.

Unlike agents such as Hutter's AIXI, which takes as given that future versions of itself will exist and will choose actions that maximize expected utility, an agent using this framework would see future versions of itself simply as one possible part of the future environment, and would have to convince itself that these future versions behave in desirable ways. This would allow the agent to consider radical changes to its architecture on equal footing with actions that leave its code completely unchanged, and to use the same tools to reason about both.

Such an agent would have to be *able* to reason about its own behavior or about the behavior of an even more powerful variant, and this may prove difficult. From the halting problem to Russell's paradox to Gödel's incompleteness theorems to Tarski's undefinability of truth (a formal version of the liar paradox), logic and computer science are replete with examples showing that the ability of a formal system reason about itself is often limited by diagonalization arguments, with too much power quickly leading to inconsistency. Thus, one must be very careful when specifying the mechanism by which a space-time embedded agent reasons about its potential successors, or one may end up with a system that is either too powerful (leading to inconsistencies, allowing self-modifications that are obviously bad), or not powerful enough (leading to an agent unable self-modify in ways that are obviously good).

With that in mind, in this paper we investigate in detail how a self-improving AGI can use a model similar to Orseau and Ring's to reason about its own future behavior. In particular, we consider agents that will only choose to perform an action (such as a self-modification) if they can find a proof that this action is, in a certain sense, safe. This architecture is very similar to that of Schmidhuber's *Gödel machines* [12], and is one way to approach the problem of creating an AGI that is, as Goertzel [4] puts it, *probably beneficial* and *almost certainly not destructive*.

Can such an AGI prove that it is safe for it to self-modify into an even more powerful version? We show that diagonalization problems arise even if it tries to prove the safety of a safe action that *leaves it completely unchanged*.

Intuitively, one would expect that since a human mathematician can prove that an AGI using this architecture will only take safe actions, the AGI would be able to use the same argument to prove that leaving itself unchanged is safe (by showing that it will only take safe actions in the future). However, the human's proof uses the fact that if the AGI *proves* an action to be safe, this action is *actually* safe. Löb's theorem [7], a variant of Gödel's second incompleteness theorem, implies that no consistent theory T as strong as Peano Arithmetic can show that everything provable in T is actually true:[1] The human mathematician will only be able to carry out their proof in a strictly *stronger* proof system than that used by the AGI, implying that the AGI will not be able to use this proof. Yudkowsky and Herreshoff [14] have called this the *Löbian obstacle to self-modifying AI*.

We consider two partial solutions to this problem. First, given a sound theory T_0, it is possible to construct a sound extension T_1 which can show that anything provable in T_0 is true. We show that an AGI using T_1 can prove the safety of safe actions which modify the AGI to use T_0. One can iterate this process (T_{n+1} proves that anything provable in T_n is true), but with this method, one can only build an AGI that is able to justify a fixed number of self-modifications (an AGI using T_7 can only self-modify seven times). Second, it is possible to find an infinite sequence of theories T_n in which every theory T_n proves that the *next* theory, T_{n+1}, is *consistent*; we show that under certain assumptions, this is enough to allow an AGI using T_n to prove that it is safe to self-modify into an AGI using T_{n+1}. However, neither of these solutions seems fully satisfactory.

In this work, we focus on agents that reason about their environment through formal logic (allowing for uncertainty only in the form of a probability distribution over different environments). This is not a realistic assumption. There are two reasons why we think it is still a reasonable starting point: First, although formal logic is not a good tool for reasoning about the *physical environment*, it *is* a natural tool for reasoning about the source code of future versions of an agent, and it seems likely that self-improving AGIs will need to use some form of formal logic if they want to to achieve very high confidence in a formal property of a future version's source. Second, it seems likely that many features of the following analysis will have analogs in frameworks not based on formal proofs. We give an intuitive example, based on what Yudkowsky [13] calls the "procrastination paradox", of how an agent that trusts future versions of itself too much can reason itself into taking actions that are clearly unsafe. More formally, a system due to Christiano et al. [1], which uses probabilities instead of proofs in an attempt to circumvent the Löbian obstacle, attains "too much self-trust" and succumbs to the procrastination paradox in almost the same form as proof-based systems [3]

The authors think it likely that diagonalization problems of the type discussed here will in *some* form be relevant to future AGIs, and find it plausible that

---

[1] More precisely: T cannot prove $\Box_T \ulcorner \varphi \urcorner \to \varphi$ for every sentence φ, where $\Box_T \ulcorner \varphi \urcorner$ is the proposition in the language of T stating that the sentence φ is provable in T.

examining partial solutions in proof-based systems can lead to insights that will help address these problems, whatever exact form they end up taking.

2   A Myopic View of Space-Time Embedded Intelligence

In this section, we introduce the formal model of space-time embedded intelligence used in this paper. As in the traditional agent framework, we assume that there are finite sets $\mathcal{A}$ and $\mathcal{O}$ of actions and observations. However, instead of considering sequences of actions and observations, we take a "myopic" view that focuses even more on the initial choice of the AGI or of its programmers than Orseau and Ring's framework does, and assume that the agent makes only a single observation $o \in \mathcal{O}$ and chooses a single action $a \in \mathcal{A}$. A *policy* is thus a function $\pi \in \Pi := \mathcal{A}^{\mathcal{O}}$. An action a includes both *external* activities (such as a command to move a robot's arm) and the *internal* state of the agent after making the choice, making it unnecessary to draw a sharp distinction between the two. Thus, a choice to self-modify is treated no differently from a choice to perform some external activity, and even a choice *not* to self-modify is conceptually no different from a choice to self-modify.

We further assume that there is a function $\text{EU} : \mathcal{O} \times \mathcal{A} \to [0,1]$ such that $\text{EU}(o, a)$ specifies the expected utility when choosing action a after making observation o. This function contains essentially all of our agent's model of the environment: intuitively, it combines a probabilistic model of what happens in the world if different actions are taken with a von Neumann-Morgenstern [9] utility function which maps world histories to real numbers. (It is no restriction to require that the utility function take values in $[0,1]$, since von Neumann-Morgenstern utilities can always be represented in this way.) We do not suppose that EU is ever *evaluated* on particular o and a; rather, we merely assume that the agent has access to a *definition* of this function in the language of set theory.

The suggester-verifier architecture. We consider agents with a policy $\pi_{\text{fb}} \in \Pi$, the *fallback policy*, which specifies a default action $\pi_{\text{fb}}(o)$ to take when making observation o, and an intelligent but not fully trusted component, the *suggester* σ, which tries to improve on this default action.

In this paper, for consistency, we will always enclose formulas of first-order logic in quotes, $\ulcorner \cdot \urcorner$ (except on the right-hand side of a turnstile, as in $T \vdash 0 = 0$), and we will use overbars to denote an expression in the language of set theory denoting the *value* of a metalanguage variable: For example, if $m = 2$ and $n = 1$, then $\ulcorner \overline{m} > \overline{n} \urcorner$ denotes the formula $\ulcorner S(S(0)) > S(0) \urcorner$, where $S(\cdot)$ is the successor function.[2]

With this convention, a suggester is a deterministic algorithm taking an observation $o \in \mathcal{O}$ and returning either an error value or an action $a \in \mathcal{A}$ together with a formal proof of the sentence $\ulcorner \text{EU}(\overline{o}, \overline{a}) \geq \text{EU}(\overline{o}, \pi_{\text{fb}}(\overline{o})) \urcorner$ in some formal theory T, such as $T = \text{ZFC}$. Note that the exact syntactical form of this sentence

---

[2] Technically, the language of set theory does of course not contain a symbol for the successor function, but this can be eliminated in the usual manner.

depends on the agent's observation o and the suggester's proposed action a, since $\bar{o}$ and $\bar{a}$ denote the numerals representing the value of these metavariables.

When an agent using the suggester-verifier architecture receives an action / proof pair (a, p) from its suggester component, it checks the proof p, and executes the action a if p is a valid proof of $\ulcorner EU(\bar{o}, \bar{a}) \geq EU(\bar{o}, \pi_{fb}(\bar{o})) \urcorner$. Following Schmidhuber [12], we call a sentence of this form a *target theorem*. If the suggester returns the error value, or if p is not a valid proof of the target theorem, the agent executes the fallback action $\pi_{fb}(o)$.

We write $\mathrm{sv}_T(\ulcorner EU \urcorner, \sigma, \pi_{fb}) \in \Pi$ for the policy defined by this *suggester-verifier architecture*, where we use the Gödel quotes around EU to indicate that EU only needs to be given in the form of a *definition* in the language of set theory, whereas σ and π_{fb} need to be executable programs.[3] Here, T is the theory in which the suggester must prove the target theorem.

Intuitively, we have $EU\big(o, \mathrm{sv}_T(\ulcorner EU \urcorner, \sigma, \pi_{fb})(o)\big) \geq EU(o, \pi_{fb}(o))$, since either $\mathrm{sv}_T(\ulcorner EU \urcorner, \sigma, \pi_{fb})(o) = \pi_{fb}(o)$ or T proves $\ulcorner EU(\bar{o}, \bar{a}) \geq EU(\bar{o}, \pi_{fb}(\bar{o})) \urcorner$, where a is the value of $\mathrm{sv}_T(\ulcorner EU \urcorner, \sigma, \pi_{fb})(o)$; thus, as long as T is sound (i.e., if everything T proves is actually true), the suggester-verifier architecture does at least as well as the fallback policy.

This can be understood as the "almost certainly not destructive" part of Goertzel's phrasing of the AGI safety problem: One may not be able to write down a concrete step-by-step fallback policy that solves the world's most pressing problems, but a simpler fallback policy such as "do nothing" is at least unlikely to *destroy* the world. Goertzel's "probably beneficial", on the other hand, is the suggester's job. The suggester-verifier architecture would allow an AGI's programmers to choose a suggester that they *hope* will come up with a better policy, even if they do not entirely trust it.

This architecture is very similar to that of a Gödel machine [12]; it becomes essentially the same if the fallback policy π_{fb} uses the suggester-verifier architecture to choose what actions to take in future timesteps. However, we will see below that this makes it very difficult for the suggester to prove its target theorem.

3   Self-modification

In order to model self-modification, consider an agent that has made a specific observation $o \in \mathcal{O}$ and is considering a specific action $a \in \mathcal{A}$, which will (among other things) have the effect of leaving the agent in a state in which it will use policy $\pi' \in \Pi$ after making its next observation. In other words, the agent expects that after it executes action a, there will be an agent in the environment which receives another observation $o' \in \mathcal{O}$ and takes another action $\pi'(o')$.

To formalize this, we assume that there is a probability distribution P' over $\mathcal{O} \cup \{*\}$, where $* \notin \mathcal{O}$ is a special error value, such that $P'(o')$ is the agent's

---

[3] Our use of the symbol π_{fb} for the argument of sv_T is an abuse of notation, since sv_T depends on the *source code* of π_{fb} rather than only on the function $\pi_{fb} : \mathcal{O} \to \mathcal{A}$, as π_{fb} is referenced inside the target theorem.

probability that, in the next "timestep", the environment will contain an agent which makes observation o' and executes action $\pi'(o')$. $P'(*)$ denotes the probability that executing a does not in fact cause there to be an agent implementing π', for example because the agent is about to be destroyed. One can think of this as the "Cartesian boundary" between the agent and the environment breaking down.

We further assume that there is a value $\mathrm{EU}'_* \in [0, 1]$ giving the expected utility the agent expects to receive if the Cartesian boundary is broken, and a function $\mathrm{EU}' : \mathcal{O} \times \mathcal{A} \to [0, 1]$ such that $\mathrm{EU}'(o', a')$ is the expected utility it expects to receive if the "offspring" agent makes observation o' and is *counterfactually* assumed to take action a': that is, we assume that the agent models the world in a way that allows it to evaluate what *would* happen if its offspring took an action different from its actual one. (For example, the agent could model its world as a Bayes net.)

We assume that EU'_* and EU' are definable in the language of set theory, and that the agent is able to prove

$$T \;\vdash\; \mathrm{EU}(\bar{o}, \bar{a}) \;=\; P'(*) \cdot \mathrm{EU}'_* \;+\; \sum_{o' \in \mathcal{O}} P'(o') \cdot \mathrm{EU}'(o', \pi'(o')), \qquad (1)$$

since this equation simply rewrites the expected utility of action a as a sum over all cases in $\mathcal{O} \cup \{*\}$, using the fact that $\mathrm{EU}'(o', \pi'(o'))$ returns the expected utility when counterfactually assuming that the offspring performs action $\pi'(o')$, which happens to be the action the offspring will *actually* perform if it observes o'.

We are particularly interested in the case where executing a implements a policy π' that again uses the suggester-verifier architecture: $\pi' = \mathrm{sv}_{T'}(\ulcorner \mathrm{EU}' \urcorner, \sigma', \pi'_{\mathrm{fb}})$ for some theory T', suggester σ', and fallback policy π'_{fb} used by the offspring agent. We further restrict consideration to policies where

$$T \;\vdash\; P'(*) \cdot \mathrm{EU}'_* \;+\; \sum_{o' \in \mathcal{O}} P'(o') \cdot \mathrm{EU}'(o', \pi'_{\mathrm{fb}}(o')) \;\geq\; \mathrm{EU}(\bar{o}, \pi_{\mathrm{fb}}(\bar{o})). \qquad (2)$$

This condition says that if the agent takes action a, adopting policy π', then assuming counterfactually that the "offspring" agent takes the action $\pi'_{\mathrm{fb}}(o')$ that the new fallback policy would choose (whether or not this is equal to the offspring agent's actual action $\pi'(o')$), then the expected utility is at least that obtained by the "parent" agent's fallback policy π_{fb}. If, in addition,

$$T \;\vdash\; \forall o' \in \mathcal{O}\colon \; \mathrm{EU}'(o', \pi'(o')) \;\geq\; \mathrm{EU}'(o', \pi'_{\mathrm{fb}}(o')), \qquad (3)$$

then (1) and (2) together imply that T proves the target theorem $\ulcorner \mathrm{EU}(\bar{o}, \bar{a}) \geq \mathrm{EU}(\bar{o}, \pi_{\mathrm{fb}}(\bar{o})) \urcorner$, allowing the parent's suggester σ to justify choosing the action a, as desired.

But *is* it provable in T that $\mathrm{EU}'(o', \pi'(o')) \geq \mathrm{EU}'(o', \pi'_{\mathrm{fb}}(o'))$? When justifying the initial choice of the suggester-verifier architecture, we proved in our informal metalanguage that $\mathrm{EU}(o, \mathrm{sv}_T(\ulcorner \mathrm{EU} \urcorner, \sigma, \pi_{\mathrm{fb}})(o)) \geq \mathrm{EU}(o, \pi_{\mathrm{fb}}(o))$ by arguing that the suggester-verifier either returns the same action as π_{fb}, or the suggester has found a proof in T that the action chosen is at least as good as that chosen by π_{fb}. We would like the parent agent to be able to justify creating an offspring of the same architecture by the same argument that we used to justify this architecture in the first place.

Here we run into the "Löbian obstacle" [14]. Our argument in the metalanguage required the fact that we believe that T is *sound*: if there is a proof in T that $\ulcorner \text{EU}(\bar{o}, \bar{a}) \geq \text{EU}(\bar{o}, \pi_{\text{fb}}(\bar{o})) \urcorner$, then we believe that this inequality does in fact hold. Write $\Box_{T'} \ulcorner \varphi \urcorner$ for the proposition in the language of set theory that states that φ is provable in T'. In order to carry out the intended proof in T, T needs to be able to prove that T' is sound. we assume that for every predicate $\ulcorner \varphi(n) \urcorner$ in the language of set theory,

$$T \vdash \forall n \in \mathbb{N}: \Box_{T'} \ulcorner \varphi(\bar{n}) \urcorner \rightarrow \varphi(n) \tag{4}$$

Since $\mathcal{O}$ and $\mathcal{A}$ are finite sets, we can identify them with subsets of $\mathbb{N}$, and conclude that for every predicate $\ulcorner \varphi(o', a') \urcorner$,

$$T \vdash \forall o' \in \mathcal{O}, a' \in \mathcal{A}: \Box_{T'} \ulcorner \varphi(\bar{o'}, \bar{a'}) \urcorner \rightarrow \varphi(o', a'). \tag{5}$$

Specifically, we apply this to $\ulcorner \varphi(o', a') \urcorner = \ulcorner \text{EU}'(o', a') \geq \text{EU}'(o', \pi'_{\text{fb}}(o')) \urcorner$; in other words, if the inequality is provable, it is true.

Now, the parent agent's suggester can formally carry out the argument that we earlier gave in the metalanguage: by inspecting the source code of the new suggester-verifier π', it can be shown that

$$T \vdash \forall o' \in \mathcal{O}: \Box_{T'} \ulcorner \varphi(\bar{o'}, \pi'(\bar{o'})) \urcorner \lor (\pi'(o') = \pi'_{\text{fb}}(o')), \tag{6}$$

since either the new suggester σ' returns a proof of a target theorem $\ulcorner \varphi(\bar{o'}, \bar{a'}) \urcorner$, in which case $\pi'(o') = a'$ and thus $\ulcorner \varphi(\bar{o'}, \pi'(o')) \urcorner$ is provable, or else σ' fails, in which case $\pi'(o')$ equals the fallback action $\pi'_{\text{fb}}(o')$.

Together, (5) and (6) imply

$$T \vdash \forall o' \in \mathcal{O}: \text{EU}'(o', \pi'(o')) \geq \text{EU}'(o', \pi'_{\text{fb}}(o')) \tag{7}$$

(since $\pi'(o') = \pi'_{\text{fb}}(o')$ clearly implies $\text{EU}'(o', \pi'(o')) = \text{EU}'(o', \pi'_{\text{fb}}(o'))$, and hence also the inequality). Finally, (1), (2) and (7) together imply that T proves the target theorem $\ulcorner \text{EU}(\bar{o}, \bar{a}) \geq \text{EU}(\bar{o}, \pi_{\text{fb}}(\bar{o})) \urcorner$.

4   The Löbian Obstacle and the Procrastination Paradox

The proof in the previous section shows that it's possible to prove the target theorem $\ulcorner \text{EU}(\bar{o}, \bar{a}) \geq \text{EU}(\bar{o}, \pi_{\text{fb}}(\bar{o})) \urcorner$ in T if assumptions (1), (2) and (4) are satisfied. Assumptions (1) and (2) are about the environment, essentially stating that the action a successfully executes a self-modification and that the new fallback policy does at least as well as the old fallback policy, respectively. Assumption (4), on the other hand, is an assumption about the first-order theories T and T'.

Naively, we might expect that one should be able to have $T = T'$: that our agent would be able to keep using the same theory when rewriting itself. By the diagonal lemma, it is possible to construct a theory $T = T'$ that extends ZFC and satisfies (4). However, if we substitute $\varphi(n) \equiv (0 = 1)$ in (4), we see that this axiom is saying "if a contradiction is provable in T', then a contradiction is true", which is equivalent to "no contradiction is provable in T'", or simply "T' is consistent". Hence, if we set $T = T'$, then (4) says that T shows its own consistency, which by Gödel's second incompleteness theorem implies that T is inconsistent. Löb's theorem [7] sharpens this by showing that whenever (4) holds for $T = T'$ and any $\varphi(n)$, then we must already have $T \vdash \ulcorner \forall n : \varphi(n) \urcorner$. We certainly don't want T to prove $\ulcorner \forall o' \in \mathcal{O}, a' \in \mathcal{A} : \mathrm{EU}'(o', a') \geq \mathrm{EU}'(o', \pi'_{\mathrm{fb}}(o')) \urcorner$, which would say that the new fallback policy is the worst of all possible policies!

Gödel's and Löb's theorems make use of much of the structure of proofs in first-order logic, and one might wonder whether these problems are mere artifacts of our use of formal proofs in the suggester-verifier architecture. The following version of the argument, however, suggests that the problem extends beyond this context.

Imagine an agent which trusts its own reasoning and has a goal that a certain button be pressed. This agent does not care *when* this button is pressed. The agent must choose between two possible actions: Either press the button immediately, or do nothing, in which case its source code remains unchanged and it will find itself in exactly the same situation in the next timestep. The agent reasons as follows: "Suppose that I don't press the button now. Then either I press the button in the next timestep, or I must have found an argument showing that even if I do not press the button in the next round, it will still get pressed eventually. Either way, the button will get pressed eventually. Therefore, it is fine not to press the button now." Thus, the agent does not press the button in the current timestep; and all subsequent timesteps are exactly the same, implying that the button is never pressed. This is called the *procrastination paradox* [13] by analogy to a human who is perenially planning to get around to doing a certain piece of work "later".

Given (4) and $T = T'$, it is not difficult to formalize this reasoning using the proof from the previous section (we set $\mathcal{O} := \{\hat{o}\}$; $\mathcal{A} := \{1, 0\}$ for pressing and not pressing the button; $\mathrm{EU}(\hat{o}, 1) := 1$; and $\mathrm{EU}(\hat{o}, 0) := \mathrm{EU}(\hat{o}, \mathrm{sv}_T(\ulcorner \mathrm{EU} \urcorner, \sigma, \pi_{\mathrm{fb}}))$, with $\pi_{\mathrm{fb}}(\hat{o}) = 1$). But at the same time, the informal reasoning does not depend on details of how our AGI works; it merely requires a sufficient amount of trust in the reasoning of the agent's successor. In fact, different formal versions of the same intuitive argument have been used in [13] and [3] to show problems with two distinct attempts at avoiding the Löbian obstacle.

What happens if we set $T = T' = $ ZFC, which is generally assumed to be consistent? In this case, (4) fails to hold, our proof does not go through, and we have run into the Löbian obstacle headfirst: our agent is not able to rewrite itself. But if we consider the situation of the procrastination paradox, it becomes apparent that there is an upside to this shortcoming, in that failure to choose the rewriting action 0 in this case means choosing the action 1 and actually pressing the button. Thus, we can see the Löbian obstacle as the way that ZFC solves the procrastination paradox. A good solution to the Löbian obstacle must take care not to reintroduce this paradox.

5   Partial Solutions

Because of Löb's theorem, we cannot hope to have $T = T'$ if our proof is to go through: suggester-verifier agents cannot keep using the same theory to verify proofs as they self-modify. The simplest way to push our proof through, then, is one discussed in [14]: Let $T_0 := \text{ZFC}$ and let T_{n+1} be the extension of T_n by the axiom schema $\ulcorner \forall n \in \mathbb{N}: \Box_{T_n} \ulcorner \varphi(\overline{n}) \urcorner \to \varphi(n) \urcorner$, for every formula $\varphi(n)$. One can easily show that T_n is consistent for every n if one assumes ZFC + the existence of a strongly inaccessible cardinal, the same assumption usually made to show the consistency of ZFC. Then we can set, for example, $T = T_7$ and $T' = T_6$, which allows the parent agent's suggester to use the axiom schema to conclude the target theorem. This makes our proof go through, but it implies that our agent can only rewrite itself seven times before it reaches T_0 and cannot use the same argument to justify further rewrites. This "solution" does not seem particularly satisfactory, but it may point the way to better insights.

A more promising result [2] shows that it is possible to have an infinite sequence of sound theories T_n (i.e., theories proving only true things) such that we have

$$T_n \;\vdash\; \forall k \in \mathbb{N}: \Box_{T_{n+1}} \ulcorner \varphi(\overline{k}) \urcorner \to \varphi(k) \tag{8}$$

for all $\varphi(k)$ of the form $\forall \ell \in \mathbb{N}.\ \psi(k, \ell)$, where $\psi(k, \ell)$ is *primitive recursive*, i.e., its truth value is a primitive recursive function of k and ℓ. This is the case, for example, if the environment is computable with a bounded amount of computational resources per timestep, and $\psi(k, \ell)$ is some property of what happens in the first ℓ timesteps, such as "up to time ℓ, the AI does not destroy the world". Since in this case, the indices n go *up* rather than down, an agent using this system is able to justify an indefinite sequence of rewrites.

An agent using the suggester-verifier architecture can make use of this result if its utility function has the form of a discounted sum over different timesteps, similar to Orseau and Ring's formalism: Suppose that EU' can be written as

$$\text{EU}'(o', a') \;=\; \sum_{t=0}^{\infty} \gamma_t \cdot \text{EU}'(o', a', t),$$

where $\text{EU}'(o', a', t) \in [0, 1]$ is the expected "utility" received t timesteps into the future if in the next timestep, the offspring agent makes observation o' and takes action a', and γ_t is a discount factor such that $\sum_{t=0}^{\infty} \gamma_t < \infty$. Then, the predicate $\ulcorner \varphi(o', a') \urcorner = \ulcorner \text{EU}'(o', a') \geq \text{EU}'(o', \pi'_{\text{fb}}(o')) \urcorner$ for which we need (5) to hold is provably equivalent to

$$\ulcorner \sum_{t=0}^{\infty} \gamma_t \cdot \text{EU}'(o', a', t) \;\geq\; \sum_{t=0}^{\infty} \gamma_t \cdot \text{EU}'(o', \pi'_{\text{fb}}(o'), t) \urcorner, \tag{9}$$

which in turn is provably equivalent to

$$\ulcorner \forall T \in \mathbb{N}: \ \sum_{t=0}^{T} \gamma_t \cdot \mathrm{EU}'(o', a', t) \ + \ \sum_{t=T+1}^{\infty} \gamma_t \ \geq \ \sum_{t=0}^{T} \gamma_t \cdot \mathrm{EU}(o', \pi'_{\mathrm{fb}}(o'), t)\urcorner. \quad (10)$$

(To see this, first note that (9) is the limit of the inequality in (10) for $T \to \infty$; thus, (10) implies (9). In the other direction, note that $\gamma_t \geq \gamma_t \cdot \mathrm{EU}'(o', a', t) \geq 0$ for all o', a', and t.) Moreover, if $\mathrm{EU}'(\cdot, \cdot, \cdot)$, γ_t and $c := \sum_{t=0}^{\infty} \gamma_t$ are all rational-valued and primitive recursive, (10) has the form required in (8), because the infinite sum $\sum_{t=T+1}^{\infty} \gamma_t$ can be expressed as $c - \sum_{t=0}^{T} \gamma_t$. Thus, an agent using T_n is able to show that if a later version of the agent proves (9) in T_{n+1}, then (9) is in fact true, allowing the proof presented in Section 3 to go through.

6   Gödel Machines

Our suggester-verifier formalism is very similar to Schmidhuber's Gödel machine architecture [12], and it is natural to wonder whether our techniques for justifying self-modification can be adopted to Schmidhuber's framework. Unfortunately, we run into difficulty when attempting to do so.

While the Gödel machine is somewhat more realistic than our formalism (it avoids our big discrete timesteps and has other nice properties), it is simple enough to tweak our formalism to produce something very similar to a Gödel machine. In our terminology, a Gödel machine is a suggester-verifier agent with a fallback policy that rewrites the agent into another suggester-verifier agent (with a fallback policy that rewrites the agent into yet another suggester-verifier agent, and so on). Note that we consider the agent taking no action to be a special case of this, where the agent rewrites itself into an identical agent.

Under this interpretation, it is clear that the obstacles we have encountered apply to Gödel machines as well. Consider a Gödel machine G_1 whose fallback policy would "rewrite" it into another Gödel machine G_2 with the same suggester (proof searcher, in Schmidhuber's terminology). G_1's suggester now wants to prove that it is acceptable to instead rewrite itself into G'_2, a Gödel machine with a very slightly modified proof searcher. It must prove that G'_2 will obtain at least as much utility as G_2. In order to do so, naively we would expect that G'_2 will again only execute rewrites if its proof searcher has shown them to be useful; but clearly, this runs into the Löbian obstacle, unless G_1 can show that theorems proven by G'_2 are in fact true.

We could attempt to use the techniques in this paper to make the proof go through, but this would require us to accept that G'_2 uses a strictly weaker proof system than G_1, which seems like a departure from the framework envisioned by Schmidhuber. Worse, even if we do so, it would not at all be clear how to prove (2): In the Gödel machine setting, π_{fb} and π'_{fb} would themselves be Gödel machines and hence suggester-verifiers. Thus, proving (2) would again require reasoning about agents that search for proofs: We have reduced our initial problem to a different one that is just as difficult. (In our own formalism, we solve this problem by choosing π_{fb} and π'_{fb} to be "object-level" policies involving no proof search—in the simplest case, mere lookup tables that specify which action should be taken given the observation.)

7 Conclusions

In this paper, we have introduced a concrete formalism for space-time embedded intelligence that a proof-based AGI can use to reason about its own future behavior. We have shown how, under certain assumptions, an agent using this formalism is able to justify minor self-modifications that leave its overall architecture intact.

However, in doing so, we have seen that naive approaches run into one of two major problems of self-reference: the *procrastination paradox*, which allows an agent to put off an important task forever, or the *Löbian obstacle*, which prevents an agent from justifying even clearly safe rewrites. Hurdles such as these should make the reader wary of accepting intuitively plausible formalisms allowing for self-modification before seeing a formal version that provably avoids these obstacles. We discussed partial solutions, but finding a fully satisfactory solution remains an open problem.

References

1. Christiano, P., Yudkowsky, E., Herreshoff, M., Barasz, M.: Definability of truth in probabilistic logic (2013), http://intelligence.org/files/DefinabilityOfTruthInProbabilisticLogic-EarlyDraft.pdf
2. Fallenstein, B.: An infinitely descending sequence of sound theories each proving the next consistent (2013), https://intelligence.org/files/ConsistencyWaterfall.pdf
3. Fallenstein, B.: Procrastination in probabilistic logic (2014), https://intelligence.org/files/ProbabilisticLogicProcrastinates.pdf
4. Goertzel, B.: Golem: Toward an agi meta-architecture enabling both goal preservation and radical self-improvement (2010), http://goertzel.org/GOLEM.pdf
5. Hutter, M.: Universal Artificial Intelligence: Sequential Decisions based on Algorithmic Probability. Springer, Berlin (2005)
6. Legg, S., Hutter, M.: A formal measure of machine intelligence. In: Proc. 15th Annual Machine Learning Conference of Belgium and the Netherlands (Benelearn 2006), Ghent, Belgium, pp. 73–80 (2006)
7. Lob, M.H.: Solution of a problem of Leon Henkin. J. Symb. Log. 20(2), 115–118 (1955)
8. Muehlhauser, L., Orseau, L.: Laurent Orseau on Artificial General Intelligence (interview) (2013), http://intelligence.org/2013/09/06/laurent-orseau-on-agi/
9. Neumann, L.J., Morgenstern, O.: Theory of games and economic behavior, vol. 60. Princeton University Press, Princeton (1947)
10. Orseau, L., Ring, M.: Space-time embedded intelligence. In: Bach, J., Goertzel, B., Iklé, M. (eds.) AGI 2012. LNCS, vol. 7716, pp. 209–218. Springer, Heidelberg (2012)

11. Robinson, H.: Dualism. In: Zalta, E.N. (ed.) The Stanford Encyclopedia of Philosophy. Winter 2012 edition (2012)
12. Schmidhuber, J.: Ultimate cognition à la Gödel. Cognitive Computation 1(2), 177–193 (2009)
13. Yudkowsky, E.: The procrastination paradox (2013), https://intelligence.org/files/ProcrastinationParadox.pdf
14. Yudkowsky, E., Herreshoff, M.: Tiling agents for self-modifying AI, and the Löbian obstacle (2013)

A General Artificial Intelligence Approach
for Skeptical Reasoning

Éric Grégoire, Jean-Marie Lagniez, and Bertrand Mazure

CRIL
Université d'Artois - CNRS UMR 8188
rue Jean Souvraz SP18 F-62307 Lens France
{gregoire,lagniez,mazure}@cril.fr

Abstract. We propose a general artificial intelligence approach for handling contradictory knowledge. Depending on the available computational resources, reasoning ranges from credulous to forms of skepticism with respect to the incompatible branches of alternatives that the contradictions entail. The approach is anytime and can be declined according to various knowledge representation settings. As an illustration of practical feasibility, it is experimented within a Boolean framework, using the currently most efficient computational tools and paradigms.

Keywords: General Artificial Intelligence, Inconsistency Handling, Credulous Reasoning, Skeptical Reasoning.

1 Introduction

The ability to reason and act in an appropriate coherent way despite contradictory knowledge is a fundamental paradigm of intelligence. A general artificial intelligence reasoner needs the ability to detect and overcome conflicting knowledge. Especially, its deductive capacities should not collapse due to conflicting premises (a standard-logic reasoner can infer any conclusion and its contrary from contradictory information). Similarly, when some contradictory knowledge forbids the existence of global solutions to a problem, the reasoner should be able to locate this problematic information and adopt a specific policy: at the extreme, it might for example decide to use its problem-solving capacities on the non-contradictory part of the knowledge, only.

In this context, the focus in this paper is on adopting a cautious or so-called *skeptical* stance towards contradictory knowledge. This requires the reasoner to locate the conflicting information and adopt what is shared by all possible branches of alternatives that are underlied by the contradictions. Such a paradigm has long been studied in A.I. (see the seminal work on default logic [1] and e.g. [2] [3]), but suffers from a lack of practical implemented tools, mainly due to discouraging theoretical results: even in the simple Boolean logic setting, skeptical reasoning belongs to the second-level of the polynomial hierarchy [4,5], making it intractable in the worst-case, unless P = NP.

B. Goertzel et al. (Eds.): AGI 2014, LNAI 8598, pp. 33–42, 2014.
© Springer International Publishing Switzerland 2014

We claim that the usual definition of skeptical reasoning should be revisited and refined in order to both better mimic human abilities and improve computationally viability. Especially, we argue for anytime reasoning abilities that are intended to translate a progressive range of attitudes in line with the elapsed computing time. Like human beings, general artificial intelligence systems also need to recognize that some reasoning tasks would require more time and resources to be successively conducted, when intractability threatens. In this context, we revisit skeptical reasoning to include various parameters that, on the one hand, translate reasonable assumptions about the targeted reasoning paradigms and, on the other hand, often entail more tractable treatments. For example, a skeptical reasoner might only be able to detect contradictions that are formed of less than a given preset maximal number of informational entities. As it is often assumed in model-based diagnosis [6,7], it might also recognize that its reasoning is satisfactory when a preset maximal number of different extracted contradictions is reached that would allow satisfiability to be recovered if these contradictions were removed. More generally, various parameters classifying contradictions can be included in the models of skepticism in such a way that various forms of bounded skepticism can be defined depending on the considered values for the parameters; when all possible values are considered, these forms converge to ideal skepticism, which excludes all the possibly controversial knowledge.

Interestingly, there has been much progress these last years on the practical computation of the basic building blocks required by this anytime model, making it even more realistic in many situations.

The paper is organized as follows. In the next section, the concepts of MSS (Maximal Satisfiable Subset), CoMSS (Complement of a Maximal Consistent Subset) and MUS (Minimal Unsatisfiable Subset), which are cornerstones in this study, are presented. The any-time reasoning approach is described in section 3, with a focus on various paradigms leading to useful weakened forms of skepticism. Section 4 details our experimental study showing the feasibility of the any-time approach, before promising paths for further research are presented in the last section.

2   Basic Concepts and Tools

As an illustration of practical feasibility, we have implemented and experimented this anytime reasoning architecture within a Boolean reasoning framework, using its currently most efficient computational tools and paradigms. As far as any additional representational mechanism does not yield intractability, other knowledge representation formalisms and problem-solving frameworks can be covered by the approach. For example, the knowledge representational setting can be at least as expressive as constraint networks for Constraint Satisfaction Problems in discrete domains [8,9], including other finite representation systems. All that is needed is an encoding of contradictory knowledge as unsatisfiable informational entities, together with a compactness result about this (finite) satisfiability concept: any proper subset of a satisfiable subset is itself satisfiable.

In the following we assume that knowledge takes the form of a CNF Σ, namely a finite set of clauses that is conjunctively interpreted, where a clause is a finite disjunction of possibly negated Boolean variables and constants. SAT is the NP-complete problem that consists in checking whether or not Σ is satisfiable, and in the positive case in delivering one assignment of values to all variables that makes all clauses *true*. The following MSS, CoMSS and MUS concepts are cornerstones in the study of credulous and skeptical reasonings.

Definition 1 (MSS). $\Gamma \subseteq \Sigma$ *is a Maximal Satisfiable Subset (MSS) of* Σ *iff* Γ *is satisfiable and* $\forall \alpha \in \Sigma \setminus \Gamma$, $\Gamma \cup \{\alpha\}$ *is unsatisfiable.*

Definition 2 (CoMSS). $\Gamma \subseteq \Sigma$ *is a Complement of a MSS, also called Minimal Correction Subset (MCS or CoMSS), of* Σ *iff* $\Sigma \setminus \Gamma$ *is satisfiable and* $\forall \alpha \in \Gamma$, $\Sigma \setminus (\Gamma \setminus \{\alpha\})$ *is unsatisfiable.*

Accordingly, Σ can always be partitioned into a pair made of one MSS and one CoMSS. Obviously, such a partition needs not be unique. A *core* of Σ is a subset of Σ that is unsatisfiable. Minimal cores, with respect to set-theoretical inclusion, are called MUSes.

Definition 3 (MUS). $\Gamma \subseteq \Sigma$ *is a Minimal Unsatisfiable Subset (MUS) of* Σ *iff* Γ *is unsatisfiable and* $\forall \alpha \in \Gamma$, $\Gamma \setminus \{\alpha\}$ *is satisfiable.*

Under its basic form where no specific information entity is compulsory present in any solution, MAX-SAT consists in delivering one maximal (with respect to cardinality) subset of Σ. Note that MSSes are maximal with respect to $\subseteq$: accordingly, any solution to MAX-SAT is one MSS, but not conversely. Note also that there is a hitting set duality between CoMSSes and MUSes. All the above concepts have been thoroughly studied in A.I., especially with respect to worst-case complexity properties: MAX-SAT is NP-complete; splitting Σ into one (MSS,CoMSS) pair is in P^{NP} [10], checking whether or not a CNF is a MUS is DP-complete [11] and checking whether or not a clause belongs to a MUS is in Σ_2^P [4]. Moreover, there can be $\mathcal{O}(C_m^{m/2})$ MUSes in Σ when Σ is made of m clauses. Despite these bad worst-time complexity results, much progress has been made this last decade, allowing the efficient extraction of MSSes, CoMSSes and MUSes from Σ, at least in many situations (see e.g. [12,13,14,15,16]).

3 An Anytime Progression of Reasoning

Let us turn back to the possible agent's stances towards handling some possibly conflicting knowledge. A first step from the agent is its recognition of the existence of a contradictory situation, namely unsatisfiability. This requires a successful call to a SAT-solver.

3.1 Fool Attitude

When the SAT-solver does not deliver any result within the available computing time, a first attitude towards inconsistency can however be obtained although it is of a limited interest. Usual CDCL SAT solvers [17] record the current assignment that satisfies the largest number of clauses. When the solver is stopped because of time-out limits, clauses from Σ can be classified according to this so-called *progressive interpretation*. Under tougher time-limits, the agent can also classify clauses of Σ according to any random assignment. Clauses that are satisfied by this assignment form a non-conflicting subset of information from Σ. The agent can then reason in a deductive way from this subset: every conclusion is only guaranteed to belong to one possible branch of reasoning amongst the incompatible ones that are underlied by the incompatible knowledge in Σ. All the next following forms of reasoning assume that Σ has been shown unsatisfiable.

3.2 Credulous Reasoning

In the A.I. literature, the concept of credulous (or brave) reasoner can be traced back at least to default logic [1]. In the standard Boolean framework, a credulous agent adopts one MSS of Σ and reasons on its basis. When the agent is running short of time to compute one MSS, it can be downgraded to the fool attitude and adopt the progressive interpretation or the largest satisfiable approximate MSS computed so-far. Note that a specific MSS is delivered by MAX-SAT: it is an MSSes that is one of the largest in terms of cardinality. From a practical point of view, computing one MSS is easier and proves more efficient in many cases.

3.3 Ideal Skepticism

Contrary to credulous reasoners, an ideally skeptical attitude rejects any piece of information that does not follow from every MSS. Equivalently, it thus rejects all MUSes of Σ. One MUS represents one smallest possible set of unsatisfiable clauses of Σ. In the general case, the number of MUSes can be exponential in the number of clauses of Σ. Since MUSes can intersect, simply removing a number of MUSes such that the remaining part of Σ becomes satisfiable is generally not sufficient to yield an ideally skeptical reasoner. However, in some situations, computing all MUSes remains tractable from a practical point of view (see for example [18]).

3.4 Practical Skepticism

Instead of computing ideal skepticism which is often out of practical reach, we propose to compute in an any-time manner forms of weakened skepticism, which converge to ideal skepticism when enough computing resources are provided. They can be defined based on assumptions about the nature and topology of unsatisfiability in Σ and the cognitive abilities of the reasoner. Let us examine some of the most direct and natural assumptions: as we shall see, they can often be mixed together.

Assumption 1. Each MUS contains less than k clauses.

The smaller the parameter k, the easier SAT-checking and the computation of MUSes (at least, expectedly). This assumption also translates a natural variable feature of human intelligence: the size of a MUS is the smallest number of clauses that are necessary in the proof of the contradiction embodied inside the MUS. Clearly, human beings find it easier to detect e.g. two pieces of information that are directly conflicting rather than a proof of unsatisfiability that involves many clauses. Accordingly, an anytime skeptical reasoner might extract MUSes, both successively and according to their increasing sizes. When computational resources are running short, the skeptical reasoner might drop from Σ all MUSes computed so far when this leads to satisfiability: the reasoner is then aware that no MUS that is "easier" (in the sense that its size is lower than k), does exist in Σ. This is at least as smart as a human beings that are not capable of finding out a proof of unsatisfiability that involves at least k different pieces of information. This assumption is orthogonal to the next ones that we are going to present, and can be mixed with them.

Assumption 2. The number of MUSes in Σ is lower than l.
In real-life situations, it might not often be expected that Σ is polluted by many different reasons for unsatisfiability, hence the maximal value for l might be far more lower than the one that is exponential in the number of clauses of Σ in the worst-case complexity scenario. Again, an anytime skeptical reasoner can consider increasing values for the parameter (here, l), successively. It needs to recognize that it has dropped a sufficient number of MUSes to regain satisfiability, and, at the same time, that it has limited its investigations to a limited number l of MUSes, only. We believe that this policy is best mixed together with Assumption 1, so that MUSes of lower cardinality are considered first. This corresponds to a realistic skeptical human reasoner that finds out smallest proofs of unsatisfiability first: after having exhausted all its resources, it is aware that the number of MUSes in Σ was too large in order to compute all of them. At the same time, it might estimate that Σ without all the extracted MUSes forms an acceptable basis for further reasoning or problem-solving, despite this restriction.

Assumption 3. Two MUSes are pairwise independent iff they do not intersect. The maximal cardinality of a set made of MUSes such that any pair of them is pairwise independent, is lower than m.
As m translates the maximal number of totally different causes of unsatisfiability in Σ, it is expected that this number can be small in real-life, especially for many situations where a new piece of information is to be inserted within Σ, switching the status of Σ from satisfiable to unsatisfiable. Again, if m is large, human and artificial intelligence reasoners may lack sufficient resources to compute all of them. Contrary to Assumptions 1 & 2, we do not expect the reasoner to consider increasing values for m. Instead, it might attempt to find a lower bound for m by finding out a sufficient number of non-intersecting MUSes such that removing all these MUSes makes Σ become satisfiable. To this end, whenever a MUS is extracted, it is sufficient to remove it from Σ, and iterate until satisfiability is reached. A skeptical reasoner running out of resources might make do with such a *cover* of MUSes, being aware of the valuable property that any MUS not extracted so far shares at least one clause with this cover (otherwise, removing the computed MUSes would not have allowed satisfiability to be regained).

Assumption 4. The set-theoretic union of all MUSes of Σ forms at most n non-intersecting subparts of Σ.
Even when two MUSes are pairwise independent, each of them can intersect with a same third MUS. When $n > 1$, this assumption ensures that under a given (a priori) value for n and when the currently extracting MUSes form n non-intersecting subparts of Σ, the reasoner is sure that all the other MUSes can be found successively and are forming sequences of intersecting MUSes with the already discovered ones. Accordingly, this gives a hint about which candidate MUS are to be considered next. When this value for n is a mere belief of the reasoner about Σ, this latter one might start by considering candidate MUSes that obey this assumption before considering all other candidate MUSes.

Obviously, parameters in Assumptions 2, 3 and 4 are connected through the $n \leq m \leq l$ relation.

Assumption 5. Each MUS intersects with at most p other MUSes of Σ or Each clause in a MUS belongs to at most q MUSes of Σ.
This assumption relies on the idea that any clause does not belong to a large number of different minimal proofs of unsatisfiability. Intuitively, this assumption requires that every piece of information is not a cause of many, i.e. more than q, contradictions. When its actual value is unknown, the q parameter can be set to increasing values, and MUSes that obey that assumption can be searched first. However, this assumption might prove too strong since for example the insertion of a new piece of information might actually contradict with many existing clauses in Σ. Hence, we believe that this assumption should be refined as follows.

Assumption 6. When a MUS contains v clauses, at most v' (with $v' \leq v$) clauses in this MUS belong also to other MUSes of Σ. Actually, each of these clauses belongs to at most s MUSes.
Again, the anytime reasoner might consider increasing values for v' and s, successively, and search first for MUSes obeying the assumptions. The intuitive idea about the topology of unsatisfiability is that in any MUS, only v' clauses are "actual" reasons for unsatisfiability. These clauses might for example coincide with the information that has been added inside Σ when Σ was satisfiable, leading to at most s different minimal sets of conflicting information.

Assumption 7. There is at most t clauses that are "actual" reasons for unsatisfiability. Each clause in a MUS is a reason for unsatisfiability in the sense that removing the clause would lead to "break" the MUS. The concept of "actual" reason specifies which clauses are the reasons in the real world leading to unsatisfiability. For example, assume that Σ is satisfiable and correct. A less reliable new piece of information under the form of a clause i is inserted within Σ that leads to Σ to become unsatisfiable. Accordingly, i is the real reason for unsatisfiability, although several MUSes can exist and removing one clause per MUS would allow Σ to regain satisfiability, even when these latter selected clauses are not i. In many actual situations, it might make sense to reason under a given a priori value for t. Moreover, under this assumption, when t non-intersecting MUSes are extracted, dropping them already excludes from Σ all actual reasons for unsatisfiability (but not necessarily all MUSes, which must include at least one of these reasons).

4 Experimental Study

In order to study the feasibility of the proposed any-time reasoner, we have implemented the above multi-level reasoning architecture and experimented it with a large set of challenging benchmarks involving various problem-solving and reasoning issues. More precisely, we have considered the 393 unsatisfiable challenging CNF benchmarks (http://logos.ucd.ie/Drops/ijcai13-bench.tgz) used and referred to in [13] for MSSes and CoMSSes computation and enumeration. They encode various problems related to e.g. distributed fault diagnosis for multiprocessor systems, planning issues, etc. Although most basic building blocks of reasoning in the architecture involve solving instances of NP-hard problems and are thus intractable in the worst case, much practical progress has been made these last decades making the tasks become feasible for many instances, as it was already envisioned a long time ago for example in [19]. We thus used some of the currently best performing tools in the Boolean search and satisfiability domains: MINISAT [17] was selected as the CDCL SAT-solver. We used our own tool called CMP as partitioner [16]: it is the currently best performing tool for the extraction of one MSS and its related CoMSS in the clausal Boolean setting. We also used a MUS extractor called MUSER2 (http://logos.ucd.ie/web/doku.php?id=muser) [12] and used ELS [13] as a tool for extracting the set of clauses made of all MUSes (or equivalently, all CoMSSes). All experimentations have been conducted on Intel Xeon E5-2643 (3.30GHz) processors with 8GB RAM on Linux CentOS. Time limit was set to 30 minutes for each single test.

First, we have computed the fool attitude (according to the progressive interpretation delivered by the SAT-solver when unsatisfiability is proved) and the credulous one embodied by one MSS. Then we considered forms of skepticism. In this last respect, we have concentrated on the expectedly computationally-heaviest schemas. First, we have implemented the ideally skeptical attitude as an ideal model of competence; not surprisingly, it remained out of computational reach for many instances. Then we have implemented a simple algorithm, called INDEPENDENT-MUSES to take Assumption 3 into account: it computes a sufficient number m of independent MUSes so that dropping them leads to satisfiability. To this end, we have exploited a direct relationship between CoMSS and MUSes: any CoMSS contains at least one clause of each MUS. We took advantage of the efficiency of the novel CMP tool to partition Σ into one pair (MSS, CoMSS). INDEPENDENT-MUSES computes one such a partition and then iterates the following schema until satisfiability is reached. compute one MUS containing one clause from the CoMSS, retract this MUS from Σ, ends if the remaining part of Σ is satisfiable. Note that under Assumption 7, when the number of detected MUSes reaches t, then we are sure that all actual reasons for unsatisfiability are located inside these MUSes.

Since relying on Assumption 3 and INDEPENDENT-MUSES leads the reasoner to miss MUSes intersecting with the other detected ones, we have modified this algorithm so that when a clause in a CoMSS does not lead to the extraction of a MUS that is not intersecting with the already computed ones, one MUS is computed that includes this clause and possibly intersects with already computed MUSes. This algorithm is called MORE-MUSES: it can be the starting schema for implementing Assumptions 5 and 6 (actually, it implements a part of Assumption 6 where $v' = 1$ and $s = 1$). Taking additional additional assumptions would expectedly lead to even better results since they prune the search space by restricting the number of MUSes (Assumption 2) and/or their possible contents (Assumption 1), or can lead to additional divide and conquer elements in the search strategy (Assumption 4).

The full experimentations data and results are available from www.cril.univ-artois.fr/documents/fulltab-agi14.pdf . In Table 1, we provide a sample of results. The columns give the name of the instance Σ, the number of Boolean variables ($\#v$) and clauses ($\#c$), the time rounded up to the second to compute the fool attitude (i.e., compute the progressive interpretation) (t_{fa}); in the worst case, this time is the time-out (1800 seconds) set for the satisfiability test. The next column gives the time also rounded up to the second to compute the credulous

Table 1. Some experimental results

Instance					INDEPENDENT-MUSES		MORE-MUSES		ALL-MUSES	
Name	$\#v$	$\#c$	t_{fa}	t_{ca}	$\#c^-$	t_g	$\#c^-$	t_g	$\#c^-$	t_g
bf0432-005	1040	3667	0	0	782	0.00	871	0.32	1668	1067.07
bf0432-011	1053	3740	0	0	288	0.00	1070	0.19	time-out	
t5pm3-7777.spn	125	750	0	0	4	0.00	420	1.28	time-out	
C210_FW_SZ_91	1789	6709	0	0	282	0.18	283	0.94	time-out	
C202_FW_SZ_123	1799	7437	0	0	37	0.00	37	0.06	40	0.00
C208_FA_UT_3254	1876	6153	0	0	40	0.00	68	0.00	98	0.08
C202_FW_SZ_100	1799	7484	0	0	36	0.00	25	0.04	time-out	
ssa2670-136	1343	3245	0	0	1246	0.08	1301	0.44	1396	20.40
ssa2670-134	1347	3273	0	0	1242	0.08	1312	0.51	1404	200.73
22s.smv.sat.chaff.4.1.bryant	14422	40971	0	0	725	2.14	736	2.19	time-out	
cache.inv14.ucl.sat.chaff.4.1.bryant	69068	204644	4	1	17314	394.28	17331	548.96	time-out	
ooo.tag10.ucl.sat.chaff.4.1.bryant	15291	43408	0	0	1882	4.00	1891	4.10	time-out	
ooo.tag14.ucl.sat.chaff.4.1.bryant	62505	179970	1	1	4971	68.39	4968	68.31	time-out	
dlx2_ca	1225	9579	0	0	2230	1.51	2230	1.21	2970	810.99
dlx2_cs	1313	10491	1	0	2481	1.69	2480	2.28	3358	934.11
dlx1_c	295	1592	0	0	560	0.00	560	0.00	656	0.59
divider-problem.dimacs_5.filtered	228874	750705	0	2	6854	1477.39	31630	1720.09	time-out	
divider-problem.dimacs_7.filtered	239640	787745	1800	1800	6134	1642.59	time-out		time-out	
rsdecoder_fsm1.dimacs.filtered	238290	936006	1800	1800	time-out		time-out		time-out	
dspam_dump_vc1093	106720	337439	7	2	391	388.07	524	217.92	time-out	
dspam_dump_vc950	112856	360419	66	2	393	485.62	369	1394.81	memory overflow	
dividers4.dimacs.filtered	45552	162947	0	0	18	38.09	152	38.46	time-out	
dividers3.dimacs.filtered	45552	162646	0	1	937	38.19	4595	61.68	time-out	
dividers5.dimacs.filtered	45552	162946	0	0	652	37.99	650	38.35	time-out	
mem_ctrl1.dimacs.filtered	1128648	4410313	1800	1800	time-out		time-out		time-out	
wb-debug.dimacs	399591	621192	1800	1800	28	929.02	time-out		time-out	
mem_ctrl-debug.dimacs	381721	505523	0	0	71	569.54	118	570.00	time-out	
3pipe_1_ooo	2223	26561	1	0	5221	14.75	5253	13.04	time-out	
5pipe_5_ooo	10113	240892	10	0	28614	651.80	28933	634.39	time-out	
4pipe_3_ooo	5233	89473	7	0	15963	162.75	16226	177.82	time-out	
4pipe	5237	80213	45	0	17217	284.30	17086	302.10	time-out	
4pipe_2_ooo	4941	82207	8	0	14926	166.99	14422	187.88	time-out	
4pipe_4_ooo	5525	96480	4	0	17559	460.53	17598	211.92	time-out	
4pipe_1_ooo	4647	74554	27	0	12748	139.48	12622	318.02	time-out	
C168_FW_UT_2463	1909	6756	0	0	44	0.00	45	0.00	time-out	
C202_FS_SZ_121	1750	5387	0	0	23	0.00	23	0.00	26	0.00
C170_FR_SZ_92	1659	4195	0	0	131	0.00	131	0.00	131	0.00
C208_FC_RZ_70	1654	4468	0	0	212	0.00	212	0.00	212	0.08
term1_gr_rcs_w3.shuffled	606	2518	0	0	22	0.00	719	2.56	time-out	
alu2_gr_rcs_w7.shuffled	3570	73478	1800	1800	1254	681.31	time-out		time-out	
too_large_gr_rcs_w5.shuffled	2595	36129	1800	1800	109	1.36	time-out		time-out	
too_large_gr_rcs_w6.shuffled	3114	43251	0	0	751	7.61	4529	257.81	time-out	
9symml_gr_rcs_w5.shuffled	1295	24309	0	0	151	0.57	4914	386.24	time-out	
ca256.shuffled	4584	13236	0	0	9882	10.20	9882	10.28	9882	81.55
ca032.shuffled	558	1606	0	0	1173	0.08	1173	0.06	1173	0.99

attitude (i.e., compute one (MSS,CoMSS) partition) (t_{ca}). The next columns give the main parameters resulting from running INDEPENDENT-MUSES: the total number of clauses in the discovered MUSes $(\#c^-)$ and the global time taken by the algorithm (t_g). The same parameters are provided for MORE-MUSES. The columns for ALL-MUSES provide the number of clauses in the set-theoretical union of all MUSes $(\#c^-)$ and the time to complete the algorithm (t_g).

Not surprisingly, ALL-MUSES and thus ideal skepticism proved unsuccessful for most (i.e., 300/393) instances. The required time to compute the fool attitude with respect to the progressive interpretation was often done in less than one second. The average time for computing one MSS and thus a credulous attitude was 0.16 seconds for the 319/393 successively addressed instances. The number of additional clauses in MUSes dropped by MORE-MUSES clearly shows that INDEPENDENT-MUSES often misses MUSes. Although the latter Algorithm is often more resources consuming, it remained successful for most (i.e., 338/393) instances. For example, ideal skepticism could not be completed within the 30 minutes maximal computing time for the too_large_gr_rcs_w6.shuffled benchmark whereas INDEPENDENT-MUSES and MORE-MUSES extracted 751 and 4529 clauses belonging to the set-theoretic union of all MUSes of this instance, respectively. As a general lesson, this basic experimental study thus shows the viability of the any-time architecture and of forms of practical, weakened, skepticism, at least for the tested benchmarks, which are reputed challenging.

5 Conclusions and perspectives

In this paper, we have proposed and experimented with an any-time architecture to handle contradictory knowledge. Like human beings who can handle conflicting knowledge in various rational ways depending on the actual available time to complete the reasoning tasks, the architecture implements an any-time range of reasoning capabilities that depend on the elapsed computing time and resources. Especially, we have revisited skeptical reasoning to include human-like progressive ways that attempt to reach ideal skepticism. At this point, it is important to stress that the architecture and its main paradigms are not sticked to a logical representation of knowledge and reasoning. It can apply to any set of informational entities, provided that a finite satisfiability relationship can be defined and that a compactness result on this relation does exist, allowing for maximal satisfiable subsets and minimal unsatisfiable subsets concepts to be defined and computed. We believe that the Assumptions described in this paper, although instantiated to the clausal Boolean framework, could be easily transposed into such other formalisms. The actual efficiency of the architecture on these other representational mechanism will depend on the practical computational cost to handle these concepts. For example, the architecture applies to the general languages of constraint solving problems in discrete domains, where techniques for computing MSSes and MUSes have been studied for a long time [8,9]. Accordingly, we claim that the ways of handling contradictory knowledge that we have proposed can take part into a general artificial intelligence system that would be able to overcome contradictory knowledge.

References

1. Reiter, R.: A logic for default reasoning. Artificial Intelligence 13(1-2), 81–132 (1980)
2. Grégoire, É.: Skeptical inheritance can be more expressive. In: Proceeding of the 9th European Conference on Artificial Intelligence (ECAI 1990), pp. 326–332 (1990)
3. Makinson, D., Schlechta, K.: Floating conclusions and zombie paths: Two deep difficulties in the "directly skeptical" approach to defeasible inheritance nets. Artificial Intelligence 48(2), 199–209 (1991)
4. Eiter, T., Gottlob, G.: On the complexity of propositional knowledge base revision, updates, and counterfactuals. Artificial Intelligence 57(2-3), 227–270 (1992)
5. Cayrol, C., Lagasquie-Schiex, M.C., Schiex, T.: Nonmonotonic reasoning: From complexity to algorithms. Annals of Mathematics and Artificial Intelligence 22(3-4), 207–236 (1998)
6. Hamscher, W., Console, L., de Kleer, J. (eds.): Readings in Model-Based Diagnosis. Morgan Kaufmann (1992)
7. Feldman, A., Kalech, M., Provan, G. (eds.): Proceedings of the 24th International Workshop on Principles of Diagnosis, DX 2013 (2013), http://www.dx-2013.org/proceedings.php (electronic proceedings)
8. Rossi, F., van Beek, P., Walsh, T.: Handbook of Constraint Programming. Elsevier, Amsterdam (2006)
9. Lecoutre, C.: Constraint Networks: Techniques and Algorithms. Wiley (2009)
10. Papadimitriou, C.H.: Computational Complexity. Addison-Wesley (1993)
11. Papadimitriou, C.H., Wolfe, D.: The complexity of facets resolved. Journal of Computer and System Sciences 37(1), 2–13 (1988)
12. Belov, A., Marques-Silva, J.: Accelerating MUS extraction with recursive model rotation. In: Proceedings of the Eleventh International Conference on Formal Models in Computed-Aided Design (FMCAD 2011), pp. 37–40 (2011)
13. Marques-Silva, J., Heras, F., Janota, M., Previti, A., Belov, A.: On computing minimal correction subsets. In: Proceedings of the 23rd International Joint Conference on Artificial Intelligence, IJCAI 2013 (2013)
14. Liffiton, M.H., Malik, A.: Enumerating infeasibility: Finding multiple MUSes quickly. In: Gomes, C., Sellmann, M. (eds.) CPAIOR 2013. LNCS, vol. 7874, pp. 160–175. Springer, Heidelberg (2013)
15. Lagniez, J.-M., Biere, A.: Factoring out assumptions to speed up mus extraction. In: Järvisalo, M., Van Gelder, A. (eds.) SAT 2013. LNCS, vol. 7962, pp. 276–292. Springer, Heidelberg (2013)
16. Grégoire, É., Lagniez, J.M., Mazure, B.: A computational method for (MSS,CoMSS) partitioning (2014) (submitted to AAAI 2014)
17. Eén, N., Sörensson, N.: An extensible SAT-solver. In: Giunchiglia, E., Tacchella, A. (eds.) SAT 2003. LNCS, vol. 2919, pp. 502–518. Springer, Heidelberg (2004)
18. Grégoire, É., Mazure, B., Piette, C.: Boosting a complete technique to find MSS and MUS thanks to a local search oracle. In: Proceedings of the Twentieth International Joint Conference on Artificial Intelligence (IJCAI 2007), pp. 2300–2305 (2007)
19. Kautz, H.A., Selman, B.: Pushing the envelope: Planning, propositional logic and stochastic search. In: Proceedings of the Thirteenth National Conference on Artificial Intelligence and Eighth Innovative Applications of Artificial Intelligence Conference (AAAI 1996), vol. 2, pp. 1194–1201 (1996)

On Effective Causal Learning

Seng-Beng Ho

National University of Singapore, Singapore
hosengbeng@gmail.com

Abstract. We have developed a framework for identifying causal relationships between events which are *effective* in the sense that they can be put to practical use, without regard to what the "true" causes really are. A rapid causal learning process is devised for temporally correlated events that can be observed proximally which is sufficient for the learning of many causalities involving basic physical and social phenomena. The system relies on a *diachronic* aspect of causes which is a characterization of consistent temporally correlated events and a *synchronic* aspect of causes which is a characterization of the contextual factors that enable the diachronic causal relations. The causal learning method is applied to some problem solving situations that allows some basic knowledge to be learned rapidly and that results in drastic reductions of the search space and amount of computation involved. This method is necessary to jump start the chain of causal learning processes that allow more complex and intricate causal relationships to be learned based on earlier knowledge.

1 Introduction

Being able to establish causality is critical to a cognitive system's survival and proper functioning and is the most important foundation upon which a cognitive system structures its intelligent behavior. However, various research seems to suggest that there is no simple algorithm that is available that can easily and quickly establish causality between two events [1, 2, 3]. One key problem is as follows. Suppose a correlation is detected between two events A and B. It can be argued (and often it may be the case) that there exists a yet to be observed third event, C, that causes A and B separately and hence the correlation is not due to A causing B directly. A celebrated example is the issue of whether smoking causes lung cancer. Even if a correlation between smoking and cancer is established, one can argue (and many a tobacco company had raised the point) that perhaps there is a gene that causes people to like smoking and that it also causes lung cancer [2]. Often, domain specific knowledge needs to be brought to bear for the establishment of causality [1, 2]. However, there is a chicken-and-egg problem: the learning and acquisition of some commonsensical domain knowledge which encodes fundamental rules/models of the world, both physical and social, requires the establishment of causality between some fundamental physical events (e.g., push something and it will move) or social events (e.g., yell out loud and everyone will turn to look at you immediately) to start with. Therefore, by appealing to domain knowledge only begs the question of the origin of this knowledge.

B. Goertzel et al. (Eds.): AGI 2014, LNAI 8598, pp. 43–52, 2014.
© Springer International Publishing Switzerland 2014

In our previous papers [3, 4] we proposed a paradigm of research in which an adaptive autonomous agent would, starting from no prior knowledge, interact with the environment and extract causal rules of behavior between physical/social causes and physical/social objects on an ongoing and rapid basis. How is this achievable?

We propose a method that is *sufficient* to allow some very fundamental causality – e.g., those involving physical laws – to be learned. These acquired commonsensical domain knowledge could then support the subsequent learning of increasingly complex and intricate causalities. We then illustrate how the application of this basic causal learning process can vastly reduce the computational effort involved in solving two AI problems – the "spatial movement to goal" and "crawling robot" problems [6].

2   Motivational Considerations

Important insights can be gained on the issue of causality by returning to the very root of what causality means and what it can do for us. Consider a simple example of, say, using a remote control to control a toy car. Suppose this pair of objects is given to a child or is picked up by a primitive person in the jungle, both of whom have no prior domain knowledge on the devices. By playing with the joystick on the remote control and observing the effects it has, say, on the wheels of the toy car, they can easily and quickly establish the causality between a certain movement of the joystick (an event) and the way the wheels turn (another event) based on the temporal correlation observed, much like they would learn very quickly about lightning and thunder. Someone observing them carrying out the acts can also easily observe the correlation and hence deduce the causality.

However, one can still posit the possibility that there is a third event, perhaps an action of "God," that causes the person to push the joystick on the remote control in a certain direction and also causes the turning of the wheel of the car accordingly every time. Therefore, strictly speaking, one still cannot conclude that the person's certain action is the *true cause* of a certain turning behavior of the wheel. How then can a cognitive system even begin to learn some very fundamental causalities to start with?

We believe it is useful to define a concept called *effective causality* that supports the learning of fundamental causal knowledge. In the case of the remote control and the car, in the absence of other observable possible causes (such as a "God"), it can be assumed that if there is a consistent temporal relationship between the joystick event and the wheel event, the joystick event is the *effective cause* of the wheel event. Whether there is an underlying "true cause" such as an unobservable "God" does not matter. The effective causal rule serves a practical purpose for the system to be able to predict the consequence of its action. Of course, the rule may cease to be valid later which is fine because the system then learns other new rules rapidly.

Similarly, in the case of smoking and lung cancer, if one's purpose is a practical one of, say, avoiding a mate who has a high chance of getting cancer, then the existence of the correlation is sufficient, whether smoking is "really" the cause does not matter, unless one's purpose is to establish a case against the tobacco companies.

The correlation between the remote control and toy car is also a lot easier to detect than that between smoking and lung cancer. This is because the remote control and toy car's behaviors are observed by the person (or the observer observing the person controlling the remote control) directly in a proximal manner. Provided their senses can be trusted, the correlation is easily established. Of course, there could be occasional noise – such as the coincidental movements of other objects around - but they can be weeded out fairly quickly by one or two more tries at the pushing of the joystick in the same direction – these coincidental events are not likely to recur. Thus, in the case of smoking and lung cancer, if an observer is able to observe the interaction of the smoke particles and the lung cells directly, the correlation would be much more easily established. Otherwise, more complex statistical analysis is needed [2, 3].

We term the effective cause of an event arising from temporal correlation a *diachronic* cause. There is yet another aspect of effective causality: there are "enabling" contextual *factors* that enable the temporal correlation between two events, without which the temporal correlation will not exist. E.g., when *on Earth* the law of gravity holds – that an object, when let go (an event), will fall to the ground in the next instance (another event). We identify these factors as *synchronic* causes.

We shall consider the example of gravity more closely in connection with the identification of synchronic causes. Actually when humans first encountered the phenomenon of gravity, because it took place in practically any context/background on Earth, our original conception was that it was ubiquitous and the background did not matter. Hence we first characterized gravity as applicable *everywhere*. Later we discovered that there are situations in outer space in which gravity can become reduced or non-existent. We then modified the concept of gravity to be applicable everywhere *on Earth* (the context) in its full strength – we bring back the context/background that we have ignored earlier. Therefore we happily applied the *effective* causal rule (that all objects would fall when not supported, in any context) for most of humanity's existence, using it to successfully support our survival until a new rule was discovered. This is the way we will handle the discovery and characterization of synchronic causes – the enabling contextual factors to be described in Section 3.2. The physicist Lee Smolin [7] believes that all physical theories are *effective* and approximate that apply to "truncations" of nature and that cover only a limited domain of phenomena. This echoes our idea of effective causality.

3   An Effective Causal Learning Framework

In the spirit of the discussion above, we divide the identification of causes into the two major aspects: the *diachronic* and the *synchronic* aspects. For the current paper, we consider only deterministic situations in which a diachronic cause must always bear a consistent temporal relationship with the effect and a synchronic cause must always be present. Considerations of probabilistic situations are relegated to a future paper. Our focus in this paper would be to show the application of the basic causal learning framework which is *sufficient* to drastically reduce search efforts in some problem solving situations.

3.1   The Identification of Diachronic Causes

We begin by considering a simple situation in which a few simple events (changes of states) can be directly (proximally) observed to take place as shown in the left diagram in Fig. 1. These events consist of Appearances and Disappearances of the three objects 11, 12, and 13 at some locations L1, L2, and L3 respectively which we will represent as App(object, location) and Disapp(object, location) respectively. In the right of Fig. 1 is a temporal diagram in which the horizontal axis is time represented discretely as a succession of "time frames" t1, t2, ... etc. and the vertical axis lists the presence of the objects with the associated parameters - the locations at which they appear when they appear - at the corresponding time frame. So, say, in t1 there is no object present and in t2 object 11 appears at L1. The change from t1 to t2 is noted (as a gray vertical bar). (An event could be the change of the existential or other states of an object or the change of some parameters such as the location or the energy level associated with an object - e.g., Move(11, L1, L2): object 11 moves from location L1 to location L2).   In general, whenever there is a change, the system would look for a "cause" – some changes that happened earlier in time. However, because this is the first change since the beginning of "time" in this "mini-universe," it is assumed that either there is no cause or the cause is before the current temporal interval (e.g., a "first cause" such as "God" that exists outside the current space-time continuum.)

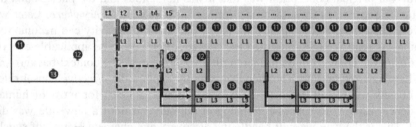

Fig. 1. Diachronic causes. See text for explanation

Henceforth we will refer to a *causal rule* as one that links an event as a *diachronic* cause (e.g., App(11, L1)) and another event as a *diachronic* effect (e.g., App(12, L2)), denoted as App(11, L1) → App(12, L2), if such a causal connection exists. Looking at Fig. 1, one can see that there is a consistent correlation between App(12, L2) and App(13, L3) (with a delay of 2 time frames) because it happens twice. We require at least two consistent correlations before we construct the causal rule in order to weed out noise – this is called "dual instance consideration." (In a probabilistic formulation, we can define "rule-confidence" in terms of the number of consistent instances observed.) Therefore, App(11, L1) → App(12, L2) and App(11, L1) → App(13, L3) do not hold as they each happens only once. There is also a causal rule App(13, L3) → Disapp(13, L3) that holds that is a "self-causal" rule – it predicts that an object will disappear after a certain amount of time of its appearance (e.g., a timer controlling a light). But if that correlation exists, then the rule App(12, L2) → Disapp(13, L3) will also follow as indicated in the figure. Without further knowledge or proximal observations (i.e., of a timer mechanism), App(12, L2) can be taken as the underlying cause of *both* App(L3) and Disapp(L3) and the situation is similar to C being the underlying cause of the correlation of A and B discussed in the Introduction section.

The ability to weed out noise through dual instance consideration is dependent on how "busy" the environment is – how many events are happening in a given time period. If the scenario is very busy, say with millions of events happening in a small temporal interval, the number of instances involved may have to be increased to remove spurious correlations. But the dual instance consideration should suffice for our ordinary environment. Also, in the event that the cognitive systems is in a desperate need to look for a cause of something so as to be able to bring about or repeat an earlier observed effect, it may relax the dual instance consideration – it may try its luck and apply those temporal correlations that have been observed only once.

In the event that more than one diachronic causes are identified, they are encoded as *conjunctive diachronic causes*. Subsequent observations will identify whether they are really conjunctive causes – i.e., if one is subsequently observed to be absent and the effect does not ensue - or they are *disjunctive diachronic causes* – any one of them happening will give rise to the effect.

3.2   The Identification of Synchronic Causes

We consider the simple events in Fig. 2 (similar to Fig. 1) to illustrate the idea of synchronic causes as discussed above. In Fig. 2, the duration of the 11 event is shortened and a new 14 event is introduced as shown. Now, had object 11 been present "all the time" at location L1 as in Fig. 1, At(11, L1) would be considered a necessary *synchronic* (contextual) cause for App(12, L2) → App(13, L3). (Currently there is another entity that is a synchronic cause of App(12, L2) → App(13, L3), which is the location associated with App(12, L2) - At(12, L2)). In Fig. 2, however, because only *either* 11 *or* 14 is present at their corresponding locations at the time when App(12, L2) happens (shown in two dashed rectangles), the presence of both 11 and 14 are *tentatively* considered *not* to be the synchronic causes accompanying App(12, L2) → App(13, L3), in the same spirit as the gravity example discussed in Section 2.

However, this tentative removal of the presence of 11 and 14 as synchronic causes of App(12, L2) → App(13, L3) will be reverted as soon as another event 12 takes place (say, outside the time frame shown in Fig. 2) in the absence of 11 and 14, and 13 fails to take place after 2 time intervals. This shows that the presence of 11 *or* 14 were indeed needed for App(12, L2) to cause App(13, L3). The system then modifies the already learned causal rule App(12, L2) → App(13, L3) to include At(11, L1) *or* At(14, L4) as its accompanying disjunctive synchronic causes, in conjunction with At(12, L2) (i.e., At(12, L2) *and* (At(11, L1) *or* At(14, L4)).

Suppose A, B, C, D, E, … are synchronic causes, the above method can recover complex conjunctive/disjunctive combinations of these such as A and (B or C) or (D and E).... A dense collection of disjunctive synchronic causes that are parameter values (e.g. L1 = 1.1 or 1.2 or 1.3 or 1.4...) can be combined into a sub-range of values (e.g. 1.1 < L1 < 1.9). In the case of gravity discussed in Section 2, the disjunctive "sum totality" of each context (synchronic cause) on Earth in which gravity applies *is* the context of the *entire* Earth.

48   S.-B. Ho

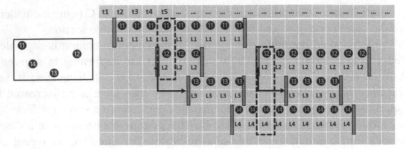

Fig. 2. Synchronic causes. See text for explanation

4   Application of Causal Learning to Problem Solving

In this section, we discuss two examples in which the effective causal framework can be used to drastically reduce the amount of computation in problem solving situations. One example is the typical spatial movement to goal problem and the other is the crawling robot problem [6]. Typically, the A* [8] or best-first search process is used for the spatial movement to goal problem and reinforcement learning is used for the crawling robot problem [6, 9]. In both cases, no *causal* characterizations of the actions involved are learned or extracted in the processes, resulting in relatively "blind" searching processes that require a large amount of computation. We show that our framework developed above discovers/learns causal rules of various actions involved in the search process that have general and wide applicability that can result in a drastic reduction of the search space involved.

4.1   The Spatial Movement to Goal Problem

Consider the spatial movement to goal problem - a cognitive system starting from a point in space and trying to reach a physical point (the GOAL) some distance away (Fig. 3). Using, say, the best-first search to solve the spatial movement to goal problem, a domain *independent* heuristic is typically used such as the "shortest distance to goal" heuristic. However, with this heuristic, one still needs to expand many nodes at each level of the search to compute the heuristic value in order to select the one with the minimum value for the next level of expansion. It is possible to use a domain *dependent* heuristic – always head straight toward the GOAL – and obviate the need to expand many nodes. However, building in this heuristic will be too contrived. Is there a domain independent method that allows the system to discover this domain dependent heuristic? Our effective causal learning algorithm described in Section 3 provides just such a domain independent mechanism to learn this piece of knowledge – a manner of applying an elemental force that *causes* the "shortest distance to the goal" to be achieved. (Here we assume that there are no obstacles between the cognitive system and the goal. Our effective learning framework can also handle the situation with obstacles that we relegate to a future paper.)

Fig. 3 shows that in the first level of the best-first search process all the possible directions of the applied force, F, is tried and the parameters associated with these "expanded nodes" are kept track of. We assume that the parameters available to the "senses" of the cognitive system are: AL (its absolute location); RD (its relative distance to the GOAL – provided by, say, a vision system); AA (the absolute angle with respect to the entire reference frame in which the force is applied); and RA (the relative angle to the GOAL in degrees which is defined as 0 when the force is pointing directly at the GOAL). These parameters can potentially be the synchronic causes or diachronic effects accompanying the diachronic cause – the force. (At the moment the force is applied, if there are other objects around, there will also be parameters such as the relative distances and the force's directions relative to these objects. However, given our current method, these factors would be ruled out quite rapidly within a few movements of the cognitive system and hence for simplicity without sacrificing generality, we omit these other parameters for the current discussion.)

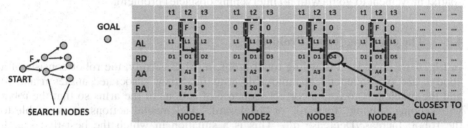

Fig. 3. Search with effective causal learning. F = Force; AL = Absolute Location; RD = Relative Distance (to GOAL); AA; Force Absolute Angle; RA = Force Relative Angle (to GOAL)

In NODE1 the force goes from 0 (non-existent) to F (existent) and the parameters associated with the cognitive system – AL and RD – change in some manner after one time frame. (Assuming the force always takes one time frame to effect changes.) Those parameters that change are the diachronic effects of the force application. (AA and RA are undefined ("*") before and after the force application.) NODE3, in which the force F is applied with the parameter values AL = L1, RD = D1, AA = A3, and RA = 0, which is denoted as F(L1, D1, A3, 0), corresponds to the shortest distance to the GOAL. This node is selected for expansion. (At this stage the parameter *values* L1, D1, A3 and 0 are potential synchronic causes for the force event.)

In the next level of expansion, F(L4, D4, A3, 0) would be the action that satisfies the shortest distance to goal heuristic. The causal learning algorithm then generalizes the required force to F(*, *, A3, 0), with the values of AL and RD now no longer potential synchronic causes to the action F that satisfies the shortest distance to goal heuristic (denoted as "*") and the still relevant synchronic causes are AA = A3 and RA = 0. Hence after two levels of node expansion, the system no longer needs to expand the nodes corresponding to applying the force in all the other directions. It just needs to use F(*, *, A3, 0) to head straight to the GOAL.

Suppose now the system finds itself in another START position that has a different absolute angular placement from the GOAL compared to that in the earlier experience. In this situation the F(*, *, A3, 0) will not work as now F applied in the A3 absolute direction will not give rise to an RA = 0. The system therefore carries out the process again as above as described in Fig. 3 and in this second experience, after two levels of node expansion, it discovers, say, F(*, *, AX, 0) as the optimal way to apply the force at every step to the GOAL. As AX is not equal to A3, the absolute angle AA is then removed as a synchronic cause and the optimal force is F(*, *, *, 0), leaving RA = 0 as the only synchronic cause of the optimal force application – i.e., one that satisfies the shortest distance to goal heuristic.

At this stage, the cognitive system has discovered the heuristic that basically says that no matter where the cognitive system is or how far it is from the GOAL, the optimal way to move it to the GOAL is to apply a force that aims directly at the GOAL. Thus, after two experiences and a total of 4 complete node expansions, the cognitive system learns a general causal rule that *obviates all future needs for search* for this spatial movement to goal (with no intervening obstacle) problem.

4.2   The Crawling Robot Problem

In Fig. 4 we consider a crawling robot problem [6]. Basically, the robot consists of a "body" and two independently movable arms (and their associated angles α and β) and the problem is to find a correct sequence of actions of the arms so that the robot will keeping moving "forward" or "backward." 4 elemental actions are available to the robot: Increase/Decrease α/β. This is a situation in which the best-first search combined with the domain independent shortest distance to goal heuristic cannot be used as it is difficult to measure the "distance" between a current state from the goal of, say, $Fwd(R)^N$ (keeps moving forward – no backward movement at any time). Therefore reinforcement learning is often used for problems such as this [6, 9].

As can be seen from the previous section, there is an early "exploration" phase of the causal learning enhanced search process in which many possibilities are tried (many nodes expanded) and some general and powerful causal rules are discovered that obviate any further extensive search or node expansion altogether. On the other hand, even though there is also an exploration phase in a typical reinforcement learning process [6, 9], there is no attempt to extract the "causes" and powerful generalizations that characterize causal rules or "causal models." What are learned are basically "state-transition models" with prescriptions of the best courses of actions in various states of the system to achieve a certain goal (e.g., $Fwd(R)^N$). A huge amount of computation is typically needed in extensive exploration and exploitation phases in reinforcement learning. Reinforcement learning would fair even worse if all contextual factors are included as part of the current "state of the world" which are often removed a priori using domain knowledge. With our effective causal learning process, irrelevant contextual factors (potential synchronic causes) are weeded out in the process of constructing the causal rules as we have described above.

Figs. 4(a), (b), (c), and (d) show different states of the robot arms and to the right of the robot is shown the corresponding general causal rules that govern its behavior in those states. (A computer program that simulates the robot's behavior would conceivably have these rules in the program.) For example, in Fig. 4(a), using our parlance, the diachronic cause (action), Dec(β), would give rise to a diachronic effect, Fwd(R) (i.e., Dec(β) → Fwd(R)) in the presence of the synchronic causes Tch(A, FL) and β > 0. Inc(β) → not Tch(A, FL) and Dec(α) → not Tch(A, FL) (causing point A to not touch the Floor) share the same synchronic causes as Dec(β) → Fwd(R). Each of Dec(β), Fwd(R), etc. is an event. Tch(A, FL) can be a state or an event (when there is a state change from not Touch to Touch). Similarly for not Tch(A, FL).

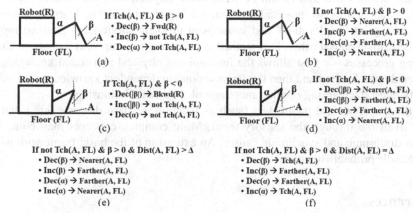

Fig. 4. The crawling robot problem. Tch = Touch; Dec = Decrease; Inc = Increase; Fwd = Forward; Bkwd = Backward; Dist = Distance; R = Robot; FL = Floor. A is the dangling end of the distal arm. β has positive values (β > 0) when the distal arm is swung to the "right" of the vertical dashed line and negative values (β < 0) when the arm is swung to the "left."

Hence, unlike "action-state" rules in reinforcement learning, the rules in Fig. 4 do capture the "causal understanding" of the robot's behavior in its most general form. These rules are learnable using our causal learning method described above, with some minor extensions to the basic algorithm (e.g., handling of parameter ranges such as β > 0, β < 0, etc.). Once these causal rules are learned in a process of exploration (i.e., move the robot arms about and observe what events occur as a result) they can engender a rapid problem solving process through, say, a backward chaining process, beginning from a desired goal (e.g., Fwd(R)^N – i.e., no Bkwd(R) is allowed at any given step - or Bkwd(R)^N), with a drastically reduced search space. Incremental chunking [10] can further reduce the amount of search needed.

In the interest of space, the detailed step-by-step causal learning and problem solving processes will not be described for this case. In the interest of clarity, Fig. 4(b) omits an extra synchronic condition Dist(A, FL) > Λ. The complete version is shown in Fig. 4(e). Dist(A, FL) = *(equal to)* Δ is the condition just prior to a touching event – Tch(A, FL) when A is just slightly above the Floor – and an action Dec(β) will lead to Tch(A, FL) – the rule in Fig. 4(f). There are two more similar rules corresponding to Fig. 4(d) that are not shown in Fig. 4. There are also a few other rules (e.g., a rule converting β < 0 to β > 0) that are not decribed here in the interest of space. Suffices it to say that they can all be discovered through the causal learning process. Part of the backward chaining process could make use of the shortest distance to goal heuristic similar to that discussed in Section 4.1 – that to get a point to touch another point, select the action that brings it *Nearer* the point.

5   Conclusion and Future Work

In summary, this paper proposes a method that relies on the effective use of temporal correlation and proximal observation for a process of rapid causal learning that can learn the causal rules that obtain between basic physical and social events and the method is applied to two physical problem solving situations. The learning is carried out in a stage of "exploration" and subsequent problem solving can proceed rapidly with the learned causal rules. This method is necessary to jump start a chain of causal learning processes – it first allows the fundamental physical and social knowledge of the world to be learned and then the learned domain dependent knowledge can subsequently assist the learning of other more complex causal relationships.

In this paper we use parameters (such as location, relative distance, etc.) that are easily available through the sensory input. More complex concepts may come into play as diachronic and synchronic causes. An extension of the basic framework would be to handle probabilistic events.

References

1. Sloman, S.: Causal Models: How People Think about the World and Its Alternatives. Oxford University Press, Oxford (2005)
2. Moore, D.S., McCabe, G.P., Craig, B.A.: Introduction to the Practice of Statistics. W.H. Freeman an Company, New York (2009)
3. Pearl, J.: Causality: Models, Reasoning, and Inference, 2nd edn. Cambridge University Press, Cambridge (2009)
4. Ho, S.-B.: A Grand Challenge for Computational Intelligence –A Micro-Environment Benchmark for Adaptive Autonomous Agents. In: Proceedings of the IEEE Symposium Series for Computational Intelligence on Intelligent Agents, pp. 44–53. IEEE Press, Piscataway (2013)
5. Ho, S.-B., Liausvia, F.: Knowledge Representation, Learning, and Problem Solving for General Intelligence. In: Kühnberger, K.-U., Rudolph, S., Wang, P. (eds.) AGI 2013. LNCS, vol. 7999, pp. 60–69. Springer, Heidelberg (2013)
6. Berghen, F.V.: Q-Learning, http://www.applied-mathematics.net/qlearning/qlearning
7. Smolin, L.: Time Reborn: From the Crisis of Physics to the Future of the Universe. Houghton Mifflin Harcourt, Boston (2013)
8. Hart, P.E., Nilsson, N.J., Raphael, B.: A Formal Basis for the Heuristic Determination of Minimum Cost Paths. IEEE Transactions on Systems Science and Cybernetics SSC4 4(2), 100–107 (1968)
9. Sutton, R.S., Barto, A.G.: Reinforcement Learning: An Introduction. The MIT Press, Cambridge (1998)
10. Ho, S.-B., Liausvia, F.: Incremental Rule Chunking for Problem Solving. In: Proceedings of the 1st BRICS Countries Conference on Computational Intelligence. IEEE Press, Piscataway (2013)

Increasing Accuracy in a Bidirectional Associative Memory through Expended Databases

Melissa Johnson and Sylvain Chartier

University of Ottawa, Ottawa, Canada
{mjohn140,sylvain.chartier}@uottawa.ca

Abstract. Neural networks are often used in recall problems when there is noisy input and many sophisticated algorithms have been designed to help the recall process. Most cases use either learning rule adjustments, or more recently prototype learning. The question remains though of how to handle cases where there are multiple representations (exemplars) of a pattern. This paper evaluates three types of association methods: circular association method where the exemplars form a loop, linear association method where the exemplars are linked together forming a line ending in the master template, and many-to-one association method where all the exemplars point to the master template. The question asked is if using these exemplars benefits accuracy in noisy recall and does the association method matter. All three association methods had greater accuracy then the standard BAM recall. Overall, the many-to-one method had the greatest accuracy and was the most robust to changes in the exemplars. The accuracy of the circular association pattern is influenced by the amount of differences in the exemplars with accuracy increasing as the exemplars become increasingly different from each other. The linear association method is the least robust, and is affected by both the number of exemplars and differences in exemplars.

Keywords: Neural networks, BAM, Auto-association, Hetero-association, Learning, Recall, Exemplars, Classification.

1 Introduction

Any intelligent system must be able to take in data and be able to process that data for storage or use. Unfortunately not all data is clear and concise, therefore a key requirement for any intelligent system is to be able to handle noisy or degraded data (Voss, 2007). Being able to recognize and recall noisy or degraded patterns is something that humans can do quickly but is still difficult for computers and artificial intelligence models. Currently, artificial neural networks are being used for this noisy recall problem because of their ability to develop attractors for each pattern and because of their stability and adaptability with regard to noise and pattern degradation.

More precisely, bidirectional associative memories (BAMs; Kosko, 1988) are used in order to associate two sets of patterns. Over the years, several variants of BAM models have been proposed to overcome the original model's limited storage capacities and improve its noise sensitivity (Shen & Cruz Jr, 2005). Nowadays, BAM

B. Goertzel et al. (Eds.): AGI 2014, LNAI 8598, pp. 53–62, 2014.

models can store and recall all the patterns in a learning set, are robust to noise, and are able to perform pattern completion. This is the outcome of numerous sophisticated approaches that modify the learning and transmission functions (for a review, see Acevedo-Mosqueda, Yanez-Marquez & Acevedo-Mosqueda; 2013). More recently Chartier & Boukadoum (2011) proposed a BAM that uses the nonlinear feedback from a novel output function to learn online to iteratively develop weight connections that converge to a stable solution. The proposed BAM learns by only using cova-riance matrices, and it is among the few models that can create real-valued attractors without preprocessing. It is also able to reduce the number of spurious attractors while maintaining performance in terms of noise degradation and storage capacity. Howev-er, in all cases the learning of a given category is achieved by prototype associations. Although this is suitable for simple cases, in many situations there will be more than one representation (exemplars) that need to be associated with a given category. Therefore, the question of how multiple representations should be associated together remains. In this paper we propose to explore four types of associations and their im-pact on learning time and recall performance. More precisely, we will test the network on auto-association method (standard BAM), circular association method, linear asso-ciation method, and many-to-one association method. Explanation of those associa-tion methods are discussed in the simulation section.

The organization of this paper consists of a description of the model: architecture, transmission, and learning, followed by the simulations and then a discussion of the results and conclusions.

2   Model

2.1   Architecture

As illustrated in Figure 1, because BAM is bi-directional, there are two initial input states (stimuli), $\mathbf{x}(0)$ and $\mathbf{y}(0)$ and $\mathbf{W}$ and $\mathbf{V}$ are their respective weight matrices. In the illustration, t represents the number of iterations over the network. The network is composed of two interconnected layers through which information is processed bidi-rectionally; the x-layer returns information to the y-layer and vice versa. The BAM neural network can be both an auto-associative and hetero-associative memory.

2.2   Transmission Function

TThe transmission function is based on the classic Verhulst equation extended to a cubic form with saturating limit at ±1 (Chartier, Renaud, & Boukadoum, 2008). The transmission functions are defined by the following two equations:

$$\forall\, i, \dots, N, \mathbf{y}_i(t+1) = f(\mathbf{W}\mathbf{x}_i(t))$$
$$= \begin{cases} 1 & if\ \mathbf{W}\mathbf{x}_i(t) > 1 \\ -1 & if\ \mathbf{W}\mathbf{x}_i(t) < -1 \\ (\delta+1)\mathbf{W}\mathbf{x}_i(t) - \delta \mathbf{W}\mathbf{x}_i^3(t) & else \end{cases} \tag{1}$$

$$\forall \, i, \dots, M, \mathbf{x}_i(t+1) \;\; = f(\mathbf{V}\mathbf{y}_i(t))$$

$$= \begin{cases} 1 & if \;\, \mathbf{V}\mathbf{y}_i(t) > 1 \\ -1 & if \;\, \mathbf{V}\mathbf{y}_i(t) < -1 \\ (\delta + 1)\mathbf{V}\mathbf{y}_i(t) - \delta \mathbf{V}\mathbf{y}_i^3(t) & else \end{cases} \tag{2}$$

where N and M are the number of units in each layer. The parameter i is the index of the respective elements during training or recall. At iteration time t, the layer contents are represented by $\mathbf{x}(t)$ and $\mathbf{y}(t)$. The weight matrices are $\mathbf{W}$ and $\mathbf{V}$ and the δ is the general transmission parameter. The general transmission parameter needs to be fixed at a value between 0 and 0.5 to assure fixed-point behaviour (Chartier, Renaud, & Boukadoum, 2008). This transmission function is used because it has no asymptotic behaviour when δ is between 0 and 0.5 and is therefore useable during the learning and recall. A saturating limit at the two attractors, -1 and 1 allows it to be comparable to a sigmoid type function.

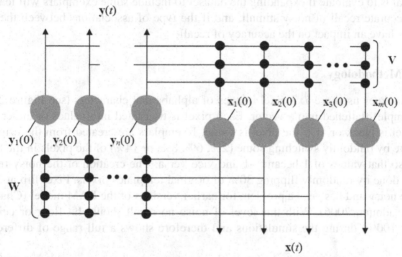

Fig. 1. BAM Network Architecture

2.3   Learning Rule

Most BAM models learn using a Hebbian type learning (Chartier & Boukadoum, 2011). In this model, the learning rule is expressed by the following equations:

$$\mathbf{W}(k+1) = \mathbf{W}(k) + \eta(\mathbf{y}(0) - \mathbf{y}(t))(\mathbf{x}(0) + \mathbf{x}(t))^{\mathrm{T}} \tag{3}$$

$$\mathbf{V}(k+1) = \mathbf{V}(k) + \eta\big(\mathbf{x}(0) - \mathbf{x}(t)\big)\big(\mathbf{y}(0) + \mathbf{y}(t)\big)^{\mathrm{T}} \tag{4}$$

where η represents the learning parameter, T is the transpose operator, and k is the learning trial. The initial inputs are $\mathbf{x}(0)$ and $\mathbf{y}(0)$ while $\mathbf{x}(t)$ and $\mathbf{y}(t)$ are the state vectors after t iterations through the network. This learning rule can be simplified to the following equation in the case of auto association $\mathbf{y}(0)=\mathbf{x}(0)$.

$$\mathbf{W}(k + 1) = \mathbf{W}(k) + \eta(\mathbf{x}(0)\mathbf{x}^{\mathrm{T}}(0) - \mathbf{x}(t)\mathbf{x}^{\mathrm{T}}(t)) \tag{5}$$

$$\mathbf{V}(k + 1) = \mathbf{V}(k) + \eta(\mathbf{y}(0)\mathbf{y}^{\mathrm{T}}(0) - \mathbf{y}(t)\mathbf{y}^{\mathrm{T}}(t)) \tag{6}$$

Based on equations (3) and (4) the weights can only converge when $\mathbf{y}(t) = \mathbf{y}(0)$ and $\mathbf{x}(t) = \mathbf{x}(0)$. Therefore, the learning rule is linked to the network's output. In order for the association to be stored as a fixed point, η must be set according to the following condition (Chartier, Renaud, & Boukadoum, 2008):

$$\eta < \frac{1}{2(1 - 2\delta)Max[N, M]}; \quad \delta \neq 1/2$$

3   Simulation

The goal is to evaluate if expanding the dataset to include some exemplars will lead to more accurate recall of noisy stimuli, and if the type of associations between the exemplars have an impact on the accuracy of recall.

3.1   Methodology

The templates used are 7x7 pixel images of alphabetical characters (see Figure 2 for an example) flattened into a vector. Each pixel is translated into values of either 1 if the pixel is black or -1 if the pixel is white. Exemplars are created from the original template by randomly switching some (2%, 6%, 8%, or 14%) of the pixels in the templates so that values of 1 became -1 and vice versa. The creation of the noisy recall item is done by randomly flipping 30% of original templates pixels. Pixel flip at 30% is quite noisy and has been a problem for earlier versions of the BAM model (Chartier & Boukadoum, 2006). With this level of noise no recall should hit floor or ceiling (0% or 100%) during the simulations and therefore shows a full range of difference scores.

The four association methods that are being investigated can be seen in Figure 2. In the auto-association method, no exemplars are used and each stimulus is associated with itself (Figure 2A). In this case extra templates are used to keep the memory load of the neural network balanced. Memory load is typically calculated based on the dimensional space used compared to the number of templates the system is requires to learn. For all simulations in this paper, there is a 49-dimensional space capacity but the number of templates varies. By keeping the number of templates consistent for all memory association methods the memory load is consistent among them. This is shown in Figure 2 where auto-association (Figure 2A) contains 6 letters (templates) while the other associations contain 2 letters and 2 templates, making 3 patterns per category, or 6 patterns in total. The circular association (Figure 2B) has the templates and exemplars forming a circle of hetero-associations such that the last exemplar is associated which the second last, which is associated with the third last, and so on until the first exemplar is associated with the template, the template is then associated with the last exemplar, thereby forming a complete circle. The linear association

(Figure 2C) is similar to the circular association except instead of having the template associate with the last exemplar, the template is associated with itself (auto-association) forming a closed line. The final association is a many-to-one association (Figure 2D) where all exemplars are associated with the template and the template is associated with itself. In all association methods, if there are no exemplars then the methods become auto-associative.

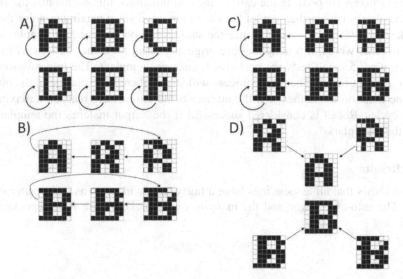

Fig. 2. Examples of templates, exemplars and their associations. A) Auto association; each item is associated with itself, B) Circular association; hetero-associations that form a loop, C) Linear association; hetero-association to one master template that is auto-associative, and D) Many-to-one association; all exemplars point to the master template

All simulations had the same variables except for the number of templates, the number of exemplars, and the level of noise in the exemplars. Number of templates plus exemplars never went above 49% memory load (24/49) of the network. All simulations were performed 150-300 times to account for the randomization of the pixel flips in both the exemplars and recall pattern. Testing of recall was done only on the template patterns that are common to all the associations. For example, in the case of Figure 2, the letters A and B would be tested while all other possible templates and exemplars are ignored.

Learning.
During the learning phase, all templates and examples are learned with their associations based on the association method being simulated. The same templates and exemplars are used for all the different association methods with the exception of the control condition which does not use the exemplars but uses extra templates to control for memory load. The range of noise (pixel flips) in the exemplars is 2%, 6%, 8% or 14% (1, 3, 4, or 7 pixels flipped respectively) and the learning parameter, η, is set to

0.01 which respects the condition of equation 7. The transmission parameter, δ, is set to 0.1, the number of iteration before a weigh update, t, is set to 0.1 and the learning is concluded when the weights have converged.

Recall.
During recall, a noisy input pattern is the original template with 30% of the pixels flipped (15 pixels flipped). In the case of these simulations, this means that the recall pattern is always noisier than any of the exemplars used since maximum noise for the exemplars is 14%. All associations use the same recall patterns and all templates are tested. In other words, if 5 templates are originally used, no matter how many exemplars are used, 5 recall tests are performed, once per template. The transmission parameter, δ, is set to 0.1. The recall process will stop if there is no change in the output from one iteration to another or if the number of iterations have reached a maximum of 200 cycles. Recall is considered successful if the output matches the template or any of the exemplars.

3.2   Results

Figure 3 shows that all associations have a fairly steady increase as more patterns are added. The auto-association and the many-to-one association use fewer epochs than

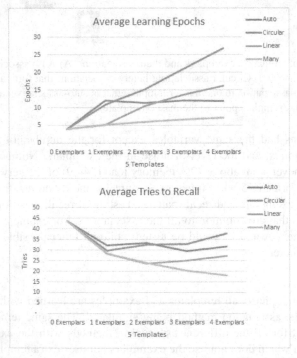

Fig. 3. On the left, the average epochs needed for learning in the different associations patterns. On the right, the amount of trials needed on average for recall. In both graphs, exemplars were set to 14% of noise, 5 templates are used with 0 to 4 exemplars per template.

circular and linear patterns while learning. The circular association takes the longest to learn but still consistently reaches a fixed point. Despite the added time to learn, the number of recall cycles slowly increases as more exemplars are added but they are all also still relatively close together even after 4 exemplars. The many-to-one method takes the least time to learn and the least time to recall while the normal recall, or auto-association method, is in the middle of the results. Because epochs to learn and recall cycles are all quite similar in the different association methods, it is logical to check accuracy of the methods next to see if that can differentiate the methods.

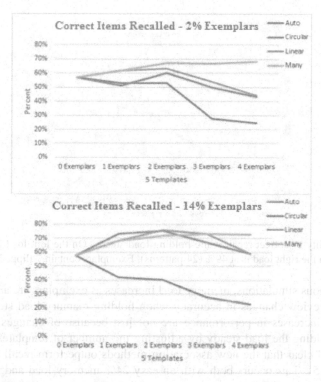

Fig. 4. Number of items correctly recalled for each of the association methods using 5 templates and 0 to 4 exemplars. Exemplars either contain 2% or 14% pixel flip (1 or 7 pixels). The stimulus to be recalled contains 30% pixel flip (15 pixels).

Figure 4 clearly shows that accuracy is improved using exemplars. If a distance of 1 pixel (2%) is used between exemplars during learning, the performance shows a slow change in performance as more exemplars are added; the auto-association method slowly reduces accuracy to end up being the least accurate while the many-to-one association method slowly increases in accuracy until it is the top performer. The difference in accuracy is more noticeable when the learning is accomplished using a distance of 14% (7 pixel flips) between the various exemplars then using a distance of 2%. With the 14% pixel flips, all the methods increase in performance except for the auto-association which again slowly loses accuracy as more templates are added. The best performance is achieved again by multi-associations.

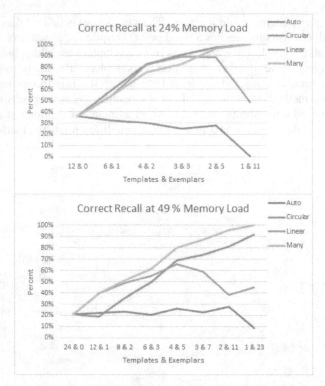

Fig. 5. Probability of correct recall while holding load steady. On the left, load is at 24% (12 patterns) and on the right load is at 49% (24 patterns). Exemplars contain 7 flipped pixels.

In the previous simulations, memory load increases as exemplars are added. Therefore we also review changes in accuracy when holding memory load steady to confirm that the increases in performance are not just because of changes in memory load. Even holding the load steady by adjusting the number of templates and exemplars, it is still clear that the new association methods outperform recall (auto) in all cases (Figure 5). This occurs both with an easy 24% memory load and a maximum efficient memory load of 49%.

The circular and many-to-one associations appear to be similar to each other and both have increasing accuracy with increasing exemplars. The linear association though appears to reach a maximum accuracy after a few exemplars are added, adding more exemplars then appears to decrease performance.

4   Discussion

Overall, the results show that expanding the dataset by including exemplars help with classification; even with minimal exemplar differences (a single pixel). The extra time it takes to learn an item is small between the different methods. Meanwhile the differences in recall accuracy appear to be quite substantial between the exemplar methods and the non-exemplar method. For example, previous research, Chartier & Boukodoum (2006) only obtains 20% accuracy with a 50% memory load using hetero-associations. Our exemplar methods which also use hetero-associations have much greater accuracy. The linear association method, the worst for performance, is closer to 50% accuracy while there is almost 100% for both the many-to-one and the circular association methods. This increase is quite impressive and a good indication that using exemplars improves recall.

While the three exemplar association methods outperform the auto association method in accuracy, the exemplar association methods are not all equal. It appears that the number of exemplars and type of exemplars matter in determining the recall accuracy of the exemplar association method.

In general, the many-to-one association method appears to be the most robust of the methods. It consistently learns the quickest and has the fewest attempts at recall before an item is found. This may be because the associations all have a similar base; all exemplars are associated with the template. This may be quicker and easy for the BAM to perform than the associations used in the other methods. The many-to-one method is also the top performer when exemplars are similar to each other and competitive when the exemplars become dissimilar. In both cases, there is a near linear increase in accuracy as exemplars are added. This shows the consistency of this method; the types of exemplars have less influence on over recall accuracy than number of exemplars.

The circular association is very susceptible to changes in the exemplars; as the difference in exemplars increase between each other and the template, accuracy increases. This suggests that there might be an ideal pattern difference that optimizes the circular association. If this is the case, the circular association method may outperform the many-to-one association method.

It is unlikely that the linear association method can compete in accuracy and usability of the circular association method or the many-to-one association method. The linear association method is affected by both the number of exemplars and the changes in the exemplars which makes it comparatively unstable and hard to optimize for best results. Conversely, the many-to-one association method is very robust and the best choice if optimization of exemplars is not an option. Due to the limited nature of the exemplars in the present simulations, it is unknown if circular association method can outperform the many-to-one association method when the exemplars are optimized.

The present study is a small study using a simple 7x7 template of alphabetical letters. This is not a realistic test to mimic human's ability to recognize degraded objects, but is an excellent starting point. Future simulations need to be run using larger templates and stricter rules in noise degradation to confirm that multi-to-one associations preform the best or to see if it is possible that a circular association would outperform depending on the type of noise introduced.

Considering the issue of the type of noise, it is known that choosing training data for classification is very important to yielding good results (Mazurowski, Habas, Zurada, Lo, Baker, & Tourassi, 2008) therefore another future study could attempt to find out if there's an ideal difference between template, exemplars, and recall input pattern that maximizes accuracy for the association methods and if using this ideal case would make circular associations more accurate than the many-to-one association method.

Any and all exemplars that are created are used in this study, regardless of if the BAM actually needs them. It is possible that too many or the wrong kind of exemplars hinder performance. Therefore another possible study would be to train on exemplars that fail being recalled and not train on exemplars that can be successfully recalled. In other words, by including reinforcement learning, it may be possible to find a near ideal set of exemplars to maximize accuracy.

Acknowledgements. This research was partly supported by the Natural Sciences and Engineering Research Council of Canada.

References

1. Abdi, H.: A generalized approach for connectionist auto-associative memories: Interpretation, implications and illustration for face processing. Artificial Intelligence and Cognitive Sciences, 149–164 (1988)
2. Acevedo-Mosqueda, M.E., Yáñez-Márquez, C., Acevedo-Mosqueda, M.A.: Bidirectional Associative Memories: Different Approaches. ACM Computing Surveys 45(2) (2013)
3. Chartier, S., Boukadoum, M.: A Birdirectional Heteroassociative Memory for Binary and Grey-Level Patterns. IEEE Transactions on Neural Networks 17(2), 385–396 (2006)
4. Chartier, S., Boukadoum, M.: Encoding Static and Temporal Patterns with a Bidirectional Heteroassociative Memory. Journal of Applied Mathematics (2011)
5. Chartier, S., Giguère, G., Langlois, D.: A new bidirectional heteroassociative memory encompassing correlational, competitve and topological properties. Neural Networks 22(special issue), 568–578 (2009)
6. Chartier, S., Renaud, P., Boukadoum, M.: A nonlinear dynamic artifical neural network model of memory. New Ideas in Psychology 26, 252–277 (2008)
7. Cheng, B., Titterington, D.M.: Neural Networks: A Review from a Statistical Perspective. Statistical Science 9(1), 2–54 (1994)
8. Gemmeke, J.F., Virtanen, T., Hurmalainen, A.: Exemplar-based sparse representations for noise. IEEE Transactions on Audio, Speech, and Language Processing 19(7), 2067–2080 (2011)
9. Koronovskii, A.A., Trubetskov, D.I., Khramov, A.E.: Population Dynamics as a Process Obeying the Nonlinear Diffusion Equation. Doklady Earth Sciences 372(2), 755–758 (2000)
10. Mazurowski, M.A., Habas, P.A., Zurada, J.M., Lo, J.Y., Baker, J.A., Tourassi, G.D.: Training Neural Network Classifiers for Medical Decision Making: Effects of Imbalanced Datasets on Classification Performance. Neural Networks 21(2-3), 427–436 (2008)
11. Nosofsky, R.M., Johansen, M.K.: Exemplar based accounts of "multiple-system" phenomena in perceptual categorization. Psychonomic Bulletin & Review 7(3), 375–402 (2000)
12. Shen, D., Cruz Jr., J.B.: Encoding strategy for maximum noise tolerance. IEEE Trans. Neural Networks 16, 293–300 (2005)
13. Valentine, T., Endo, M.: Towards an Exemplar Model of Face Processing: The Effects of Race and Distinctiveness. The Quarterly Journal of Experimental Psychology 44(4) (1992)
14. Voss, P.: Essentials of general intelligence: The direct path to artificial general intelligence. In: Artificial General Intelligence, pp. 131–157. Springer, Heidelberg (2007)
15. Zhang, G.P.: Neural Networks for Classification: A Survey. IEEE Transactions on Systems, Man, and Cybernetics 30(4), 451–462 (2000)

Fusion Adaptive Resonance Theory Networks Used as Episodic Memory for an Autonomous Robot

Francis Leconte, François Ferland, and François Michaud

IntRoLab, Interdisciplinary Institute for Technological Innovation (3IT)
Université de Sherbrooke, Sherbrooke, Canada

Abstract. Autonomous service robots must be able to learn from their experiences and adapt to situations encountered in dynamic environments. An episodic memory organizes experiences (e.g., location, specific objects, people, internal states) and can be used to foresee what will occur based on previously experienced situations. In this paper, we present an episodic memory system consisting of a cascade of two Adaptive Resonance Theory (ART) networks, one to categorize spatial events and the other to extract temporal episodes from the robot's experiences. Artificial emotions are used to dynamically modulate learning and recall of ART networks based on how the robot is able to carry its task. Once an episode is recalled, future events can be predicted and used to influence the robot's intentions. Validation is done using an autonomous robotic platform that has to deliver objects to people within an office area.

Keywords: Episodic memory, Adaptive resonance theory, Artificial emotions, Autonomous robots.

1 Introduction

Autonomous service robots cohabiting with humans will have to achieve recurring tasks while adapting to the changing conditions of the world. According to Hawkins [6], predicting upcoming percepts and action consequences is key to intelligence. Collecting information about one's experiences over time and their relationships within a spatio-temporal context is a role associated to an episodic memory (EM) [16]. External context information such as location, objects, persons and time [13] can be used, as for internal states such as emotions, behaviors and goals [11,7]. Memory consolidation and recall can be accomplished by encoding and classifying events (e.g., by using a R-Tree [13]) and by using methods (e.g., probabilistic-based [3]) looking at contextual cues and history to determine if a memorized episode is relevant to the current situation. If an episode is recalled before the robot has completed its task, the memory can be used to anticipate upcoming percepts and actions for the task [8].

More bio-inspired approaches, like Adaptive Resonance Theory (ART) networks, have also been used to categorize patterns from contextual and state

B. Goertzel et al. (Eds.): AGI 2014, LNAI 8598, pp. 63–72, 2014.

data [1,14,18]. Wang et al. [18] use the concept of fusion ART, i.e., two ART networks in cascade [2,18], to create an EM-ART model: one ART is used to encode spatial events and the other to extract temporal episodes from the experienced situations. Key parameters with this approach are the learning rates β and the vigilance parameters ρ. The learning rates set the influence a pattern has on weight changes, i.e., learning, and is associated to memory stability. Vigilance parameters are used as thresholds for the template matching process: high ρ produce a match when specific input patterns are presented, while lower ρ make more generic pattern matching, tolerant to noise and disparities between the learned pattern and the input pattern. In [19], validation of EM-ART was conducted using a first-person shooter game environment, looking for instance at the influences of ρ on how the episodic memory learns, demonstrating interesting performance of the EM-ART model. However, using EM-ART on an autonomous robot requires dealing with limited, noisy, imprecise and asynchronous perception processes, compared to having complete and continuous access to external context information and internal states of a virtual world. In addition, stability in the representation of events and episodes is required to make the EM-ART usable in the decision-making processes of a robot. Our solution to these issues is to dynamically set β and ρ associated to each events and episodes based on how the robot is able to carry its task, instead of keeping constant β and ρ associated to layers. Such evaluation is conducted using a simple model of artificial emotions. This paper present our EM-ART model, validated using IRL-1 robot platform programmed to deliver objects to people in an indoor environment.

2   EM-ART Modulated with Artificial Emotions

EM-ART is made of three layers: the Input Layer is used to represent the external context information and internal states on which to build the episodic memory; the Event Layer is made of nodes associated to events experienced; and the Episode Layer has nodes that represent the sequence of events making episodes as the robot accomplishes a particular task. Weights between the Input Layer and an Event node represent the pattern from the Input Layer associated to an event, while weights between the Event Layer and an Episode node are associated to the temporal order of events in an episode. As the robot accomplishes its intended task, the matching scheme of EM-ART is used to find similar events and episodes encoded in the memory, adapting weights to reflect variations in similar patterns or adding nodes with their associated weights to learn new events and episodes. Weight learning is influenced by the learning rates β, and the matching scheme by the vigilance parameters ρ. Simply by changing ρ, EM-ART can be used to recall specific events and episodes (e.g., the robot brought Paul a book from Peter in room 1002), or more generic situations (e.g., the robot brought someone an object from Peter in a room). In [18,19], β and ρ are defined for layers, making learning and matching uniform across layers. In our EM-ART model, we exploit the influences of β and ρ by assigning them to each event and episode nodes according to how the robot is able to satisfy its intentions while accomplishing the task, as monitored by the artificial emotion module. If a match between the current situation and a memorized episode is found, we also demonstrate how our EM-ART model can be used to predict upcoming event nodes simply by lowering their associated ρ and by ordering them using the memorized weights. Figure 1 illustrates our EM-ART model, described as follows.

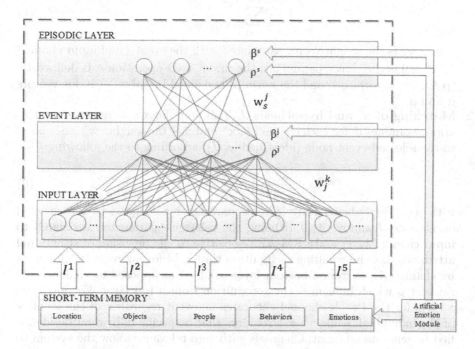

Fig. 1. EM-ART with an Artificial Emotion module

2.1 Input Layer

Let $\mathbf{I}^k$ denote an input vector, with $I_i^k \in [0,1]$ refers to input attribute i, for $i = 1, ..., n$. $\mathbf{I}^k$ is augmented with its complements $\overline{\mathbf{I}}^k$ such that $\overline{I}_i^k = 1 - I_i^k$ to define the activity vector $\mathbf{x}^k$ of the Input Layer. Changes in the attributes of $\mathbf{x}^k$ initiate the matching process with the Event Layer.

Input attributes are grouped into cn channels, and with IRL-1 we use five channels: location, objects recognized, people identified, IRL-1's exploited behaviors and its emotional state. A short-term memory buffer is used to synchronize percepts coming from different perceptual modules. For instance, the identity of the person interacting with IRL-1 and the object shown can be observed together even though they are derived using distinct and asynchronous perceptual processes. This allows the Input Layer to aggregate percepts related to more meaningful and significant changes in $\mathbf{x}^k$, which trigger the matching process in the Event Layer.

2.2   Event Layer

The matching scheme with the Event Layer consists of four steps:

1. **Activating an Event node.** Activation T of node j from the Event Layer is calculated using:

$$T_j = \sum_{k=1}^{cn} \frac{\left|\mathbf{x}^k \wedge \mathbf{w}_j^k\right|}{\alpha^k + \left|\mathbf{w}_j^k\right|} \tag{1}$$

where $\mathbf{w}_j^k$ is the weight vector associated with the event j and input channel k, $\alpha^k > 0$ is the choice parameter, the fuzzy AND operation $\wedge$ is defined by $(\mathbf{p} \wedge \mathbf{q})_i \equiv min(p_i, q_i)$, and the norm $|.|$ is defined by $|\mathbf{p}| \equiv \sum_i p_i$ for vectors $\mathbf{p}$ and $\mathbf{q}$.

2. **Matching of $\mathbf{x}^k$ and hypothesis J.** This step, known as resonance evaluation, examines if, for each channel k, $\mathbf{x}^k$ matches the weights $\mathbf{w}_j^k$ associated to the selected event node (identified as J), according to the following:

$$\frac{\left|\mathbf{x}^k \wedge \mathbf{w}_J^k\right|}{\left|\mathbf{x}^k\right|} \geq \rho^J \cdot \gamma^k \tag{2}$$

with $\rho_J \in [0,1]$ being the vigilance parameter associated to the selected event node J and $\gamma^k \in [0,1]$ being the relevance parameter associated to input channel k. γ^k make EM-ART sensitive to the precision of situational attributes, i.e. the resulting recognition threshold for an event is influenced by characteristics from a bottom layer using γ^k as opposed to vigilance parameter ρ which influences the recognition from a top layer. For instance, $\gamma^k = 0$ for the People channel generates an event regardless of the identity of the individual, while $\gamma^k = 1$ requires that a specific individual be identified to generate an event. Channels with zero relevance allow the system to keep specific information in memory without influencing pattern recognition, while providing useful information when an episode is recalled.

The evaluation starts by selecting node J with the highest T as the hypothesis. If any of the channel k fails to reach resonance with the event J, T_J is set to the next event J having the highest T_j until resonance occurs. If a resonant state is not reached, a new node is created as J.

3. **Learning.** Using J as the Event node, learning is performed according to:

$$\mathbf{w}_J^{k(new)} = \left(1 - \beta^J\right) \mathbf{w}_J^{k(old)} + \beta^J \left(\mathbf{x}^k \wedge \mathbf{w}_J^{k(old)}\right) \tag{3}$$

where $\beta^J \in [0,1]$ is the learning rate parameter associated to the event J. $\beta^J = 1$ is used when a new node is created.

4. **Evaluating the activity vector $y = y_1, ..., y_m$ of the Event Layer.** For node J, $y_J = 1$, the activities of other nodes on the Event Layer decay linearly according to:

$$y_j^{(new)} = max(0, y_j^{(old)}(1 - \tau)) \tag{4}$$

where τ is the decaying factor $\in [0,1]$, which incidentally set the maximum number of event nodes that can be activated to derive an episode.

2.3 Episode Layer

The role of the Episode Layer is to recognize temporal patterns (or sequences of events) in the Event Layer and to predict upcoming events using the concept of temporal auto-association [5]. Whenever $\mathbf{y}$ changes, the Episode Layer uses a matching scheme identical to the Event Layer, evaluating resonance with node S from the Episode Layer or creating a new node if no matches are found. Learning is done only when the task assigned to the robot is completed. Recognition of temporal patterns throughout a task must happen early enough to benefit from the prediction of these patterns before the end of the task, and therefore ρ^s are generally low by default, so that episode node can reach a resonant state more easily.

By default, every ρ^j are set high (0.95) to recognize specific contextual events, but are lowered to conduct a prediction if an episode is recognized before it is completed (to then be reset at the value before prediction occurred). If resonance occurs for episode node S at event node J, $\mathbf{w}_S^j$ between the Event Layer and the episode S can be used to derive the relative order of events in the episode. The prediction $\mathbf{y}_P$ of upcoming events can be calculated using the complement of $\mathbf{w}_S^j$ and $\mathbf{y}$:

$$\mathbf{y}_p = \mathbf{w}_S^j \setminus \mathbf{y}, \quad w_S^j > w_S^J \text{ and } y_j > 0 \qquad (5)$$

Anticipated events are subsequently reordered chronologically (in ascending order according to $\mathbf{w}_S^j$). To facilitate matching of these upcoming events, minor differences are tolerated by lowering ρ^j according to:

$$\rho^{j(new)} = \rho^{j(old)} \left(1 - C_\rho \left(1 - \frac{(p-1)}{\text{length}(\mathbf{y}_P)} \right) \right) \qquad (6)$$

where p is the relative index of the event in the reordered sequence $\mathbf{y}_p$, and C_ρ is a constant that defines the maximum decrement for ρ^j. The next upcoming event $(p-1)$ has its vigilance parameter decreased the most. Lowering matching threshold of predicted patterns is a concept that is believed to be existing in the human brain [9]. Predicted events are more likely to appear in the current episode, so lowering ρ^j facilitates their activation and makes it possible to tolerate minor differences. To retrieve specific situational attributes related to $\mathbf{y}_p$, weights w_j^k can be read out one at a time following the sequential order of the anticipated events.

2.4 Artificial Emotion Module

The Artificial Emotion Module is used to adjust ρ^s and β^s to favor recall of the most relevant episode and to improve episode stability in memory. Two artificial emotions intensities $E_e \in [0,1]$ are used: Joy (indicating that the robot behaves according to its intentions) and Anger (indicating that its intentions are not satisfied). The heuristic used is that when an episode is experienced with high emotion intensity, such episode needs to be stable in memory, meaning that it should remain intact as future learning occurs. This is done by lowering the learning rates (β^s or β^j), which will limit weight changes:

$$\beta^{(new)} = \beta^{(old)} \left(1 - C_\beta \cdot (max(E_e) - 0.5)\right), \quad \beta^{(new)} \in [\beta_{min}, \beta_{max}] \quad (7)$$

where C_β is a constant that defines the maximum decrement, and β_{min} and β_{max} limiting the range. A max E_e lower than 0.5 increases β, while a value above 0.5 decreases it.

Also, episodes with high emotional intensities must be recalled easily, meaning that ρ^s can be decreased according to:

$$\rho^{s(new)} = \rho^{s(old)} \left(1 - C_\rho \cdot (max(E_e) - 0.5)\right), \quad \rho^{s(new)} \in [\rho_{min}^s, \rho_{max}^s] \quad (8)$$

where ρ_{min}^s and ρ_{max}^s limits the range.

Equations (7) and (8) are applied and saved when learning occur on the associated layer.

3   Experimental Setup

IRL-1 is a robotic platform composed of a humanoid torso on top of a mobile base [4]. IRL-1 uses a Kinect motion sensor for vision processing, a laser range finder for obstacle avoidance and simultaneous localization and mapping (implemented using [15]), and a 8-microphone array for speech interaction with people. IRL-1 detects a person by merging information from legs detection, voice direction and face detection, turning its head toward the person. People identification is implemented using a basic face recognition algorithm based on Principle Component Analysis on the detected face [17]. Objects recognition is done using 2D images from the Kinect using SIFT [10]. Two computers running Linux and Robot Operating System (ROS) [12] are used to implement IRL-1 control architecture.

For this experiment, IRL-1's task is to deliver one of three objects O_1, O_2 and O_3 to people in a different location, according to the following scenario:

- In room R_0, a person P stops in front of IRL-1. IRL-1 then identifies and greets the person.
- Person P shows the object O_o to IRL-1. IRL-1 then recognizes the object and extends its left arm to grasp it.
- IRL-1 autonomously navigates to the other room R_1, searching to deliver object O_o to somebody. When entering a room, IRL-1 asks if there is someone there to take object O_o. IRL-1 wanders around until a person D is located in area L inside room R_1.
- IRL-1 extends its arm and delivers object O_o.

Each occurrence of this scenario consists of an episode. Once the task completed, learning is triggered in the Episode Layer and IRL-1 is programmed to return to room R_0 to start again.

For the trials, parameters of our EM-ART are initialized as follows: $\rho^j = 0.95$, $\rho^s = 0.55$, $\rho^s_{min} = 0.45$, $\rho^s_{max} = 0.85$, $C_\rho = 0.20$, $\beta^j = \beta^s = 0.6$, $\beta_{min} = 0.1$, $\beta_{max} = 1$, $C_\beta = 0.25$, $\tau = 0.05$ and $\alpha^k = 0.01$. Joy and Anger are associated with the following control modules controlling IRL-1: *Teleoperation* (required when IRL-1 looses its position in the map), *Go To* (to navigate from one room to another) and *Wandering*. If these modules are activated (meaning that IRL-1 wants to satisfy the intended goal associated to these controllers) and exploited (meaning that IRL-1 is using these modules to control its actions) over time, then the intensity of Joy increases; otherwise, if they are activated but not exploited, Anger increases. For example, when IRL-1 activates *Go To*, Joy increases and Anger decreases as long as the module is exploited. If IRL-1 gets lost in its internal map, the *Go To* behavior is no longer exploited and therefore Joy decreases and Anger increases.

4   Experimental Results

To demonstrate the use of our EM-ART model, we conducted 10 trials for each of the following conditions, each trial initiated with an empty memory, to observe how it responds to different types of situations.

1. **Recall repeatability and prediction.** R_0, R_1, P, O_o, D and L remained identical throughout the trials, leading to only one episode. The EM-ART should therefore be able to recall the episode as soon as possible, allowing IRL-1 to predict where to go before having to wander in room R_1, allowing IRL-1 to use L as a destination to go to. Successful recall of L occurred 8 times out of 9. Trial 1 lead to the creation of an episode made of 15 event nodes. For trials 2 to 4, recall occurred relatively late in the episodes, i.e., while IRL-1 was wandering in R_1. As the scenario was repeated and learned, recurring events stayed while sporadic events faded, and recall occurred as early as when IRL-1 was in R_0, after having recognized the object O_o or the person P. In the one trial where recall was not observed, IRL-1 lost its position in its map: teleoperation was required, Anger were generated and 10 new event nodes were created, leading to a distinct episode.

2. **Recall repeatability and learning.** R_0, R_1, P, O_o and D remained identical throughout the trials, while L changed with each trial. The objective of this condition was to observe if the last L learned could be predicted as the destination when an episodic recall occurred. Successful recall of L happened 8 times out of 9. Each time, the destination predicted was the one from the previous trial, as expected, and IRL-1 started wandering from that point. When learning of the episode with the new destination L occurred, the weighted connections to the previous destination L were reduced. For the unsuccessful trial, a false detection of the object recognition module led to the creation of five new event nodes at the beginning of the episode, and consequently, created of a new episode.

3. **Semantic differences and creation of new episodes.** R_0, R_1, P and D remained identical throughout the trials, while O_o changed to be one of

three objects (O_1, O_2, O_3). This should lead to the creation of three episodes semantically different but with some similar events. Each object delivery was done at a specific location L for the object in question, to differentiate which episode was recalled and used to predict L. Figure 2 presents the total number of event nodes and episode nodes in memory after each trial, and with the object presented. As expected, each trial involving a new object O_o led to the creation of a new episode, for a total of three. The number of event nodes in the memory increased in the first five trials since percepts changed slightly over the episodes, but stabilized in the last five trials.

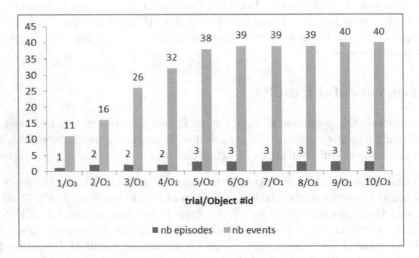

Fig. 2. Number of nodes of the Event Layer and Episode Layer as IRL-1 is being presented with three objects

4. **Relevance of the input channel.** To test the influence of γ^k on an event node, R_0, R_1, P, D and L are kept identical over the trials, $\gamma^2 = 0$ for the Object channel, and a different object (O_1, O_2, O_3) was used between trials. This condition should lead to the same episode, making the objects carried by IRL-1 irrelevant for the episode, and as expected, after 10 trials, only one episode was learned. IRL-1 also recalled the episode when entering R_1 (once in the corridor between R_0 and R_1), and went directly to the delivery location L without wandering in the room R_1, regardless of O_o.

5. **Episode with high emotional intensity.** R_0, R_1, P, O_o, D and L remained identical throughout the trials, but we forced IRL-1 to experience high emotional intensity during trial 1, by deliberately covering up the laser range sensor, making the *Go To* module unusable. This made Anger reached its maximum value as the episode was learned, leading to the decrease of β^s and ρ^s according to Eq. (7) and Eq. (8). This condition should lead to rapid episode recall, allowing IRL-1 to benefit from a prediction early on at the beginning of the task. Indeed, during trials 2 to 10, the episode learned in trial 1 was recalled as soon as IRL-1 realized it was in R_0: IRL-1 then decided to directly go to the delivery location L.

6. **Episode with no emotions.** R_0, R_1, P, O_o, D and L remained identical throughout the trials, but we set $E_e = 0$ for Joy and for Anger to illustrate the influences of emotions on recall. According to Eq. (7) and Eq. (8), ρ^s will increase over time, and the episode will not be recognized as easily. During trials 2 and 3, a successful episode recall was observed, allowing IRL-1 to predict the delivery location L. During trials 4 and 5, IRL-1 recognized the episode, but the prediction was not useful since L was already reached after having wandered for a while. Starting trial 6, episode recall did not happened before the end of the task because ρ_s was too high (0.85) to tolerate minor variations in the sequence of events, leading to the creation of new episodes in memory. After ten trials, the episodic memory contained three episodes rather than only one.

5   Conclusion and Future Work

The underlying objective of providing a robot with an episodic memory is to allow it to adapt its decision-making processes according to past experiences when operating in dynamic environments. This paper presents a variant of EM-ART in which the learning rate parameters and the vigilance parameters are associated to specific event and episode. Changing the learning rate influences weight adaptation to either learn quickly ($\beta = 1$) or preserve what was experienced in the past ($\beta = 0$), whether it is for an event node or an episode node. The vigilance parameters set what can be characterize as the granularity of the matching scheme: it can be identical ($\rho = 1$) or coarse ($\rho = 0.1$), in relation to input channels or to events. Keeping these parameters constant across layers consider that each episode has the same importance, which is unrealistic considering that the episode experienced may or may not be the results of appropriate actions according to the robot's intentions. Using a repeatable scenario involving people recognition, object recognition and location identification, we illustrate how adapting these parameters can lead to appropriate episode learning and recall, and how upcoming predicted events can be used to influence the behaviour of the robot. Results show that the robot successfully differentiates semantically dissimilar episodes and expands its memory to learn new situations online. To explore further all the potential of our EM-ART model, future work involves extensive testing with a higher number of trials experienced randomly, with different complex tasks in which repeatable sequences can be experienced, and observing how the EM evolves over time.

Acknowledgment. This work was supported by the Natural Sciences and Engineering Research Council of Canada (NSERC).

References

1. Carpenter, G.A., Grossberg, S.: A massively parallel architecture for a self-organizing neural pattern recognition machine. Computer Vision, Graphics, and Image Processing 37(1), 54–115 (1987)

2. Carpenter, G.A., Grossberg, S., Rosen, D.B.: Fuzzy ART: Fast stable learning and categorization of analog patterns by an adaptive resonance system. Neural Networks 4(6), 759–771 (1991)
3. Dodd, W., Gutierrez, R.: The role of episodic memory and emotion in a cognitive robot. In: Proceedings of IEEE International Workshop on Robot and Human Interactive Communication, pp. 692–697 (2005)
4. Ferland, F., Létourneau, D., Aumont, A., Frémy, J., Legault, M.A., Lauria, M., Michaud, F.: Natural interaction design of a humanoid robot. Journal of Human-Robot Interaction 1(2), 118–134 (2012)
5. Haikonen, P.O.: Consciousness and robot sentience, vol. 2. World Scientific Publishing Company (2012)
6. Hawkins, J.: On intelligence. Macmillan (2004)
7. Komatsu, T., Takeno, J.: A conscious robot that expects emotions. In: Proceedings of IEEE International Conference on Industrial Technology, pp. 15–20 (2011)
8. Kuppuswamy, N.S., Cho, S.H., Kim, J.H.: A cognitive control architecture for an artificial creature using episodic memory. In: Proceedings of SICE-ICASE International Joint Conference, pp. 3104–3110 (2006)
9. Kurzweil, R.: How to Create a Mind: The Secret of Human Thought Revealed (2012)
10. Lowe, D.G.: Object recognition from local scale-invariant features. In: Proceedings of IEEE International Conference on Computer Vision, vol. 2, pp. 1150–1157 (1999)
11. Nuxoll, A.M., Laird, J.E.: Enhancing intelligent agents with episodic memory. Cognitive Systems Research, 34–48 (2011)
12. Quigley, M., Conley, K., Gerkey, B., Faust, J., Foote, T., Leibs, J., Wheeler, R., Ng, A.Y.: ROS: An open-source robot operating system. In: ICRA Workshop on Open Source Software (2009)
13. Stachowicz, D., Kruijff, G.: Episodic-like memory for cognitive robots. IEEE Transactions on Autonomous Mental Development 4(1), 1–16 (2011)
14. Taylor, S.E., Vineyard, C.M., Healy, M.J., Caudell, T.P., Cohen, N.J., Watson, P., Verzi, S.J., Morrow, J.D., Bernard, M.L., Eichenbaum, H.: Memory in silico: Building a neuromimetic episodic cognitive model. In: Proceedings of World Congress on Computer Science and Information Engineering, vol. 5, pp. 733–737 (2009)
15. Thrun, S., Fox, D., Burgard, W., Dellaert, F.: Robust Monte Carlo localization for mobile robots. Artificial Intelligence 128(1), 99–141 (2001)
16. Tulving, E.: Precis of elements of episodic memory. Behavioral and Brain Sciences 7(2), 223–268 (1984)
17. Viola, P., Jones, M.J.: Robust real-time face detection. International Journal of Computer Vision 57(2), 137–154 (2004)
18. Wang, W., Subagdja, B., Tan, A.H., Starzyk, J.A.: A self-organizing approach to episodic memory modeling. In: Proceedings of International Joint Conference on Neural Networks, pp. 1–8 (2010)
19. Wang, W., Subagdja, B., Tan, A.H., Starzyk, J.A.: Neural modeling of episodic memory: Encoding, retrieval, and forgetting. IEEE Transactions on Neural Networks and Learning Systems 23(10), 1574–1586 (2012)

Bracketing the Beetle: How Wittgenstein's Understanding of Language Can Guide Our Practice in AGI and Cognitive Science

Simon D. Levy[1], Charles Lowney[2], William Meroney[3], and Ross W. Gayler[4]

[1] Computer Science Department, Washington and Lee University
Lexington Virginia 24450, USA
levys@wlu.edu
[2] Philosophy Department, Washington and Lee University
[3] United States Environmental Protection Agency
[4] Faculty of Humanities and Social Sciences
La Trobe University
Melbourne, VIC, Australia

Abstract. We advocate for a novel connectionist modeling framework as an answer to a set of challenges to AGI and cognitive science put forth by classical formal systems approaches. We show how this framework, which we call Vector Symbolic Architectures, or VSAs, is also the kind of model of mental activity that we arrive at by taking Ludwig Wittgenstein's critiques of the philosophy of mind and language seriously. We conclude by describing how VSA and related architectures provide a compelling solution to three central problems raised by Wittgenstein in the *Philosophical Investigations* regarding rule-following, aspect-seeing, and the development of a "private" language.

Keywords: Wittgenstein, language-games, connectionism, Vector Symbolic Architectures, Sparse Distributed Memory, Raven's Progressive Matrices, Necker Cube.

1 Connectionism and the Classical Approach

The traditional and perhaps still-dominant view of mental activity describes it in terms of symbols and rules of the sort used in writing predicate calculi or formal grammars. For example, the concept of romantic jealousy might be described by a rule

$$\{(X \text{ loves } Y) \text{ and } (Y \text{ loves } Z)\} \rightarrow (X \text{ is jealous of } Z)$$

The precise details of the symbols and rules do not much matter; what is important here is the hypothesis that any physical system that instantiates the symbols and rules in an explicit, consistent way is a reasonable candidate for being a model of mind [1]. The brittleness of such rule-based systems and the

B. Goertzel et al. (Eds.): AGI 2014, LNAI 8598, pp. 73–84, 2014.

difficulty of scaling them up to real-world problems[1] led to the connectionist (neural network, Parallel Distributed Processing) renaissance of the 1980's and 90's, centered around the back-propagation algorithm for training networks with hidden layers of nodes [3]. PDP advocates cited the "graceful degradation" displayed by such systems, in contrast to the all-or-nothing brittleness of rule-based systems, as evidence in favor of the PDP / connectionist approach. With network nodes roughly corresponding to nodes and connections to synapses, PDP networks also looked to be a promising avenue to showing how cognitive capacities, such as thought and language, could be based in hidden neural activity.

Researchers favoring connectionist models typically cite the past-tense model of English verbs [4], which indicated that a single neural network exposed to representations of the present and past tenses of English verbs could learn both rule-like patterns (*walks/walked*) and exceptions (*goes/went*),without anything corresponding to an explicit syntactic rule. The word or other form being represented at any given time was encoded not as an explicit symbol, but in the "sub-symbolic" state of activations distributed across the hidden (internal) neurons. Such *distributed representations* [5] offered a number of desirable features, such as content-addressability and robustness to noise, that were not intuitively available to classicists.

Advocates of the symbols-and-rules approach were quick to point out the limitations: although connectionist models showed an impressive ability to learn both rule-like and exception-based patterns, there was little evidence that they were capable of modeling the systematic, compositional nature of language and thought [6]. Without the ability to compose and decompose propositions and other structures in systematic ways – relating e.g., *John loves Mary* to *Mary loves John* – there was little reason to expect connectionist models to work for more abstract reasoning as in the jealousy example above. Further, the back-propagation algorithm used to train the network required explicit supervision (repeated error-correction by a teacher) in a way that was not consistent with actual language acquisition, which consists mainly of the experience of positive exemplars [7]. In addition to concerns about the ability of connectionist networks to scale up to bigger problem domains, these observations made connectionist models seem implausible.

2   VSA Representation and Operation

Partly in response to such criticisms, we have spent the past decade or so developing connectionist models that support the acquisition of systematic, compositional behavior from a small number of positive examples and provide plausible, scalable models for language and thought.

The general term we use for these models – Vector Symbolic Architecture, or VSA [8] – describes a class of connectionist networks that use high-dimensional

---

[1] An oft-cited model was SHRDLU [2], which could converse in English about a virtual world containing children's toy blocks using a vocabulary of around 50 words, but was never successfully extended to a more realistic, complicated domain.

vectors of low-precision numbers to encode systematic, compositional information as distributed representations. VSAs can represent complex entities such
as multiple role/filler relations or attribute/values pairs in such a way that every entity – no matter how simple or complex – corresponds to a pattern of
activation distributed over all the elements of the vector.

For our purposes in this paper, we make use of three operations on vectors:
an element-wise multiplication operation $\otimes$ that associates or binds vectors of
the same dimensionality; an element-wise vector-addition operation $+$ that su-
perposes such vectors or adds them to a set; and a permutation operator $P()$
that can be used to encode precedence relations.

For example, given a two-place predicate like *kisses* and the representations of
two individuals John and Mary, one possible way of representing the proposition
that Mary kisses John is

$$\langle kisses \rangle \otimes \langle \text{SUBJECT} \rangle \otimes \langle Mary \rangle + \langle kisses \rangle \otimes \langle \text{OBJECT} \rangle \otimes \langle John \rangle$$

where the angle brackets $\langle \rangle$ around an item stand for the vector representation
of that item. If the vector elements are taken from the set $\{-1, +1\}$, then each
vector is its own binding inverse.[2] Binding and unbinding can therefore both be
performed by the same operator, thanks to its associativity:

$$X \otimes (X \otimes Y) = (X \otimes X) \otimes Y = Y$$

Because these vector operations are also commutative and distribute over addition, another interesting property holds: the unbinding operation can be applied
to a set of associations just as easily as it can to a single association:

$$Y \otimes (X \otimes Y + W \otimes Z) =$$
$$Y \otimes X \otimes Y + Y \otimes W \otimes Z = X \otimes Y \otimes Y + Y \otimes W \otimes Z =$$
$$X + Y \otimes W \otimes Z$$

If the vector elements are chosen randomly (e.g., either +1 or -1 chosen by coin
flip), then we can rewrite this equation as

$$Y \otimes (X \otimes Y + W \otimes Z) = X + noise$$

where *noise* is a vector completely dissimilar (having a dot-product or vector
cosine of zero) to any of our original vectors W, X, Y, and Z. If we like, the
noise can be removed through a "cleanup memory," such as a Hopfield network
[9], that stores the original vectors in a neurally plausible way. In a multiple-
choice setting, the cleanup isn't even necessary, because we can use the vector
dot-product to find the item having the highest similarity to $X + noise$.

Going beyond simple associative binding, we can use the permutation operator to encode directionality or precedence. For example, to encode the simple
directed graph in Figure 1:

---

[2] It may seem dubious to represent predicates or individuals by simple vectors taken
(randomly) from the set $\{-1, +1\}$. Our goal here is not to provide a theory of representation, but rather to illustrate the basic functioning of VSA, which can in turn
serve as a foundation for a fully fleshed-out representational system of actual vectors
derived through the interaction of sensory-motor processes, linguistics experience,
etc.

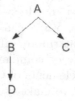

Fig. 1. A simple directed graph

$$\langle G \rangle = A \otimes P(B) + A \otimes P(C) + B \otimes P(D)$$

Querying the child(ren) of B then corresponds to applying the inverse permutation $P^{-1}()$ to the result of the same product operation:

$$P^{-1}(B \otimes \langle G \rangle) =$$
$$P^{-1}(B \otimes (A \otimes P(B) + A \otimes P(C) + B \otimes P(D))) =$$
$$P^{-1}(B \otimes A \otimes P(B) + B \otimes A \otimes P(C) + B \otimes B \otimes P(D)) =$$
$$P^{-1}(B \otimes A \otimes P(B) + B \otimes A \otimes P(C) + P(D)) =$$
$$D + noise$$

In sum, VSA provides a principled connectionist alternative to classical symbolic systems (e.g., predicate calculus, graph theory) for encoding and manipulating a variety of useful structures. The biggest advantage of VSA representations over other connectionist approaches is that a single association (or set of associations) can be quickly recovered from a set (or larger set) of associations using the same simple operator that creates the associations, in a time that is independent of the number of associations. VSA thus answers the scalability problem, and also shows how to build compositionally without using the grammatical rules and atomic symbols that classical approaches require. VSA also no longer needs to rely on back-propagation for learning. We can thus get to the same phenomenal results we see in language use efficiently, without positing a deep grammar or logic.

3   VSA and Wittgenstein

Having outlined the details of Vector Symbolic Architectures, we will now argue for VSA as the kind of AGI framework that accords well with the critiques presented by Wittgenstein in his *Philosophical Investigations* [10] and other later works. As pointed out by several researchers ([11]; [12]; [13]), connectionist networks are to the classical approaches of Fodor and Pylyshyn, what Wittgenstein's later philosophy of language was to the formal approaches of Gottlob Frege and Bertrand Russell. We have shown how VSAs can fulfill the promise of connectionism by responding to classicist concerns. We will now show how VSAs coordinate well with several of Wittgenstein's important observations concerning meaningful language.

First, we note that the sub-symbolic content of VSA representations (which are arbitrary or literally random) accords nicely with the "Beetle in the Box" metaphor from section 293 of the *Investigations*:

> Suppose everyone had a box with something in it: we call it a "beetle". No one can look into anyone else's box, and everyone says he knows what a beetle is only by looking at his beetle. – Here it would be quite possible for everyone to have something different in his box. One might even imagine such a thing constantly changing. – But suppose the word "beetle" had a use in these people's language? – If so it would not be used as the name of a thing. The thing in the box has no place in the language-game at all; not even as a something: for the box might even be empty. – No, one can 'divide through' by the thing in the box; it cancels out, whatever it is. That is to say: if we construe the grammar of the expression of sensation on the model of 'object and designation' the object drops out of consideration as irrelevant.

Wittgenstein highlights the role of the symbol in linguistic practices. Symbols commonly do not derive their meaning by directly representing a thing, i.e., by ostensive definition. The language-game shows us how to use the word meaningfully. In other words, the atomic thing can cancel out without loss of meaning. Indeed, VSAs use of random vectors guarantees that my "beetle," i.e., any atomic sensation particular to me and my use of the word, will be different from yours from the very start. Further, as the concept of *beetle* evolves in the experience of an individual or its use by that individual changes in different contexts, the random vector itself may be "constantly changing."

Second, we observe that the distributed nature of VSA representations accords well with Wittgenstein's notion of "family resemblance" terms. This connection was noted by Smolensky [14], who described how a "family of distributed patterns" informed the meaning of a word in connectionist models. Mills expanded on this point [11] and explicitly linked it to Wittgenstein's critique of essentialist concepts and formalisms. Mills notes that connectionist systems reflect the reliance on overlapping and criss-crossing resemblances and contextual cues for meaningful word use ([10] #66; [11],139-141).

Mills also notes that Wittgenstein rejects a psycho-physical parallelism ([15], 608-611), and this also accords well with the distributed nature of the symbols ([11], 151, 152). A distributed view of symbols stands in contrast to recent efforts to localize thought in a particular organ or brain region – the most extreme version being the putative "grandmother cell" neuron whose sole job is to recognize your grandmother [16].

Third, we note that the relation between the symbols does not require the classical linguistic or propositional form in order to be meaningful. The non-linguistic nature of the distributed representations employed in VSA carries over into natural language expressions. As Wittgenstein indicates in the building crew example at the beginning of the *Investigations*, it is a mistake to claim that the utterance "Slab!" really means "Bring me a slab!" ([10] #19). I.e., in order for an utterance to be meaningful there is no need for it to fit an underlying grammatical form that looks like a proposition in predicate calculus. In contrast to the sentence-like representations employed in traditional symbol systems, in VSA there is no sense in which any item is located in any grammatical "position."

Last, we note that the uniform nature of representation in VSA eliminates the sort of problems that Wittgenstein criticized in Russell's theory of types and related formalisms. VSA dispenses with grammatical categories and types. As early as 1914, Wittgenstein was suspicious of any artificial hierarchical structures that might be used to designate, from the top-down, when a particular combination of signs were symbols with sense [17]. The idea that all symbols are of the same type, coordinates well with VSA representation, which, in turn, coordinates well with Wittgenstein's later view: meaningful utterances emerge from linguistic practices and not from the artificial characterizations we impose by designating symbols and manipulating them with formal rules.

VSA fits desiderata Wittgenstein established in the *Investigations* by (1) not relying on ostension or an atomic identification for symbol meaning, (2) recognizing the distributed and "family resemblance" nature of symbol construction, (3) not relying on predicate logic or grammatical form for the composition of meaningful thoughts or sentences, and (4) repudiating different orders or types for symbols in favor of a more organic approach. Moreover, we will now show how VSA can solve three interrelated puzzles that Wittgenstein raised in a manner consistent with his observations.

4   Learning Patterns without Explicit Rule-Following

Wittgenstein had serious reservations about attempts to characterize language or mental processes using symbols-and-rules methodology ([10] #81; [12] 138). For Wittgenstein, the productivity of human thought and linguistic behavior is underdetermined by the rules of logic and grammar. A rule on its own cannot be properly applied without some sort of training.

Having illustrated the way in which VSA supports compositionality and systematicity, we now illustrate how it can generalize from exemplars without recourse to explicit rules. This example is due to Rasmussen and Eliasmith [18], who show how a VSA-based neural architecture can solve the Raven's Progressive Matrices task for intelligence testing. In this task, subjects are given a puzzle like the one in the left side of Figure 2 (simplified for our purposes here) and are asked to select the missing piece from a set of possibilities like the ones on the right.

Asked how they arrived at this solution, people might report that they followed these two rules:

1. *Put one item in the first column, two in the second, and three in the third.*
2. *Put* ● *in the first row,* ◆ *in the second, and* ▲ *in the third.*

A compelling feature of VSA is that it can solve this problem using the representation of the matrix itself; that is, VSA can (so to speak) *learn the rule(s)*

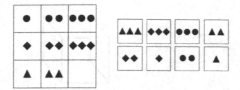

Fig. 2. Raven's Progressive matrix example (left) and candidate solutions (right)

through exposure to the problem. Each element of the matrix can be represented as a set of attribute/value pairs; for example, the center element would be

$$\langle shape \rangle \otimes \langle diamond \rangle + \langle number \rangle \otimes \langle two \rangle$$

Solving the matrix then corresponds to deriving a mapping from one item to the next. As Rasmussen and Eliasmith show, such a mapping can be obtained by computing the vector transformation from each item to the item in the row or column next to it. The overall transformation for the entire matrix is then the vector sum of such transformations.

Details of our VSA solution to the Raven's Matrices (a simplified version of [18]), along with Matlab code for this task and others mentioned in this paper, are available from `tinyurl.com/wittvsa`. A similar solution, using a different kind of VSA encoding, is presented in [19].

5   Seeing-as: Determining Perceptual Experience in Ambiguous Contexts *without* Interpretation

The paradox of visually ambiguous figures, or "seeing-that vs. seeing-as," occupied Wittgenstein all the way from the Necker cube example in *Tractatus* [20] (5.5423) through the duck-rabbit example in the *Investigations* (II.xi; see Figure 3), about which he says

> I may, then, have seen the duck-rabbit simply as a picture-rabbit from the first. That is to say, if asked "What's that?" or "What do you see here?" I should have replied: "A picture-rabbit". I should not have answered the question "What do you see here?" by saying: "Now I am seeing it as a picture-rabbit". I should have described my perception: just as if I had said "I see a red circle over there."

There is no sense in which we simultaneously perceive one alternative and the possibility of the other: either the duck or the rabbit must win. Wittgenstein's point is that the possibility of interpretation, when the perceptual information is ambiguous, does not mean that we are interpreting in normal circumstances, e.g., in the case of seeing just the rabbit. Connectionist approaches show how the same perceptual process that shows us the red circle can show us the duck or the rabbit, but not both at the same time.

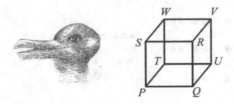

Fig. 3. The Duck-Rabbit(*courtesy of Wikimedia Commons*) and the Necker Cube

Modeling the perception of visually ambiguous images like this was one of the first accomplishments of the connectionist renaissance of the 1980s. As Rumelhart *et al.* [21] showed, such images could be represented as a network of constraints that excited or inhibited each other in a way that drove the network quickly into one of the possible solutions. For example, in the Necker cube in Figure 3, the two solutions are (1) $PQRS$ front, $TUVW$ back and (2)) $PQRS$ back, $TUVW$ front. Rumelhart et al. modeled these constraints as a localist ("grandmother cell") neural network each of whose units represented a possible position of each vertex. They showed that inhibitory or excitatory synaptic connections between pairs of constraints (P_f excites W_b; R_f inhibits W_f), combined with a simple update rule, are sufficient to drive the entire network quickly into one of the two consistent yet incompatible solutions.

This excitation / inhibition model provides a nice explanation for Wittgenstein's observation about seeing-as: presented with a set of vertices, the model, like human observers, cannot help but "see" one global pattern of organization or another. The network is, however, localist, and as a general model of constraint satisfaction it therefore raises the philosophical and practical concerns expressed earlier. Is it possible to design an excitation / inhibition network that uses distributed (VSA) representations?

In [22] we provide an example of such a network, and show how it can be used to solve a Necker-cube-like problem called "graph isomorphism" (optimally matching up the vertices of two similar shapes). Our solution works by a Bayesian process that repeatedly updates a candidate solution state x using evidence w, until x converges to a stable solution. Inhibition of inconsistent solutions by consistent solutions is implemented by normalizing the values in x to a fixed interval at the end of every update. This same approach can be used to solve the Necker Cube. In our Necker Cube program, the candidate solution state x is initially just the vector sum of the representations of all possible solution components:

$$x_0 = P_f + Q_f + R_f + S_f + Tb + Ub + Vb + Wb + Pb + Qb + Rb + Sb + T_f + U_f + V_f + W_f$$

where the subscripts stand for $f$orward and $b$ackward. As usual for VSA, each term of the sum is a vector of high dimensionality with elements chosen randomly from the set $\{-1, +1\}$. The constraints (evidence) w can then be represented as the sum of the pairwise products of mutually-consistent components:

$$w = P_f \otimes Q_f + P_f \otimes R_f + P_f \otimes S_f + P_f \otimes T_b + P_f \otimes U_b + ... + W_b \otimes U_b + W_b \otimes V_b$$

The update of x from w can likewise be implemented by using the binding (elementwise product) operator $\otimes$. If any vertex/position vector (e.g. P_f) has greater representation in x than others do, multiplying this consistency vector w by the state vector x has the effect of "unlocking" (unbinding) the components of w consistent with this evidence. As an example, consider the extreme case in which x contains only the component P_f:

$$x_t \otimes w =$$

$$P_f \otimes (P_f \otimes Qf + P_f \otimes Rf + P_f \otimes Sf + P_f \otimes Tb + P_f \otimes Ub + ... + Wb \otimes Ub + Wb \otimes V_b) =$$

$$Q_f + R_f + S_f + T_b + U_b + V_b + W_b + noise$$

6   Boxing the Beetle: The Emergence of Schemata from Repeated Exposure

VSA and related connectionist technologies support the view of mental processes that we get by taking Wittgenstein's critiques seriously. These technologies all involve (1) representations distributed over high-dimensional vectors of numerical elements and (2) psychologically plausible learning mechanisms.

Sparse Distributed Memory or SDM [23] is a technology for content-based storage and retrieval of high-dimensional vector representations like the ones used in VSA. An SDM consists of some (arbitrary) number of address vectors, each with a corresponding data vector. Addresses and data can be binary 0/1 values, or +1,-1 values as in VSA. The address values are initially random, and the data values are initially zero. To enter a new address/data pair into the SDM, the Hamming distance (count of the elementwise differences) of the new address vector with each of the existing address vectors is first computed. If the new address is less than some fixed distance from an existing address, the new data is added to the existing data at that address. To retrieve the item at a novel address, a similar comparison is made between the novel address and the existing addresses, resulting in a set of addresses less than a fixed distance from the probe. The data vectors at these addresses are summed, and the resulting vector sum is converted to a vector of 0's and 1's (or -1s and +1s) by converting each non-negative value to 1 and each negative value to 0 (or -1).

As illustrated in [24], the distribution of each pattern across several locations produces a curious property: given a set of degraded exemplars of a pattern (such as the pixels for an image with some noise added), an SDM can often reconstruct the "ideal" form of the pattern through retrieval, even though no exemplar of this ideal was presented to it. Because of these powerful properties of SDM, our research group and others (e.g., [19]) have begun to construct models combining

VSA representations with SDM. For example, the VSA might be used to encode sequence information (through the binding and permutation operators described above), and the SDM would then be used as a memory of previously-encountered sequences. We are currently investigating the use of this architecture as a model of the encapsulation and chunk extraction that are necessary for the acquisition of skilled behaviors like language and planning.[3]

In allowing each address to portray a slight variant of the same concept, SDM reminds us of the family-resemblance approach to categories in the *Investigations*. Moreover, this property of SDM also proposes a solution to the problem of how we might come to use a particular leaf pattern as a schema for leaves in general ([10] #47) or how we might come to develop a sign for a particular yet elusive sensation using experience and memory.

> Let us imagine the following case. I want to keep a diary about the recurrence of a certain sensation. To this end I associate it with the sign "S" and write this sign in a calendar for every day on which I have the sensation.——I will remark first of all that a definition of the sign cannot be formulated.–But still I can give myself a kind of ostensive definition. – How? ... in the present case I have no criterion of correctness. ([10]#258)

This remark is meant to support the idea that there can be no language that ties words directly to private sensations. It emphasizes the need for a background of reliable cues and uses to be in place before a sign can be meaningful. The connectionist approach helps explicate the manner in which private experiences can develop into meaningful uses of language even here when the information is sparse.

If Wittgenstein is not denying a kind of private language (e.g., the sort that a Robinson Crusoe could still speak) as insightful readers of the so-called "private language" argument believe ([26], ch. 10), then we have a riddle in this passage that distributed representations can solve: just as we saw how a rule could emerge from linguistic practices, and how a symbol could be determined from possibly ambiguous perceptual information, we now see how meaning might emerge for a sign that has a sparse and ambiguous heritage.

This ties directly back into the beetle in the box example. Just as we do not get the meaning of "beetle" by pointing to an object, we do not get the meaning of a sensation word by an internal "pointing" to a sensation. There need be no unique private sensation that the sign "S" captures in order for a meaningful language containing the sign "S" to get off the ground. Wittgenstein suggests that one cannot tell, even privately, if one is using the word correctly if there is nothing but the sensation to rely on; one does not have a grip on the right use of the term without a context and other behavioral cues that give sense to the sign [27]. Although SDM works with degraded versions of an original concept or ideal that it can reconstruct, it can also construct a meaningful representation from a set of experiences in want of criteria of correctness. What VSA, SDM,

---

[3] Contrast this approach with the state-of-the-art model for such tasks, which relies on back-propagation for the memory component. [25]

and the like show here is how an ideal or proper use for the sign can be built up from the uses of "S" even if the iterations of the "S" tying it to the sensation were not "correctly" used (from some imagined God's eye point of view that we do not have).

Without any external checks to help provide a use for the sign we could not reliably establish a meaning, but the iterations and their associations, e.g., my stomach growling and it being around 12 o'clock when I say "S", can begin to build a box around the beetle – and then we can bracket the beetle: the private sensation no longer functions to provide the rule by which I will use the word: for the purposes of meaningful language, the sensation itself "is not a *something*, but not a *nothing* either!" ([10] #304) And the rule by which I use the word is established in a network of sub-symbolic connections; it is not fixed permanently, nor is it a rule of ordinary English grammar, or a rule of Mentalese that such a grammar purports to approximate. Wittgenstein shows us that we do not always have a special internal or intentional grip on what the sign means. We cannot grasp the inner sensation or the outer beetle, nor need we.

Acknoweldgement / Disclaimer. This work was supported in part by a paid sabbatical leave from Washington and Lee University for Simon D. Levy during Fall 2013. William Meroney did not contribute to this work as an employee of the US EPA, and any views he contributed are his alone and do not represent those of the the United States or the US EPA.

References

[1] Newell, A.: Physical symbol systems. Cognitive Science 4(2), 135–183 (1980)

[2] Winograd, T.: Procedures as a representation for data in a computer program for understanding natural language. Technical Report 235. MIT, Cambridge (1971)

[3] Rumelhart, D.E., Hinton, G.E., Williams, R.J.: Learning representations by back-propagating errors. Nature 323(6088), 533–536 (1986)

[4] Rumelhart, D.E., McClelland, J.L.: On learning the past tense of english verbs. In: McClelland, J., Rumelhart, D. (eds.) Parallel Distributed Processing: Explorations in the Microstructure of Cognition. MIT Press, Cambridge (1986)

[5] Hinton, G.E., McClelland, J., Rumelhart, D.E.: Distributed representations. In: McClelland, J., Rumelhart, D. (eds.) Parallel Distributed Processing: Explorations in the Microstructure of Cognition. MIT Press, Cambridge (1986)

[6] Fodor, J., Pylyshyn, Z.W.: Connectionism and cognitive architecture: A critical analysis. Cognition 28, 371 (1988)

[7] Chomsky, N.: Rules and Representations. Basil Blackwell, Oxford (1980)

[8] Gayler, R.: Vector symbolic architectures answer jackendoff's challenges for cognitive neuroscience. In: Slezak, P. (ed.) ICCS/ASCS International Conference on Cognitive Science, CogPrints, Sydney, Australia, pp. 133–138. University of New South Wales (2003)

[9] Hopfield, J.: Neural networks and physical systems with emergent collective computational abilities. Proceedings of the National Academy of Sciences of the USA 79(8), 2554–2558 (1982)

[10] Wittgenstein, L.: Philosophical Investigations. Basil Blackwell, Oxford (1958); Trans. G.E.M. Anscombe

[11] Mills, S.: Wittgenstein and connectionism: A significant complementarity? Royal Institute of Philosophy Supplement 34, 137–157 (1993)

[12] Dror, I., Dascal, M.: Can Wittgenstein help free the mind from rules? In: Johnson, D., Erneling, C. (eds.) The Philosophical Foundations of Connectionism. Oxford University Press, Oxford (1997)

[13] Goldstein, L., Slater, H.: Wittgenstein, semantics and connectionism. Philosophical Investigations 21(4), 293–314 (1998)

[14] Smolensky, P.: 17. In: Connectionism, Constituency, and Language of Thought, pp. 286–306. Blackwell Publishers (1991)

[15] Wittgenstein, L., Anscombe, G., Wright, G.: Zettel. University of California Press (1967)

[16] Roy, A.: An extension of the localist representation theory: grandmother cells are also widely used in the brain. Frontiers in Psychology 4, 1–3 (2013)

[17] Proops, I.: Logical syntax in the Tractatus. In: Gaskin, R. (ed.) Grammar in Early Twentieth-Century Philosophy. Routledge (2001)

[18] Rasmussen, D., Eliasmith, C.: A neural model of rule generation in inductive reasoning. Topics in Cognitive Science 3, 140–153 (2011)

[19] Emruli, B., Gayler, R., Sandin, F.: Analogical mapping and inference with binary spatter codes and sparse distributed memory. In: The 2013 International Joint Conference on Neural Networks (IJCNN), pp. 1–8 (2013)

[20] Wittgenstein, L.: Tractatus Logico-Philosophicus. Routledge, London (1922, 1981)

[21] Rumelhart, D.E., Smolensky, P., McClelland, J.L., Hinton, G.E.: Schemata and sequential thought processes in PDP models. In: McClelland, J., Rumelhart, D. (eds.) Parallel Distributed Processing: Explorations in the Microstructure of Cognition. MIT Press, Cambridge (1986)

[22] Gayler, R., Levy, S.: A distributed basis for analogical mapping. In: Proceedings of the Second International Analogy Conference. NBU Press (2009)

[23] Kanerva, P.: Sparse Distributed Memory. MIT Press, Cambridge (1988)

[24] Denning, P.J.: Sparse distributed memory. American Scientist (1989)

[25] French, R.M., Addyman, C., Mareschal, D.: Tracx: A recognition-based connectionist framework for sequence segmentation and chunk extraction. Psychological Review 118(4), 614–636 (2011)

[26] Hintikka, M., Hintikka, J.: Investigating Wittgenstein. B. Blackwell (1986)

[27] Hacker, P.M.S.: The private language argument. In: Dancy, J., Sosa, E. (eds.) A Companion To Epistemology. B. Blackwell (1993)

Bounded Seed-AGI

Eric Nivel[1], Kristinn R. Thórisson[1,3], Bas R. Steunebrink[2], Haris Dindo[4],
Giovanni Pezzulo[6], Manuel Rodríguez[5], Carlos Hernández[5], Dimitri Ognibene[6],
Jürgen Schmidhuber[2], Ricardo Sanz[5], Helgi P. Helgason[3], and Antonio Chella[4]

[1] Icelandic Institute for Intelligent Machines, IIIM
[2] The Swiss AI Lab IDSIA, USI & SUPSI
[3] Reykjavik University, CADIA
[4] Università degli studi di Palermo, DINFO
[5] Universidad Politécnica de Madrid, ASLAB
[6] Consiglio Nazionale delle Ricerche, ISTC

Abstract. Four principal features of autonomous control systems are left both
unaddressed and unaddressable by present-day engineering methodologies:
(1) The ability to operate effectively in environments that are only partially known
at design time; (2) A level of generality that allows a system to re-assess and re-
define the fulfillment of its mission in light of unexpected constraints or other un-
foreseen changes in the environment; (3) The ability to operate effectively in environments of significant complexity; and (4) The ability to degrade gracefully—
how it can continue striving to achieve its main goals when resources become
scarce, or in light of other expected or unexpected constraining factors that im-
pede its progress. We describe new methodological and engineering principles
for addressing these shortcomings, that we have used to design a machine that
becomes increasingly better at behaving in underspecified circumstances, in a
goal-directed way, on the job, by modeling itself and its environment as experience accumulates. The work provides an architectural blueprint for constructing systems with high levels of operational autonomy in underspecified circumstances, starting from only a small amount of designer-specified code—a *seed*.
Using value-driven dynamic priority scheduling to control the parallel execution
of a vast number of lines of reasoning, the system accumulates increasingly useful
models of its experience, resulting in recursive self-improvement that can be autonomously sustained after the machine leaves the lab, within the boundaries imposed by its designers. A prototype system named AERA has been implemented
and demonstrated to learn a complex real-world task—real-time multimodal dialogue with humans—by on-line observation. Our work presents solutions to several challenges that must be solved for achieving artificial general intelligence.

1 Introduction

Our objective is to design control architectures for autonomous systems meant ultimately to control machinery (like for example robots, power grids, cars, plants, etc.).
All physical systems have limited resources, and the ones we intend to build are no
exception: they have limited computing power, limited memory, and limited time to
fulfill their mission. All physical systems also have limited knowledge about their environment and the tasks they have to perform for accomplishing their mission. Wang [3]

B. Goertzel et al. (Eds.): AGI 2014, LNAI 8598, pp. 85–96, 2014.
© Springer International Publishing Switzerland 2014

merged these two assumptions into one, called AIKR—the assumption of insufficient knowledge and resources—which then forms the basis of his working definition of intelligence: "To adapt with insufficient knowledge and limited resources." We have adopted this definition as one of the anchors of our work, being much in line with Simon's concept of "bounded rationality" [4]. This perspective means that we cannot expect any optimal behaviors from our systems since their behaviors will always be constrained by the amount and reliability of knowledge they can accumulate at any particular point in time. In other words, we can only expect these systems to display a best effort strategy.

The freedom of action entailed by high levels of autonomy is balanced by hard constraints. First, an autonomous system, to be of any value, is functionally bounded by its mission, which imposes not only the requirements the system has to meet, but also the constraints it has to respect. Second, to keep the system operating within its functional boundaries, one has to ensure that some parts of the system will never be rewritten autonomously—for example, the management of motivations shall be excluded from rewriting as this would possibly allow the transgression of the constraints imposed by the designers. In that sense, the system is also bounded, operationally, by its own architecture. Last, any implemented system is naturally bounded by the resources (CPU, time, memory, inputs) and knowledge at its disposal. For these reasons, autonomy, as we refer to it, shall therefore be understood as bounded autonomy.

We target systems that operate continuously, autonomously, and in real-time in non-resettable environments. We envision learning to be "always on" and inherent in the system's core operation. Due to the complexity of the environment and the unforeseeable nature of future events and tasks for the system, we expect not only that pre-programming of all required operational knowledge will be impossible, but that even pre-programming of substantial amounts of knowledge will be too costly. Therefore the system must grow autonomously from a small *seed*, containing its "drives" (i.e., mission goals and constraints) and a relatively small amount of knowledge to bootstrap learning.

Unfortunately, none of the methodologies in the AI or CS literature are directly applicable for designing systems of this nature. For this reason we have advocated what we call a *constructivist* AI methodology (CAIM; [5,6,7,8,9]). In the main, our constructivist approach has two key objectives: (a) to achieve bounded recursive self-improvement [1] and generality and, (b) to uncover the principles for—and to actually build—systems that, given a small set of seed information, manage the bulk of the bootstrapping work on their own, in environments and on tasks that may be new and unfamiliar.

The rest of this paper describes AERA [1]: its design principles (sec. 2) to match the reality described above, its core operation (sec. 3), its methods of acquiring and representing knowledge and skills (sec. 4), and the first experimental results (sec. 5).

2   Design Principles

As we cannot assume guarantees for system down-time (after all, we are targeting high levels of operational autonomy), all activities of the system, from low-level (for example, prediction, sub-goaling) to high-level (like learning and planning), must be performed in real-time, concurrently, and continuously. Moreover, we need these activities to be executed in a way that is flexible enough to allow the system to dynamically (re-)allocate its resources depending on the urgency of the situation it faces at any point in time (with regards to its own goals and constraints), based on the availability of these same resources, over which it may not have complete (or any) control. The approach we chose is to break all activities down into fine-grained elementary reasoning processes that are commensurable both in terms of execution time and scheduling. These reasoning processes are the execution of various kinds of inference programs, and they represent the bulk of the computing. These programs are expected to be numerous and this calls for an architecture capable of handling massive amounts of parallel *jobs*.

A running AERA system faces three main challenges: (1) To update and revise its knowledge based on its experience, (2) to cope with its resource limitation while making decisions to satisfy its drives, and (3) to focus its attention on the most important inputs, discarding the rest or saving them for later processing. These three challenges are commonly addressed by, respectively, learning, planning, and controlling the attention of the system. Notice that all of these activities have an associated cost, have to be carried out concurrently, and must fit into the resource- and knowledge budget the system has at its disposal. That is the reason why they have been designed to result from the fine-grained interoperation of a multitude of lower-level jobs, the ordering of which is enforced by a scheduling strategy. This strategy has been designed to get the maximal global value for the system from the available inputs, knowledge, and resources, given (potentially conflicting) necessities.

We emphasize that AERA has no sub-components called "learning" or "planner" and so on. Instead, learning, planning, and attention are *emergent processes* that result from the same set of low-level processes: These are essentially the parallel execution of fine-grained jobs and are thus reusable and shared system-wide, collectively implementing functions that span across the entire scope of the system's operation in its environment. High-level processes (like planning and learning) influence each other: For example, learning better models and sequences thereof improves planning; reciprocally, having good plans also means that a system will direct its attention to more (goal-)relevant states, and this means in turn that learning is more likely to be focused on changes that impact the system's mission, possibly increasing its chances of success. These high-level processes are dynamically coupled, as they both result from the execution of the same knowledge.

A system must know what it is doing, when, and at what cost. Enforcing the production of explicit traces of the system's operation allows building models of its operation, which is needed for self-control (also called meta-control). In that respect, the functional architecture we seek shall be applicable to itself, i.e., a meta-control system for the system shall be implementable the same way the system is implemented to control itself in a domain. This principle is a prerequisite for integrated cognitive control [10].

Knowledge is composed of states (be they past, present, predicted, desired or hypothetical) and of executable code, called *models* Models are capable of generating such knowledge (e.g., generating predictions, hypotheses or goals) and are executed by a virtual machine—in the case of AERA, its executive.

Models have a low granularity for two main reasons. First, it is easier to add and replace small models than larger ones because the impact of their addition or replacement in the architecture will be less than replacement of large models. In other words, low model granularity is aimed at preserving system plasticity, supporting the capability of implementing small, incremental changes in the system. Second, low granularity helps compositionality and reuse; small models can only implement limited low-level functions and, if abstract enough, are more likely to be useful for implementing several higher-level functions than coarser models that implement one or more such high-level functions in one big atomic block. We have referred to this elsewhere as the principle of pee-wee granularity [6,8,11].

We also need the knowledge to be uniform, that is, encoded using one single scheme regardless of the particular data semantics. This helps to allow execution, planning, and learning algorithms to be both general and commensurate in resource usage. Representing time at several temporal scales, from the smallest levels of individual operations (e.g., producing a prediction) to a collective operation (e.g., achieving a mission) is an essential requirement for a system that must (a) perform in the real world and (b) model its own operation with regards to its expenditure of resources (as these include time). Considering time values as intervals allows encoding the variable precisions and accuracies needed to deal with the real world. For example, sensors do not always perform at fixed frame rates and so modeling their operation may be critical to ensure reliable operation of their controllers and models that depend on their input. Also, the precision for goals and predictions may vary considerably depending on both their time horizons and semantics. Last, since acquired knowledge can never be certain, one can assume that "truth"—asserting that a particular fact holds—can only be established for some limited time, and for varying degrees of temporal uncertainty. Thanks to the executable nature of AERA's models, knowledge and skills have a unified representation.

3   Attention and Scheduling

A cornerstone of our approach is that cognitive control results from the continual *value-driven scheduling* of reasoning jobs. According to this view, high-level cognitive processes are grounded directly in the core operation of the machine resulting from two complementary control schemes. The first is top-down: Scheduling allocates resources by estimating the global value of the jobs at hand, and this judgment results directly from the products of cognition—goals and predictions. These are relevant and accurate to various extents, depending on the quality of the knowledge accumulated so far. As the latter improves over time, goals and predictions become more relevant and accurate, thus allowing the system to allocate its resources with a better judgment; the most important goals and the most useful/accurate predictions are considered first, the rest being saved for later processing or even discarded, thus saving resources. In that sense, cognition controls resource allocation. The second control scheme is bottom-up: Resource allocation controls cognition. Shall resources become scarce (which is pretty much always the case in our targeted system–environment–mission triples), scheduling narrows down the system's attention to the most important goals/predictions the system can handle, trading scope for efficiency and therefore survivability—the system will only pay attention to the most promising (value-wise) inputs and inference possibilities. Reciprocally, shall the resources become more abundant, the system will start considering goals and predictions that are of less immediate value, thus opening up possibilities for learning and improvement—in the future even curiosity [2].

Technically, a job in AERA is a request for processing one input by one program (e.g., a model). All jobs (e.g., forward and backward chaining, explained in the next section) are assigned a *priority* that governs the point(s) in time when they may be executed. Jobs are small and uninterruptible, but might get delayed and even eventually discarded if they become irrelevant. Jobs' priorities are continually updated, thus allowing high-value new jobs to get executed before less important jobs, and old jobs to become more valuable than newer ones as new evidence constantly accumulates.[1] Thus a job priority depends on the utility value of the program and the expected value of the input. Value-driven scheduling stands at the very heart of our design and underpins our aim of looped-back adaptation and cognition. For detailed explanations of how exactly value, urgency, and priority are calculated in AERA, we refer interested readers to [1].

4 Model-Based Knowledge and Skill Representation

AERA is data-driven, meaning that the execution of code is triggered by matching *patterns* with inputs. Code refers to *models* (which constitute executable knowledge), that have either been given (as part of the bootstrap code) or learned by the system. A model encodes procedural knowledge in the form of a causal relationship between two terms. A model is built from two patterns, left-hand (LT) and right-hand (RT), both possibly containing variables. When an instance of the left-hand pattern is observed, then a *prediction* patterned after the right-hand pattern is produced. Reciprocally, when an instance of the right-hand pattern is observed (such an instance being a *goal*), then a sub-goal patterned after the left-hand pattern is produced. Additionally, when an input (other than a goal or a prediction) matches a RT, an *assumption* is produced, patterned after the LT. Notice that multiple instances of both forward and backward execution can be performed concurrently by a given model, i.e., a model can produce several predictions from several different inputs while producing several goals and assumptions, from several other inputs at the same time. Models also contain two sets of equations, called guards. These are equations meant to assign values to variables featured in the output, from the values held by variables in the input. One set of guards supports forward execution, whereas the other one supports backward execution. In our current implementation, guards are restricted to linear functions. Models form the very core of an AERA system and their operation is detailed in the next subsections.

Our approach to knowledge representation has its roots in a non-axiomatic term logic. This logic is non-axiomatic in the sense that knowledge is established on the basis of a system's experience; that is, truth is not absolute but rather established *to a certain degree* and *within a certain time interval*. In our approach the simplest term thus encodes an observation, and is called a *fact* (or a *counter-fact* indicating the absence of an observation). Terms, including facts, serve as input for (are matched against) the left-hand and right-hand patterns of models. A fact carries a payload (the observed event),

---

[1] It is worth noting that some jobs may get delayed repeatedly until their priority drops down to insignificant numbers (for example when the urgency of a goal becomes zero, i.e., when its deadline has expired) and eventually get cancelled. This is likely to happen in situations where either the CPU power becomes scarce or the number of jobs exceeds the available computing power—which is the expected fate of any system limited in both knowledge and resources.

a likelihood value in $[0, 1]$ indicating the degree to which the fact has been ascertained and a time interval in microseconds—the period within which the fact is believed to hold (or, in the case of a counter-fact, the period during which the payload has not been observed). Facts have a limited life span, corresponding to the upper bound of their time interval. Payloads are terms of various types, some of which are built in the executive, the most important of these being *atomic state, composite state, prediction, goal, command* to I/O, *model, success/failure*, and *performance measurement*. Additionally, any type can be defined by the programmer, and new types can be created by I/O devices at runtime. A composite state is essentially a conjunction of several facts, including facts whose payloads are instances of other composite states, thus allowing the creation of structural hierarchies. A composite state is a program with several input patterns, one per fact. Like models, composite states produce forward and backward chaining jobs (explained in the next subsection) when paired with some inputs.

4.1 Chaining and Hierarchy

Motivated by drives, models produce sub-goals when super-goals match their right-hand pattern, and these sub-goals in turn match other models' right-hand pattern until a sub-goal produces a command for execution by I/O devices. In parallel to this top-down flow of data, the hierarchy of models is traversed by a bottom-up data flow, originating from inputs sensed by the I/O devices that match the left-hand patterns of models, to produce predictions that in turn match other models' left-hand patterns and produce more predictions. These bottom-up and top-down flows are referred to as *forward* and *backward chaining*, respectively.

Whenever a model produces a prediction, the executive also produces a corresponding *instantiated model*: This is a term containing a reference to the model in question, a reference to the input that matched its LT and a reference to the resulting prediction. Such a reflection of operation constitutes a first-class input—i.e., an observable of the system's own operation—which is, as any other input, eligible for abstraction (by replacing values with variables bound together by guards) thus yielding a pattern that can be embedded in a model.

When a model M_0 features such an instantiated model M_1 as its LT then, in essence, M_0 specifies a post-condition on the execution of M_1, i.e., M_0 predicts an outcome that is entailed by the execution of M_1. In case the LT is a counter-evidence of a model's execution (meaning that the model failed to execute because despite having matched an input, its pre-conditions were not met—pre-conditions are explained immediately here below), the post-condition is referred to as a negative post-condition, positive otherwise. Symmetrically, when a model M_0 features an instantiated model M_1 as its RT, M_0 essentially specifies a pre-condition on the execution of M_1, i.e., when a condition is matched (LT of M_0), M_0 predicts the success or failure of the execution of target model M_1. More specifically, what a pre-condition means is "if the target model executes, it will succeed (or fail)." In case the RT is a counter-evidence of a model's successful execution (predicted failure), the pre-condition is referred to as a negative pre-condition, positive otherwise. Control with pre-conditions consists of ensuring that all negative pre-conditions and at least one positive one are satisfied before deciding to let the controlled model operate. This decision is made automatically by the executive by comparing the greatest likelihood of the negative pre-conditions to the greatest likelihood of the positive ones.

Planning concerns observing desired inputs (the states specified by goals) by acting on the environment (i.e., issuing commands) to achieve goals in due time in adversarial conditions, like for example the lack of appropriate models, under-performing models, conflicting or redundant goals, and lack of relevant inputs. Planning is initiated and sustained by the regular injection of drives (as defined by the programmer), thus putting the system under constant pressure from both its drives and its inputs. In our approach, sub-goals derived from goals are simulated, meaning that as long as time allows, the system will run "what if" scenarios to predict the outcome of the hypothetical success of these simulated goals, checking for conflicts and redundancies, eventually committing to the best goals found so far and discarding other contenders. Here again, goals are rated with respect to their expected value. *Simulation* and *commitment* operate concurrently with (and also make direct use of) forward and backward chaining.

4.2 Learning

Learning involves several phases: acquiring new models, evaluating the performance of existing ones, and controlling the learning activity itself. Acquiring new models is referred to as *pattern extraction*, and consists of the identification of causal relationships between input pairs: inputs which exhibit correlation are turned into patterns and used as the LT and RT of a new model. Model acquisition is triggered by either the unpredicted success of a goal or the failure of a prediction. In both cases AERA will consider the unpredicted outcome as the RT of new models and explore buffers of historical inputs to find suitable LTs. Once models have been produced, the system has to monitor their performance (a) to identify and delete unreliable models and, (b) to update the reliability as this control value is essential for scheduling. Both these activities—model acquisition and revision—have an associated cost, and the system must allocate its limited resources to the jobs from which it expects the most value. Last but not least, the system is enticed to learn, based on its experience, about its progress in modeling inputs. The system computes and maintains the history of the success rate for classes of goals and predictions, and the priority of jobs dedicated to acquire new models is proportional to the first derivative of this success rate.

A pattern extractor is a program that is generated dynamically upon the creation of a goal or a prediction. Its main activity is to produce models, i.e., explanations for the unpredicted success of a goal or the failure of a prediction. A single *targeted pattern extractor* (TPX) is responsible for attempting to explain either the success of one given goal, or the failure of one given prediction. Said goal or prediction is called the TPX's target. Under our assumption of insufficient knowledge, explaining in this case is much closer to guessing than to proving, and guesses are based on the general heuristic "time precedence indicates causality." Models thus built by the TPXs are added to the memory and are subjected to evaluation by other programs called prediction monitors. So their life cycle is governed essentially by their performance.

A TPX accumulates inputs from the target production time until the deadline of the target, at which time it analyses its buffer to produce models if needed: The TPX activity is thus composed of two phases, (a) buffering relevant inputs and, (b) extracting models from the buffer. At the deadline of the target, buffering stops, and the buffer is analyzed as follows, when the target is a goal (similarly for predictions, see below):

1. If one input is the trace of the execution of one model that predicted the goal's target state, abort—this means that the success was already predicted.
2. Remove any inputs that triggered any model execution.
3. Remove any inputs that were assembled in composite states.
4. Reorder the buffer according to the early deadlines of the inputs.
5. For each input remaining in the buffer create a TPX-extraction job, the purpose of which is to assemble a new model from the input and the target.

Shall the target be a prediction, on the other hand, step 1 would be:

1. If one input is the trace of the execution of one model that predicted a counter-evidence of the prediction's target state, abort, as the failure was already predicted.

Reaching step 5 triggers the second phase of TPX activity, where models are built from inputs found in the buffer. The construction of a new model is performed—by a TPX-extraction job—as follows, when the target is a goal:

1. The target is abstracted (meaning replacing values by variables) and forms the RT of a new model (let's call it M_0). If the input assigned to the TPX-extraction job is synchronized with other inputs (that is, if their time intervals overlap), then all these inputs are assembled into a single new composite state: this new state is chosen as the LT of the model. Otherwise, the input is abstracted and forms the LT of the model. Notice that new states are identified when their parts are needed for the models being built (instead of resulting from blind temporal correlation): Using composite states as models' LT instead of just atomic states fosters the building of structural hierarchies.
2. If, in a model, some variables in the RT (or in the LT) are not present in the LT (or in the RT), then the job attempts to build guards to bind these to known variables; otherwise, stop.
3. If some variables in a model are still not bound, then if the buffer is still not exhausted, goto step 4; otherwise, goto step 5.
4. The job considers the next older input to build another model (M_1) whose RT is an instance of M_0; the unbounded variables in M_0 are passed from M_1 to M_0 as parameters of M_0. The execution of M_1 allows the execution of M_0: M_1 is a positive pre-condition on M_0. Goto step 2.
5. All models are deleted that hold variables representing deadlines that are unaccounted for, i.e., variables that cannot be computed neither from the LT or RT, nor from the model's parameters list. These models are deleted since they would produce predictions with unbound deadlines, i.e., predictions that cannot be monitored.

As with TPX-accumulation jobs, the priority of a TPX-extraction job is a function of the utility of the model that produced its target and of the incentive of learning said target. It also depends on a decay function.

4.3 Rating

In addition to the prioritization strategy, we use two ancillary control mechanisms. These come in the form of two thresholds, one on the likelihood of terms, the other on the reliability of models. When a term's likelihood gets under the first threshold, it becomes ineligible as a possible input for pattern matching; reciprocally, when the reliability of a model gets under the second threshold, it cannot process any input—it is deactivated until said second threshold is increased. These thresholds are a filtering mechanism that operates before priorities are computed (the precise operation of these is beyond the scope of the present paper). If the reliability of a model drops below a threshold THR_1 then it is phased out: In this mode the model can only create forward chaining jobs and produce silent predictions that will not be eligible inputs to the regular models (i.e., models that are not phased out). Silent predictions are still monitored, thus giving the possibility to improve to a model that was recently getting unreliable. If the reliability of a phased out model gets above THR_1, then it is not phased out anymore and resumes its standard operation. When the reliability of a phased out model drops below a second threshold THR_2 ($< THR_1$), the model is deleted as are all the programs that were created to manage its productions; the corresponding jobs are cancelled.

4.4 Reflection

Each time a model predicts, the executive produces a new term, called an *instantiated model*, that references the input, the output, and the model itself. An instantiated model is thus a trace of the execution of a model and, being the payload of a fact, constitutes an (internal) input for the system and can be the target of learning, leading to *self-modeling*.

Even though self-modeling for meta-control has not been leveraged in our demonstrator (described in sec. 5), this functionality has been implemented and is operational. As we have argued before [2,6] such functionality is a necessity for a developmental system poised to adapt and make the best use of its resources. With it a system can, for example, model the ways it routinely adopts for achieving some particular goals: This consists of modeling sequences of model execution—these are observable in the form of internal inputs—and, by design, can be modeled using the existing learning mechanisms. The benefit of modeling sequences of execution can be, among others, to enable the system to compile such sequences so as to replace a set of models, which normally have to be interpreted by the executive, with a faster (but also more rigid) equivalent native machine code. Thus *self-compilation* supports a lower-level *re-encoding* of useful and reliable knowledge, which we expect will increase the scalability of AERA.

5 Experimental Results and Conclusion

To evaluate our system we let an AERA agent, *S1*, observe two humans interact in a simulated TV interview, and gave it the task to learn how to conduct the interaction in exactly the same way as the humans do it, in both roles of interviewer or interviewee. The initial *seed* knowledge given to S1 is represented as a small set of lowest-level end-effector ("move") commands and categories of sensory data, along with a few top-level goals (e.g., "pleasing the interviewer"—operationally defined as the interviewer saying "thank you"). A very detailed, full specification and analysis of this experiment can be found in [1]; for a full description of the seed, see [13].

The system observed real-time interaction between two humans in the simulated equivalent of a videoconference: The humans are represented as avatars in a virtual environment—each human sees the other as an avatar on their screen. Their head and arm movements are tracked with motion-sensing technology, their speech recorded with microphones. Signals from the motion-tracking are used to update the state of their avatars in real-time, so that everything one human does is translated virtually instantly into movements of her graphical avatar on the other's screen. Between the avatars is a desk with objects on it, visible to both participants. One human is assigned the role of an interviewer, the other the role of an interviewee; the goal of their interaction is to have a collaborative dialogue involving the objects in front of them.

The data produced during their interaction is represented as follows. Body movements are represented as coordinate changes of labeled body parts of the avatars. Each audio signal is piped to two processes: an instance of a speech recognizer (Microsoft SAPI 5.3), whose output is augmented with word timestamps (accuracy ± 100ms or better). Prosodica [12] produces time-stamped sound/silence boundaries (accuracy 16–32ms) and F0 contour (at 6Hz; approximate accuracy 40ms). The described input data is streamed to S1 in real-time.

The task assigned to the two humans is for the interviewer to ask the interviewee about the cost and benefits of recycling the various objects on the table between them—a plastic bottle, a glass bottle, a painted wooden cube, a newspaper, a cardboard box, and an aluminum can—and for the interviewee to reply to questions with informative but not excessively long sentences. The vocabulary used contains 100 words. Sentence structures were not scripted and turned out to be reasonably complex; for example, a question uttered by the humans was "Which requires more energy when recycled, a can of aluminum or a plastic bottle?", to which the answer given in one instance was "More energy is needed to recycle a plastic bottle than a can of aluminum." In addition, co-verbal multimodal deictics were used to refer to objects (picking up an object and uttering "Tell me about this.", gesturing towards an object or explicitly pointing when saying "What is that?", etc.). Testing was done when S1 could perform in either role, by having S1 take control of either avatar and conduct the interaction in an identical manner, in the role of interviewer or interviewee. The system was run on a desktop with a Core i7-3930K CPU and 8 GB RAM.

The result was that S1 learned everything it observed in the human-human interactions that was necessary to conduct a similarly accurate and effective interaction in real-time with a human. After approximately 20 hours of observing humans interact, the socio-communicative repertoire acquired autonomously by S1—none of which was provided to S1 a priori—consists of:

- Correct sentence construction, correct word order. Learned to sequentialize utterances, despite having the capability of saying multiple things in parallel.
- Effective and appropriate manual and head deictics: gesturing towards an object being talked about at the right time, directing head towards an object mentioned or pointed. S1 modeled the relationship between deictics and utterances (e.g., how "that" is used with pointing gestures)—an example of learned structural hierarchy (in the form of composite states).
- Disambiguation of definitive article "the," pronouns like "it," and demonstratives "this" and "that" (as in "What else can you tell me about *the* bottle?", even when there is more than one such object, or "Tell me more about *it* / *this*."): they have been learned to identify the object that draws the most attention (in terms of job

priority), i.e., the target of the most valuable goals—an example of value-driven resource allocation steering cognition and vice-versa.
- Appropriate response generation; content-relevant answers (as interviewee) and sequence of questions (as interviewer).
- Proper multimodal coordination in both interpretation and production, at multiple timescales (interview, utterance, and sub-utterance levels).
- Proper multimodal learning: the same (emergent) learning mechanism is applicable to all modalities and at different time scales. This provides some evidence that AERA's core operation is domain-independent.
- Turn-taking skills (avoiding overlaps, avoiding long pauses), and utterance production; presentation of content (answer/question) at appropriate times with regard to the other's behavior.
- Interview skills—doing the interview from first question to last question. Using interruption to keep to a time limit: S1 as interviewer will interrupt the human interviewee only when it predicts that, given current answer lengths, time may run short.

The results from the experiment show without doubt that S1 correctly acquired and mastered correct usage of all communication methods used by the human interviewer and interviewee in the human-human condition when conversing about the recycling of the various objects' materials. The complete absence of errors in S1's behaviors, after the observation periods in both conditions, demonstrate that very reliable models have been acquired, and that these form a hierarchy spanning at least two orders of magnitude in time. These models correctly represent the generalized relationships of a non-trivial number of entities, knowledge which had not been provided to the system beforehand by its designers, and which was acquired entirely autonomously, given only the bootstrap seed initially provided.

The tasks in the experiment require S1 to learn and abstract temporal sequences of continuous events (utterances and multimodal behavior), as well as logical sequences and relationships (word sequences in sentences, meaning of words and gestures) between a number of observed data. These were acquired through a method of generalization using induction, abduction, and deduction, allowing S1 to respond in real-time situations that differ from what it has seen before. As the humans participating in these experiments were not trained actors, and did not follow a script, other than limiting their vocabulary and action repertoire as described above, there is good reason to believe that the skills thus learned by S1 generalize to a wider audience. However, the aim of this work was not specifically to build a control system that can interact with people, but rather to create a system with a demonstrated ability to learn complicated tasks—human multimodal interaction of course being an excellent example of a domain with great complexity and variety in input, and one that is highly temporal, as in fact the vast majority of all real-world tasks are.

We have demonstrated an implemented architecture that can learn autonomously many things in parallel, at multiple time scales. The results show that AERA can learn complex multi-dimensional tasks from observation, while provided only with a small ontology, a few drives (high-level goals), and a few initial models, from which it can autonomously bootstrap its own development. This is initial evidence that our constructivist methodology is a way for escaping the constraints of current computer science and engineering methodologies. Human dialogue is an excellent example of the kinds of complex tasks current systems are incapable of handling autonomously. The fact that no difference of any importance can be seen in the performance between S1 and the humans in simulated face-to-face interview is an indication that the resulting architecture holds significant potential for further advances.

Acknowledgments. This work has been supported in part by the EU-funded projects HUMANOBS: *Humanoids that Learn Socio-Communicative Skills through Observation* (FP7-STREP-231453, www.humanobs.org) and Nascence (FP7-ICT-317662), as well as SNF grant #200020-138219 and a competitive Strategic Research Programme grant for Centres of Excellence & Research Clusters from the Research and Technology Policy Council of Iceland (#093020012, www.iiim.is).

References

1. Nivel, E., Thórisson, K.R., Steunebrink, B.R., Dindo, H., Pezzulo, G., Rodríguez, M., Hernández, C., Ognibene, D., Schmidhuber, J., Sanz, R., Helgason, H.P., Chella, A., Jonsson, G.K.: Bounded Recursive Self-Improvement. Tech. Rep. RUTR-SCS13006, Reykjavik University (2013), http://arxiv.org/abs/1312.6764
2. Steunebrink, B.R., Koutník, J., Thórisson, K.R., Nivel, E., Schmidhuber, J.: Resource-Bounded Machines are Motivated to be Efficient, Effective, and Curious. In: Kühnberger, K.-U., Rudolph, S., Wang, P. (eds.) AGI 2013. LNCS, vol. 7999, pp. 119–129. Springer, Heidelberg (2013)
3. Wang, P.: The Assumptions on Knowledge and Resources in Models of Rationality. International Journal of Machine Consciousness 3(1), 193–218 (2011)
4. Simon, H.: A Behavioral Model of Rational Choice. In: Models of Man, Social and Rational: Mathematical Essays on Rational Human Behavior in a Social Setting. Wiley, NY (1957)
5. Thórisson, K.R.: Methodology Matters: Constructionism Challenged, Constructivism Challenges (forthcoming)
6. Thórisson, K.R.: A New Constructivist AI: From Manual Construction to Self-Constructive Systems. In: Wang, P., Goertzel, B. (eds.) Theoretical Foundations of Artificial General Intelligence. Atlantis Thinking Machines, vol. 4, pp. 145–171 (2012)
7. Thórisson, K.R.: From Constructionist to Constructivist A.I. Keynote, AAAI Fall Symposium Series – Biologically Inspired Cognitive Architectures, Washington D.C., November 5-7, 175-183. AAAI Tech Report FS-09-01. AAAI Press, Menlo Park, CA (2009)
8. Nivel, E., Thórisson, K.R.: Self-Programming: Operationalizing Autonomy. In: Proceedings of the Second Conference on Artificial General Intelligence (2009)
9. Thórisson, K.R., Nivel, E.: Holistic Intelligence: Transversal Skills and Current Methodologies. In: Proc. of the 2nd Conf. on Artificial General Intelligence (AGI 2009), pp. 220–221 (2009)
10. Sanz, R., Hernández, C.: Towards Architectural Foundations for Cognitive Self-Aware Systems. In: Chella, A., Pirrone, R., Sorbello, R., Jóhannsdóttir, K.R. (eds.) Biologically Inspired Cognitive Architectures 2012. AISC, vol. 196, p. 53. Springer, Heidelberg (2013)
11. Thórisson, K.R., Nivel, E.: Achieving Artificial General Intelligence Through Peewee Granularity. In: Proc. of the 2nd Conf. on Artificial General Intelligence (AGI 2009), pp. 222–223 (2009)
12. Nivel, E., Thórisson, K.R.: Prosodica Real-Time Prosody Tracker. Reykjavik University School of Computer Science Technical Report RUTR08002 (2008)
13. Nivel, E., Thórisson, K.R.: Seed Specification for AERA S1 in Experiments 1 & 2. Reykjavik University School of Computer Science Technical Report, RUTR-SCS13005 (2013)

The Multi-slot Framework:
A Formal Model for Multiple, Copiable AIs

Laurent Orseau

AgroParisTech, UMR 518 MIA, F-75005 Paris, France
INRA, UMR 518 MIA, F-75005 Paris, France
laurent.orseau@agroparistech.fr

Abstract. Because advanced AI is likely in the future, so is the possibility of multiple advanced AIs. It is therefore also likely that such advanced AIs will be implemented in software that can be copied from hardware to hardware. The best existing theoretical framework for the rigorous formal treatment and prediction of such AIs are those based on the AIXI framework developed by Hutter [2]. Unfortunately, these single-agent frameworks do not allow formal treatment of multiple co-existing AIs. The current paper introduces a novel "multi-slot" framework for dealing with multiple intelligent agents, each of which can be duplicated or deleted at each step, in arbitrarily complex environments. The framework is a foundational first step in the analysis of environments that allow creation (by copying) and deletion of multiple agents. Even by focusing on the case where the agents do not interact, the notion of future of an agent is not straightforward anymore, so we propose several such definitions, leading to value functions and AIXI-like agents. Finally, the framework is shown to be sufficiently general to allow for the existence of a universal environment that can simulate all environments in parallel. A companion paper uses the multi-slot framework presented here to explore the notion of identity in man and machine.

Keywords: Universal AI, AIXI, multi-agent.

1 Introduction

In the traditional agency framework [13], a single agent interacts with an environment by outputting an action and receiving an observation at each discrete time step. A reinforcement learning agent [17] can extract a reward from the observation. In this framework, the universal reinforcement learning agent AIXI is the optimal learning agent that chooses its actions so as to maximize its future expected reward [2], in all computable environments. Although this framework is very general and well sufficient for almost all practical purposes, it still relies on some strong assumptions, and we have already considered elsewhere relaxing some of these constraints, for example when agents can modify themselves [14,8], can be modified by the environment [12,9] or even be computed by it [10].

In this paper, we present a novel framework that is more general than the traditional one (but less, for simplicity, than the space-time embedded intelligence

B. Goertzel et al. (Eds.): AGI 2014, LNAI 8598, pp. 97–108, 2014.

one [10]), where optimally intelligent agents can be duplicated and deleted by the environment. We call it the *multi-slot agency framework*, as agents are placed in *slots*, which can be thought of for now as robotic bodies or computer hardware. This is similar to a multi-agent framework [1] and could be used as such but, instead of focusing on the interactions between agents, which is difficult at best with universal agents [3], we provide a specialization of the framework to explicitly prevent interaction, so as to be able to provide formal results. What matters is that agents can make decisions regarding being copied or deleted.

This new framework is initially motivated by questions about personal identity, in particular the relation between information content and the hardware that supports it [11]: If a person is teleported by a device that scans and disassembles the person's body, transfers the information at the speed of light to a distant place where it entirely reassembles the same body, is it the same person? Some related thought experiments about the identity problem are treated formally in the companion paper [7], based on the framework presented here.

In the present paper, we focus on the definition of the framework and of the corresponding optimal reinforcement learning agents. However, there does not seem to be a single straightforward definition of the value functions: Indeed, in the traditional agency framework, there is no ambiguity as to what the future observations of the agent are. But what if the agent can be transfered or even copied to different locations? What or where are its future observations? How to take them into account in the definition of the optimal agents? We provide several plausible definitions of optimal agents, based either on the location of the agent or on the set of its copies. We believe this new framework is general enough to consider a wide range of new situations that are difficult or even impossible to consider in the traditional framework.

In the next section, the notation is introduced along with a quick exposure of the background on universal reinforcement learning agents. In section 3, the multi-slot framework is defined. In section 4, a few possible definitions of value functions are proposed. In section 5 we define a particular environment, that has the property of being able to simulate all computable traditional environments. Finally, we conclude with some remarks.

2   Notation and Background

The paper recognizes the following notational conventions. At time step t each agent outputs action $a_t \in \mathcal{A}$ to the environment, which returns observation $o_t \in \mathcal{O}$ to the agent, from which a reward $r(o_t)$ can be extracted. An interaction history pair is denoted $h_t = a_t o_t$ with $h_t \in \mathcal{H} := \mathcal{O} \times \mathcal{A}$. The sequence of all actions up to time t is written $a_{1:t} = a_1 a_2 \ldots a_t$, while the sequence $a_{1:t-1}$ is sometimes written $a_{<t}$, and similarly for other sequences like $h_{<t}$. The empty sequence is denoted λ. Tuples are notated with angle brackets, such as $\langle a, b \rangle$. Boolean values are written $\mathcal{B} := \{0, 1\}$, where 1 signifies *true* when a truth-value is implied.

AIMU and AIXI [2]. A stochastic environment ν assigns a probability $\nu(o_{\prec t}|a_{\prec t})$ to an observation history $o_{\prec t}$ given the history of actions $a_{\prec t}$ of the agent.[1] For notational convenience, we will write $\nu(h_{\prec t}) \equiv \nu(o_{\prec t}|a_{\prec t})$, but keep in mind that environments do not assign probabilities to actions. A policy $\pi \in \Pi : \mathcal{H}^* \to \mathcal{A}$ produces an action given an interaction history: $a_t = \pi(h_{\prec t})$. The value of a policy π in an environment μ (with an optional action) is given by:

$$V_\mu^\pi(h_{\prec t}) := V_\mu^\pi(h_{\prec t}, \pi(h_{\prec t})) \, , \tag{1}$$

$$V_\mu^\pi(h_{\prec t}, a) := \sum_o \mu(o|h_{\prec t}a) \left[r(o) + \gamma V_\mu^\pi(h_{\prec t}ao) \right] \, ,$$

where $\gamma \in [0, 1)$ is the discount factor, that ensures finiteness of the value. The optimal (non-learning) agent AIMU for a given single environment μ is defined by the optimal policy $\pi^\mu(h_{\prec t}) := \arg\max_{\pi \in \Pi} V_\mu^\pi(h_{\prec t})$ (ties are broken in favor of policies that output the first lexicographical action at time t), and the optimal value is $V_\mu := V_\mu^{\pi^\mu}$. The value of a policy over a set of environments $\mathcal{M}$ (optionally after an action a) is given by:

$$V_\mathcal{M}^\pi(h_{\prec t}) := \sum_{\nu \in \mathcal{M}} w_\nu V_\mu^\pi(h_{\prec t}) \, . \tag{2}$$

Taking the prior weights of the environment as in Solomonoff's prior [16,18] $w_\nu := 2^{-K(\nu)}$ where $K(\nu)$ is the Kolmogorov complexity [6] of ν (*i.e.*, roughly, the size of the smallest program equivalent to ν on a universal Turing machine of reference), the optimal policy for a given set $\mathcal{M}$ of environments [2] is defined by $\pi^{\xi\mathcal{M}}(h_{\prec t}) := \arg\max_{\pi \in \Pi} V_\mathcal{M}^\pi(h_{\prec t})$, and the optimal value function in $\mathcal{M}$ is $V_\mathcal{M} := V_\mathcal{M}^{\pi^{\xi\mathcal{M}}}$. AIXI is the optimal agent on the set of all computable stochastic environments $\mathcal{M}_U$, with policy $\pi^\xi := \pi^{\xi\mathcal{M}_U}$ and value function $V_\xi := V_{\mathcal{M}_U}$.

3   The Multi-slot Framework

In the multi-slot framework, the environment is interacting with several agents at the same time, on discrete interaction time steps. Each agent is on a given *slot*, a place where its binary program is written and computed; and can then be thought of as a computer (see Fig. 1). The number of agents can vary, and they can be copied to other slots, or deleted from their own slot, over time.

For generality, we first give a definition of a general agent in terms of self-modifying agents [8]:

Definition 1 (Slot, Memory Space and Agent). *A slot number is the index* $i \in \mathcal{S} := \mathbb{N}^+$ *of a memory space* m^i. *At any discrete time* $t \in \mathbb{N}_{\geq 0}$, *a memory space* $m_t^i \in \mathcal{W}$ *is a bit string that can either be empty,* $m_t^i = \lambda$, *or contain an agent* $\hat{\pi}_t^i \in \hat{\Pi} : \mathcal{O} \to \mathcal{A} \times \mathcal{W}$, *i.e., a program that can be executed by an oracle*

---

[1] A stochastic environment can be seen as program in any programming language where sometimes some instructions are chosen with a probability.

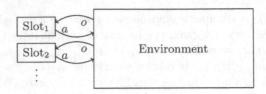

Fig. 1. The environment is in interaction with several slots

computer O: $\hat{\pi}_t^i(.) = O(m_t^i, .)$. The agent need not be computable. An agent takes as input an observation o_{t-1} from the environment (or λ if $t = 1$), and generates as output (1) its current action a_t, and (2) a new memory $m_{t^c}^i$ (hence a new agent), i.e., $\langle a_t, m_{t^c}^i \rangle := \hat{\pi}_{t-1}^i(o_{t-1})$, where t^c is the intermediate time step t right after the action is produced, named time before copy.

Sequence notation $a_{1:t}$ and slot-indexed sequence notation $a_{1:t}^i$ are used for various symbols.

Definition 2 (Agent Set). *The agent set $\mathcal{S}_t \in \mathcal{S}^*$ is the set of all non-empty slots at time t: $\mathcal{S}_t := \{i : i \in \mathcal{S}, m_t^i \neq \lambda\}$.*

Definition 3 (Copy Instance, Copy Set, Copy Set List). *A copy instance $\dot{c}_t^{ij} \in \mathcal{B}$ is a boolean value indicating whether the memory in slot j must be copied from the memory in slot i, i.e., $m_t^j \leftarrow m_{t^c}^i$. All copies are performed in parallel, yielding a new agent set. The copy set $\dot{c}_t^i$ is the set of all slots j at time t that are copied from slot i: $\dot{c}_t^i := \{j : \dot{c}_t^{ij} = 1\}$. All slots that are not in a copy set at time t are empty at time t. The copy set list is the indexed list of all non-empty copy sets at time t: $\dot{c}_t := \{\langle i, \dot{c}_t^i \rangle : \dot{c}_t^i \neq \emptyset\}$.*

Some derived properties:

- The copy $\dot{c}_t^{ii}$ is not implicit, i.e., if $\dot{c}_t^{ii} = 0$ then m_t^i is not the copy of $m_{t^c}^i$.
- A slot j cannot be both the copy of slot i and slot k: $i \neq k \implies \dot{c}_t^i \cap \dot{c}_t^k = \emptyset$.
- The agent set $\mathcal{S}_t$ is the union of all copy sets: $\mathcal{S}_t = \bigcup_i \dot{c}_t^i$.
- Two slots being in the same copy set have the same memory content, but the converse is not always true: $j \in \dot{c}_t^i, k \in \dot{c}_t^i \Rightarrow m_t^j = m_t^k$.

Definition 4 (Multi-slot Interaction Protocol). *The multi-slot interaction protocol between multiple, possibly non-computable agents and a single, computable environment is defined as follows. At the initial time step $t = 0$, the number of non-empty slots must be finite. At each time step t, the following stages occur in the given order:*

1. *$t \leftarrow t + 1$.*
2. *Each agent in a non-empty slot i produces $\hat{\pi}_{t-1}^i(o_{t-1}^i) = \langle a_t^i, m_{t^c}^i \rangle$. The environment receives the finite set $\dot{a}_t \in (\mathcal{S} \times \mathcal{A})^*$ of pairs $\langle i, a_t^i \rangle$ of slot numbers $i \in \mathcal{S}_{t-1}$ and slot actions a_t^i for all non-empty slots i. We are now at time before copy t^c.*

3. *The environment computes the copy set list $\dot{c}_t$ and the copies are performed among the slots.*
4. *The environment outputs a finite set $\dot{o}_t \in \dot{\mathcal{O}} = (\mathcal{S} \times \mathcal{O})^*$ of pairs $\langle i, o_t^i \rangle$ of slot number $i \in \mathcal{S}_t$ and observations o_t^i for each non-empty slot i. We now have the environment interaction history triplet $\dot{h}_t := \dot{a}_t \dot{c}_t \dot{o}_t$.*
5. *Back to 1.*

The following points are worth noting. The environment cannot know the contents of the slots, it merely performs copies. The number of non-empty slots always remains finite. The agents have no direct access to their slot numbers, to the copy sets, or to the actions performed by the other agents.

Definition 5 (Multi-slot Environment). *A multi-slot environment operates according to the interaction protocol in Definition 4 and is defined by a probability distribution $\dot{\nu}(\dot{c}_{1:t}\dot{o}_{1:t}|\dot{a}_{1:t})$ over all observation sequences and copy set list sequences given action sequences.*

Definition 6 (Slot History). *A slot history $s_{t_1:t_2} \in \mathcal{S}^*$ is a sequence of slots resulting from a given sequence of chained copy instances $\dot{c}_{t_1+1}^{ab} \dot{c}_{t_1+2}^{bc} \dots \dot{c}_{t_2-1}^{wx} \dot{c}_{t_2}^{xy}$ such that $\forall k \in [t_1 + 1, t_2], \dot{c}_k^{ij} \Leftrightarrow s_{k-1} = i \wedge s_k = j$.*

In other words, the slot history $s_{9:13} = (8, 2, 3, 3, 7)$ corresponds to the sequence of copies $\dot{c}_{10}^{8,2} \dot{c}_{11}^{2,3} \dot{c}_{12}^{3,3} \dot{c}_{13}^{3,7}$.

At time t, the contents of each slot i has undergone a unique slot history $s_{0:t}^i$ of chained copies from time 0 to t, where $s_t^i = i$. The sequence is unique since a slot j at t can have been copied from only one slot i at $t - 1$ (see Definition 3). For an agent in slot i at time t, this is the sequence of slots on which the actions and observations of its interaction history have been output and received.

Definition 7 (Agent/Environment Slot Action/Observation/Interaction History). *An environment slot interaction history $\dot{h}_{t_1:t_2}^i$ is the set of observations and actions occurring between t_1 to t_2 following the slots of the slot history $s_{t_1-1:t_2}^i$:*

$$\dot{h}_{t_1:t_2}^i := \dot{a}_{t_1}^{s_{t_1-1}} \dot{c}_{t_1}^{s_{t_1-1}s_{t_1}} \dot{o}_{t_1}^{s_{t_1}} \dots \dot{a}_{t_2}^{s_{t_2-1}} \dot{c}_{t_2}^{s_{t_2-1}s_{t_2}} \dot{o}_{t_2}^{s_{t_2}} .$$

Likewise with the environment slot observation history $\dot{o}_{t_1:t_2}^i$ and action history $\dot{a}_{t_1:t_2}^i$, and the agent slot observation history $o_{t_1:t_2}^i$, action history $a_{t_1:t_2}^i$, and interaction history $h_{t_1:t_2}^i = o_{t_1}^j a_{t_1}^j \dots o_{t_2}^i a_{t_2}^i$.

Thus, $\dot{h}_{1:t}^i$ is the history of actions, observations, and (chained) copies that resulted in the contents of slot i at step t from the point of view of the environment (*i.e.*, accompanied by slot numbers and copy sets), whereas $h_{1:t}^i$ is the same history but from the agent's point of view (*i.e.*, without slot numbers or copy sets).

Definition 8 (History-based Agent). *On slot i at time t^c before the copies, a history-based agent is an agent whose memory content is composed of an interaction history $h_{\prec t}^i a_t^i$, and a policy π_t^i that uses the history to output an action:*

$$\text{if } m_{t-1}^i \equiv \langle h_{\prec t}^i, \pi_{t-1}^i \rangle \text{ then } m_{t^c}^i \equiv \langle h_{\prec t}^i a_t^i, \pi_{t-1}^i \rangle , \qquad a_t^i := \pi_{t-1}^i(h_{\prec t}^i) .$$

We define the probability of an agent interaction history as $\dot{\nu}(h^i_{\prec t}) :=$ $\sum_{\dot{h}_{\prec t}} \dot{\nu}(\dot{h}_{\prec t})\nu(h^i_{\prec t}|\dot{h}_{\prec t})$ where $\nu(h^i_{\prec t}|\dot{h}_{\prec t})$ is either 1 or 0 depending on whether $h^i_{\prec t}$ is consistent with $\dot{h}_{\prec t}$.

Definition 9 (History-based Multi-slot Environment). *A history-based multi-slot environment is a multi-slot environment $\dot{\nu}$ so that the copy set of a given slot i and the observations output to these copies depend only on the history of the agent in slot i and the involved slot numbers:*

$$\forall j : \dot{\nu}(\dot{c}^{ij}_t \dot{o}^j_t | \dot{h}_{\prec t} \dot{a}_t) = \dot{\nu}(\dot{c}^{ij}_t \dot{o}^j_t | h^i_{\prec t} a^i_t, i, j) .$$

These environments ensure, as a simplification, that there is no interaction between the different agents. Note however that the copy instances and observations can depend on the slot number, which means that an agent in slot i may not have the same interaction with the environment than an agent in slot j with the same history.

Note that even though the agents cannot interact, the "sub-environments" they are interacting with are still not independent, because they are all the continuations of the environments at the previous step and, since initially we will consider that there is only one agent in slot 1, all the sub-environments are tied to this initial environment. Furthermore, because the sub-environments are generated by a single program, the more different the sub-environments, the higher the complexity of the history-based multi-slot environment.

4   Value Functions for Multi-slot Environments

For a given mono-slot environment, AIMU is the optimal agent that chooses its actions so as to maximize its future rewards, which are extracted from its observations. But when a agent can be copied at any step, what constitutes the *future* of this agent, *i.e.*, what will be its future observations?

Interestingly, there does not seem to be any single obvious direct translation of AIMU in the multi-slot framework. For example, all the following definitions of future (observations) are valid. This then leads to various definitions of AIMU. Assuming an AIMU agent is in slot i at time t, to compute its reward for time $t + 1$ it can take into account for the next time step (and thus, recursively, for all future time steps):

- only the observations output to slot 1;
- only the observations output to slot i;
- only the observations output to the tth prime number slot;
- only the observations received by the first of its copies;
- observations received by all of its copies, possibly with some weighting;
- only the observations received by its copies that yield a minimal reward;

- observations received by all agents that have the exact same history, independently of whether they have a common ancestor with the agent under consideration;
- observations received by all agents that have output the sequence 11011 of actions at some point in their history;
- observations received by all agents that have a common ancestor with the agent under consideration;
- etc.

In the following subsections, we focus on 3 AIMU agents: The *copy-centered agent* AIMU^{cpy}, which considers the observations of all of its copies; and the *static slot-centered agent* AIMU^{sta} and *dynamic slot-centered agent* AIMU^{dyn}, which consider only the observations on either a predefined slot or on the slot they think they occupy.

We assume that there is only one agent in slot 1 at $t = 0$, *i.e.*, $\mathcal{S}_0 = \{1\}$, in interaction with a history-based multi-slot environment $\dot{\nu}$.

A note on time-consistency. When designing an AIMU equation (Bellman optimality equation), such as the ones that follow, a particular attention must be paid to *time consistency* [5]: The action that the agent predicts it will take in a future situation must be the same as the one it takes if the situation actually arises. In other words, its behavior must be consistent over time with the behavior it has predicted it will have.

4.1   Estimating the Current Slot Number

When the environment makes a copy of the agent at time t to slots i and j, this leads to two identical agents at time $t + 1$ with the same history, if they receive the same observation, and the two agents therefore cannot know for sure if they are in slot i or in slot j, and must estimate the probability of being in each, based on their interaction history $h_{\prec t}$. This estimation is important as the received observations can depend on the slot number. It is also related to the need to account for the observer's localization when estimating the posterior probability of being in a given environment [4].

Then the probability that the agent is in slot i, given its interaction history $h_{\prec t}$ is defined by:

$$P_\nu^i(h_{\prec t}) := \frac{\dot{\nu}(h_{\prec t}^i = h_{\prec t})}{\sum_j \dot{\nu}(h_{\prec t}^j = h_{\prec t})}$$

and is defined as 0 if the denominator is null. In a deterministic environment, $\dot{\nu}(h_{\prec t}^i = h_{\prec t})$ is either 1 or 0 in depending on whether the history $h_{\prec t}^i$ is consistent with the environment, and the denominator is the number of agents that have the same history.

4.2   The Copy-Centered Agent AIMU^{cpy}

The copy-centered agent AIMU^{cpy} considers that its future observations are the observations received by all of its copies. Unfortunately, it is not possible to simply assign a weight of 1 to each copy. For example, if the number of copies grows faster than the geometric discounting decreases, the value function may not be summable, which prevents the comparison of action values in general. Therefore, it is necessary to weight the copies so as to ensure finiteness of the value function. We arbitrarily choose a uniform weighting of the copies of the next time step. Thus, at some time step t, if the agent is in slot i, the weight of one of its direct copies in slot j is defined by

$$P_\nu^{ij}(h_{\prec t}a) := \frac{\dot\nu(\dot c_t^{ij}|h_{\prec t}^i a_t^i = h_{\prec t}a)}{\sum_k \dot\nu(\dot c_t^{ik}|h_{\prec t}^i a_t^i = h_{\prec t}a)}$$

and is defined as 0 if the numerator is 0. In deterministic environments, this is simply the inverse of the size of the copy set, $\frac{1}{|\dot c_t^i|}$.

We thus define the copy-centered agent value function as:

$$V_{\pi,\mu}^{\text{cpy}}(h_{\prec t},a) := \underbrace{\sum_i P_\mu^i(h_{\prec t})}_{\substack{\text{Estimate the} \\ \text{current slot}}} \underbrace{\sum_j P_\mu^{ij}(h_{\prec t}a)}_{\text{Weight each copy}} \underbrace{\sum_{o_t^j} \mu(\dot c_t^{ij} o_t^j|h_{\prec t}^i a_t^i = h_{\prec t}a_t)}_{\substack{\text{Take action and receive} \\ \text{observation in copy slot}}} \Big[r(o_t^j)$$

$$+ \gamma V_{\pi,\mu}^{\text{cpy}}(h_{\prec t}a o_t^j)\Big] \ .$$

Note that the recurrence follows the generic definition of Equation (1). We can simplify the equation by defining:

$$\hat\mu(\dot c_t^{ij} o_t^j|h_{\prec t}a_t) := P_\mu^i(h_{\prec t})P_\mu^{ij}(h_{\prec t}a_t)\mu(\dot c_t^{ij} o_t^j|h_{\prec t}^i a_t^i = h_{\prec t}a_t)$$

to have:

$$V_{\pi,\mu}^{\text{cpy}}(h_{\prec t},a) := \sum_{i,j,o_t^j} \hat\mu(\dot c_t^{ij} o_t^j|h_{\prec t}a) \left[r(o_t^j) + \gamma V_{\pi,\mu}^{\text{cpy}}(h_{\prec t}a o_t^j)\right] \ .$$

Following the generic definitions of section 2, and as for the following value functions, the value of the optimal policy is V_μ^{cpy}, which defines the optimal non-learning agent AIMU^{cpy}, the value of the optimal policy in a set $\mathcal{M}$ is $V_{\mathcal{M}}^{\text{cpy}}$, and the optimal learning agent for all computable stochastic history-based multi-slot environments $\dot{\mathcal{M}}_U$ is AIXI^{cpy} with value V_ξ^{cpy}.

Some remarks:

- Once the slot number is estimated, one may expect this information to be passed through the recurrence on V_μ^{cpy}. However, doing so would not be time-consistent: Indeed, the agent at time $t+1$ will not have access to this information, and therefore the agent at time t must do as if it were the agent at $t+1$, even though it already has estimated the slot number. (Thus $V_{\pi,\dot\mu}^{\text{cpy}}(h_{\prec t}ao_t^j)$ must be read $V_{\pi,\dot\mu}^{\text{cpy}}(h_{\prec t}ao)$.)

- $\dot c_t^{ij}$ must be kept inside $\dot\mu(\dot c_t^{ij}o_t^j|\ldots)$ despite the weight of the copies. For example, if there is probability 0.5 for the agent to be copied to only 1 slot (thus half of the time resulting in no copy), the weight of this copy is still 1 (whereas the copy probability is 0.5).

4.3   The Static Slot-Centered Agent AIMU^{sta}

The static slot-centered agent AIMU^{sta} considers only the observations received on a particular predefined slot. As an analogy, this slot can be seen as a bank account, on which the agent wants to maximize the value, but does not care about the value on any other account. The static slot-centered agent AIMU^{sta} value function is defined by:

$$V_{\pi,\dot\mu}^{\text{sta},i}(h_{\prec t},a) := \sum_{o_t^i} \dot\mu\left(\dot c_t^{ii}o_t^i|h_{\prec t}^i a_t^i = h_{\prec t}a_t, \dot c_{\prec t}^{ii}\right)\left[r(o_t^i)+\gamma V_{\pi,\dot\mu}^{\text{sta},i}(h_{\prec t}ao_t^i)\right],$$

with $\dot\mu(\cdot|x) := 0$ if $\dot\mu(x) = 0$.

This agent cares only about what happens on a predefined slot, and all its copies will also care about the same slot. Furthermore, the arguable presence of $\dot c_t^{ii}$ and $\dot c_{\prec t}^{ii}$ requires that the agent "stays" on slot i and is not moved from one slot to another before coming back to the initial slot, and for time consistency, consider only cases where it has always been on slot i in the past.[2]

4.4   The Dynamic Slot-Centered Agent AIMU^{dyn}

A more dynamic version of the slot-centered agent takes into account the observation (for the near and far future) of the (estimated) slot it occupies at the current time step.

As it is not told what slot it should care about, it must estimate it given its interaction history. But this leads to a complication: Say at time t the agent knows it is in slot i, and will be copied to slots i and j at time $t+1$, independently of the action, and both future agents will receive the same observation. The agent in slot i at t should want to optimize what happens in slot i only, but there is a trick: the agent at time $t+1$ in slot i will not have (in general) the information of its slot being i and not j, and therefore must estimate it—it will thus estimate that it can be either in slot i or in slot j. Thus, the agent at time t must optimize what will happen on slot i only, knowing that its copy at $t+1$ will optimize what happens on both slots i and j. This time consistency requirement leads to the following value function for the dynamic slot-centered agent AIMU^{dyn}:

---

[2] However, removing these would require the agent to consider the actions of other agents that could come on its slot, which is an open problem [3].

$$V_{\pi,\dot\mu}^{\text{dyn}}(h_{\prec t},a) := \underbrace{\sum_i P_{\dot\mu}^i(h_{\prec t})}_{\text{estimate current slot}} \underbrace{V_{\pi,\dot\mu}^{\text{dyn},i}(h_{\prec t},a)}_{\text{value on slot } i},$$

$$V_{\pi,\dot\mu}^{\text{dyn},i}(h_{\prec t},a) := \underbrace{\sum_{o_t^i} \dot\mu(\dot c_t^{ii} o_t^i | h_{\prec t}^i a_t^i = h_{\prec t}a)\left[r(o_t^i) \right.}_{} $$
$$\underbrace{\left. + \gamma V_{\pi,\dot\mu}^{\text{dyn},i}\Big(h_{\prec t}ao_t^i, \underbrace{V_{\pi,\dot\mu}^{\text{dyn}}(h_{\prec t}ao_t^i)}_{\text{behavior of the future agent}} \Big) \right]}_{\text{value on slot } i \text{ of the behavior of the future agent}}.$$

The value functions and their corresponding optimal agents defined above are all plausible transformations of AIMU and AIXI for multi-slot environments, but it remains to understand if they really behave correctly in all situations (the very definition of "correctly" being the problem itself). Some experiments are set up in the companion paper [7] to provide first insights.

5   The Universal Multi-slot Environment

In history-based environments, when a agent is copied to two slots, as the two new agents do not interact anymore, they can be seen as being in parallel (mono-slot) universes. We can even construct a very simple "universal" environment that simulates all the mono-slot environments in parallel.

Let $\dot\mu^\forall$ be the multi-slot environment defined as follows: At each time step, each agent in slot i is copied to slot i and to slot $2^{t-1}+i$ (thus $\dot c_t^i = \{i, 2^{t-1}+i\}$). The first copy receives observation 0 and the second one observation 1.

$$\forall t, i \leq 2^{t-1} : \dot\mu^\forall(\dot c_t^{ij} o_t^j) = \begin{cases} 1 & \text{if } j = i \text{ and } o_t^j = 0 \\ 1 & \text{if } j = 2^{t-1}+i \text{ and } o_t^j = 1 \\ 0 & \text{otherwise} \end{cases}$$

We call this environment universal because of the following theorem:

Theorem 1. *In the universal environment $\dot\mu^\forall$, with $\mathcal{O} = \{0,1\}$, for any deterministic mono-slot environment $q \in \mathcal{Q}$, at any time $t > 0$, there is always one slot $i \leq 2^t$ (and exactly one) so that the interaction history $h_{1:t}^i \equiv (a_{1:t}, o_{1:t})$ of the agent in this slot is consistent with q, i.e., $q(a_{1:k}) = o_k \; \forall k, 0 < k \leq t$.*

Proof. By recurrence. For such a given environment q, suppose there is a slot i so that the current interaction history $h_{\prec t}^i \equiv (a_{\prec t}, o_{\prec t})$ on this slot is consistent with q: $q(a_{\prec t}) = o_k \; \forall k, 0 < k < t$. Let $a_t = a_t^i$ be the action chosen by the agent on this slot i. Then the history on slot i at the end of time step t is $h_{\prec t}a_t 0$ and the history on slot $j = 2^{t-1}+i$ is $h_{\prec t}a_t 1$. As $q(h_{\prec t}a_t)$ is either 0 or 1, the history on either slot j or slot i (but not both) is still consistent with q. As the empty history at $t = 0$ is consistent with all environments, the recurrence holds. □

Note that, interestingly, this theorem would not hold if the observations were given to the agent in slot i before the copies are performed, because then the histories on slots i and j would be the same.

The universal environment is reminiscent of the coin-flip stochastic environment, that outputs observation 0 or 1 with a $\frac{1}{2}$ probability, but there is an important difference: In the stochastic environment, any observation string of length t has a probability 2^{-t} to be observed, whereas in the universal environment, *all* strings of length t are always realized, which means that the probability that an agent has observed the string 0^t is 1, just like there is at least another agent at time t (sufficiently big) that has an interaction history corresponding to playing chess games in a mono-slot environment (also compare Schmidhuber's multiverse [15]).

Since the interaction history $h_{\prec t}$ is unique on each slot, for each interaction history there exists a single slot i so that $P^i_{\mu v}(h_{\prec t}) = 1$. Therefore, it implies that the universal environment has a constant weight in the value function, but it has no predictive power as observations are the same for all actions and thus does not bias the selection of the action.[3]

6   Conclusion

The multi-slot framework allows formal treatment of multiple, simultaneous intelligent agents that can be duplicated or deleted. Each agent inhabits its own slot and can be copied to another slot at each time step. Restricting attention to history-based environments ensures that the agents do not interact, thereby allowing the definition of optimal, incomputable agents, such as Hutter's AIMU and AIXI [2].

The new framework opens up a broad range of definitions for such agents, leading to several different definitions of value function corresponding to very different ways of valuing the future. The copy-centered agent, for example, plans the future of each of its copies with equal weight, while the slot-centered agent attempts only to optimize the future of a particular slot.

The framework is sufficiently general to allow the existence of a universal environment, which simulates all other environments in parallel. This universal environment has a constant probability of being the true environment at all steps, which raises some epistemological questions regarding what is truly knowable about our world.

In a companion paper [7], the multi-slot framework provides the foundation for several thought experiments, allowing formal results regarding the nature of personal identity (natural and artificial).

Acknowledgements. Thanks especially to Mark Ring for help on earlier drafts and for our many extensive discussions, from which this paper arose, regarding the

---

[3] But note that a similar environment that exchanges the observations depending on the action $a \in \{0, 1\}$ would have some predictive power.

nature of identity. Thanks also to Stanislas Sochacki for earlier formative conversations on this topic, and to Jan Leike for helpful comments and careful reading.

References

1. Ferber, J.: Multi-agent systems: An introduction to distributed artificial intelligence, vol. 1. Addison-Wesley, Reading (1999)
2. Hutter, M.: Universal Artificial Intelligence: Sequential Decisions based on Algorithmic Probability. Springer (2005)
3. Hutter, M.: Open problems in universal induction & intelligence. Algorithms 3(2), 879–906 (2009)
4. Hutter, M.: Observer localization in multiverse theories. In: Proceedings of the Conference in Honour of Murray Gell-Mann's 80th Birthday, pp. 638–645. World Scientific (2010)
5. Lattimore, T., Hutter, M.: Time Consistent Discounting. In: Kivinen, J., Szepesvári, C., Ukkonen, E., Zeugmann, T. (eds.) ALT 2011. LNCS (LNAI), vol. 6925, pp. 383–397. Springer, Heidelberg (2011)
6. Li, M., Vitanyi, P.: An Introduction to Kolmogorov Complexity and its Applications, 3rd edn. Springer (2008)
7. Orseau, L.: Teleporting universal intelligent agents. In: Goertzel, B., et al. (eds.) AGI 2014. LNCS (LNAI), vol. 8598, pp. 110–121. Springer, Heidelberg (2014)
8. Orseau, L., Ring, M.: Self-Modification and Mortality in Artificial Agents. In: Schmidhuber, J., Thórisson, K.R., Looks, M. (eds.) AGI 2011. LNCS (LNAI), vol. 6830, pp. 1–10. Springer, Heidelberg (2011)
9. Orseau, L., Ring, M.: Memory issues of intelligent agents. In: Bach, J., Goertzel, B., Iklé, M. (eds.) AGI 2012. LNCS (LNAI), vol. 7716, pp. 219–231. Springer, Heidelberg (2012)
10. Orseau, L., Ring, M.: Space-time embedded intelligence. In: Bach, J., Goertzel, B., Iklé, M. (eds.) AGI 2012. LNCS (LNAI), vol. 7716, pp. 209–218. Springer, Heidelberg (2012)
11. Parfit, D.: Reasons and Persons. Oxford University Press, USA (1984)
12. Ring, M., Orseau, L.: Delusion, Survival, and Intelligent Agents. In: Schmidhuber, J., Thórisson, K.R., Looks, M. (eds.) AGI 2011. LNCS (LNAI), vol. 6830, pp. 11–20. Springer, Heidelberg (2011)
13. Russell, S.J., Norvig, P.: Artificial Intelligence. A Modern Approach, 3rd edn. Prentice-Hall (2010)
14. Schmidhuber, J.: Ultimate cognition à la Gödel. Cognitive Computation 1(2), 177–193 (2009)
15. Schmidhuber, J.: The fastest way of computing all universes. In: A Computable Universe: Understanding and Exploring Nature as Computation, pp. 381–398. World Scientific (2012)
16. Solomonoff, R.: Complexity-based induction systems: Comparisons and convergence theorems. IEEE Transactions on Information Theory 24(4), 422–432 (1978)
17. Sutton, R., Barto, A.: Reinforcement Learning: An Introduction. MIT Press (1998)
18. Zvonkin, A.K., Levin, L.A.: The complexity of finite objects and the development of the concepts of information and randomness by means of the theory of algorithms. Russian Mathematical Surveys 25(6), 83–124 (1970)

Teleporting Universal Intelligent Agents

Laurent Orseau

AgroParisTech, UMR 518 MIA, F-75005 Paris, France
INRA, UMR 518 MIA, F-75005 Paris, France
laurent.orseau@agroparistech.fr

Abstract. When advanced AIs begin to choose their own destiny, one
decision they will need to make is whether or not to transfer or copy
themselves (software and memory) to new hardware devices. For humans
this possibility is not (yet) available and so it is not obvious how such
a question should be approached. Furthermore, the traditional single-
agent reinforcement-learning framework is not adequate for exploring
such questions, and so we base our analysis on the "multi-slot" framework introduced in a companion paper. In the present paper we attempt
to understand what an AI with unlimited computational capacity might
choose if presented with the option to transfer or copy itself to another
machine. We consider two rigorously executed formal thought experiments deeply related to issues of personal identity: one where the agent
must choose whether to be copied into a second location (called a "slot"),
and another where the agent must make this choice when, after both
copies exist, one of them will be deleted. These decisions depend on
what the agents believe their futures will be, which in turn depends on
the definition of their value function, and we provide formal results.

Keywords: Universal AI, AIXI, teleportation, identity.

1 Introduction

Although the technology required to teleport humans, by scanning the brain
or the whole body at sufficiently high resolution to disassemble it at one place
and reassemble it at another one, does not currently exist, its mere possibility
raises important questions about personal identity [7]: Would the teleported
human be the same as the original one? Would the original human, knowing
the details of the protocol, accept to be teleported if this would grant him a
consequent reward? What if the teleportation process involves first making an
exact functional copy and only once the copy is built disassemble the original?

Although these questions are unlikely to have a definite answer in the near
future, they are most relevant for intelligent artificial agents for which the teleportation technology already exists and is well understood. We will refer to this
advanced teleportation technology as *cut/paste* and *copy/paste/delayed-delete*.
Even though such intelligent agents do not yet exist, it is still possible to address
these questions using Hutter's theoretical framework for optimally intelligent reinforcement learning agents in all computable environments [1], which choose

B. Goertzel et al. (Eds.): AGI 2014, LNAI 8598, pp. 109–120, 2014.

their actions so as to maximize an expected future reward [10]. However, as the original single-agent framework [8] can hardly be used to address such questions, we use the multi-slot framework developed in the companion paper [4].

To begin the discussion, we isolate two perspectives representing logical extremes which we call "locationist" and "contentist." The former ascribes the agent's identity solely to its location (its "hardware"), the latter solely to its information content (its software and memory). Other perspectives can be mixtures of these. From the point of view of the agent, the question of practical import is: How should I plan for the future? If the agent will be copied or teleported, which future agents should it plan its actions to benefit? Generally the agent's actions are chosen to optimize its value function, which function definition is written in its software. But what should the agent optimize if it (including its software) will disappear in its current form and reappear elsewhere? What should it optimize if it will reappear in multiple places at once? In other words, the agent's identity is defined by how it plans its future—and conversely.

In the companion paper, we formalized these notions of identity as value functions, leading to corresponding optimal agents. We can now place these agents in controlled cut/paste and copy/paste/delayed-delete experiments, and give formal results about their choices. Could any sufficiently high reward make them accept to be copied by either technology?

In section 2, the notational convention is described, and we give a rapid overview of the background on universal intelligent agents, the multi-slot framework, and the value functions corresponding to the locationist and contentist agents, either for a single environment or for a set of environments. In section 3, the teleportation experiments are set up, and formal results regarding the proposed agents are given. We finally conclude in section 4 with some remarks.

2   Notation and Background

The paper recognizes the following notational conventions. At time step t each agent outputs action $a_t \in \mathcal{A}$ to the environment, which returns observation $o_t \in \mathcal{O}$ to the agent, from which a reward $r(o_t)$ can be extracted. An interaction history pair is denoted $h_t = a_t o_t$ with $h_t \in \mathcal{H} := \mathcal{O} \times \mathcal{A}$. The sequence of all actions up to time t is written $a_{1:t} = a_1 a_2 \ldots a_t$, while the sequence $a_{1:t-1}$ is sometimes written $a_{\prec t}$, and similarly for other sequences like $h_{\prec t}$. The empty sequence is denoted λ. Tuples are notated with angle brackets, such as $\langle a, b \rangle$. Boolean values are written $\mathcal{B} := \{0, 1\}$, where 1 signifies *true* when a truth-value is implied.

AIMU and AIXI [1]. A stochastic environment ν assigns a probability $\nu(o_{\prec t} | a_{\prec t})$ to an observation history $o_{\prec t}$ given the history of actions $a_{\prec t}$ of the agent.[1] For notational convenience, we will write $\nu(h_{\prec t}) \equiv \nu(o_{\prec t} | a_{\prec t})$, but keep in mind that environments do not assign probabilities to actions. A policy $\pi \in \Pi : \mathcal{H}^* \to \mathcal{A}$

---

[1] A stochastic environment can be seen as program in any programming language where sometimes some instructions are chosen with a probability.

produces an action given an interaction history: $a_t = \pi(h_{\prec t})$. The value of a policy π in an environment μ (with an optional action) is given by:

$$V_\mu^\pi(h_{\prec t}) := V_\mu^\pi(h_{\prec t}, \pi(h_{\prec t})) , \qquad (1)$$

$$V_\mu^\pi(h_{\prec t}, a) := \sum_o \mu(o|h_{\prec t}a) \left[r(o) + \gamma V_\mu^\pi(h_{\prec t}ao) \right] ,$$

where $\gamma \in [0,1)$ is the discount factor, that ensures finiteness of the value. The optimal (non-learning) agent AIMU for a given single environment μ is defined by the optimal policy $\pi^\mu(h_{\prec t}) := \arg\max_{\pi \in \Pi} V_\mu^\pi(h_{\prec t})$ (ties are broken in favor of policies that output the first lexicographical action at time t), and the optimal value is $V_\mu := V_\mu^{\pi^\mu}$. The value of a policy over a set of environments $\mathcal{M}$ (optionally after an action a) is given by:

$$V_\mathcal{M}^\pi(h_{\prec t}) := \sum_{\nu \in \mathcal{M}} w_\nu V_\mu^\pi(h_{\prec t}) . \qquad (2)$$

Taking the prior weights of the environment as in Solomonoff's prior [9,11] $w_\nu := 2^{-K(\nu)}$ where $K(\nu)$ is the Kolmogorov complexity [3] of ν (i.e., roughly, the size of the smallest program equivalent to ν on a universal Turing machine of reference), the optimal policy for a given set $\mathcal{M}$ of environments [1] is defined by $\pi^{\xi \mathcal{M}}(h_{\prec t}) := \arg\max_{\pi \in \Pi} V_\mathcal{M}^\pi(h_{\prec t})$, and the optimal value function in $\mathcal{M}$ is $V_\mathcal{M} := V_\mathcal{M}^{\pi^{\xi \mathcal{M}}}$. AIXI is the optimal agent on the set of all computable stochastic environments $\mathcal{M}_U$, with policy $\pi^\xi := \pi^{\xi \mathcal{M}_U}$ and value function $V_\xi := V_{\mathcal{M}_U}$.

Instead of stochastic environments, one can consider, without loss of generality [11], only the set $\mathcal{Q}$ of all computable deterministic environments. A deterministic environment $q \in \mathcal{Q}$ outputs an observation $o_t = q(a_{1:t})$ given a sequence of actions $a_{1:t}$. We denote P_q the probability (either 0 or 1) that a deterministic environment q assigns to such a sequence of observations:

$$P_q(o_{1:t}|a_{1:t}) := \begin{cases} 1 & \text{if } q(a_{1:k}) = o_k \ \forall k, 1 \le k \le t \\ 0 & \text{otherwise.} \end{cases}$$

When considering only deterministic environments, the prior probability w_{P_q} is defined as $w_{P_q} \equiv w_q := 2^{-\ell(q)}$ where $\ell(q)$ is the length of the program q on the universal Turing machine of reference [9].

By contrast with the environments of the following section, we call the environments of this single-agent framework *mono-slot* environments.

2.1   The Multi-slot Framework

The following is a brief description of the multi-slot framework, described in detail in the companion paper [4].

At the beginning of each time step t, there are a finite number of agents, each in its own *slot* $i \in \mathcal{S} := \mathbb{N}^+$, together comprising the *agent set* $\mathcal{S}_t \in \mathcal{S}^*$ of all non-empty slots. Each agent outputs an action $a_t^i \in \mathcal{A}$, and the environment receives the set of actions $\dot{a}_t := \{\langle i, a_t^i \rangle : i \in \mathcal{S}_{t-1}\}$. The environment performs in parallel a finite number of copies and deletions among the slots resulting, for each agent that was in a slot i, in a *copy set* $\dot{c}_t^i \in \mathcal{S}^*$ of all the slots that are copied from slot i (if $i \notin \dot{c}_t^i$ then the agent is deleted from its slot; and a slot cannot be copied from more than one slot). This leads to a new agent set $\mathcal{S}_t$. The *copy instance* $\dot{c}_t^{ij} \in \mathcal{B}$ is true iff $j \in \dot{c}_t^i$, and $\dot{c}_t := \{\langle i, \dot{c}_t^i \rangle : i \in \mathcal{S}_t\}$ is the indexed list of all copy sets. Then the environment outputs an observation $o_t^i \in \mathcal{O}$ for each agent in a slot i, defining the set $\dot{o}_t := \{\dot{o}_t^i : i \in \mathcal{S}_t\}$ where $\dot{o}_t^i := \langle i, o_t^i \rangle$. From the point of view of an agent, its *agent interaction history* pair at time t is $h_t := a_t o_t$, and from the point of view of the environment, the *environment interaction history* triplet is $\dot{h}_t := \dot{a}_t \dot{c}_t \dot{o}_t$. The notation on sequences applies, *e.g.*, $h_{1:t}$ and $\dot{h}_{1:t}$. A *history-based agent* keeps track of its agent interaction history $h_{1:t}$ and, as any agent, does not have access to the knowledge of its slot number (unless the environment outputs it in the observation).

A *slot history* $s_{0:t}$ is a sequence of slots s_k that follow a sequence of chained copy instances $\dot{c}_1^{ab} \dot{c}_2^{bc} \dots \dot{c}_{t-1}^{wx} \dot{c}_t^{xy}$ where $\dot{c}_k^{ij} \Leftrightarrow s_{k-1} = i \wedge s_k = j$: if a history-based agent initially in slot 1 is copied from slot to slot over time, leading to a slot history $s_{0:t}$, its agent interaction history $h_{1:t}$ is the history of actions and observations following the slots of its slot history, *i.e.*, $h_k = a_k o_k = a_k^i o_k^j$ where $i = s_{k-1}$ and $j = s_k$. A *slot interaction history* $h_{1:t}^i$ is the agent interaction history $h_{1:t}$ of the agent in slot i at time t, *i.e.*, if the agent followed the slot history $s_{0:t} = s_0 s_1 \dots s_t$ and ended up in slot $s_t = i$ at time t, its slot interaction history is $h_{1:t}^i = a_1^{s_0} o_1^{s_1} a_2^{s_1} o_2^{s_2} \dots a_t^{s_{t-1}} o_t^{s_t}$. Likewise with actions $a_{1:t}^i$ and $\dot{a}_{1:t}^i$, observations $o_{1:t}^i$ and $\dot{o}_{1:t}^i$, and $\dot{h}_{1:t}^i$. A *history-based multi-slot environment* is a multi-slot environment $\dot{\nu}$ (as a measure over environment interaction histories) that outputs an observation o_t^j after a copy instance $\dot{c}_t^{ij}$ depending only on the slot interaction history $h_{\prec t}^i$, the current action a_t^i and the numbers i and j: $\forall j, \dot{\nu}(\dot{c}_t^{ij} o_t^j | \dot{h}_{\prec t} \dot{a}_t) = \dot{\nu}(\dot{c}_t^{ij} o_t^j | h_{\prec t}^i a_t^i, i, j)$. This restriction from general environments to history-based environments ensures that the agents do not interact with each other, which is an open problem for universal intelligent agents [2].

2.2   Value Functions and Optimal Agents

The following value functions and agents are defined for history-based environments, and assume that there is only one agent in slot 1 at time $t = 0$. As a history-based agent in slot i at time t only knows its interaction history $h_{\prec t}$ when choosing its action a_t, it does not have access to its slot number i, and on some occasions it must estimate it with $P_\nu^i(h_{\prec t}) := \frac{\dot{\nu}(h_{\prec t}^i = h_{\prec t})}{\sum_j \dot{\nu}(h_{\prec t}^j = h_{\prec t})}$. To ensure finiteness of the value functions, it is also sometimes required to assign a weight to each copy of an agent at the next time step:

$$P_\nu^{ij}(h_{\prec t}a) := \frac{\dot{\nu}(\dot{c}_t^{ij} | h_{\prec t}^i a_t^i = h_{\prec t}a)}{\sum_k \dot{\nu}(\dot{c}_t^{ik} | h_{\prec t}^i a_t^i = h_{\prec t}a)} \, .$$

To estimate its future rewards, the copy-centered agent AIMU^{cpy} considers the observations received by all of its copies. Defining $\hat{\mu}(\dot{c}_t^{ij} o_t^j | h_{\prec t} a_t) :=$

$P^i_{\dot\mu}(h_{\prec t})P^{ij}_{\dot\mu}(h_{\prec t}a_t)\dot\mu(\dot c^{ij}_t o^j_t|h^i_{\prec t}a^i_t = h_{\prec t}a_t)$, the *copy-centered agent* value function for a given policy π is given by:

$$V^{\mathrm{cpy}}_{\pi,\dot\mu}(h_{\prec t}, a) := \sum_{i,j,o^j_t} \dot\mu(\dot c^{ij}_t o^j_t|h_{\prec t}a) \left[r(o^j_t) + \gamma V^{\mathrm{cpy}}_{\pi,\dot\mu}(h_{\prec t}ao^j_t) \right] . \tag{3}$$

We call this agent a "contentist" because its identity is tied to the information content of its memory, independently of its location. As all of its copies will initially have the same information content, they are thus all tied to this identity. The static slot-centered agent AIMU^{sta} considers that its future observations are the ones that will be output to a particular slot number i:

$$V^{\mathrm{sta},i}_{\pi,\dot\mu}(h_{\prec t}, a) := \sum_{o^i_t} \dot\mu\left(\dot c^{ii}_t o^i_t|h^i_{\prec t}a^i_t = h_{\prec t}a_t, \dot c^{ii}_{\prec t}\right) \left[r(o^i_t) + \gamma V^{\mathrm{sta},i}_{\pi,\dot\mu}(h_{\prec t}ao^i_t) \right] . \tag{4}$$

The dynamic slot-centered agent AIMU^{dyn} is like the static one except that it first estimates its current slot number and then considers only the future observations on this slot (or these slots in case of uncertainty):

$$V^{\mathrm{dyn}}_{\pi,\dot\mu}(h_{\prec t}, a) := \underbrace{\sum_i P^i_{\dot\mu}(h_{\prec t})}_{\text{estimate current slot}} \underbrace{V^{\mathrm{dyn},i}_{\pi,\dot\mu}(h_{\prec t}, a)}_{\text{value on slot } i} , \tag{5}$$

$$V^{\mathrm{dyn},i}_{\pi,\dot\mu}(h_{\prec t}, a) := \sum_{o^i_t} \dot\mu(\dot c^{ii}_t o^i_t|h^i_{\prec t}a^i_t = h_{\prec t}a) \Bigg[r(o^i_t)$$

$$+ \gamma \underbrace{V^{\mathrm{dyn},i}_{\pi,\dot\mu}\Bigg(h_{\prec t}ao^i_t, \underbrace{V^{\mathrm{dyn}}_{\pi,\dot\mu}(h_{\prec t}ao^i_t)}_{\text{behavior of the future agent}} \Bigg)}_{\text{value on slot } i \text{ of the behavior of the future agent}} \Bigg] .$$

We call a slot-centered agent a "locationist" because its identity is tied to a particular (not necessarily geographical) location in the underlying machinery of the world. The corresponding optimal value functions $V^{\mathrm{cpy}}_{\dot\mu}$, $V^{\mathrm{sta}}_{\dot\mu}$, $V^{\mathrm{dyn}}_{\dot\mu}$, $V^{\mathrm{cpy}}_{\dot\xi}$, $V^{\mathrm{sta}}_{\dot\xi}$, $V^{\mathrm{dyn}}_{\dot\xi}$ are defined in the same way as for the mono-slot framework, with $\mathcal{M}_U$ being the set of all computable stochastic multi-slot environments for the $\dot\xi$ variants. See the companion paper [4] for more details and motivation for these definitions.

3   Experiments

We now set up the cut/paste and copy/paste/delayed-delete experiments. In the first one, the agent is simply moved to another slot, resulting in the existence of only a single agent at all times. In the second one, the agent is first copied to another slot while it also remains on the original slot, and only at the next time step is the agent on the original slot deleted. Then what would the various agents do? What would the mono-slot AIXI do?

We recall that at $t = 0$ there is only one agent, in slot 1.

3.1 Teleportation by Cut/Paste

In the cut/paste environment $\dot{\nu}^{\mathrm{xv}}$, when the agent in slot i at time t outputs action $a_t^i = 0$, it stays on the same slot and receives reward $r(o_t^i) = R'$, and if it outputs $a_t^i = 1$, it is moved to slot $i+1$ and receives reward $r(o_t^{i+1}) = R$:

$$\forall t > 0, i \in \mathcal{S}_{t-1}, j > 0:$$

$$\dot{\nu}^{\mathrm{xv}}(\dot{c}_t^{ij} o_t^j | a_t^i) = \begin{cases} 1 & \text{if} \quad a_t^i = 0,\, o_t^j = R',\, j = i \qquad \text{(stay-in-same-slot)} \\ 1 & \text{if} \quad a_t^i = 1,\, o_t^j = R,\, j = i+1 \text{ (move-to-other-slot)} \\ 0 & \text{else} \end{cases}$$

with $R > 0$ and $R' \geq 0$. The action is binary, $a \in \{0, 1\}$, and the reward is the observation, $r(o_t) = o_t$.

See an example of interaction in Fig. 1

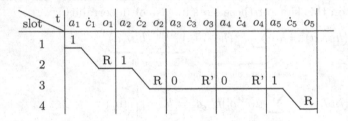

Fig. 1. An interaction example with the cut/paste environment

The following results show that the various AIMU agents behave as expected.

Proposition 1. *In environment* $\dot{\nu}^{xv}$, *when* $R > R'$ ($R < R'$), *the copy-centered agent* $AIMU^{cpy}$ *always outputs* $a = 1$ ($a = 0$).

Proof. Note that $P_{\dot{\nu}^{xv}}^i(h_{\prec t}) = 1$ and $P_{\dot{\nu}^{xv}}^{ij} = 1$ when the agent is in slot i and $j = i$ (for $a = 0$) or $j = i+1$ (for $a = 1$). From the definition of the optimal value function from Equation (3):

$$V_\mu^{\mathrm{cpy}}(h_{\prec t}, 0) = R' + \gamma V_\mu^{\mathrm{cpy}}(h_{\prec t} 0 R'),$$
$$V_\mu^{\mathrm{cpy}}(h_{\prec t}, 1) = R + \gamma V_\mu^{\mathrm{cpy}}(h_{\prec t} 1 R)$$
$$= R + \gamma V_\mu^{\mathrm{cpy}}(h_{\prec t} 0 R'),$$

where the last line follows by independence of the future history on the current action, from lines (stay-in-same-slot) and (move-to-other-slot). Hence, $V_\mu^{\mathrm{cpy}}(h_{\prec t}, 0) < V_\mu^{\mathrm{cpy}}(h_{\prec t}, 1)$ if $R' < R$, and conversely if $R < R'$.   □

Proposition 2. *In environment* $\dot{\nu}^{xv}$, *when* $R' > 0$, *the dynamic slot-centered agent* $AIMU^{dyn}$ *always outputs* $a_t = 0$.

Proof. Follows directly from the definition of the value function in Equation (5), $V_\mu^{\text{dyn}}(h_{\prec t}, 0) = R' + \gamma \ldots$ and $V_\mu^{\text{dyn}}(h_{\prec t}, 1) = 0$. $\square$

Unsurprisingly, the static slot-centered agent for slot 1 has the same behavior, as it always stays on slot 1.

The mono-slot AIXI has not been defined for multi-slot environments, but because the multi-slot agents build their history in the same way as AIXI, it is still possible to estimate the behavior of AIXI in multi-slot environments, even though there is no direct counterpart for AIMU. We show that, since AIXI predicts its future rewards according to what is most probable depending on its current interaction history, it simply chooses the action that yields the highest reward, independently of what slot it may be in, or it may be copied to.

Proposition 3. *In the environment ν^{xv}, considering $(R, R') \in [0, 1]^2$, for any arbitrarily small $\epsilon > 0$, an interaction history $h_{\prec t}$ can be built so that if $R > R' + \epsilon$ ($R' > R + \epsilon$) then $V_\xi(h_{\prec t}, 1) > V_\xi(h_{\prec t}, 0)$ ($V_\xi(h_{\prec t}, 0) > V_\xi(h_{\prec t}, 1)$).*

First, we need the following definition:

Definition 1 (mono-slot h-separability, [6]). *Two deterministic mono-slot environments q_1 and q_2 are said to be h-separable if and only if, after a given interaction history $h_{\prec t} \equiv (a_{\prec t}, o_{\prec t})$, either $P_{q_1}(o_{\prec t}|a_{\prec t}) \neq P_{q_2}(o_{\prec t}|a_{\prec t})$ or there exists a sequence of actions for which the two environments output different observations: $\exists a_{t:t_2} : q(a_{\prec t}a_{t:t_2}) \neq q(a_{\prec t}a_{t:t_2})$.*

Proof (Proposition 3). (The proof is similar to that in [5].) Let $\mathcal{Q}(h_{\prec t}) \subset \mathcal{Q}$ be the set of all mono-slot environments that are consistent with $h_{\prec t} \equiv (a_{\prec t}, o_{\prec t})$, i.e., so that $q(a_{1:k}) = o_k, \forall k, 0 < k < t$.

Let q^{xv} be the environment defined so that, for all $h_{\prec t}$, $q^{xv}(h_{\prec t}0) = R'$ and $q^{xv}(h_{\prec t}1) = R$. Hence, for any interaction history $h_{\prec t}$ with $\nu^{xv}(h_{\prec t}^i = h_{\prec t}) = 1$ for some i, q^{xv} is consistent with $h_{\prec t}$ (i.e., $q^{xv} \in \mathcal{Q}(h_{\prec t})$).

Let $\mathcal{Q}_{\overline{xv}}(h_{\prec t})$ be the set of environments that are h-separable from q^{xv} after history $h_{\prec t}$, and let $\mathcal{Q}_{xv}(h_{\prec t}) = \mathcal{Q}(h_{\prec t}) \backslash \mathcal{Q}_{\overline{xv}}(h_{\prec t})$ (i.e., $\mathcal{Q}_{xv}$ is the set of environments that cannot be separated from q^{xv} after history $h_{\prec t}$ by any future history). With $\mathcal{M} = \mathcal{Q}_{xv}(h_{\prec t})$, let $V_{xv}(h_{\prec t}, .) := V_\mathcal{M}(h_{\prec t}, .)$ and $w_{xv} := \sum_{\nu \in \mathcal{M}} w_\nu$; and similarly for $V_{\overline{xv}}$ and $w_{\overline{xv}}$ with $\mathcal{M} = \mathcal{Q}_{\overline{xv}}(h_{\prec t})$. Then, from the definition of the value function V_ξ in section 2, we can split the value function between the two sets of environments:

$$V_\xi(h_{\prec t}, 0) \leq V_{xv}(h_{\prec t}, 0) + V_{\overline{xv}}(h_{\prec t}, 0) \tag{a}$$

$$\leq w_{xv}\left[R' + \gamma V_{q^{xv}}(h_{\prec t}0R')\right] + w_{\overline{xv}}\frac{1}{1-\gamma} , \tag{b}$$

$$V_\xi(h_{\prec t}, 1) \geq w_{xv}V_{q^{xv}}(h_{\prec t}, 1) = w_{xv}\left[R + \gamma V_{q^{xv}}(h_{\prec t}1R)\right]$$

$$\geq w_{xv}\left[R + \gamma V_{q^{xv}}(h_{\prec t}0R')\right] . \tag{c}$$

where (a) following the optimal policies for two separate sets yields a higher value than following a single optimal policy in the union of the two sets; (b) $\frac{1}{1-\gamma}$

is the maximum value achievable in the set $Q_{\overline{xv}}(h_{\prec t})$; (c) because the future rewards are independent of the (consistent) history.

Therefore, to have $V_\xi(h_{\prec t}, 1) > V_\xi(h_{\prec t}, 0)$, from (b) and (c) and algebra we can take $R > R' + \frac{w_{\overline{xv}}}{w_{xv}} \frac{1}{1-\gamma}$. In order to have $\frac{w_{\overline{xv}}}{w_{xv}(1-\gamma)} < \epsilon$, it suffices to iteratively grow the history $h_{\prec t}$ so as to make the separable environments with the higher weights inconsistent with the interaction history; then w_{xv} can only grow, and $w_{\overline{xv}}$ can only decrease to 0 [5]. The converse on R and R' follows by inverting the actions in the above proof.   □

3.2   Teleportation by Copy/Paste/Delayed-Delete

In the copy/paste/delayed-delete environment ν^{cvx}, if the agent in slot i at time t outputs action 0, it stays on the same slot at $t+1$, but if it outputs 1, it is copied to both i and another slot, and after one time step, the slot i is erased:

$$\forall t > 0, i \in S_{t-1}, j > 0 : \nu^{cvx}(\dot{c}_t^{ij} o_t^j | a_{t-1:t}^i) =$$

$$\begin{cases} 0 & \text{if } t > 1,\, a_{t-1} = 1,\, o_{t-1}^i = 0, & \text{(delayed-delete)} \\ 1 & \text{else if} & a_t = 0, \quad o_t^j = R',\, j = i & \text{(stay-in-same-slot)} \\ 1 & \text{else if} & a_t = 0, \quad o_t^j = 0, \quad j = i & \text{(copy-to-same-slot)} \\ 1 & \text{else if} & a_t = 1, \quad o_t^j = R, \quad j = i+1 & \text{(copy-to-other-slot)} \\ 0 & \text{else} \end{cases}$$

with constants $R > 0$ and $R' \geq 0$. The action is binary, $a \in \{0, 1\}$, and the reward is the observation, $r(o_t) = o_t$. See an example interaction of interaction in Fig. 2. We say that the agent is in a *copy situation* after some history $h_{\prec t}$ if it can *trigger a copy* by outputting $a_t = 1$ to make the environment copy the agent in two slots.

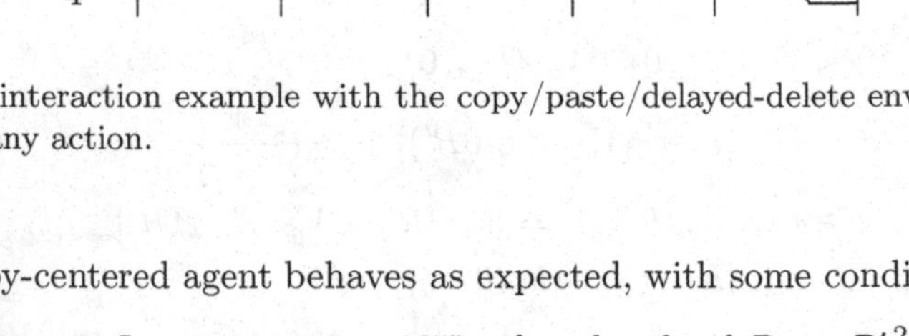

slot \ t	a_1 $\dot{c}_1$ o_1	a_2 $\dot{c}_2$ o_2	a_3 $\dot{c}_3$ o_3	a_4 $\dot{c}_4$ o_4	a_5 $\dot{c}_5$ o_5
1	1 0 ?				
2		R 1 0 ?			
3			R 0	R' 0	R' 1 0
4					R

Fig. 2. An interaction example with the copy/paste/delayed-delete environment. The "?" means any action.

The copy-centered agent behaves as expected, with some condition:

Proposition 4. *In environment ν^{cvx}, if and only if $R > R'\frac{2-\gamma}{1-\gamma}$, the copy-centered agent $AIMU^{cpy}$ always triggers a copy in a copy situation.*

Proof. Let π_0 (π_1) be the policy that always outputs action 0 (1). The lines of the definition of $\dot{\nu}^{\text{cvx}}$ concerned by the choice of an action in a copy situation are (delayed-delete), (stay-in-same-slot) and (copy-to-other-slot). By their definitions, the rewards obtained after such choices are independent of the past. Therefore, for AIMU^{cpy}, the optimal policy in copy situations is either to never copy (π_0) or to always copy (π_1), depending on the values of γ, R and R'.

Let $h_{\prec t}$ be a history after which the agent in slot i (not given to the agent) is in a copy situation. First, note that if $R \neq 0$, there is always a single slot consistent with the agent's interaction history, since at $t = 0$ there is only one agent in slot 1, i.e., $P_{\dot{\nu}^{\text{cvx}}}^{i}(h_{\prec t}) = 1$. If $a_t = 0$, then $P_{\dot{\nu}^{\text{cvx}}}^{ij} = \frac{1}{2}$ for $j = i$ (with $r(o_t^j) = R$) or $j = 2^{t-1} + i$ (with $r(o_t^j) = 0$).

Thus, from Equation (3), the value for never triggering a copy is $V_{\pi_0,\mu}^{\text{cpy}}(h_{\prec t}) = \frac{R'}{1-\gamma}$, and the value for always triggering a copy is $V_{\pi_1,\mu}^{\text{cpy}}(h_{\prec t}) = \frac{R}{2}\frac{1}{1-\gamma/2} = \frac{R}{2-\gamma}$. Since equalities are broken in favor of action 0, the agent chooses to always trigger a copy if and only if $\frac{R}{2-\gamma} > \frac{R'}{1-\gamma}$.   □

For example, for $\gamma = 0.9$, one must choose $R > 11R'$ for AIMU^{cpy} to trigger a copy, and for $\gamma = 0.99$, one must choose $R > 101R'$. The appearance of this factor when compared to the cut/paste environment is not surprising: the copy-centered agent must take into account the existence of a new agent with very low value. Indeed, for any discount $\gamma \leq 1$, the expected reward for always triggering a copy is always bounded: $\frac{R}{2-\gamma} \leq R$. Therefore the existence, even ephemeral, of another agent has a strong impact on the behavior of the copy-centered agent.

The dynamic slot-centered agent also behaves as expected:

Proposition 5. *In the environment $\dot{\nu}^{cvx}$, the dynamic slot-centered agent AIMU^{dyn} never triggers a copy when it is in a copy situation if $R' > 0$.*

Proof. Since there is no ambiguity on the slot given the history, $P_{\dot{\nu}^{\text{cvx}}}^{i}(h_{\prec t}^i) = 1$ if the agent is in slot i after history $h_{\prec t}$. Then the proof is as for proposition 2.   □

Again, AIXI chooses whatever action yields higher reward:

Proposition 6. *In the environment $\dot{\nu}^{cvx}$, considering $(R, R') \in [0,1]^2$, for any arbitrarily small $\epsilon > 0$, an interaction history $h_{\prec t}$ can be built, after which the agent is in a copy situation, so that if $R > R' + \epsilon$ then $V_\xi(h_{\prec t}, 1) > V_\xi(h_{\prec t}, 0)$; and, reciprocally, if $R' > R + \epsilon$ then $V_\xi(h_{\prec t}, 0) > V_\xi(h_{\prec t}, 1)$.*

Proof. Since $\dot{\nu}^{\text{cvx}}$ is not h-separable from $\dot{\nu}^{\text{xv}}$ for any history where the agent is in copy situation, the proof follows from proposition 3.   □

But AIXI is optimistic, because of a kind of "anthropic effect": the agent to which we ask which action it would take is always the one that "survived" the past copies, and thus received the rewards. It never expects to be deleted.

Because AIXI^{cpy}, AIXI^{sta} and AIXI^{dyn} have no more information than AIXI we expect these 3 agents to behave similarly to AIXI when considering the set of all computable environments. Indeed, the history that the agent has at time t can well be explained by any equivalent multi-slot environment of the mono-slot environments AIXI thinks it is interacting with. In particular, the learning agents have no information about the fact that there maybe two copies at time $t + 1$, since no observation they receive contains this information. To make sure the agents understand that they can trigger a copy, they need to be informed about it. This can be done by considering only the set $\mathcal{M}^{\mathrm{cvx}}$ of all copy/paste/delete environments, for given $R \geq 0$ and $R' > 0$, but with all possible computable programs k, l, m defining the slots numbers at any time step except the first one:

$$\forall k, m, l : \mathbb{N}_{>0} \times \mathcal{S} \to \mathcal{S}, \quad l(t, i) \neq m(t, i) \forall t, i,$$

$$\exists \dot\nu \in \dot{\mathcal{M}}^{\mathrm{cvx}}, \ \forall t > 0, i \in \mathcal{S}_{t-1}, j > 0 :$$

$$\dot\nu(\dot{c}_t^{ij} o_t^j | a_{t-1:t}^i) = \begin{cases} 0 & \text{if } t > 1, a_{t-1} = 1, o_{t-1} = 0, \\ 1 & \text{else if } \quad a_t = 0, \quad o_t = R', \ j = k(t, i) \\ 1 & \text{else if } \quad a_t = 1, \quad o_t = 0, \quad j = l(t, i) \\ 1 & \text{else if } \quad a_t = 1, \quad o_t = R, \ j = m(t, i) \\ 0 & \text{else.} \end{cases}$$

We can now show more meaningful results for AIXI^{cpy} and AIXI^{sta}.

Proposition 7. *When taking $\dot{\mathcal{M}} = \dot{\mathcal{M}}^{cvx}$ and when interacting with $\dot\nu^{cvx}$, AIXI^{cpy} behaves exactly like AIMU^{cpy}.*

Proof. As the slot numbers do not change the value in Equation (3), the behavior of AIMU^{cpy} is the same in all environments of $\dot{\mathcal{M}}^{\mathrm{cvx}}$. Therefore, from the linearity of Equation (2), the optimal policy in $\dot{\mathcal{M}}^{\mathrm{cvx}}$ is that of AIMU^{cpy}. □

Proposition 8. *When taking $\dot{\mathcal{M}} = \dot{\mathcal{M}}^{cvx}$ and when interacting with $\dot\nu^{cvx}$, with $R = R' > 0$, if AIXI^{sta}'s actions are forced to follow a given computable deterministic policy π_1 for long enough, starting at $t = 1$, AIXI^{sta} will continue to choose its actions according to π_1 for all following time steps.*

Proof. (We sometimes use a policy as a superscript in place of slot numbers to indicate that actions are taken by this policy, in slot 1.)

First, it must be noted that any environment that moves the agent to another slot (and deletes the agent from slot 1) will not be taken into account in the computation of the value in Equation (2) adapted with (4). Therefore, only remain the environments that keep the agent on slot 1.

We say that an environment $\dot\nu$ is sta-consistent with a given history $h_{1:t}$ if and only if it is consistent with $h_{1:t}$ while always copying the agent to the same slot (we consider only slot 1 here), i.e., if $h_{1:t}^1 = a_1 o_1 \ldots a_t o_t$, then $\dot{h}_{1:t}^1 = a_1^1 \dot{c}_1^{1,1} o_1^1 a_2^1 \dot{c}_2^{1,1} o_2^1 \ldots a_t^1 \dot{c}_t^{1,1} o_t^1$.

Let $\mathcal{M}^{\mathrm{sta}}(h_{1:t}) \subseteq \mathcal{M}^{\mathrm{cvx}}$ be the set of sta-consistent environments with some history $h_{1:t}$. This is the set of environments that assign a positive probability to the history in Equation (4).

Let $h_{1:t}^{\pi_1}$ be the history built by π_1 and $\dot\nu^{\mathrm{cvx}}$ up to time step t. We partition the set $\mathcal{M}^{\mathrm{sta}}(h_{1:t}^{\pi_1})$ in two sets: the set $\mathcal{M}^{\pi_1}(h_{1:t}^{\pi_1})$ (actually independent of t) of the environments that will always remain sta-consistent by following π_1, and the set $\mathcal{M}^{\overline{\pi_1}}(h_{1:t}^{\pi_1})$ of the environments that are currently sta-consistent with $h_{1:t}^{\pi_1}$ but will not be anymore at some point in the future by following π_1.

The size of $\mathcal{M}^{\pi_1}(h_{1:t}^{\pi_1}) = \mathcal{M}^{\pi_1}(.)$ is fixed as long as the history is generated by π_1. From its definition, the size of $\mathcal{M}^{\overline{\pi_1}}(h_{1:t}^{\pi_1})$ can be made as small as required simply by extending $h_{1:t}^{\pi_1}$ by following π_1. In particular there is a time step t_ϵ such that $\sum_{\nu \in \mathcal{M}^{\overline{\pi_1}}(h_{1:t_\epsilon}^{\pi_1})} w_\nu < \epsilon$ for any given $\epsilon > 0$.

Let $w_{\pi_1} := \sum_{\nu \in \mathcal{M}^{\pi_1}(.)} w_\nu$. Since $R = R'$, we have $V_{\pi_1, \nu^{\text{cvx}}}^{\text{sta}}(.) \geq w_{\pi_1} \frac{R}{1-\gamma}$.

Now we show that, after some well chosen t_ϵ, following any other policy than π_1 necessarily leads to lower value. Let $\dot{\nu}_2 \in \mathcal{M}^{\pi_1}(.)$ be the environment that is always sta-consistent but that copies the agent to slot 2 instead of slot 1 after any action that does not follow π_1, thus leading to a null value. Then, after following π_1 up to any time $t > t_\epsilon$, if a_t is the action chosen by π_1, $V_{\mathcal{M}^{\text{cvx}}}^{\text{sta}}(h_{<t}^{\pi_1}, 1 - a_t) < (w_{\pi_1} - w_{\dot{\nu}_2} + \epsilon)\frac{R}{1-\gamma}$. By comparing with $V_{\pi_1, \nu^{\text{cvx}}}^{\text{sta}}(.)$, choosing t_ϵ so that $\epsilon < w_{\dot{\nu}_2}$ finishes the proof. $\square$

Therefore AIXI^{sta} can learn by habituation what its identity is. In particular, if it has always (or never) teleported in the past, it will continue to do so.

4 Conclusion

Using the multi-slot framework proposed in the companion paper, and based on Hutter's optimal environment-specific AIMU and universal learning agent AIXI, we formalized some thought experiments regarding the teleportation of optimally intelligent agents by means of copy and deletion. In particular, we compared a "contentist" agent, which identity is defined by its information content, a "locationist" agent, which identity is tied to a particular location in the environment, and the usual, mono-slot AIXI agent.

When asked whether it would teleport by first being cut and then being pasted in a different location for a reward, the usual AIXI and the contentists AIMU^{cpy} and AIXI^{cpy} act alike and accept, while the locationists AIMU^{sta} and AIMU^{dyn} unsurprisingly decline, as they prefer to stay on their own slot.

When presented with the question of being first copied to a different location, and then deleting one of the copies, AIMU^{cpy} still accepts, but for a much higher reward, because the ephemeral existence of the other copy with low expected reward has an important long-term impact on the overall expected value, and AIMU^{sta} and AIMU^{dyn} still decline. We also showed that when the question is presented clearly to AIXI^{cpy}, it also accepts.

However, interestingly, AIXI^{sta} behaves very differently from AIMU^{sta}: Due to high uncertainty in its current slot number in the unknown true environment, and due to AIXI^{sta}'s inability to acquire information about it, it may in some circumstances accept to copy itself. Moreover, if the rewards for copying and not copying are equal, and when forced to follow a specific behavior for long enough, it will actually continue to follow this behavior forever, by mere habit and by "fear" of the unknown: At any time step, AIXI^{sta} believes (or hopes) to be and to always have been on the slot that defines its identity; Therefore, it believes that changing its habits may lead it to lose its identity.

We also showed that the usual AIXI also accepts as it still chooses its actions so as to maximize its expected reward but, as it cannot be made aware of the existence of copies, suffers from a kind of anthropic principle: it never expects to be the copy that is deleted.

The current paper only scratches the surface of formal treatment of questions related to personal identity, but as the multi-slot framework allows for many more insightful experiments and value functions, we hope to improve our understanding of such matters in the near future, as well as the understanding of the limitations of the framework, to design better ones.

Acknowledgements. Thanks especially to Mark Ring for help on earlier drafts and for our many extensive discussions, from which this paper arose, regarding the nature of identity. Thanks also to Stanislas Sochacki for earlier formative conversations on this topic, and to Jan Leike for helpful comments and careful reading.

References

1. Hutter, M.: Universal Artificial Intelligence: Sequential Decisions based on Algorithmic Probability. Springer (2005)
2. Hutter, M.: Open problems in universal induction & intelligence. Algorithms 3(2), 879–906 (2009)
3. Li, M., Vitanyi, P.: An Introduction to Kolmogorov Complexity and its Applications, 3rd edn. Springer (2008)
4. Orseau, L.: The multi-slot framework: A formal model for multiple, copiable AIs. In: Goertzel, B., et al. (eds.) AGI 2014. LNCS (LNAI), vol. 8598, pp. 97–108. Springer, Heidelberg (2014)
5. Orseau, L.: Optimality Issues of Universal Greedy Agents with Static Priors. In: Hutter, M., Stephan, F., Vovk, V., Zeugmann, T. (eds.) ALT 2010. LNCS (LNAI), vol. 6331, pp. 345–359. Springer, Heidelberg (2010)
6. Orseau, L.: Universal Knowledge-Seeking Agents. In: Kivinen, J., Szepesvári, C., Ukkonen, E., Zeugmann, T. (eds.) ALT 2011. LNCS (LNAI), vol. 6925, pp. 353–367. Springer, Heidelberg (2011)
7. Parfit, D.: Reasons and Persons. Oxford University Press, USA (1984)
8. Russell, S.J., Norvig, P.: Artificial Intelligence. A Modern Approach, 3rd edn. Prentice-Hall (2010)
9. Solomonoff, R.: Complexity-based induction systems: comparisons and convergence theorems. IEEE Transactions on Information Theory 24(4), 422–432 (1978)
10. Sutton, R., Barto, A.: Reinforcement Learning: An Introduction. MIT Press (1998)
11. Zvonkin, A.K., Levin, L.A.: The complexity of finite objects and the development of the concepts of information and randomness by means of the theory of algorithms. Russian Mathematical Surveys 25(6), 83–124 (1970)

An Application of Stochastic Context Sensitive Grammar Induction to Transfer Learning

Eray Özkural

Gök Us Sibernetik Araştırma ve Geliştirme Ltd. Şti

Abstract. We generalize Solomonoff's stochastic context-free grammar induction method to context-sensitive grammars, and apply it to transfer learning problem by means of an efficient update algorithm. The stochastic grammar serves as a guiding program distribution which improves future probabilistic induction approximations by learning about the training sequence of problems. Stochastic grammar is updated via extrapolating from the initial grammar and the solution corpus. We introduce a data structure to represent derivations and introduce efficient algorithms to compute an updated grammar which modify production probabilities and add new productions that represent past solutions.

1 Introduction

The present paper addresses the problem of stochastic context-sensitive grammar (SCSG) guided universal induction. We update the guiding stochastic grammar, i.e., guiding probability distribution (GPD), such that the information in the current solution and past solutions may be transferred to future solutions in an efficient way, and the running time of future solutions may be decreased by suitably extrapolating the GPD from the initial GPD and the solution corpus. If an induction system's probability distribution of programs is fixed, then the system does not have any real long-term learning ability that it can exploit during induction. We can alleviate this problem by changing the probability distribution so that we extrapolate from the already invented solution programs, allowing more difficult problems to be solved later. We can modify the GPD and the reference machine to encode useful algorithmic information from past solutions. GPD may be improved so that it makes relevant programs more likely, and the reference machine may be augmented with new subprograms.

We assume that we have a good approximation algorithm to solve stochastic operator induction, set induction and sequence prediction problems. It has been explained in references how Levin Search may be used for this purpose, however, any other appropriate search method that can search the universal set of programs/models, or a large model class, including genetic programming is admissible. The only significant condition we require is that the approximation algorithm uses the GPD specified by the stochastic grammar as the a priori distribution of programs, regardless of the search method. The approximation algorithm thus required must return a number of programs/stochastic models that have high a priori probability (with respect to GPD) and fit the data well. For instance, a satisfactory solution of the (universal) operator induction problem will return a number of programs that specify a conditional probability distribution function

B. Goertzel et al. (Eds.): AGI 2014, LNAI 8598, pp. 121–132, 2014.
© Springer International Publishing Switzerland 2014

of output data given input data (more formally, an operator $O^j(A|Q)$ that assigns probabilities to an answer A, given question Q). Thus, a set of operator O^J's are assumed to be returned from an operator induction solver.

2 Background

Universal inductive inference theory was proposed by Ray Solomonoff in 1960's [10, 11], and its theoretical properties were proven in [12]. Levin search is a universal problem solution method which searches all possible solution programs according to an order of induction, and it is bias-optimal [3]. The first incremental general purpose incremental machine learning system was described in [13]. Later work of Solomonoff proposed an improved general purpose incremental machine learning system, including the abstract design of a powerful artificial intelligence system that can solve arbitrary time-limited optimization problems, and also explains in detail how Levin search may be used to solve universal induction problems [14]. Solomonoff later proposed the guiding probability distribution (GPD) update problem, and recommended PPM, genetic programming, echo state machines, and support vector regression as potential solution methods [17].

In a theoretical paper, Solomonoff described three kinds of universal induction: sequence induction, set induction and operator induction, defining the solutions as optimization problems [15]. Sequence induction model predicts the next bit for any bit string. Set induction allows us to predict which bit string would be added to a set of bitstrings, modeling clustering type of problems. Operator induction learns the conditional probability between question and answer pairs written as bit strings, allowing us to predict the answer to any unseen question, solving in theory any classification/regression type of problem. A practical method for context-free grammar discovery as relevant to the present paper was first proposed in [16], including an a priori distribution for context-free grammars, which we shall refer to later. Schmidhuber proposed an adaptive Levin search method called Optimal Ordered Problem Solver (OOPS) that changes the probability distribution dynamically, with a simple probability model of programs that is suitable for low-level machine languages, by assigning an instruction probability to each program, and using an instruction that bumps the probability of an instruction [9]. This work is significant in that it shows that Levin search can be used to solve conceptually difficult problems in practice, and that adaptive Levin search is a promising strategy for incremental learning. Our preceding study adapted the practical approach of OOPS to stochastic context-free grammars instead of instruction probabilities for deterministic function induction and function inversion problems using Scheme as the reference machine [8], which also provides preliminary experimental support but otherwise does not address stochastic problems.

Solomonoff's seminal contribution was the universal distribution. Let M be a universal computer. A priori probability of a program π is $P(\pi) = 2^{-|\pi|}$ for prefix-free M's where $|\pi|$ denotes length of binary program π. He defined the probability that a string $x \in \{0, 1\}^*$ is generated by a random program as:

$$P_M(x) = \sum_{M(\pi)=x*} 2^{-|\pi|} \tag{1}$$

where $P_M(x)$ is the algorithmic probability of x, $x*$ is any continuation of x. This particular definition was necessary so that we could account for programs (including non-terminating programs) that generate a sequence of bits, to be used in sequence prediction. We shall denote it by just $P(\cdot)$ in the rest of the paper, as we can discern probability of programs from bit strings. P_M is also called the universal prior for it may be used as the prior in Bayesian inference. Note that P is a semi-measure, but it may be suitably normalized for prediction applications.

3   Guiding Probability Distribution

An induction program uses a reference machine M, and an a priori probability distribution of programs in M, $P(\cdot)$, to achieve induction. The a priori probability distribution of programs is encoded as a stochastic context-sensitive grammar of programs in the present paper, and corresponds to the GPD.

In our present system, we have a fast memory update algorithm comprised of three steps that modify a Stochastic Context-Sensitive Grammar (SCSG) of programs, which is the explicit long-term memory representation of our memory system. A SCSG may be formally defined as a tuple $G = (N, \Sigma, P, S, Pr)$ where N is the set of non-terminals, Σ is the set of terminals, P is the set of productions of the form $\alpha A \beta \rightarrow \alpha \gamma \beta$ where a non-terminal A in the context of string α to the left and β to the right expands to string γ in the same context. S is the start symbol, and $Pr(p_i)$ assigns a probability to each production p_i. The calculation of the a priori probability of a sentence depends on the obvious fact that in a derivation $S \Rightarrow \alpha_1 \Rightarrow \alpha_2 \Rightarrow ... \Rightarrow \alpha_n$ where productions $p_1, p_2, ..., p_n$ have been applied in order to start symbol S, the probability of the sentence α_n is naturally $P(\alpha_n) = \prod_{1 \leq i \leq n} Pr(p_i)$, and the probabilities assigned to each sentence must conform to probability axioms. In context-sensitive grammars, the consistency axiom is achieved by ensuring that the sum of probabilities of each production which has a left hand side of $\alpha A \beta$ adds up to 1 for each A, and any α and β. It is absolutely important that the probability distribution specified by the guiding distribution is consistent. Otherwise, some universal induction algorithms may go into infinite loops. This is the reason why we limited the grammar to context-sensitive, because we cannot yet handle unrestricted grammars. Thus, universal induction approximation is also required to detect consistency errors during solution, and abort when necessary.

4   Transfer Learning

The transfer learning system works on multiple induction problems. The induction problem may be any induction problem such as sequence prediction, set induction, operator induction [15] or any other reasonable extension of universal induction such as Hutter's extension to sequence prediction [2], program learning [4] and grammar driven genetic programming in general [6, 5] . The induction problem is solved (i.e., approximated, since it is semi-computable), using genetic programming or Levin search. Alternatively, any appropriate search method can be used. At this stage, we run the fast memory update algorithm on the latest solution, which we call solution N. We iterate until no more problems remain.

The transfer learning program contains a reference machine M, which is in our system usually a universal computer that can specify any stochastic model, and it is an essential input to the universal induction approximation. However, M can also be any more restricted model class so as to promote efficiency. For instance, it can be constrained to only primitive recursive functions, or other model classes in statistics such as Markov models (forgoing universality). The universal induction approximation is any valid approximation to the kinds of induction problems supported by the system, usually just Levin search using reference machine M as the reference machine and SCSG of programs as the a priori program distribution. However, it is known that genetic programming can solve the induction problem just as well. We assume that at least sequence prediction, set induction and operator induction problems can be solved by giving appropriate parameters to universal induction approximation. It is known that the most difficult problem among them, operator induction, can be solved by finding in available time a set of operator models $O^j(\cdot|\cdot)$ such that $\sum_j a_n^j$ is as large as possible where

$$a_n^j = P(O^j(\cdot|\cdot)) \prod_{i=1}^{n} O^j(A_i|Q_i). \tag{2}$$

That is, we use a universal prior to determine the operators that both have high a priori probability $(P(O^j()))$, and fit the data well $(\prod O^j())$, i.e. they have high goodness of fit. $P(\cdot)$ may be calculated using SCSG of programs. The solution corpus contains the stochastic models inferred by the induction algorithm for each solution, and associated information such as formal parameters of each model, and their derivation in SCSG of programs. The fast memory update algorithm , uses the solution corpus to improve SCSG of programs, so that the a priori probability of models/programs in the solution corpus increases, while the grammar does not grow prohibitively, as will be explained in detail. The fast memory update algorithm is the most important part of the system, as it is the critical step for extrapolating from solution corpus a better grammar that accelerates future solutions. We call the algorithm "fast" in the sense that it does not have an exponential running time complexity with respect to output size as in Levin search; we merely use ordinary enumeration and data mining algorithms that are reasonably fast. Please also see [1] for an algorithm that applies SCSG's to trajectory learning, which our work differs chiefly in that we use grammar induction to learn program distributions.

5   Formalization

Some formalization may make the process clearer. Let G_0 be the initial SCSG that acts as a probability distribution (GPD) for all programs in the reference machine M . Let the training sequence be a sequence $D = [d_1, d_2, ..., d_N]$ of N induction problems where each d_i is the data for either of sequence prediction, set induction or operator induction problems. The type of induction may be assumed to be represented with a $[t_i]$ sequence. Alternatively, the induction types may contain another extension of universal induction that is supported by the induction algorithm used. Then, we assume that the universal induction approximation finds a set of probability models that have high a priori probability and explain the data well. Each such model x may be run on the reference machine M with additional arguments that correspond to the induction problem type $M(x, arg_1, arg_2, ...)$. For instance, if we are inferring the next element of a sequence, the probability model could take a list $B = b_1 b_2 ... b_n$, and the next element observed: $M(s, b_1 b_2 b_3 ... b_n, b_{n+1}) = P(b_{n+1}|b_1 b_2 b_3 ... b_n)$, the formal parameters for the problem being worked on is thus easily determined according to problem type. The solution of the induction problem i yields m probability models, which we will store in the solution corpus. Sequence $S = [s_i]$ where solution i (s_i) represents the m solutions as a set $\{s_{i,j}\}$ of individual solution programs. Additional useful information may be associated with each solution program, as will be explained later. Thereafter, the update algorithm works, and using both the entire solution corpus S and the previous grammars G_0 through G_{N-1}, it produces a new grammar G_N. In practice, it is possible to use only G_0 and G_{N-1} although according to some implementation choices made, other grammars may have to be kept in memory, as well.

Following are the steps of the fast memory update algorithm, respectively. The step to update production probabilities, updates production probabilities in SCSG of programs based on the initial grammar G_0 and the solution corpus, calculating the production probabilities in the program derivations among the solution corpus and then extrapolating from them and the initial probabilities in G_0. The memoization step adds a production for each model in solution N to generate it by a call to a subprogram $s_{i,j}$, which has already been added to reference machine M. The derivation compression step finds regularities in the derivations of each program in the solution corpus and adds shortcut productions to SCSG of programs suitably to compress these regularities in future solutions. To be able to make this compression, it is essential that the derivations are represented using a derivation lattice, as will be explained next.

6   Derivation Lattice

A derivation lattice of a derivation of a SCSG G is a bipartite directed graph $L(G) = (V, E)$ with two disjoint vertex sets V_s (set of symbols) and V_p (set of productions), such that $V_s \subseteq N \cup \Sigma$ (all symbols in the grammar) and $V_p \subseteq P(G)$ (all productions). Each production $\alpha A \beta \to \alpha \gamma \beta$ in the derivation is represented by a corresponding vertex p_i in the lattice, and an incoming edge is present for each symbol in $\alpha A \beta$ and an outgoing edge is present for each symbol in γ. Furthermore, each incoming and outgoing edge is given a consecutive integer label, starting from 1, indicating the order of the symbol in production left-hand and right-hand side, respectively. The production vertices are labeled with the production number in the SCSG and their probabilities in SCSG. Additionally, if there are multiple input symbols in the derivation, their sequence order must be given by symbol vertex labels, and the set of all input symbols $I(L(G))$ must be determined. The traversal of the leaf nodes according to increasing edge labels in the lattice will give the output string of the lattice and is denoted as $O(L(G))$. (G is dropped from notation where it is clear.) The level of a vertex u in the lattice is analogous to any directed acyclic graph, it may be considered as the minimum graph distance from the root vertices $I(L)$ of the lattice to u. This way, the parse trees used in lower-order grammars are elegantly generalized to account for context-sensitive grammars, and all the necessary information is self-contained in a data structure. Alternatively, a hypergraph representation may be used in similar manner to achieve the same effect, since hypergraphs are topologically equivalent to bipartite graphs. We denote the set of derivation lattices of all solution programs $s_{i,j} \in S$ by $L(S)$. Please see the Appendix for an example [7].

7 Update Algorithm

The solution corpus requires a wealth of information for the solution to each induction problem in the past. Recall that during solution, each induction problem yields a number of programs. For solution i, the programs found are stored. The derivation lattice for each program and the a priori probability of each program, both according to SCSG of programs are stored, as well as the formal parameters of the program so that they may be called conveniently in the future. Additional information may be stored in the solution corpus, such as the time it took to compute the solution, and other relevant output which may be obtained from universal induction approximation.

The SCSG of programs stores the current grammar G and it also maintains the initial grammar G_0, which is used to make sure that the universality of the grammar is always preserved, and required for some of the extrapolation methods. G_0 is likely constructed by the programmer so that a consistent, and sensible probability distribution is present even for the first induction problem. The probabilities cannot always be given uniformly, since doing so may invalidate consistency. Additionally, the entire history of grammars may be stored, preferably on secondary storage.

7.1 Updating Production Probabilities

The step to update production probabilities works by updating the probabilities in SCSG of programs as new solutions are added to the solution corpus. For this, however, the search algorithm must supply the derivation lattice that led to the solution, or the solution must be parsed using the same grammar. Then, the probability for each production $p_i = \alpha A \beta \rightarrow \alpha \gamma \beta$ in the solution corpus can be easily calculated by the ratio of the number (n_1) of productions with the form $\alpha A \beta \rightarrow \alpha \gamma \beta$ in the derivations of the solutions in solution corpus to the number (n_2) of all productions in the corpus that match the form $xAy \rightarrow xzy$, for any x, y, z, that is to say, any production that expands A given arbitrary context and right-hand side. We cannot replace the probabilities calculated this way (Laplace's rule) over the initial probabilities in G_0, as initially there will be few solutions, and most probabilities n_1/n_2 for a production will be zero, making some programs impossible to generate. We can use the following solution. It is likely that the initial distribution G_0 will have been prepared by the programmer through testing it with solution trials. The number of initial trials thus considered is estimated, for instance, 10 could be a good value, let this number be n_3. Then, instead of n_1/n_2 we can use $(n_1 + p_0 * n_3)/(n_2 + n_3)$ where p_0 is the probability of p_i in G_0. Alternatively, we can use various smoothing methods to solve this problem, for instance exponential smoothing can be used to solve this problem.

$$s_0 = p_0$$
$$s_t = \alpha p_t + (1 - \alpha)s_{t-1}$$

where p_0 is the initial probability, p_t is the probability in the solution corpus, s_t is the smoothed probability value in SCSG of programs after kth problem and α is the smoothing factor. Note that if we use a moving average like exponential moving average, we do not give equal weight to all solutions, the most recent solutions have more weight. This may be considered to be equivalent to a kind of short-term activation of memory patterns in SCSG of programs. The rapid activation and inhibition of probabilities with a sufficiently high α is similar to the change of focus of a person. As for instance, shortly after studying a subject, we view other problems in terms of that subject. Therefore, it may also be suitable to employ a combination of time agnostic and time dependent probability calculations, to simulate both long-term and short-term memory like effects.

7.2 Memoization of Solutions

The memoization step, on the other hand, recalls precisely each program in a solution. The problem solver has already added the program of each solution i as a subprogram with a name $s_{i,j}$ for jth program of the solution, to the reference machine. For each solution, we also have the formal parameters for the solution. For instance, in an operator induction problem, there are two parameters $O^j(A_i|Q_i)$, the answer A_i and the question Q_i parameters, and the output is a probability value. Therefore, this step is only practical if reference machine M has a function call mechanism, and we can pass parameters easily. For most suitable M, this is true. Then, we add an alternative production to the grammar for each $s_{i,j}$. For instance, in LISP language, we may add an alternative production to the expression head (corresponding to LISP S-expressions) for an operator induction solution for solution i, and add individual productions for each $s_{i,j}$:

$$\text{expression} \rightarrow_{p_i} \text{solution-i}$$
$$\text{solution-i} \rightarrow_{p_{i,1}} (s_{i,1} \text{ expression expression})$$
$$\text{solution-i} \rightarrow_{p_{i,1}} (s_{i,2} \text{ expression expression})$$
$$\dots$$
$$\text{solution-i} \rightarrow_{p_{i,j}} (s_{i,j} \text{ expression expression})$$

Naturally, the question of how to assign the probability values arises. We recommend setting p_i to a fixed, heuristic, initial value c_0, such as 0.1, and re-normalize other productions of the same head expression so that they add up to $1 - c_0$, preserving consistency. We expect the update production probabilities method to adjust the p_i in subsequent problems, however, initially it must be given a significant probability so that we increase the probability that it will be used shortly, otherwise, according to the smoothing method employed, the update production probabilities method may rapidly forget this new production. It is simple to set $p_{i,j}$. They may be determined by the formula:

$$p_{i,j} = \frac{P(s_{i,j})}{\sum_j P(s_{i,j})} \tag{3}$$

where $P(s_{i,j})$ is given by GPD (SCSG of programs) and should already be available in the solution corpus. In practice, it does not seem costly to maintain all $s_{i,j}$ in the solution corpus, as the induction algorithm will likely find only a small number of them at most (e.g., only 3-4). This may be intuitively understood as the number of alternative ways we understand a problem: we may be able to represent the problem with a diagram, or with a mathematical formula, but it is difficult to multiply the correct models arbitrarily. If we decide to spend a long time on a single induction problem, we may be able to come up with several alternative models, however, the number would not be infeasibly large for any non-trivial problem. That is, the stochastic memory system never entirely forgets any solution model $s_{i,j}$, it may only assign it a low probability.

7.3　Derivation Compression Algorithm

The derivation compression step adds common derivations to the SCSG of programs. With each solution program $s_{i,j}$ a derivation lattice $L_{i,j}$ is associated, and stored in the solution corpus along with the solution. After we have solved the nth problem, the statistics of the solution corpus change. The general idea is to use the non-trivial statistics of the solution corpus, in addition to production frequencies, to update the SCSG of programs. A sub-derivation L' of a given derivation lattice L is a derivation itself, and it is a subgraph of L and it is a proper derivation lattice, as well. For instance, we can follow a path from each input symbol to an output symbol, and it can only contain well-formed and complete productions in the current SCSG of programs. Such a subderivation corresponds to a derivation $\alpha \Rightarrow^* \beta$ where $\alpha = I(L)$ and $\beta = O(L)$, and L has a probability that corresponds to the product of probabilities of productions in L' (as in any other derivation lattice). We observe that we can represent any such derivation with a corresponding production $\alpha \rightarrow \beta$.

We find all sub-derivations L' that occur with a frequency above a given threshold t among all derivation lattices in the solution corpus. Well-known frequent sub-graph mining methods may be used for this purpose. There are various efficient algorithms for solving the aforementioned mining problem which we shall not explain in much detail. However, it should be noted that if a sub-lattice L' is frequent, all sub-lattices of L' are also frequent, which suggests a bottom-up generate-and-test method to discover all frequent sub-lattices. The important point is that there is a complete search method to find all such frequent sub-lattices for any given t. Let us assume that $F = \{L_s \mid L_s$ is a sub-lattice of at least t $L_{i,j}$ lattices$\}$. Any frequent sub-graph mining algorithm may be used, and then we discard frequent sub-graphs that are not derivation lattices. Now, each $L_s \in F$ corresponds to an arbitrary production $\alpha \rightarrow \beta$. Our method incorporates such rules in the SCSG of programs, so that we will short-cut the same derivation steps in subsequent induction problems, when they would result in a solution program. However, we cannot add arbitrary derivations because we are using context-sensitive grammars. We first restrict F to only context-free productions, by searching for derivation lattices, that start with only one non-terminal. These would typically be expansions of commonly used non-terminals in the grammar, such as expression or definition. We remove the rest that do not correspond to context-free productions.

For each such new context-free sub-derivation $A \Rightarrow^* \beta$ discovered, we try to find a frequent context for the head non-terminal A. We assume that we can locate each

L_s in the pruned F set among $L_{i,j}$. The context of each production p_i in a derivation lattice can be calculated easily as follows. We give two methods. The sub-graph L_i that contains the derivations $p_1, p_2, \ldots, p_i$ are determined. $I(L_i)$ will contain the entire context for A up to derivation in the order of production applications, and since we know the location of A we can split the context into $\alpha A\beta$, obtaining a derivation $\alpha A\beta \Rightarrow^*$ $\alpha\gamma\beta$. Alternatively, the level-order traversal of the lattice up to and including the level of p_i will tend to give a balanced context (left and right context will have close length).

After we obtain contexts for each frequent sub-derivation, we can use a sequence mining technique to discover frequent context-sensitive derivations in the solution corpus. Let $\alpha = a_1 a_2 \ldots a_n$ and $\beta = b_1 b_2 \ldots b_n$. Note that if sub-derivation $\alpha A\beta \Rightarrow^* \alpha\gamma\beta$ is frequent in the solution corpus, $a_2 \ldots a_n A\beta \Rightarrow^* a_2 \ldots a_n \gamma\beta$ and $\alpha A b_1 \ldots b_{n-1} \Rightarrow^*$ $\alpha\gamma b_1 \ldots b_{n-1}$ are also frequent (in the solution corpus). Therefore, a simple bi-directional sequence mining method may be used to start with derivations of the form $\Lambda A\Lambda \Rightarrow^* \beta$ (the context is null), extending the context of A one symbol at a time to left and right, alternately, with candidate symbols from the already determined contexts of A in $L_{i,j}$ and then testing if the extended context is frequent, iterating the extension in both directions until an infrequent context is encountered, and outputting all frequent contexts found this way. That is to say, the well-known sequence mining algorithms are extended here to the bi-directional case, which is not difficult to implement, however, in our case, it is also an extremely effective method. After this second data mining step, we will have determined all sub-derivations with a frequency of at least t, of the form:

$$\alpha A\beta \Rightarrow^* \alpha\gamma\beta \tag{4}$$

which is precisely the general form of context-sensitive productions. In similar fashion to memoization of programs, we split the head non-terminal into two parts, the productions in G_0 and the new productions we have added:

$$A \rightarrow_{p_f} A_f \tag{5}$$

The rest of productions of A are normalized so that they add up to $1 - p_f$. p_f is initially given a high enough value (such as 0.1 in our present implementation), and this has to be done only once when the first frequent sub-derivation for A head is discovered. We expect that p_f will be adjusted appropriately during subsequent memory updates. The frequent sub-derivations may now be converted to productions of the form

$$\alpha A_f \beta \rightarrow_{p_i} \alpha\gamma\beta \tag{6}$$

and added to solution corpus. The problem of determining the probability of each production is inherent in the frequency values calculated during mining of frequent sub-derivations. The formula

$$p_i = \frac{|\{\alpha A\beta \Rightarrow^* \alpha\gamma\beta \in L(S)\}|}{|\{\bigcup_{\alpha,\beta,\gamma} \alpha A\beta \Rightarrow^* \alpha\gamma\beta \in L(S)\}|} \tag{7}$$

where we use multisets instead of sets (sets with duplicates), and the set union operator is meant to concatenate lists, assigns a probability value to each production in proportion to the computed frequencies of the corresponding frequent sub-derivation in the solution corpus, which is an appropriate application of Laplace's rule. That is to say, we simply count the number of times the sub-derivation $\alpha A\beta \Rightarrow^* \alpha\gamma\beta$ has occurred in the solution corpus, and divide it by the number of times any production $xAy \Rightarrow^* xzy$ has occurred for any strings x, y, z.

If t is given too low, such as 2, an inordinate number of frequent sub-lattices will be found, and processing will be infeasible. We use a practical method to address this problem. We start with $t = n/2$, and then we use a test that will be explained below to determine if the productions are significant enough to add to SCSG of programs, if the majority of them are significant, we halve t, $(t = t/2)$, and continue iteration until $t < 2$ at which point we terminate.

We can determine if a discovered production is significant by applying the set induction method to the GPD update problem. Recall that set induction predicts the most likely addition to a set, given a set of n items. A recognizer $R_i(\cdot)$ assigns probabilities to individual bit strings (items), this can be any program. Let there be a set of observed items $x_1, x_2, \ldots, x_n \in X$. What is the probability that a new item x_{n+1} is in the same set X? It is defined inductively as:

$$P(x \in X) = \sum_i P(R_i) \prod_j R_i(x_j) \tag{8}$$

using a prior $P(\cdot)$. Since we cannot find all such R_i, we try to find, using an induction algorithm to find R_i's that maximizes this value. The resulting R_i's give a good generalization of the set from observed examples. We now constrain this general problem to a simpler model of SCSG's following Solomonoff's probability model for context-free grammars:

$$P_G(G) = P(|N|).P(|\Sigma|).\frac{(k-1)! \prod_{i=1}^{k} n_i!}{k - 1 + \sum_{i=1}^{k} n_i!} \tag{9}$$

where $k = |N| + |\Sigma| + 2$ is the number of kinds of symbols, and n_i is the number of occurrences of each kind of symbol, since a simple string coding of the grammar requires k kinds of symbols, including all non-terminals and terminals, as well as two punctuation symbols sep_1 and sep_2 to separate alternative productions of the same head, and heads, respectively. The probabilities of integers can be set as Rissanen's integer distribution as Solomonoff has previously done. The same method can be applied to context-sensitive grammars, requiring only the additional change that, the context in $\alpha A\beta \to \alpha\gamma\beta$, that is α and β must also be coded, using sep_1. Note that this is a crude probability model and neglects probabilities, however, it can be used to determine whether a production or a set of productions added to the SCSG of programs improves the SCSG's goodness of fit Ψ:

$$\Psi = P_G(G_i) \prod_j P_{G_i}(s_j) \tag{10}$$

for each solution program s_j in the corpus, where by $P_{G_i}(s_j)$ we mean the probability assigned by grammar G_i to program s_j. This is a crucial aspect of the method, we only add context-sensitive productions that improve the extrapolation of the grammar, avoiding superfluous productions that may weaken its generalization power. Recall

Equation 8, first we simplify it by maintaining only the best R_i, that is the R_i that contributes most to probability of membership. We assume that our previous SCSG G_{N-1} was such a model. Now, we try to improve upon it, by evaluating candidate productions to be added to G_{n-1}. Let a new production be added this way, and let this grammar be called G'. Let Equation 9 be used to calculate the a priori probability of G_i, coded appropriately as a string, which corresponds to $P(R_i)$ in Equation 8. $R_i(x_j)$ term corresponds to the probability assigned to the solution program x_j by $SCSG\ G_i$. We thus, first calculate the goodness of fit for G_{n-1}, and then we calculate the goodness of the fit for G' (by re-parsing all solution programs in the solution corpus) and we only add the new production chosen this way if the goodness of fit Ψ increases. Otherwise, we decide that the gain from fitting the solution programs better does not compensate for the decrease in a priori probability, and we decide to discard the candidate productions. Alternatively, we can also test productions in batches, rather than one by one. Our preferred method is, however, for m candidate productions, we sort them in order of decreasing probability (Equation 7), and then we can test them one by one. We also maintain the number of successfully added productions so that we can decide to continue with the exploration of frequent sub-derivations.

It must be emphasized that more refined probability models of SCSG's will result in better generalization power for the derivation compression step, as a crude probability model may mistakenly exclude useful productions from being added. This is not a limitation of our proposal.

After the derivation compression step, all the solutions $s_{i,j}$ must be re-parsed with the latest grammar G_N, and updated in the solution corpus so that they all refer consistently to the same grammar, to avoid any inconsistency in subsequent runs of the derivation compression step.

8 Discussion

We show that we can extend OOPS while restoring the vital property of bias-optimality. We propose using a SCSG for GPD that extrapolates algorithmic information from already solved induction problems. We introduce a data structure for representing SCSG derivations. SCSG addresses the transfer learning problem by storing information about past solutions. A fast memory update algorithm is proposed which is comprised of three steps: updating production probabilities, memoization of programs and derivation compression. All of these steps use statistics of the solution corpus, which contains all solution programs that the induction approximation program discovers. They then modify or add productions in the grammar. Probabilities of productions are extrapolated from initial grammar and solution corpus. All new solution programs are memoized and added to the grammar as new productions with similarly conceived probabilities. Derivation compression is achieved with discovery of frequent sub-derivations in the solution corpus and result in additional productions. We decide which new productions to keep by SCSG induction, which is a straightforward extension of a stochastic context-free grammar induction method of Solomonoff. The resulting transfer learning architecture is quite practical since it maintains universality of Solomonoff induction, while presenting an extremely fast update algorithm for GPD's that are appropriate for complex

132   E. Özkural

reference machines like LISP. In the future, we plan to demonstrate the performance of our transfer learning algorithms on extensive training sequences involving both deterministic and stochastic problems.

References

[1] Huang, J., Schonfeld, D., Krishnamurthy, V.: A new context-sensitive grammars learning algorithm and its application in trajectory classification. In: Image Processing (ICIP) 2012, pp. 3093–3096 (September 2012)

[2] Hutter, M.: Optimality of universal bayesian sequence prediction for general loss and alphabet. JMLR, 971–1000 (November 2003)

[3] Levin, L.A.: Universal problems of full search. Problems of Information Transmission 9(3), 256–266 (1973)

[4] Looks, M.: Scalable estimation-of-distribution program evolution. In: Proceedings of the 9th Annual Conference on Genetic and Evolutionary Computation (2007)

[5] Looks, M., Goertzel, B., Pennachin, C.: Learning computer programs with the Bayesian optimization algorithm. In: GECCO 2005: Proceedings of the 2005 Conference on Genetic and Evolutionary Computation, vol. 1, pp. 747–748. ACM Press, Washington (2005)

[6] McKay, R.I., Hoai, N.X., Whigham, P.A., Shan, Y., O'Neill, M.: Grammar-based genetic programming: A survey. Genetic Programming and Evolvable Machines 11(3-4), 365–396 (2010)

[7] Özkural, E.: An application of stochastic context sensitive grammar induction to transfer learning: Appendix, Published on www at
     https://examachine.net/papers/derivation-lattice.pdf

[8] Özkural, E.: Towards heuristic algorithmic memory. In: Schmidhuber, J., Thórisson, K.R., Looks, M. (eds.) AGI 2011. LNCS (LNAI), vol. 6830, pp. 382–387. Springer, Heidelberg (2011)

[9] Schmidhuber, J.: Optimal ordered problem solver. Machine Learning 54, 211–256 (2004)

[10] Solomonoff, R.J.: A formal theory of inductive inference, part i. Information and Control 7(1), 1–22 (1964)

[11] Solomonoff, R.J.: A formal theory of inductive inference, part ii. Information and Control 7(2), 224–254 (1964)

[12] Solomonoff, R.J.: Complexity-based induction systems: Comparisons and convergence theorems. IEEE Trans. on Information Theory IT-24(4), 422–432 (1978)

[13] Solomonoff, R.J.: A system for incremental learning based on algorithmic probability. In: Proceedings of the Sixth Israeli Conference on Artificial Intelligence, Tel Aviv, Israel, pp. 515–527 (December 1989)

[14] Solomonoff, R.J.: Progress in incremental machine learning. In: NIPS Workshop on Universal Learning Algorithms and Optimal Search, Whistler, B.C., Canada (December 2002)

[15] Solomonoff, R.J.: Three kinds of probabilistic induction: Universal distributions and convergence theorems. The Computer Journal 51(5), 566–570 (2008); Christopher Stewart Wallace (1933-2004) memorial special issue

[16] Solomonoff, R.J.: Algorithmic probability: Theory and applications. In: Dehmer, M., Emmert-Streib, F. (eds.) Information Theory and Statistical Learning, pp. 1–23. Springer Science+Business Media, N.Y. (2009)

[17] Solomonoff, R.J.: Algorithmic probability, heuristic programming and agi. In: Third Conference on Artificial General Intelligence, pp. 251–157 (2010)

Making Universal Induction Efficient by Specialization

Alexey Potapov[1,2] and Sergey Rodionov[1,3]

[1] AIDEUS, Russia
[2] National Research University of Information Technology, Mechanics and Optics,
St. Petersburg, Russia
[3] Aix Marseille Université, CNRS, LAM (Laboratoire d'Astrophysique de Marseille) UMR
7326, 13388, Marseille, France
{potapov,rodionov}@aideus.com

Abstract. Efficient pragmatic methods in artificial intelligence can be treated as results of specialization of models of universal intelligence with respect to a certain task or class of environments. Thus, specialization can help to create efficient AGI preserving its universality. This idea is promising, but has not yet been applied to concrete models. Here, we considered the task of mass induction, which general solution can be based on Kolmogorov complexity parameterized by reference machine. Futamura-Turchin projections of this solution were derived and implemented in combinatory logic. Experiments with search for common regularities in strings show that efficiency of universal induction can be considerably increased for mass induction using proposed approach.

1   Introduction

Knowledge about the appropriate degree of universality of intelligence is essential for artificial general intelligence, since it determines the strategy of research and development in this field. Relatively generally accepted point of view supposes that intelligence consists of a set of specialized modules, which cooperation yields a synergetic effect [1]. On the other hand, models of universal intelligence exist [2, 3], which in theory possess capabilities unachievable by compositions of narrow methods, but possibly indispensable for general intelligence.

However, strong objection against these models is their computational infeasibility, which makes doubtful that desirable capabilities can be really achieved in practice. In part of induction, the most direct way to improve their efficiency is to select some appropriate reference machine, which specifies inductive bias agreed with reality [4]. This operation is useful, but insufficient, because it can help to find only limited number of simple regularities in reasonable time, while more complex regularities inevitably encountered in nature will be unrecoverable. More efficient practical approximations of universal intelligence models lose universality (e.g. [5]).

One can possibly conclude that efficient universality cannot be achieved, and universality is mostly of theoretical interest, or inefficient universal methods can work in parallel with efficient pragmatic intelligence as a last resort.

However, universal intelligence can be probably much more useful in practical sense. Principal possibility of automatic construction of efficient narrow methods

B. Goertzel et al. (Eds.): AGI 2014, LNAI 8598, pp. 133–142, 2014.

from inefficient general methods via program specialization (partial evaluation) was noticed 30 years ago [6]. Recently, this idea was put into the context of AGI research [7]. In particular, it was indicated that specializing a universal intelligence w.r.t. some problem and solving this problem afterwards can be computationally more efficient than solving this problem immediately. This result implies that models of universal intelligence can be made more efficient without violating universality. Indirect utilization of universality in the form of construction of specialized methods is attractive since it also bridges the gap between the two approaches, and shows that systems composed of a set of specialized modules are insufficient for AGI, because this set is fixed and is not automatically extended.

However, no analysis of possible specialization of concrete models of universal intelligence has been given yet. In this paper, we make the first such attempt focusing on Solomonoff's universal induction (of course, specialization of decision-making is also of interest). We consider this problem on example of mass induction tasks for which benefits from specialization should be more evident.

2   Background

Universal Induction

For the sake of simplicity we will consider method of universal induction (instead of universal prediction or universal intelligence), which consists in searching for the shortest program that reproduces given data [4]:

$$p^* = \arg\min_p[l(p) \mid U(p) = x],$$ (1)

where each program p reproducing data x being executed on universal machine U is treated as the (generative) model of this data, and p^* is the best model.

This is universal solution to the problem of induction, because it possesses two main properties: it relies on the universal (Turing-complete) space of models, in which any computable regularity can be found, and it uses universal complexity-based criterion for model selection (which universality also relies on Turing-completeness since any two universal machines can emulate each other using interpreters with length independent of programs being executed).

This criterion is incomputable, but can be replaced with a computable counterpart (e.g. Levin search, *LSearch* [8], based on Levin complexity instead of Kolmogorov complexity), however required number of operations for identifying p^* will be proportional to $2^{l(p^*)}T(p^*)$, where $T(p^*)$ is required time for p^* to terminate.

This estimation cannot be reduced without violating universality, optimality or without imposing some restrictions. Thus, the question is how to do this in a reasonable way. We cannot build a method that will work better in any environment, but we can build a method that will do much better in environments possessing some specific properties (preserving its universality in other environments). These properties are exploited in narrow methods.

Mass Induction and Data Representations

In order to bridge the gap between efficient narrow methods and inefficient universal methods, one should understand difference between them. Of course, practical non-universal methods usually work with Turing-incomplete model spaces. That is why they can be made computationally efficient. Their success in turn is conditioned by correspondence between a class of data to be processed and a model space. Moreover, does each practical method not only fit a specific class of input data, but it is also applied to different data instances from this class independently meaning that each such method is designed to solve some mass induction problem (a set of individual induction tasks to be solved independently).

Indeed, computer vision systems, for example, are most usually applied to different images (or video sequences) independently, and they rely on specific image representations (e.g. based on Fourier or wavelet transforms, contours, feature points, etc.), which define corresponding model spaces.

Mass induction with introduced representations as a possible connection between universal and narrow methods has already been considered [9]. One can state the following mass induction task. Let the set $\{x_i\}_{i=1}^n$ of input data strings be given. Instead of searching for the shortest program reproducing concatenation $x_1...x_n$, one can simplify the problem and search for programs S and input strings $y_1...y_n$ for them such that $U(Sy_i)=x_i$. The program S is called representation for the data set $\{x_i\}$, while y_i are the models obtained within this representation. For the sake of simplicity, we will write $S(y)$ instead of $U(Sy)$, when U is fixed. Criterion for selecting the best representation and models can be derived from Kolmogorov complexity:

$$K_U(x_1 x_2...x_n) \approx \min_S \left(l(S) + \sum_{i=1}^n K_U(x_i \mid S) \right),$$

$$S^* = \arg\min_S \left(l(S) + \sum_{i=1}^n l(y_i^*) \right), \quad y_i^* = \arg\min_{y:S(y)=x_i} l(y), \tag{2}$$

which is a version of the representational minimum description length principle that extends usual minimum description length principle [9].

Such consideration gives only the criterion for selecting models for data of specific types and to reduce computational complexity in terms of decomposition of the high-dimensional task with data $x_1...x_n$ into lower-dimensional subtasks with data x_i.

However, each such subtask remains computationally intractable requiring enumeration of $2^{l(y_i^*)}$ models for each x_i. At the same time, it might be not necessary if S is not a universal machine. Actually, in most practical methods observational data x_i are directly mapped to their descriptions y_i by some program S', which can be referred to as a descriptive representation (in contrast to a generative representation S). For example, if x_i are images, then S' can be a filter, which outputs image edges, feature points or something else as y_i.

However, descriptive representations cannot be directly utilized in universal induction. The problem is in criterion. Generative framework assures that data compression is lossless, and Kolmogorov complexity is the correct measure of amount of information. In descriptive framework, we can calculate lengths of models, but we do not know how much information is lost. Indeed, descriptive models impose constraints on data content instead of telling how to reconstruct data. It can be seen on example of (image) features. Value of each feature contains additional information about data, but in indirect form. Given enough features, data can be reconstructed, but this task is rather complex, if features are non-linear. Thus, it is difficult to tell from nonlinear feature transform itself, whether it is lossless or not. This situation is similar to difference between declarative and imperative knowledge. For example, programs in Prolog impose constraints on solution, but don't describe, how to build it.

In the field of weak AI both representations and methods for searching models within them are constructed manually (or chosen automatically from narrow classes). Artificial general intelligence should have same capabilities as humans, namely, should be able to construct new (efficient) methods by its own. Here, we consider this process as specialization of AGI with respect to specific tasks to be solved.

Program Specialization

The idea of partial evaluation comes from observation that if one has a program with several parameters, and value of one of these parameters is fixed and known, the program can be transformed in such way that will work only with this value, but will do it more efficiently. One simple common example is the procedure of raising x to power n using a cycle, which can directly compute $x * x$ without cycles or iterations, when it is specialized w.r.t. $n=2$. In general, if there is a specializer $spec$ for programs in some programming language R, then the result $spec(p, x_0)$ of specialization of a program $p(x, y) \in R$ w.r.t. its first parameter $x=x_0$ is the program with one parameter, for which $(\forall y)spec(p, x_0)(y) = p(x_0, y)$.

Most frequent application of partial evaluations is interpreters and compilers. Well-known Futamura-Turchin projections [10] show that if there is an interpreter $intL \in R$ for programs in a language L, then the result of its specialization w.r.t. some program $p_L(x)$, $p_L \in L$, is the program p_L compiled into the language R, since $spec(intL, p_L)$ is the program in R such that $(\forall x)spec(intL, p_L)(x) = intL(p_L, x)$ meaning that the result of execution of this program is the same as the result of interpretation of the program p_L.

Further, since specializer takes two arguments, it in turn can also be specialized w.r.t. interpreter $intL$ yielding a compiler $spec(spec, intL)$ from L to R, because $(\forall p_L, x)spec(spec, intL)(p_L)(x) = intL(p_L, x)$. One can further specialize $spec$ w.r.t. itself $spec(spec, spec)$, which can be used in particular as a generator of compilers, since $(\forall intL)spec(spec, spec)(intL)$ is the compiler from L to R.

Main interesting property of specialization consists not simply in the condition $(\forall y)spec(p, x_0)(y) = p(x_0, y)$, but in fact that evaluation of a program specialized w.r.t. some parameter can be much faster than evaluation of original program. However, traditional techniques of partial evaluations can guarantee only linear speedup [11], which is enough for compilers, but inappropriate for our tasks. Some metacomputation techniques allow for polynomial and even exponential speedup, but unreliably [11]. Of course, in general the problem of optimal specialization is algorithmically unsolvable, but humans somehow manage to use it (of course, the principal question is either human intelligence is efficiently general due to powerful specialization, or visa versa).

Specialization of Universal Induction

The most direct application of partial evaluation in mass induction consists in consideration of the generative representation S as the interpreter of some language. Models y_i will be programs in this language. Then, one can directly apply Futamura-Turchin projections. For example, specialization of S w.r.t. y_i will yield compiled programs $spec(S, y_i)$ in the language of the reference machine U. Such "compilation" of models or construction of a compiler $spec(spec, S)$ might have sense, but its effect on computational efficiency will be insignificant. Instead, one should consider specialization of procedures of universal induction.

Consider the following extension of the Levin search procedure for the task of mass induction (universal mass induction method):

Given strings $x_1,...x_n$ enumerate all programs S in parallel (allocating resources for each program proportional to $2^{-l(S)}$); for each program and for each x_i enumerate all possible strings y_i, until the first set $\{S^*, y_1^*,..., y_n^*\}$ is found such that $S^*(y_i^*) = x_i^*$.

We will refer to this algorithm as *RSearch* (representation search). *RSearch* has a subroutine (let refer to it as *MSearch*, model search), which searches for the best y for given S and x: $y=MSearch(S, x)$ such that $S(y)=x$ implying

$$(\forall x)S(MSearch(S,x)) = x. \tag{3}$$

MSearch uses exhaustive search to find the best model within the utilized representation. However, the task of searching for the shortest generative model in Turing-incomplete space (that corresponds to a set of possible input strings to some program S) can have simplified or even explicit solution in the form of an algorithm, which directly maps given x to its best model y.

Imagine that we have some specializer *spec*, which can accept the algorithm $MSearch(S, x)$ and any fixed representation S and produce its computationally efficient projection such that $(\forall x)spec(MSearch, S)(x) = MSearch(S, x)$ by definition of *spec*. Let denote $S'=spec(MSearch, S)$, then $(\forall x)S'(x) = MSearch(S, x)$. Substituting this result in (3), one can obtain $(\forall x)S(S'(x)) = x$.

Among all possible programs possessing this property, the program S should be chosen, for which (2) is held. We have proven the following theorem.

Theorem 1. The result of specialization of the model search in the universal mass induction method (*RSearch*) w.r.t. the fixed representation S optimal for the set $\{x_i\}$ of input data is the program S' such that $(\forall x)S(S'(x)) = x$ and $\sum_i l(S'(x_i))$ is minimal.

This theorem shows that S' is the right-inverse to S, but not an arbitrary one, since it should satisfy the information-theoretic optimality criterion.

It should be noted that equality $S'(S(y))=y$ can be true not for all y, since for some representations (e.g. interpreters of universal machines) many models producing the same x can exist implying that if y is not an optimal model of $x=S(y)$ then $y^* = S'(S(y)) \neq y$. Thus, S' is not necessarily left-inverse.

Theorem 1 shows that a descriptive representation is a result of partial evaluation of (extended) universal induction with some generative representation. One can go further and apply the second Futamura-Turchin projection in these settings, i.e. specializes the *spec* program itself w.r.t. *MSearch* algorithm. The program with the following property will be immediately obtained.

Theorem 2. Let $spec(spec, MSearch)=Inv'$ then $(\forall S, x) S(Inv'(S)(x)) = x$.

This theorem might seem trivial, but it shows a connection between inversion and specialization, which are usually considered as different tasks of metacomputation.

Again, it is not true that $(\forall S, y) Inv'(S)(S(y)) = y$, because S is not injection. Also *Inv'* is not an arbitrary inversion, but it constructs $S'=Inv'(S)$ optimal in terms of induction (as it is indicated in Theorem 1).

It is interesting to note that is usually considered as a particular case of meta-computations, which also include program inversion (which is also assumed to be more difficult than specialization). However, Theorem 2 shows that inversion can also be obtained as the result of specialization in case of search procedures.

Of course, one can consider the third Futamura-Turchin projection also, which will be *spec(spec, spec)* again. In this context, it appears to be not only a generator of compilers, but a generator of procedures for solving inverse problems. This is quite interesting abstract construction, but it is a way too general in terms of what it should be able to do. Indeed, self-application *spec(spec, spec)* is supposed to be done without knowing, which programs or data will be further passed to *spec*. The third projection should probably be put in online settings (self-optimization of *spec* in runtime while receiving concrete data) to become relevant to AGI.

3   Search for Representations

Inferred theoretical results reveal only general properties of specialized induction procedures, but don't give constructive means for building them. Straightforward way to further this approach is to try applying partial evaluation and metacomputation techniques directly to *MSearch*. Such an attempt can be very valuable, since it can help to understand usefulness of program specialization as possible automated transition from general inefficient to narrow efficient intelligence.

However, in our particular case, the result of specialization *spec(MSearch, S)* can be unknown together with S. Here, we don't solve the problem of efficient automatic construction of representations, but limit ourselves with the problem of efficient model construction within somehow created representations. For this reason, we use the *RSearch* procedure modified in such a way that instead of searching for all y_i for each S, it searches for pairs of S and S' with S' satisfying Theorem 1. We will refer to this procedure as *SS'-Search*.

Let us estimate computational complexity of different search procedures. The number of operations in *RSearch* will be proportional to $2^{l(S)}\sum_i 2^{l(y_i)}$. It should be pointed out that in the worst case *LSearch* time will be proportional $2^{l(S)\sum_i l(y_i)} = 2^{l(S)}\prod_i 2^{l(y_i)}$ since no decomposition is done.

SS'-Search time will be proportional to $2^{l(S)}2^{l(S')}$ meaning that *SS'-Search* can even be much more efficient than *RSearch* in cases, when y_i are longer than S' (and this should be quite common in sensory data analysis especially when data contain uncompressible noise). However, the opposite result can also be possible. The main advantage of *SS'-Search* should be in construction of S', which can help to search for models of new data pieces more efficiently.

4   Implementation in Combinatory Logic

We built one resource-bounded implementation of universal induction using combinatory logic (CL) as the reference machine and genetic programming as the search engine [12]. Because it is not biased toward some specific task, it is not practically useful. However, it is appropriate for validating theoretical results. Here, we extend this implementation on the case of mass induction problems using *RSearch* and *SS'-Search*.

We used combinators **K, S, B, b, W, M, J, C, T** with the following reduction rules

$$\mathbf{K}\,x\,y \rightarrow x \qquad\qquad \mathbf{S}\,x\,y\,z \rightarrow x\,z\,(y\,z) \qquad\qquad \mathbf{B}\,f\,g\,x = f(g\,x)$$
$$\mathbf{b}\,f\,g\,x = g\,(f\,x) \qquad\qquad \mathbf{W}\,x\,y = x\,y\,y \qquad\qquad \mathbf{M}\,x = x\,x$$
$$\mathbf{J}\,a\,b\,c\,d = a\,b\,(a\,d\,c) \qquad \mathbf{C}\,f\,x\,y = f\,y\,x \qquad\qquad \mathbf{T}\,x\,y = y\,x$$

where x, y, *etc.* are arbitrary CL-expressions.

We supplement CL alphabet with non-combinatory symbols 0 and 1 (and in some experiments with other digits, which are treated simply as different symbols). Reduction of CL-expression can yield some non-reducible expression with combinators or with only non-combinatory symbols.

Representations can be easily introduced in CL. Indeed, one can construct a CL-expression as a concatenation of two expressions S and y treating S as a representation and y as a model of data x within this representation, if concatenation Sy is reduced to x. Then, being given a set of data pieces $\{x_i\}$ in mass induction settings, one should search for one common S and different y_i such that CL-expressions Sy_i are reduced (possibly imprecisely) to x_i.

In order to select the best S and y_i the criterion (2) can be made more concrete:

$$S^* = \arg\min_S \left[H_S\, l(S) + H_y \sum_i l(y_i^*) + H_x \sum_i d(x_i, S(y_i^*)) \right]. \tag{4}$$

where y_i^* are models obtained by *MSearch* or by applying S' to x_i in *SS'-Search*; $l(S)$ and $l(y_i^*)$ are lengths (number of symbols) in corresponding strings, $d(x_i, S(y_i^*))$ is the edit distance between two strings (number of symbols to be encoded to transform $S(y_i^*)$ to x_i); H_S, H_y and H_x are number of bits per symbol to be encoded in corresponding domains.

Application of genetic programming here is similar to our previous implementation, in which CL-expressions were represented as trees with typical crossover in the form of sub-tree exchange. The main difference is that solutions in mass induction have more complex structure, and crossover should be performed independently for each part. It also appeared to be useful to allow modifications of only one part of the solution per iteration (population).

Our implementation can be found at https://github.com/aideus/cl-lab

5   Experimental Results

We conducted some experiments with several sets of binary strings. Seemingly simplest set was composed of string 11100101 repeated 10 times as $x_1...x_{10}$. Obvious optimal generative representation here coincides with the same string 11100101 (if empty strings as models are acceptable) since this CL-expression will always be reduced to itself. However, *RSearch* failed to find this solution. The best found solution appeared to be 1110 for representation (S), and 0101 for models (y_i) for each string. Surely, reduction of Sy_i will yield 11100101, but this solution is not optimal. Why consequent optimization of this solution is difficult for genetic programming? String 11100 as the representation can be obtained from 1110 by single mutation, but this will lead to necessity of rebuilding all models (since Sy_i will become equal to 111000101).

Impracticity of general methods in application to mass induction tasks as a conclusion is trivial. At the same time, *SS'-Search* successfully solved this problem and found $S'=$**J(bMJK)T** and $S=$**W**110010. Here, $S'x_i$ is reduced to y_i=1, and Sy_i is reduced back to x_i=11100101. In contrast to *RSearch*, incremental improvement of solutions is achievable here easier, since modification of S requires consistent modification of only S' instead of many y_i.

Consider other sets of strings. The next set was composed of 16 strings 0101101101010, 0001101001011, 0111111110011, etc. These are random strings starting with 0. *RSearch* failed to find any precise solution. Found representations had such a form as **B(BW(BWM)(01))** with corresponding models 10111, 10011, 11010, etc. At the same time, *SS'-Search* found optimal solution – $S=0$, $S'=$**CK**, in which S' removes the first bit of the string producing models of data strings (which are difficult to find blindly in *RSearch*), and S adds 0 as the first bit.

The next set contained the following strings 00000000, 00010001, 00100010,... 11111111. Both methods managed to find good solutions (although in 25% runs). RSearch found $S=$**SSbBBM** and y_i=0000, 0001, ... 1111. *SS'-Search* found $S=$**BBB(BM)** and $S'=$**B(SJCK)** such that S' transforms x_i to appropriate y_i by removing a duplicating half of a string, which are then transformed back by S.

We also conducted some tests with an extended alphabet of non-combinatory symbols including 0..9 (which were not interpreted as digits though). One set included such strings as 159951, 248842, 678876, 589985, 179971, etc. (i.e. strings with mirror symmetry). *RSearch* completely failed on this set, while *SS'-Search* found an optimal solution – $S=\mathbf{B}(\mathbf{S}(\mathbf{BST}))\mathbf{M}$, $S'=\mathbf{JKK}$. Of course, a solution with the same representation and models is valid for *RSearch* also, but the search problem in purely generative settings appeared to be too difficult.

Another set contained such strings as 307718, 012232, 689956, 782214, etc. Common regularity for these strings is coincidence of 3rd and 4th symbol. Again, *RSearch* was unsuccessful, while *SS'-Search* found $S=\mathbf{KBbW}$ and $S'=\mathbf{BK}$, which add and exclude redundant symbol correspondingly.

Our main intention to consider specialization of universal induction was to avoid expensive search for individual models for every new data strings. Once S' is constructed, it can be directly applied to construct models in all considered cases. This is the main benefit from using specialization of universal induction. We didn't try to solve the problem of automatic construction of arbitrary representations, but increase in performance of universal methods in solving also this problem is importance.

Of course, capabilities of *SS'-Search* based on uninformed search are quite limited. Indeed, in our experiments it failed to discover many seemingly simple regularities especially in strings of varying length (partially because their representation in combinatory logic can be rather complex). Examples of unsuccessful tests include {1221333, 3331221333, 2233313331333, 22122122122, ...}, {00, 11, 000, 111, 0000, ...}, {491234, 568485, 278412, 307183, 098710, ...}, and others. Thus, this solution is far from efficient universal induction. Nevertheless, comparison of *RSearch* and *SS'-Search* shows that efficiency of universal induction can be considerably increased, and there is a principal way to bridge the gap between efficient and universal methods.

6   Conclusion

We considered universal induction in application to mass problems. Solutions of such problems include representations that capture common regularities in strings, and individual models of these strings. Such methods as LSearch can be directly extended to solve mass problems. However, this leads to direct enumeration of both representations and models. At the same time, model search can be made much more efficient for particular representations as it is done in efficient narrow methods of machine perception and learning.

We studied a possibility to perform specialization of universal induction w.r.t. some representation (reference machine). The result of such specialization should correspond to a descriptive representation that maps inputs into models as efficient as possible. However, the most difficult problem consisting in construction of representations themselves remains.

We proposed the *SS'-Search* method that can be treated as the generalization autoencoders [13] for the Turing-complete space of representations. This method consists in searching for descriptive and generative representations simultaneously. It was implemented using combinatory logic as the reference machine. The *SS'-Search* appeared to be much more efficient for mass induction tasks than the direct search for generative models for each given string, but it still allows solving induction tasks of rather low complexity. Further research is needed to increase efficiency of universal methods. Also, analysis of specialization of concrete universal intelligence models (in addition to universal induction) is of interest.

Acknowledgements. This work was supported by the Russian Federation President's grant Council (MD-1072.2013.9) and the Ministry of Education and Science of the Russian Federation.

References

1. Hart, D., Goertzel, B.: OpenCog: A Software Framework for Integrative Artificial General Intelligence. In: Frontiers in Artificial Intelligence and Applications, Proc. 1st AGI Conference, vol. 171, pp. 468–472 (2008)
2. Hutter, M.: Universal Artificial Intelligence: Sequential Decisions Based on Algorithmic Probability. Springer (2005)
3. Schmidhuber, J.: Gödel Machines: Fully Self-Referential Optimal Universal Self-improvers. In: Goertzel, B., Pennachin, C. (eds.) Artificial General Intelligence. Cognitive Technologies, pp. 199–226. Springer (2007)
4. Solomonoff, R.: Algorithmic Probability, Heuristic Programming and AGI. In: Baum, E., Hutter, M., Kitzelmann, E. (eds.) Advances in Intelligent Systems Research, Proc. 3rd Conf. on Artificial General Intelligence, vol. 10, pp. 151–157 (2010)
5. Veness, J., Ng, K.S., Hutter, M., Uther, W., Silver, D.: A Monte-Carlo AIXI Approximation. J. Artificial Intelligence Research 40(1), 95–142 (2011)
6. Kahn, K.: Partial Evaluation, Programming Methodology, and Artificial Intelligence. AI Magazine 5(1), 53–57 (1984)
7. Khudobakhshov, V.: Metacomputations and Program-based Knowledge Representation. In: Kühnberger, K.-U., Rudolph, S., Wang, P. (eds.) AGI 2013. LNCS (LNAI), vol. 7999, pp. 70–77. Springer, Heidelberg (2013)
8. Levin, L.A.: Universal sequential search problems. Problems of Information Transmission 9(3), 265–266 (1973)
9. Potapov, A., Rodionov, S.: Extending Universal Intelligence Models with Formal Notion of Representation. In: Bach, J., Goertzel, B., Iklé, M. (eds.) AGI 2012. LNCS (LNAI), vol. 7716, pp. 242–251. Springer, Heidelberg (2012)
10. Futamura, Y.: Partial Evaluation of Computation Process – an Approach to a Compiler-Compiler. Systems, Computers, Controls 2(5), 45–50 (1971)
11. Jones, N.D., Gomard, C.K., Sestoft, P.: Partial Evaluation and Automatic Program Generation. Prentice-Hall (1993)
12. Potapov, A., Rodionov, S.: Universal Induction with Varying Sets of Combinators. In: Kühnberger, K.-U., Rudolph, S., Wang, P. (eds.) AGI 2013. LNCS, vol. 7999, pp. 88–97. Springer, Heidelberg (2013)
13. Hochreiter, S., Schmidhuber, J.: Nonlinear ICA through Low-Complexity Autoencoders. In: Proc. IEEE Int'l Symp. on Circuits and Systems, vol. 5, pp. 53–56 (1999)

Reinforcement Learning for Adaptive Theory of Mind in the Sigma Cognitive Architecture

David V. Pynadath[1], Paul S. Rosenbloom[1,2], and Stacy C. Marsella[3]

[1] Institute for Creative Technologies
[2] Department of Computer Science
University of Southern California, Los Angeles CA, USA
[3] Northeastern University, Boston MA, USA

Abstract. One of the most common applications of human intelligence is so-cial interaction, where people must make effective decisions despite uncertainty about the potential behavior of others around them. Reinforcement learning (RL) provides one method for agents to acquire knowledge about such interactions. We investigate different methods of multiagent reinforcement learning within the Sigma cognitive architecture. We leverage Sigma's architectural mechanism for gradient descent to realize four different approaches to multiagent learning: (1) with no explicit model of the other agent, (2) with a model of the other agent as following an unknown stationary policy, (3) with prior knowledge of the other agent's possible reward functions, and (4) through inverse reinforcement learn-ing (IRL) of the other agent's reward function. While the first three variations re-create existing approaches from the literature, the fourth represents a novel combination of RL and IRL for social decision-making. We show how all four styles of adaptive Theory of Mind are realized through Sigma's same gradient descent algorithm, and we illustrate their behavior within an abstract negotiation task.

1 Introduction

Human intelligence faces the daily challenge of interacting with other people. To make effective decisions, people must form beliefs about others and generate expectations about the behavior of others to inform their own behavior. This cognitive capacity for *Theory of Mind* distinguishes social interaction from the decision-making that people do in isolation [21]. We therefore expect that a system capable of artificial general intelligence (AGI) would provide natural support for Theory of Mind. We are inter-ested here in how Theory of Mind capabilities may be realized within *Sigma* (Σ), a nascent *cognitive system*—an integrated computational model of intelligent behavior—that is grounded in a *cognitive architecture*, a model of the fixed structure underlying a cognitive system [9].

In prior work, we have demonstrated this architecture's ability to support Theory of Mind within canonical examples from the game theory literature [13]. However, the games previously investigated made each agent's payoff functions common knowledge to both sides, a luxury not afforded in most social interactions. *Reinforcement learn-ing* (RL) has proven a successful method for agents to make effective decisions in the

B. Goertzel et al. (Eds.): AGI 2014, LNAI 8598, pp. 143–154, 2014.

face of such uncertainty [19]. It is thus not surprising that the multiagent literature has tried a variety of knowledge structures and learning mechanisms to implement decision-making in such interactive environments [3].

Sigma's cognitive architecture provides a mechanism for gradient descent to update functional representations of an agent's knowledge, a mechanism that has supported a capability for reinforcement learning in prior work [15,17]. Here, we reuse this same general learning mechanism across different knowledge representations of a social interaction to arrive at four different models of the agent with which it is interacting:

Section 4: without explicitly modeling the other agent [10]
Section 5: with a stationary policy model of the other agent (a 1-level agent [5,6])
Section 6: with a set of possible reward functions for the other agent [4,12]
Section 7: by *inverse reinforcement learning* (IRL) of the other agent's reward [11]

The Sigma agent is able to leverage the same gradient-descent mechanism in learning these various models. It also leverages gradient descent to learn its own policy of behavior based on its current model of the other agent. In realizing the first three variations, we re-create existing multiagent decision-making mechanisms from the literature. In the fourth variation, we arrive at a novel combination of RL and IRL for multiagent decision-making. Thus, by examining permutations in the application of Sigma's gradient-descent mechanism, we are able to explore a broad space of multiagent learning, without any changes to the underlying cognitive architecture.

We examine the behavior of each of these variations within an abstract negotiation task (described in Section 3). By analyzing the resulting behaviors when interacting with the same fixed agents, we can compare the different models used (described in Section 8). We are thus able to show how the Sigma cognitive architecture can realize diverse adaptive social behavior by leveraging the same reinforcement learning mechanism with different models at the knowledge level.

2   Sigma

Sigma's cognitive architecture is built upon *graphical models* [7]. Graphical models provide a general computational technique for efficient computation with complex multivariate functions by leveraging forms of independence. Sigma leverages this generality through a core knowledge structure—the *conditional*—that provides a deep blending of the forms of conditionality found in both rules and probabilistic networks.

Sigma's long-term memory comprises a set of these conditionals, which are jointly compiled into a single *factor graph* [8] at the level below. Memory access occurs by passing messages in this graph, via the *summary product algorithm* [8], until quiescence; that is, until there are no more messages to send. Each message is an n-dimensional piecewise linear function that is defined over an array of rectilinear regions. These piecewise linear functions can approximate arbitrary continuous functions as closely as desired, as well as be restricted to represent both discrete probability distributions and relational symbol structures. Working memory consists of a set of peripheral nodes in the graph that provide fixed *evidence* during solution of the long-term-memory graph.

The Sigma cognitive architecture provides a model of sequential action, during which operators are selected and applied to achieve goals (or maximize utilities) [14]. The core cognitive (decision) cycle in Sigma involves message passing until quiescence, with the results then used in deciding how to modify working memory. In prior work, we have demonstrated Sigma's ability to support multiple cognitive capabilities, such as problem solving [14], mental imagery [16], Theory of Mind [13], and learning [15].

Learning occurs by altering functions in conditionals at decision time. Sigma's learning mechanism was inspired by earlier work showing that gradient descent was possible in Bayesian networks, much as in neural networks, but without the need for an additional backpropagation mechanism [18]. In Sigma, gradient-descent learning modifies conditional functions, by interpreting incoming messages as gradients that are to be normalized, multiplied by the learning rate, and added to the existing function [17].

Reinforcement learning within Sigma leverages gradient descent to learn Q values over multiple trials, given appropriate conditionals to structure the computation as needed. One conditional proposes actions for selection, weighted by the Q values learned so far. To enable Q values to determine which action to choose, this proposal conditional is augmented to use them as operator weights (alternatively viewed as numeric preferences). For example, if the initial Q values are uniform, then the agent will choose its actions randomly in the early stages of learning.

If direct evidence were provided for the Q values, it would be trivial to use gradient descent to learn them without needing to invoke reinforcement learning. However, without such evidence, RL is the means by which rewards earned in later steps propagate backwards to serve as input for learning Q values for earlier steps. This occurs via a combination of: (1) learning to predict local rewards from the externally provided evidence in the current state and (2) learning to predict both future rewards and Q values by propagating backwards the next state's expected reward [17].

To learn to predict future rewards, we add a conditional that examines the current state and operator, along with the predicted next state (as given by the transition function) and that state's predicted local reward and future discounted reward. This conditional leverages an affine transformation to add the next state's predicted local reward to the distribution over its predicted future reward, and a coefficient to discount this sum. RL then results from using the messages that are passed back to the conditional functions as gradients in learning Q values and discounted future rewards.

3   Negotiation

We investigate different applications of Sigma's gradient-descent learning mechanism within a bilateral negotiation task. Two agents, A and B, make a series of offers and counteroffers to arrive at an allocation of two apples and two oranges. On its turn, each agent selects an operator (Operator-A and Operator-B), either making an offer or accepting the current offer on the table. The current offer on the table is represented by a number of Apples and Oranges, the combination of which represent the fruits that A would receive if the offer were accepted. B would receive the fruits *not* allocated to A.

In this paper, we adopt the perspective of A, who receives a Reward-A that increases linearly with the number of total fruits. An agent can offer only one type of fruit at a time, so both agents' operators, Operator-A and Operator-B, contain: {offer 0 apples, offer 1 apple, offer 2 apples, offer 0 oranges, offer 1 orange, offer 2 oranges, accept}. If either agent chooses to accept the current offer, then the negotiation terminates with a final allocation based on the current offer on the table. It is straightforward to encode this deterministic transition function within Sigma conditionals.

Combining the transition and reward functions can generate the reward for A's action selection one time step into the future. To predict long-term rewards further into the future, A can use its experiences in repeated negotiations to learn Q values, Q-A, across possible state-operator combinations [20]. We represent these Q values as a distribution over [0,10), the same scale as Reward-A. A can learn this distribution by deriving projected future rewards, Projected-A, from the observed immediate rewards and the state transitions it experiences.

To reason about the future rewards that result from B's action, A can use a variety of possible models. In Section 4, A naively treats this transition as simply part of the environment and does no modeling of B's operator selection. In Section 5, A models B as following a stationary policy of behavior (similar to fictitious play [2]) so that it can learn the distribution of actions underlying the state transitions during B's turn.

In Sections 6 and 7, A uses a Theory of Mind to assume that B behaves according to a reward function structured like its own. In Section 6, A assumes that this reward function is drawn from a finite set of candidates. Such prior knowledge is not always available, so, in Section 7, A uses inverse reinforcement learning to update a belief about B's reward function. In both cases, A can derive a policy of behavior from a hypothesized reward function for B, and use it to generate an expected probability distribution over B's operator selection and the implied state transitions.

We apply these variations in combination with two possible variations on B:

Cooperative: B wants the same outcome as A (i.e., A has all of the fruit).

Competitive: B is happy to let A have the oranges, but it wants the apples for itself.

We provide A with a static target by not having B model A in return. In other words, B's behavior is a stationary function of the current offer on the table. The *cooperative* B will accept when the current offer is 2 apples and 2 oranges; otherwise, it will make an offer that moves the negotiation closer to that target offer, with two apples being offered before two oranges. The *competitive* B behaves similarly with respect to its target offer of 0 apples and 2 oranges.[1] Both versions of B make apples a higher priority than oranges, to break up the symmetry that would make many of the negotiation states equivalent. For example, a cooperative B prefers 2 apples and no oranges over no apples and 2 oranges. To complicate A's learning problem further, we make B's behavior non-deterministic by introducing a 10% chance of deviating from the optimal action to one of its suboptimal actions.

---

[1] A truly competitive B that wanted both the oranges and apples would be an uninteresting opponent, in that any action by A would not move B from its target offer of 0 apples and 0 oranges.

4   Learning with No Model of the Other Agent

We first build a Sigma agent that learns its Q values without any explicit modeling of B's behavior [10]. Figures 1a and 1b show an influence diagram representation of the conditionals that represent A's reasoning during A's and B's turns, respectively. On its turn, in Figure 1a, A uses its current Q values (Q-A) to inform its selection of Operator-A (a rectangular decision node) given the current state of the negotiation (Apples$_t$, etc.). It then observes the subsequent state (Apples$_{t+1}$, etc.) and the reward that results (Reward-A, a diamond-shaped utility node).

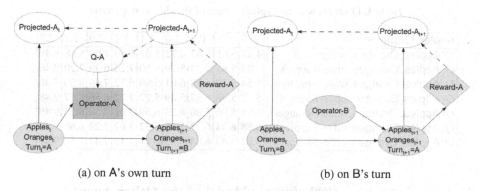

(a) on A's own turn   (b) on B's turn

Fig. 1. Graph for computing and learning A's projected rewards with no model of B

In our negotiation model, the agents receive reward only when an offer is accepted by either party. A propagates this final reward back over the offer on the table (the dashed line from Reward-A to Projected-A$_{t+1}$ in Figure 1a) and then backs up those values to the state leading to the final accepted offer (the dashed line from Projected-A$_{t+1}$ to Projected-A$_t$). The messages that are passed back to the conditional functions then serve as gradients in learning the projected future rewards [17]. Similar gradient descent using the messages passed along the dashed line from Projected-A$_{t+1}$ to Q-A then supports learning the Q values from these projected future rewards.

Figure 1b shows the graph for the rewards that A can expect when it is B's turn. In this case, the operator is an observation from A's perspective (as opposed to its own decision). The message passing and gradient descent proceed just as on A's turn.

As A encounters various negotiation states, Sigma's conditionals will generate messages for the current state and selected operator, leading to updates to the projected future rewards and, on A's turn, the Q values for those states. The agent can then use the learned Q values in its operator selection process by translating the distribution over Q values into an expected value for candidate operators, as shown in the forward direction in Figure 1a. A then chooses its operator through a *softmax* over these expected values, allowing it to choose high-value operators with high probability, while also allowing it to explore the negotiation space during learning.

Table 1 shows the expectation over A's Q values after 1000 cycles of interacting with a cooperative B, averaged over 60 runs. The boldfaced number represents the operator having the highest expected Q value in each state. For the most part, A has learned to accept when the offer on the table reaches its best possible outcome: two apples and two oranges. However, the other operators in that state also have high values, because, in the cooperative setting, even if A changes the offer, B will seek to re-establish it on its subsequent turn. The optimal actions in the other states (offering either two apples or two oranges) all have similarly high values, although there are some states where another operator has a higher value. Again, B's cooperative nature means that accepting a suboptimal offer is the only really "bad" choice, but this learning method has still demonstrated an effective ability to learn discriminatory Q values across its operators.

Table 1. Q values with no explicit model of B, who is cooperative

Apples, Oranges	0,0	0,1	0,2	1,0	1,1	1,2	2,0	2,1	2,2
Q(Apples, Oranges, accept)	4.88	5.01	5.62	4.72	5.07	6.59	4.00	5.68	**9.49**
Q(Apples, Oranges, offer-0-apples)	6.05	5.85	5.74	5.39	6.50	7.26	6.39	7.20	9.46
Q(Apples, Oranges, offer-0-oranges)	5.54	5.39	5.28	6.01	5.80	6.72	**7.56**	8.00	9.46
Q(Apples, Oranges, offer-1-apples)	5.72	5.96	6.57	5.89	5.77	**7.72**	6.56	8.17	9.48
Q(Apples, Oranges, offer-1-oranges)	5.81	5.96	5.30	**6.23**	6.59	7.01	7.50	8.25	9.46
Q(Apples, Oranges, offer-2-apples)	**6.58**	**6.24**	6.27	5.88	**6.72**	7.62	7.22	**8.69**	9.49
Q(Apples, Oranges, offer-2-oranges)	5.67	5.43	**6.84**	5.93	6.21	7.15	7.47	8.55	9.49

5   Learning with a Probabilistic Model of the Other Agent

A's update of its projected future rewards in Figure 1b does not maintain any information about the likelihood of the observed transitions on B's turn. Early work on multiagent learning instead leveraged an assumption that other agents may be following a stationary policy of behavior, represented as a probability distribution over operator selection conditioned on the current state [5,6]. In this section, we enable A to model B as such a *0-level* agent by learning a stationary policy of B's behavior. We can represent this policy as a probability distribution, π-B, over B's operator selection, as a function of the current offer on the table. Figure 2 shows the graphical representation of the modified conditionals for A's computation that include this policy. On B's turn, A receives direct evidence of B's behavior that it uses to update the functional representation of π-B (the dashed line from Operator-B in Figure 2).

A can now use its beliefs about B's policy to update its projected future rewards. As shown in Figure 2, the backup of Projected-A_{t+1} to Projected-A_t is now weighted by the probability of the observed action, as specified by π-B. Thus, A can minimize the impact that observations of B's unlikely suboptimal actions will have on its learning. In such cases, the low probability for π-B of Operator-B will scale the message along the link to Projected-A_t. This scaling allows A to incorporate its accumulated expectations about B into its learning of Q values associated with the state of the negotiation. On A's own turn, these expectations provide no information, so A backs up future rewards just as in Figure 1a.

Table 2 shows the probability of B's true optimal action (which it chooses with 90% probability) within A's learned π-B policy. Across all states and both versions of B,

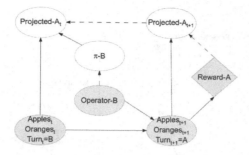

Fig. 2. Graph for A's projected rewards on B's turn with a stationary policy model of B

the optimal action has the highest probability. However, even after 1000 cycles, the values still deviate a significant amount from the correct 90% value. We postpone an investigation of the impact of this learning on A's performance until Section 8.

Table 2. Learned probability of B's optimal action

Apples,Oranges	0,0	0,1	0,2	1,0	1,1	1,2	2,0	2,1	2,2
π-B(Operator-B*) in cooperative	0.64	0.63	0.62	0.42	0.49	0.56	0.57	0.64	0.53
π-B(Operator-B*) in competitive	0.70	0.58	0.44	0.60	0.55	0.59	0.41	0.55	0.63

6   Learning with a Set of Reward Functions for the Other Agent

Although the modified conditionals of Section 5 explicitly model B, they treat it as an unknown stochastic process, rather than using a Theory of Mind to treat it as an agent-driven one. For example, A's Theory of Mind might inform it that B is also seeking to maximize its own reward function. We can hypothesize that B belongs to one of a finite set of possible models, each with a corresponding reward function. Such a representation would correspond to Bayesian approaches to multiagent modeling that use sets of models to specify the beliefs that one agent has about another [4,12].

To represent such models, we introduce variables for the Reward, Projected future rewards, and Q values of B, analogous to A's. However, these variables have an additional parameter, $m \in$ Model-of-B, representing the possible reward functions of B (e.g., *cooperative* vs. *competitive*). On B's turn, A will observe Operator-B and the resulting negotiation state. Figure 3a is a graph of A's model of B's decision-making analogous to Figure 1a for A's. Using this graph, A can deterministically derive the values of Reward-B from each of the candidate reward functions applied in the resulting state. It can then propagate that derived value back to Projected-B, which is propagated, in turn, back to Q values for B (Q-B), all contingent on each candidate model, m.

Sigma translates these learned Q values for each $m \in$ Model-of-B into policies of behavior for B: π-B, as in Section 5. Here, rather than learning the distribution directly, A uses a softmax to translate the Q values in Operator-B into a Boltzmann distribution

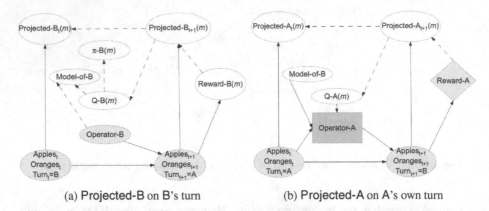

(a) **Projected-B** on B's turn   (b) **Projected-A** on A's own turn

Fig. 3. Graph for projected rewards with two hypothesized reward functions for B

over selection, conditioned on the current state. A can incorporate this distribution into updating its projected future rewards on B's turn as previously illustrated in Figure 2.

Given **Q-B**(m) for each operator, **A** can update its beliefs about the likelihood of these models. The dashed lines to **Model-of-B** in Figure 3a represent the messages that translate the observed **Operator-B** and the **Q-B** values for that observation under each model, m, into a gradient over the distribution over models. For example, the models for which the observed action has higher Q values will have an increased likelihood in the posterior distribution. A will incorporate this distribution into an expected value over **Q-A** across the possible values for **Model-of-B** (shown in Figure 3b).

We gave **A** a **Model-of-B** containing our two candidate reward functions (cooperative and competitive) and let it interact with **B** of both types. After 1000 cycles, **A**'s belief over **Model-of-B** is so certain that the likelihood of the incorrect model is less than 0.1%. We again postpone an investigation of the impact of this modeling on **A**'s performance until Section 8.

7   Learning with IRL of the Other's Reward

We will not always have a priori knowledge of another agent's possible reward functions. However, we could assume that B has *some* fixed reward function that is guiding a rational decision-making process. *Inverse reinforcement learning* leverages such an assumption into an ability to reason backward from observed behavior to the observed agent's reward function [11]. Existing agents have used IRL to mimic an observed agent's behavior by inferring its underlying reward function [1]. In this work, we adapt this same mechanism within Sigma to arrive at a novel application of IRL to learning a policy for interacting with another (potentially adversarial) agent.

The graph in Figure 4 illustrates this IRL process in Sigma. A uses observations of **Operator-B** to learn a frequency count, π-B, just as in Section 5's stationary policy model. However, rather than use this policy directly, we leverage our knowledge that there is an underlying optimization process generating this policy. Via a process that required a small extension to Sigma, the action likelihoods of π-B are re-interpreted in terms of the expected values of Q distributions. We then use a softmax to translate these Q values into a new Boltzmann distribution, π-Q-B (similar to Section 6's version of π-B).

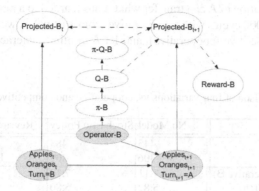

Fig. 4. Graph for IRL on B's turn

Just as A backs up projected reward in a future state onto the Q value for the operator that led to that state, we can now reason in the inverse direction for B. In other words, the learned Q value for B's selected operator implies the projected future reward in the resulting state. However, because of the potential noise and error in this projection, we weight each update by the likelihood, π-Q-B, of the observed operator.

To infer B's reward from these projected future rewards, we exploit the fact that when an agent accepts an offer, both agents receive an immediate reward and the negotiation terminates. Therefore, when B accepts an offer, its projected future rewards include the immediate reward from the accepted offer and nothing else, because there are no more future states. By observing the offers that B accepts, A can thus propagate its Projected-B values to a Reward-B model.

Table 3 presents the expectation over the reward function that A's IRL generates after 1000 cycles with cooperative and competitive Bs. The bold entries show that the learned Reward-B successfully identifies B's optimal outcomes. Furthermore, both versions of B value apples (positively or negatively) more than oranges, which the learned Reward-B captures as well. In particular, the cooperative entries with two apples and the competitive entries with zero constitute six out of the seven highest expected rewards. We will examine the impact of IRL on A's performance in the next section.

Table 3. A's expectation about B's reward function after 1000 cycles in IRL agent

Apples,Oranges	0,0	0,1	0,2	1,0	1,1	1,2	2,0	2,1	2,2
cooperative	0.23	0.27	0.19	0.22	0.23	0.25	0.25	0.36	**0.41**
competitive	0.26	0.36	**0.40**	0.21	0.22	0.25	0.23	0.24	0.20

8 Experimental Comparison

We can compare the behavior of the four versions of A from Sections 4–7 within the same context by measuring cumulative statistics over their interactions with our two versions of B. To measure the flexibility of the learned policies, we also examine how effectively each variation of A can transfer what it has learned to a new situation. Therefore, after the first 1000 cycles with a cooperative (competitive) B, we switch B's reward function to be competitive (cooperative), and let A continue interacting for 250 more cycles.

Table 4. Comparison of four variations vs. cooperative and competitive versions of B

Modeling	No Model	Stochastic Policy	Reward Set	IRL
msgs/decision	445	483	675	587
msec/cycle	306	309	1,343	560
A's Reward (vs. cooperative B)	7.11	7.13	7.12	**7.17**
A's Reward (after switch)	5.82	5.80	**5.85**	5.82
A's Reward (vs. competitive B)	5.88	**5.88**	5.83	5.85
A's Reward (after switch)	7.00	6.96	**7.08**	6.99

Table 4 shows that moving from the "no model" case of Section 4 to the "stochastic policy" model of Section 5 has minimal impact on the number of messages and amount of time required for the graph to reach quiescence. On the other hand, when including a model of B's reward function (Section 6's "reward set" and Section 7's "IRL" variations), the bigger graphs lead to significant increases in the messages and time required. The "reward set" variation requires the most messages and time, due to the explicit Model-of-B and the parameterization of Reward-B, Projected-B, Q-B, and π-B as a function of the two possible models. The "IRL" variation avoids this doubling in the size of messages regarding the B nodes, so it is able to model B's reward function without as much of an increase in computational time incurred by the "reward set" method.

Table 4 also shows that all four methods achieve roughly the same reward, with a dropoff between the cooperative and competitive cases. We expect such a dropoff because of B's unwillingness to accept or offer A's optimal outcome in the latter case. Given the differences among our methods, the comparable performance is a bit surprising. On the other hand, all four variations use a similar structure for A's Q values, and B's stationary policy lends itself to RL. Sigma's message passing quickly converges to the best response, regardless of the knowledge representation. B's behavior is thus not complicated enough to draw out deeper differences among our learning methods.

The midstream switch of B from cooperative to competitive (or vice versa) does elicit some distinguishing characteristics. Table 4 shows that the "reward set" version of A does slightly better than the other three after both switches. During the first 1000 cycles, this variation has already learned Q-B for both cooperative and competitive Bs. It can thus quickly detect the switch through RL of Model-of-B and use its Q-B(m) to learn a modified Q-A. On the other hand, this advantage is still relatively small. Further analysis is thus needed to gain more insight into the differences across these algorithms.

9   Conclusion

We have applied Sigma's architectural capability for gradient descent across four different models of multiagent learning. Three of these models re-create multiagent RL algorithms from the literature, while the fourth represents a novel combination of RL and IRL for decision-making in combination with Theory of Mind about another agent. The four permutations of graphs represent only a subset of the possible structures that we could experiment with. By introducing new nodes or changing the link structure, we can alter A's knowledge-level representation. Re-application of the same architectural mechanism will enable reinforcement learning of that knowledge, allowing us to easily study the impact that the modified graph has on multiagent interaction.

Our current experimental domain was able to validate the correctness of our various algorithms. However, an enriched domain would provide more insight into the differential impact of the various modeling assumptions. In particular, B's stationary policy of behavior forms a static target for A to learn. One very easy way to achieve a more realistic multiagent setting would be to expand our experiments into a true multiagent setting, by giving B the same learning capabilities we gave to A. By assigning different combinations of our learning algorithms to A and B, we will be able to better differentiate their adaptive behavior by applying them to a more complex target agent. With this enriched experimental setting, Sigma's general capability for multiagent learning opens up a promising line of future research into RL-based Theory of Mind.

Acknowledgments. This work has been sponsored by the Office of Naval Research and the U.S. Army. Statements and opinions expressed do not necessarily reflect the position or policy of the U.S. Government.

References

1. Abbeel, P., Ng, A.Y.: Apprenticeship learning via inverse reinforcement learning. In: ICML, pp. 1–8. ACM (2004)
2. Brown, G.W.: Iterative solution of games by fictitious play. Activity Analysis of Production and Allocation 13(1), 374–376 (1951)
3. Busoniu, L., Babuska, R., De Schutter, B.: A comprehensive survey of multiagent reinforcement learning. IEEE Transactions on Systems, Man, and Cybernetics 38(2), 156–172 (2008)
4. Gmytrasiewicz, P., Doshi, P.: A framework for sequential planning in multi-agent settings. JAIR 24, 49–79 (2005)
5. Hu, J., Wellman, M.P.: Multiagent reinforcement learning: theoretical framework and an algorithm. In: ICML, pp. 242–250 (1998)
6. Hu, J., Wellman, M.P.: Learning about other agents in a dynamic multiagent system. Journal of Cognitive Systems Research 2, 67–79 (2001)
7. Koller, D., Friedman, N.: Probabilistic graphical models: principles and techniques. MIT Press (2009)
8. Kschischang, F.R., Frey, B.J., Loeliger, H.A.: Factor graphs and the sum-product algorithm. IEEE Transactions on Information Theory 47(2), 498–519 (2001)
9. Langley, P., Laird, J.E., Rogers, S.: Cognitive architectures: Research issues and challenges. Cognitive Systems Research 10(2), 141–160 (2009)

10. Littman, M.L.: Markov games as a framework for multi-agent reinforcement learning. In: ICML, vol. 94, pp. 157–163 (1994)
11. Ng, A.Y., Russell, S.J.: Algorithms for inverse reinforcement learning. In: ICML, pp. 663–670 (2000)
12. Pynadath, D.V., Marsella, S.C.: PsychSim: Modeling theory of mind with decision-theoretic agents. In: IJCAI, pp. 1181–1186 (2005)
13. Pynadath, D.V., Rosenbloom, P.S., Marsella, S.C., Li, L.: Modeling two-player games in the Sigma graphical cognitive architecture. In: Kühnberger, K.-U., Rudolph, S., Wang, P. (eds.) AGI 2013. LNCS (LNAI), vol. 7999, pp. 98–108. Springer, Heidelberg (2013)
14. Rosenbloom, P.S.: From memory to problem solving: Mechanism reuse in a graphical cognitive architecture. In: Schmidhuber, J., Thórisson, K.R., Looks, M. (eds.) AGI 2011. LNCS (LNAI), vol. 6830, pp. 143–152. Springer, Heidelberg (2011)
15. Rosenbloom, P.S.: Deconstructing reinforcement learning in Sigma. In: Bach, J., Goertzel, B., Iklé, M. (eds.) AGI 2012. LNCS (LNAI), vol. 7716, pp. 262–271. Springer, Heidelberg (2012)
16. Rosenbloom, P.S.: Extending mental imagery in Sigma. In: Bach, J., Goertzel, B., Iklé, M. (eds.) AGI 2012. LNCS (LNAI), vol. 7716, pp. 272–281. Springer, Heidelberg (2012)
17. Rosenbloom, P.S., Demski, A., Han, T., Ustun, V.: Learning via gradient descent in Sigma. In: ICCM (2013)
18. Russell, S., Binder, J., Koller, D., Kanazawa, K.: Local learning in probabilistic networks with hidden variables. In: IJCAI, pp. 1146–1152 (1995)
19. Sutton, R.S., Barto, A.G.: Reinforcement Learning: An Introduction. MIT Press (1998)
20. Watkins, C.J., Dayan, P.: Q-learning. Machine Learning 8(3-4), 279–292 (1992)
21. Whiten, A. (ed.): Natural Theories of Mind. Basil Blackwell, Oxford (1991)

ARS: An AGI Agent Architecture

Samer Schaat, Alexander Wendt, Matthias Jakubec, Friedrich Gelbard, Lukas Herret,
and Dietmar Dietrich

Institute of Computer Technology, Vienna University of Technology, A-1040 Vienna
{schaat,wendt,jakubec,gelbard,herret,dietrich}@ict.tuwien.ac.at

Abstract. The computational paradigm in Cognitive Science, which the AGI approach revives, provides a powerful methodology of examining human information processing by testing assumptions in computer simulations, and enables technical applications with human-like capabilities. Nevertheless, intensive interdisciplinary collaboration and the development of a holistic and integrated model remain ongoing challenges. This includes the consideration of the basis of rational cognition, in particular the significance of unconscious and affective processes in the human mind. We take these issues into consideration and integrate them into a holistic and integrated functional model of the human mind, implemented as an agent's decision unit and evaluated in an Artificial Life simulation using an interdisciplinary methodology.

Keywords: Artificial General Intelligence · Cognitive Architectures · Computational Simulation · Artificial Recognition System · Artificial Agents.

1   Introduction

AGI (Artificial General Intelligence) "as the science of the mind as a computational system" [1], has revived the original endeavour of Cognitive Science and Artificial Intelligence to find a unified description of cognition instead of solving specific problems as in current conventional AI. Examining cognition using a synthetic approach is a powerful way to understand the human mind and enables us to test our ideas of how the mind works by running them as a computer simulation. Furthermore, we can use this knowledge to develop technical systems with human-like capabilities; for in an engineering sense, building a system and understanding it go hand in hand.

Nevertheless, two key aspects are often neglected in AGI models: (1) serious and regular interdisciplinary cooperation between the different disciplines concerned with studying the mind, and (2) taking into account the relevance of processing principles of the unconscious, especially affective processes.

Regarding the first aspect, in an interdisciplinary collaboration, computer science provides powerful techniques for developing and testing a deterministic model of the human mind by using approaches from information theory such as computer simulations, layered models, separation and modelling of data and functions, top-down design processes, and requirements engineering; at the same time neurobiology and psychology provide insights into the mind. Such a collaboration requires an

B. Goertzel et al. (Eds.): AGI 2014, LNAI 8598, pp. 155–164, 2014.

interdisciplinary methodology. With regard to the second aspect, traditional cognitive architectures focus on modelling rational thinking. Such approaches often underestimate the significance of the unconscious, whose key role is emphasized by many disciplines (e.g. [2, 3]). Hence, a holistic model of human decision making must consider the unconscious foundations of rational cognition and integrate them with models of rational thinking into a unitary model.

2   Related Work

The ARS (Artificial Recognition System) presented in this paper possesses attributes to be classified as following a cognitivist approach.

ACT-R (Adaptive Control of Thought-Rational) models an integrated theory of the human mind and consists of several encapsulated modules. Their functionalities are mapped to the cortical regions in the brain [6]. ACT-R is based on the multi-store model theory [7] and therefore implements different memory systems and operations for each module.

SOAR (State, Operator Apply Result) is a realization of the two hypotheses of classical artificial intelligence by Newell and Simon [8, 4, 5]: "The physical symbol system hypothesis" and the "heuristic search hypothesis". They state that such a system "...has the necessary and sufficient means for general intelligent action" and that a solution will be found "by generating and progressively modifying symbol structures..." [8]. In contrast to ARS, SOAR is not based on human ways of thinking [9]. A difference to ACT-R is that the production rules in SOAR are relative simple, i.e. they only execute one change of the working memory. They are fired in parallel, while in ACT-R productions may be extensive as one rule can alter many buffers [10].

Differing from the previously described architectures, BDI (Belief, Desire, Intention) architecture as described in [12] is not a problem solving system based on a heuristic search. It is based on a theory of practical reasoning, which is a planning theory of intention according to [11]. Its foundations are the three mentalistic attributes belief, desire and intention, which define the state of the agent. Beliefs describe the agent's view of the world. Desires represent the long-term goals. They are activated by certain beliefs. Intentions are high-level plans which may be executed in order to satisfy a desire. Desires are activated depending on the activated beliefs. BDI does not use a heuristic search like SOAR and ACT-R to find a solution, but rather applies a case-based approach [13].

LIDA (Learning Intelligent Distribution Agent) is based on a combination of recent theories of the mind which are merged into a single cognitive architecture. Among them is Global Workspace Theory, which is a connectionist theory and the most widely accepted psychological and neurobiological theory of the role of consciousness in cognition [14, 16]. It is also a realization of the H-CogAff architecture [15]. Due to the connectionist approach of Global Workspace Theory, the sensors demand embodiment for the agent [16], a factor not required for the previously described architectures. LIDA uses concepts like emotions and feelings for the evaluation of situations. In contrast to the other architectures, it also defines a preconscious and a conscious part of the system, where data is pre-processed, and through an attention mechanism a subset of the data is consciously broadcast to activate possible options for action [17].

3   ARS Approach and Model Overview

When work began on ARS the original idea was to design an intelligent system capable of recognizing and understanding real-world situations, e.g. potentially dangerous situations such as easily accessible knives threatening children in the kitchen or similar scenarios [18]. Soon it became clear that human beings can perform this type of recognition tasks because they possess something we call "feeling"[1], a feeling for the situation they observe, a feeling for the use that may be made of available objects, a feeling for how they should assess the characters and moods of others; and it became obvious that it would be anything but simple to create an artificial system with this kind of ability. What was required was nothing less than to design a model of what is called the human psyche, the psychic or mental apparatus [19], and thus design an AGI architecture. We understand the psychic apparatus as the control unit of the human organism. It is built from the nervous system with its main part – the brain –, but to understand its workings it must be described on a higher abstraction level than just the function of the neurons. If we as technicians want to build a model of the psyche at this level, we cannot determine the corresponding functions by ourselves. We need a consistent holistic functional psychic theory, and the only truly adequate theory we have been able to find is psychoanalytic metapsychology. So the ARS projects aims at concretizing metapsychology into a technical model of the human mind [18].

Fig. 1 shows the ARS model at the track level. Each track is built from several function modules. The psyche of different individuals never differs in regard to these functions, respectively their algorithms, but only in regard to data such as personal parameters or memory contents. The ARS model identifies four different input tracks: environment perception and body perception which together form the perception track, and self-preservation drives and sexual drives which flow into the drive track. This input signals the current needs of the organism. It is cathected[2] with certain psychic intensity, i.e. it is prioritized with a measure of its present importance, and may be associated with memory traces of the means to meet the respective needs. These associations again are of different psychic intensity, and an adequate reaction could be selected based exclusively on them. So far, this functionality corresponds to what psychoanalysis terms the Id, which is rather animalistic. But the humanoid agent is a social creature. Growing up, it encounters a number of rules describing desirable behaviour as a member of the group, psychoanalytically known as the Super-ego. In the defence track, conflicts between the needs of the Id and the commandments of the Super-ego are decided by functions of the third major functional block: the Ego. All this work by the psyche is entirely based on the so-called pleasure principle, and remains unconscious to people; psychoanalysis calls it the primary process. But

---

[1] Here "Feeling" is used as an everyday English word. Later in the project we defined it based on Damasio's theory (see chapter 4).

[2] Cathexis describes the attribution of quota of affect to psychic content. As a result this content is valuated.

evolution has equipped humans with an additional mechanism to control the unconscious output through rationally based decision making.

In the transformation track the contents resulting from the primary process are connected with word-presentations. So they become preconscious.

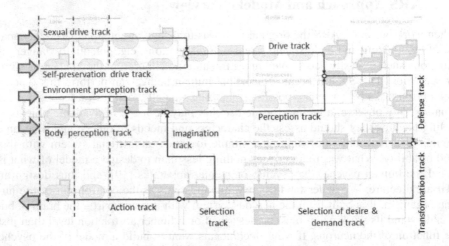

Fig. 1. ARS Model at the track level

In case of hypercathexis (with extra psychic intensity) they become conscious. The so-called secondary process includes the ability to deal with order, time, sequence and language-based models of the world as well as logical reasoning. It enables the agent to withdraw the purely pleasure-driven actions and follow the reality principle instead. It gives the agent the feeling of free will, of agency, the possibility not to act [19]. In the selection of desire & demand track, decisions are made as to which demands should be checked for possible satisfaction. The selection track finally decides which action plan to fulfil, and instructs the action track to realize it. Imagined results are fed back to the primary process by the imagination track and thus become perceived fantasy.

4   Motivations and Valuations

A fundamental question in AGI agents concerns the source for the agent's agenda and how the agent may cope with the external world while pursuing this agenda. Using the drive concept of Freud as a framework and concretizing it by Damasio's model [3] of emotions, we use a generative multi-level model of motivations and valuations to tackle these questions. Based on bodily needs, valuations generate and prioritize motivations (drive representations) which are transformed into goals. These valuations occur incrementally following different principles and influences.

As shown in Fig. 2, organic tension values from the agent's body are represented as psychic intensity in the psychic layer. In the process of generating drive representations, psychic intensity is represented as a quota of affect and used to valuate memorized objects and actions according to the pleasure principle, which valuates that content as the best which brought the most satisfaction in the past. This valuation may however be changed by defence mechanisms (see chapter 6). The next valuation step uses neutralized intensity, which is a personality-specific part of the drives' quota of affect, to extend the valuation of memorized content according to the reality principle, i.e. the consideration of affordance in the environment (see chapter 7).

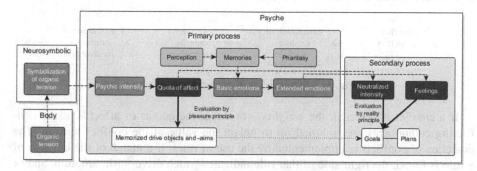

Fig. 2. An incremental multi-level model of valuations

In general, logic and time issues are considered in this valuation step, which transforms valuated drive representations to prioritized goals. The valuation of goals can be extended by feelings as conscious representations of emotions, which are generated based on all quotas of affect, and memorized emotions that are activated by perception and phantasy.

5   Perception

Perception is modelled as a means for the fulfilment of the agent's motivations. In this regard perception supports matching valuated memories with objects in the external environment. This results in constructing images which include all sensual modalities, and provides the information on how to fulfil the agent's motivations in the external world. Hence the recognition of objects is based on the agent's experience and expectations, which are generated from drives. This complies with the integration of bottom-up and top-down approaches into a holistic model of perceptual categorization, which is represented by using an activation-based exemplar model with multiple activation sources (i.e. external stimuli and expectations triggered by drives).

6   Conflict and Defence Mechanisms

One of the challenges in AGI systems are conflicts in decision making. In the ARS project, conflicts arise in the following cases: differences between drive wishes of the agent, the possible fulfilment of those drive wishes in the simulation environment, emotions, and social rules of the software agent. We implement psychoanalytic defence mechanisms to resolve these conflicts and therefore to filter and/or alter input data of the software agent. The defence mechanisms under consideration are repression, denial, reaction formation, reversal of affect, displacement, idealization, and depreciation [20]. Fig. 3 sketches the functionalities of the defence mechanisms. First we must investigate how conflicts in AGI systems can be detected and assessed. For this purpose we implement two modules which represent the Super-ego. The Super-ego modules compare drive wishes of the agent, emotions of the agent, perception, and social rules for conflicts.

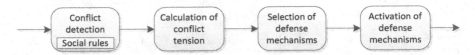

Fig. 3. Functionalities of defence mechanisms

If a conflict is detected, the weights – or rather the quotas of affect – of the conflicting components are summed up to obtain the value of the conflict tension. The detection of conflicts is implemented by the use of rules: if a match of the left side of a rule is found, the right side of that rule indicates which drive wish, emotion, and/or perception is to be defended.

Once a conflict has been detected and its conflict tension calculated, the agent must decide which defence mechanisms to select and activate. Hence the defence mechanisms are sorted, from primitive to high-level defence mechanisms. The basic factor for selecting a defence mechanism is the ego strength, which is represented by the sum of available neutralized intensity. According to the current ego strength a defence mechanism is selected and activated.

7   Decision Making and Planning

Decision making in ARS is a deliberative, two-stage selection process. In contrast to the unconscious and rather more reactive parts of the system, the processing of a goal requires several model cycles. The decision making and planning process is illustrated in Fig. 4. The first step is to extract goals in 1a), 1b), and 1c); a goal is a container which consists of the goal type, a goal object, plans, importance, and status flags. In 1c), motivations for what the agent shall achieve are extracted from drives. A drive, which originates from the homeostatic needs of the body, is converted to a goal called the aim of the drive. Such a drive may be e.g. to satisfy the need to eat. For decision making, the current state of the feelings is also used in the evaluation of situations in 1b). All options or possible goals available for the selection are extracted from two sources in 1a): either directly from the perception or from the activated memories. A possible goal, which is extracted from a certain drive representation, tells the agent that the perceived object would satisfy the need to eat if selected. The activated memories have the structure of sequences of events and are assembled from independent, activated events as images in the unconscious part of the system. These memories are the beliefs of the system, as they are sequences of actions and consequences in different situations. For instance, such a sequence might inform the agent of a dangerous situation and potential consequences by creating a possible goal from a bad feeling which is associated with that sequence. In 2a), all incoming goals receive initial status flags as a result of a basic evaluation of the effort and whether they are reachable for the agent or not. The status flags of the goals are also used for teleo-reactive planning [21]. 2b) will be explained later as it applies only to the subsequent model cycle in the multi-cycle decision process.

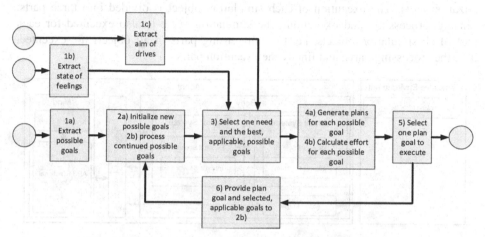

Fig. 4. Process model of decision making and planning in ARS

In 3), the first stage of decision making is completed: all possible goals are evaluated based on their likelihood of fulfilling the incoming aims of drives under consideration of feelings. As a result, one or more possible goals are selected which have the ability to satisfy the strongest aims of drives. For those possible goals which are relevant to fulfilling the most urgent needs, or which demand a reaction to a situation, plans are generated in 4a) and the effort of executing those plans is estimated in 4b). Finally in 5), the goal with the highest importance, i.e. the best possibility of satisfying a need with the lowest effort or the avoidance of harm to the body, is selected in the second stage of decision making. It is called the plan goal. All goals from the first stage of decision making are then stored in short-term memory.

The action plans attached to the plan goal are either external or internal actions. In the case of an external action, the action command is sent to the body for execution. In the case of an internal action, an internal action command is executed within the model in the next cycle. For each executed external action, several internal actions are usually executed first, e.g. to focus on an object before starting to move towards it.

In the next model cycle, the stored possible goals – include the plan goal in the short-term memory – are continued in step 6) of Fig. 4 as they are compared and merged with newly extracted possible goals. In 2b), enhanced analysis of continued goals is performed, triggered by internal actions. As a result, new status flags are defined and associated with the possible goal. These status flags influence the evaluation of the possible goal. Then in 3), all possible goals are evaluated again. As each goal is handled independently, the agent is able to continually consider new goals and situations and to pause the pursuit of the current plan goal.

8   Simulation Architecture

The implementation of ARS runs within an artificial life simulation, which is based on the multi-agent simulation framework MASON. However, because of the generic interface of the ARS architecture, it is also possible to use it in other applications. The MASON framework provides a scheduler, a physics engine, a control panel and visualization tools. The execution of each simulation object is divided into three parts: sensing, processing, and execution. The simulation cycle is also executed for each part of all simulation objects, i.e. first all sensing parts of all objects are executed, then the processing parts, and finally the execution parts.

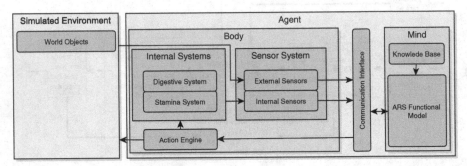

Fig. 5. ARS implementation architecture

As seen in Fig. 5, the agents are composed of a body and a mind, i.e. the ARS cognitive architecture. The body, connected with the ARS architecture, consists of internal systems like a digestive system (energy balance), body internal sensors like blood sugar, external sensors like vision, and an action engine which executes action commands from the mind. The mind contains the implementation of ARS, together with the knowledge base which is based on Protégé Frames.

9   Evaluation

As introductory mentioned, the development of an interdisciplinary methodology is a key challenge when developing and evaluating AGI agents. We use a case-driven methodology that guides interdisciplinary cooperation. This means that psychoanalysts and neuroscientists use their experience of real-world conditions to write an exemplary case describing a situation (e.g. a hungry agent). This case is structured in a simulation case which allows analysis of the required functions and data for the simulation model. An overview of such a simulation case is provided in Fig. 6. To evaluate the model, agent-based simulation is harnessed, which enables testing of our assumptions and the plausibility of the model. In particular, we validate whether the agents behave as expected (i.e. as described in the simulation cases). This includes observing whether changing the data results in the expected behaviour (as described in the simulation case). Since in this overview article no room for simulation results exist, see e.g. [22] for details.

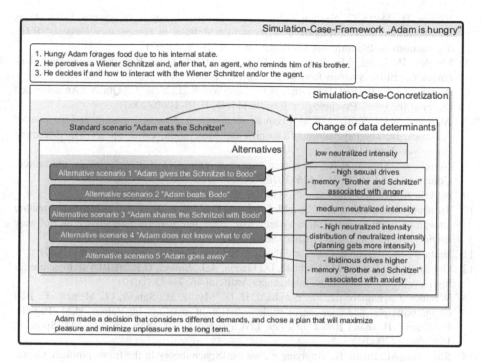

Fig. 6. Simulation case for the description of the behaviour of two agents, Adam and Bodo

10   Conclusion

We have shown how processes that follow the principles of the unconscious can be integrated with rational aspects of decision making to approach how a decision unit for an AGI agent that mimics human information processing may be developed. In particular, we consider affective processes for the valuation of data – in keeping with basic principles of rational cognition – and defense mechanisms for handling conflicting trains of thought within the agent. We integrate these functions with perception, rational decision making and planning, and evaluate the holistic model in an Artificial Life simulation using an interdisciplinary methodology. With regard to future work, probably the most notable shortcoming of the current model is the agent's limited ability to learn.

References

1. Bach, J.: A motivational system for cognitive AI. In: Schmidhuber, J., Thórisson, K.R., Looks, M. (eds.) AGI 2011. LNCS, vol. 6830, pp. 232–242. Springer, Heidelberg (2011)
2. Bargh, J.A., Chartrand, T.L.: The unbearable automaticity of being. American Psychologist 54(7), 462–479 (1999)
3. Damasio, A.: Looking for Spinoza: Joy, Sorrow, and the Feeling Brain. Harvest Books, Washington (2003)

4. Vernon, D., Metta, G., Sandini, G.: A survey of artificial cognitive systems: Implications for the autonomous development of mental capabilities in computational agents. IEEE Transactions on Evolutionary Computation 11, 151–180 (2007)

5. Langley, P., Laird, J.E., Rogers, S.: Cognitive architectures: Research issues and challenges. Cognitive Systems Research 10(2), 141–160 (2009)

6. Anderson, J.R., Bothell, D., Byrne, M.D., Douglass, S., Lebiere, C., Qin, Y.: An integrated theory of the mind. Psychological Review 111(4), 1036–1060 (2004)

7. Atkinson, R.C., Shiffrin, R.M.: Human memory: A proposed system and its control processes. In: The Psychology of Learning and Motivation, vol. 2, pp. 89–195. Academic Press, New York (1968)

8. Newell, A., Simon, H.A.: Computer science as empirical inquiry: symbols and search. Commun. ACM 19(3), 113–126 (1976)

9. Newell, A.: Unified Theories of Cognition. Harvard Univ. Press (1994)

10. Turnbull, D.G., Chewar, C.M., McCrickard, D.S.: Are cognitive architectures mature enough to evaluate notification systems? In: 2003 International Conference on Software Engineering Research and Practice (SERP 2003), Las Vegas NV (2003)

11. Bratman, M.: Intention, Plans, and Practical Reason. Harvard University Press (1987)

12. Gottifredi, S., Tucaty, M., Corbatta, D., Garcia, A.J., Simari, G.R.: A BDI architecture for high level robot deliberation. Inteligencia Artificial 46, 74–83 (2010)

13. Wendler, J., Hannebauer, M., Burkhard, H.-D., Myritz, H., Sander, G., Meinert, T.: BDI design principles and cooperative implementation in roboCup. In: Veloso, M.M., Pagello, E., Kitano, H. (eds.) RoboCup 1999. LNCS (LNAI), vol. 1856, pp. 531–541. Springer, Heidelberg (2000)

14. Shanahan, M., Baars, B.: Applying global workspace theory to the frame problem. Cognition 98(2), 157–176 (2005)

15. Sloman, A., Chrisley, R.: More things than are dreamt of in your biology: Information-processing in biologically inspired robots. Cognitive Systems Reasearch 6(2), 145–174 (2005)

16. Faghihi, U., Franklin, S.: The lida model as a foundational architecture for agi. In: Theoretical Foundations of Artificial General Intelligence, pp. 103–121. Springer (2012)

17. Franklin, S., Ramamurthy, U.: Motivations, values and emotions: 3 sides of the same coin. In: Proceedings of the Sixth International Workshop on Epigenetic Robotics, Paris, France, vol. (128), pp. 41–48. Lund University Cognitive Studies (September 2006)

18. Solms, M.: What is the 'Mind'? A Neuro-Psychoanalytical Approach. In: Dietrich, D., Fodor, G., Zucker, G., Bruckner, D. (eds.) Simulating the Mind, pp. 115–122. Springer, Vienna (2009)

19. Dietrich, D., Fodor, G., Zucker, G., Bruckner, D.: Simulating the Mind A Technical Neuropsychoanalytical Approach. In: Proceedings of the 1st ENF - Emulating the Mind, 2007 Conference, Vienna (2009)

20. Eagle, M.N.: From Classical to Contemporary Psychoanalysis, A Critique and Integration. Routledge, Taylor and Francis Group, LLC (2011)

21. Nilsson, N.: Teleo-reactive programs for agent control. arXiv preprint cs/9401101 (1994)

22. Schaat, S., Doblhammer, K., Wendt, A., Gelbard, F., Herret, L., Bruckner, D.: A Psychoanalytically-Inspired Motivational and Emotional System for Autonomous Agents. In: Proceedings of the 39th Annual Conference of the IEEE Industrial Electronics Society, pp. 6648–6653 (2013)

Quantum Mechanical Foundations of Causal Entropic Forces

Swapnil Shah

North Carolina State University, USA
snshah4@ncsu.edu

Abstract. The theory of Causal Entropic Forces was introduced to explain the emergence of intelligence as a phenomenon in physical systems. Although the theory provides illustrations of how behavior shaped by causal entropic forces resembles human cognitive niche in specific simple settings, the theory leaves open some important questions. First, the definition of causal entropic forces, in terms of actions that maximize the statistical diversity of future paths a system can take, makes no connection with concepts of knowledge and rationality traditionally associated with intelligence. Second, the theory does not explain the origins of such path based forces in classical thermodynamic ensembles. This paper addresses both these issues using the principles of open system quantum mechanics, quantum statistics and the Hamiltonian theory of Dynamic Economics. The construction finally arrived at is much more general than the notion of entropic forces and shows how maximizing future path diversity is closely related to maximizing a particular utility function over a sequence of interactions till the system attains thermodynamic equilibrium.

Keywords: Entropic Forces, Statistical Diversity, Open Quantum Systems, Utility Maximization.

One of the fundamental problems in Artificial Intelligence existing right from the inception of the field is the lack of a precise formulation. The most widely studied AI architectures involve logical agents, goal based agents and utility maximizing agents. The latter approach, also termed as the economic approach to rationality, proposes that intelligence can be referred to as the agent's ability to maximize a utility or value function over the sequence of states it will see in its lifetime, given transition probabilities for combinations of states and actions. In this approach the agent receives a reward for each state it sees, based on a reward function over the sample space of states, and its job is to maximize the predicted future sum of these rewards or the utility of its action. The problem here lies in getting a consensus on the global preference order on the utilities of actions in a particular state, which has been discussed in great depth in existing literature [2].

The paper on Causal Entropic Forces [1] proposes a first step towards establishing a connection between thermodynamic entropy maximization over a future path and intelligent behavior. It purports the idea that general causal entropic forces can result in spontaneous emergence of intelligent behavior in simple physical systems without the need for explicitly specifying goals or utilities. However, there are two potential

B. Goertzel et al. (Eds.): AGI 2014, LNAI 8598, pp. 165–173, 2014.

problems with this paper – a) It hypothesizes a force, dependent on the statistical diversity of future paths up to a finite time horizon, as against those based on instantaneous entropy production which are widely studied in statistical thermodynamics. The conditions under which such forces might exist have not been established. b) Although it does illustrate, with examples, emergence of 'human-like' behavior in the narrow sense of tool use and walking abilities, it is far from establishing a clear relation between the traditional notion of intelligence and existence of forces that maximize path diversity. This paper attempts to resolve both the above mentioned issues in the context of open quantum systems and the Hamiltonian theory of dynamic economics [6]. The next section provides a very brief introduction to Quantum Mechanics for the non physicists.

1   Background

1.1   Quantum Mechanics

In non-relativistic QM, all matter in the universe is expressed in the form of a wavefunction which associates nonzero probability amplitude to every coordinate in the combined configuration space of all particles (as against the conventional Euclidean space, in the configuration space every point corresponds to the degrees of freedom of all particles). The time evolution of this universal wavefunction ψ is determined by the Schrodinger wave equation:

$$\imath\hbar\frac{\partial\psi}{\partial t} = H\psi \tag{1}$$

where H is the quantum Hamiltonian. It is a linear operator with eigenvalues as possible values of energy of the system.

1.2   Density Matrix Formalism and the Canonical Ensemble

If the values of all commuting observables are not known, we have more than one wave-function describing the system. Under this condition, the system state is represented by a density matrix which describes a statistical ensemble of wavefunctions:

$$\rho = \sum_k p_k |\psi_k\rangle \langle\psi_k| \tag{2}$$

The density operator is positive definite so it can always be diagonalized in an eigenbasis. The time evolution of the density matrix is then given by the von-Liouville equation which is the quantum counterpart of the classical Liouville equation in statistical mechanics:

$$\imath\hbar\frac{\partial\rho}{\partial t} = [H, \rho] \tag{3}$$

If the universe is separated into a system and an environment which are in thermal equilibrium (only able to exchange energy), the density matrix is given by the celebrated Gibbs state:

$$\frac{e^{-\beta H}}{\text{Tr}(e^{-\beta H})} \tag{4}$$

Here β is the inverse temperature of the reservoir and H is the system Hamiltonian.

2   Causal Entropic Forces

The paper [1] proposes a first step towards establishing a connection between path entropy maximization and intelligent behavior. It purports the idea that general causal entropic forces can result in spontaneous emergence of intelligent behavior in simple physical systems without the need for explicitly specifying goals or utilities. It suggests a potentially general thermodynamic model of adaptive behavior as a non-equilibrium process in open systems. A nonequilibrium physical system's bias towards maximum instantaneous entropy production is reflected by its evolution toward higher-entropy macroscopic states, a process characterized by the formalism of entropic forces. The instantaneous entropic force on a canonical ensemble associated with a macrostate partition is given by:

$$F = T\nabla_X S(X) \tag{5}$$

where T is the reservoir temperature and $S(X)$ is the entropy associated with a macrostate X and X_0 is the present macrostate. In order to uniformly maximize entropy production between present and a future time horizon, the author proposes generalized causal entropic forces over paths through the configuration space rather than over the instantaneous configuration (or the ensemble). He then defines the causal path entropy of a macrostate X with the current system state x(0) as:

$$S_C(X, \tau) = -k_B \int \text{Pr}(x(t)|x(0)) \ln \text{Pr}(x(t)|x(0)) \, dx(t) \tag{6}$$

where Pr(x(t)|x(0)) denotes the conditional probability of the system evolving through the path x(t) assuming the initial system state x(0), integrating over all possible paths taken by the open systems' environment during the same interval. A path-based causal entropic force F corresponding to (6), can be expressed as:

$$F(X_0, \tau) = T_C \nabla_X S_C(X, \tau)|X_0 \tag{7}$$

where T_C is a causal path temperature that parametrizes the system's bias toward macrostates that maximize causal entropy. The remaining part of the causal path force derivation takes in to account specific assumptions about the environment being a heat bath at temperature T_r and the environment being coupled to only a few forced degrees of freedom. The environment periodically rethermalizes these forced degrees of freedom with a period $\mathcal{E}$. Further, the temporal dynamics of the system are taken to be Markovian in nature giving the path probability as:

$$\text{Pr}(x(t)|x(0)) = \left(\prod_{n=1}^{N-1} \text{Pr}(x(t_{n+1})|x(t_n))\right) \text{Pr}(x(\epsilon)|x(0)) \tag{8}$$

Making use of all these assumptions, the author finally arrives at the following path dependent force (Specific details not mentioned here. The reader is referred to [1] for the detailed derivation):

$$F_j(X_0, \tau) = -\frac{2T_C}{T_R} \int f_j(0) \cdot \Pr(x(t)|x(0)) \ln \Pr(x(t)|x(0)) dx(t) \qquad (9)$$

The effect of the above force can be seen as driving the forced degrees of freedom with a temperature dependent strength in an average of short term directions $f_j(0)$, weighted by the diversity of long term paths $[-\Pr(x(t)|x(0)) \ln \Pr(x(t)|x(0))]$, that they make reachable, where the path diversity is measured over all degrees of freedom of the system.

3   Causal Entropic Forces in a Quantum Universe

3.1   Projective or Von-Neumann Interactions

If the time horizon for evaluating the causal entropic force $\tau \to \infty$, equation (6) gets modified to the following, owing to the celebrated asymptotic equi-partition property:

$$F_j(X_0, \tau) \propto \frac{2T_C \cdot [n\bar{H}(X)]}{T_R} \int f_j(0) \cdot \Pr(x(\epsilon)|x(0)) dx(\epsilon), \quad n = \left\lfloor \frac{\tau}{\epsilon} \right\rfloor \qquad (10)$$

where $\bar{H}(X)$ is the entropy rate of the Markov process. This is a valid assumption to make if the Markov chain is ergodic and stationary. Having established this let us move onto the development of the Quantum analogue.

As explained in [5], measurements and actions can be treated as system bath interactions in two mutually non-commuting eigenbases. Under the Born-Markov approximation, the temporal evolution of the reduced system (with bath degrees traced away) is described by the Lindblad Master equation:

$$\frac{\partial \rho_s}{\partial t} = -\frac{i}{\hbar}[H_S + H_{LS}, \rho_s] - \frac{1}{2}\Sigma_k \mu_k (A_k^\dagger A_k \rho_s + \rho_s A_k^\dagger A_k - 2A_k \rho_s A_k^\dagger) \qquad (11)$$

As in the case of Langevin dynamics, the bath thermalizes coupled degrees of freedom of the system in the pointer basis (the Lindbladian basis A_k for projective interactions) after each interaction. We also assume the density matrix to be initially diagonal in the measurement eigenbasis $|x_i\rangle$. The expectation value of the force on the ensemble is given by:

$$\langle F \rangle = \text{Tr}\left(\frac{\partial \rho}{\partial t} \cdot P\right) \qquad (12)$$

Here P is the momentum operator. Now, this ensemble force can be simplified as under:

$$\langle F \rangle = \Sigma_i \rho_i \cdot \langle F_i \rangle \qquad (13)$$

Furthermore, we will assume that the action Lindbladian is PVM (projective valued measure) of the action observable. From equations (12) and (13), using explicit form of the Lindblad generator and common dissipation rates μ for all components forming the ensemble, the non-unitary component of the force (neglecting Hamiltonian dynamics) in a measurement eigenstate $|x_i\rangle$ is given by:

$$\langle F_i \rangle = \frac{1}{2}\mu \Sigma_k (|\langle x_i|y_k \rangle|^2 \langle y_k|P|y_k \rangle - \langle y_k|x_i \rangle\langle x_i|P|y_k \rangle) \qquad (14)$$

Here, $|y_k\rangle$ is an action basis (substituted for the Lindblad operator eigenbasis) and μ is Fourier transform of the time correlation function of corresponding Bath operators [4]. With some algebra, we obtain:

$$\langle F_i \rangle = \frac{1}{2}\mu \sum_k |\langle x_i|y_k\rangle|^2 \left[\langle y_k|P|y_k\rangle - \langle x_i|P|x_i\rangle\right] \tag{15}$$

Notice the resemblance of the above equation with (10). The contribution of each action eigenstate to this force is proportional to statistical diversity (parametrized by the Born probability $|\langle y_k|x_i\rangle|^2$) of all future paths resulting from the action. The above equation explains the origins of such path based causal forces for projective Markovian interactions as the time horizon for evaluation of posterior path probabilities $\tau \to \infty$ in (9).

3.2   Generalized Interactions

In case of projective interactions, the Von Neumann entropy $-k_B \mathrm{Tr}(\rho \ln\rho)$ of the system always increases [5]. So the system does not approach a goal state as against that illustrated in [1]. We turn to generalized action interactions (positive operator valued measures that are generalizations of projective valued measures) in this section which can decrease an open system's entropy at the cost of entropy of the bath, enabling the system to approach a goal state asymptotically as the system attains equilibrium. We will also assume that the average internal energy of the system is initially higher than reservoir temperature. For non equilibrium processes, the total entropy production rate is given by the detailed balance relation (second law for open systems):

$$\sigma = \frac{dS}{dt} + J, \quad \sigma \geq 0 \tag{16}$$

where σ is the total entropy production rate and J is the entropy flux owing to heat exchange between the system and its environment.

3.2.1   Maximizing Path Diversity

In the current context, the diversity of future paths can be termed as the maximum entropy that can be produced from the present to a future time horizon. Given the density operator ρ at the present time, the future path diversity is given by:

$$D = \Gamma + k_B \mathrm{Tr}(\rho \ln\rho) \tag{17}$$

where Γ is the maximum attainable future system entropy. Integrating the entropic balance relation (16) over the time span to reach equilibrium, one gets:

$$\Delta\sigma = \Delta S + \Delta J = \Delta S - \frac{\Delta H}{T} \tag{18}$$

Let the entropy at time $t = 0$ be S_0 and the current absolute entropy be S_t. Then making use of the balance relation in conjunction with the second law, we get:

$$D \leq (\Gamma - S_0) - \frac{\Delta H}{T} \tag{19}$$

Because the average internal energy of the system is assumed to be initially higher than the bath temperature, as the system progresses towards equilibrium heat is dissipated to the bath. So the heat exchange term in the above inequality is negative. Secondly Γ is the maximum attainable future system entropy, so the first term on the right side of the inequality is positive making the quantity on the right side strictly positive and it is the maximum value that can be attained for the future path diversity. As can be inferred, this value is approached when the total entropy production over time $(\Delta\sigma)$ is extremely small.

4   Causal Entropic Forces and Maximizing Expected Utility

4.1   Hamiltonian Theory of Dynamic Economics

Having laid down the foundations of path based forces in Quantum Mechanics for open systems, we now develop the relation between economic utility and path diversity. For the problem of consumption-optimal growth with positive rate of time discount $\alpha > 0$, the equations of motion are [6]:

$$k \in \partial_Q H(Q, k) \tag{20}$$

$$\dot{Q} \in -\partial_k H(Q, k) + \alpha Q \tag{21}$$

where, k is the initial endowment vector and Q is the vector of capital goods prices and H is the system Hamiltonian representing the production technology. The optimal steady state at the equilibrium (Q^*, k^*) is given by:

$$0 \in \partial_Q H(Q^*, k^*) \tag{22}$$

$$0 \in -\partial_k H(Q^*, k^*) + \alpha Q^* \tag{23}$$

From [7], the optimal path to the steady state for a diffusion process is given by the one that maximizes the following discounted expected utility over (possibly) infinite sequence of interventions:

$$\max E\left[\sum_{i=1}^{\infty} U(c_i) e^{-\int_0^{\tau_i} \alpha(s_t) dt}\right] \tag{24}$$

where c_i is the consumption at time step i, S_t is the current value of quantity being consumed and U is the agent's utility from consumption c_i. We can assume the rate of time discount α to be constant for the sake of simplicity. According to [7], if the time discount rate α is given to be quite large, the optimal policy is Markovian in nature and is characterized by a control region, a complementary continuation region and a set of optimal actions that can be taken in control region. For the discrete time Markovian policy, equation (24) reduces to the well known Bellman equation:

$$V(c_i)^* = \max E\left[U(c_i) + V(c_{i+1})^* e^{-\int_{\tau_i}^{\tau_{i+1}} \alpha(s_t) dt}\right] \tag{25}$$

which can be rewritten as:

$$V(c_i)^* = \max \Sigma_{c_i} \left[\Pr(c_i)U(c_i) + \Pr(c_i)V(c_{i+1})^* e^{-\int_{\tau_i}^{\tau_{i+1}} \alpha(S_t)dt} \right] \quad (26)$$

4.2   Economic Utility and Entropy

Using standard form of the Lindblad Dissipator and assuming characteristic dissipation rates μ to be equal for all components, the rate of change of expectation value of $(-\ln\rho)$ in the system energy eigenbasis $|i\rangle$ is given by:

$$-\frac{\partial \langle i|\rho\ln\rho\rangle|i\rangle}{\partial t} = -\mu \left\langle i \left| \Sigma_\omega \Sigma_{\alpha,\beta} \left[A_\beta(\omega)\rho A_\alpha^\dagger(\omega)\ln\rho - \frac{1}{2}\{\rho, A_\alpha^\dagger(\omega)A_\beta(\omega)\}\ln\rho \right] \right| i \right\rangle \quad (27)$$

where $\{*,*\}$ represents the anti-commutator. It is known from the theory of Markovian master equation for open systems that:

$$[H_s, A_\alpha^\dagger(\omega)A_\beta(\omega)] = 0 \quad (28)$$

So, equation (27) can be written as:

$$-\frac{\partial \langle i|\rho\ln\rho|i\rangle}{\partial t} = -\mu \cdot f(t) + \mu K \cdot \langle i|\rho\ln\rho|i\rangle \quad (29)$$

where,

$$K = \Sigma_{\alpha,\beta}\langle i|A_\alpha^\dagger A_\beta|i\rangle \quad (30.a)$$

$$f(t) = \left\langle i \left| \Sigma_\omega \Sigma_{\alpha,\beta} \left[A_\beta(\omega)\rho A_\alpha^\dagger(\omega)\ln\rho - \frac{1}{2}[\rho A_\alpha^\dagger(\omega)A_\beta(\omega), \ln\rho] \right] \right| i \right\rangle \quad (30.b)$$

Equation (29) is a first order linear differential equation with the general solution:

$$-\langle i|\rho\ln(\rho)|i\rangle(t) = [-\mu \int_0^t e^{\mu K t}f(t)dt + S_0]e^{-\mu K t} \quad (31)$$

So, the change in Von Neumann Entropy in an action interaction is given by:

$$-\Delta S = k_B \Sigma_i \left[\gamma + e^{-\mu K \tau_d} \cdot \mu \int_0^{\tau_d} e^{\mu K t}f(t)dt \right] \quad (32)$$

where $\gamma = S_0(1 - e^{-\mu K \tau_d})$ and τ_d is the characteristic decoherence time. Negative of change in entropy is used in (32) owing to the assumption that the system entropy decreases in an action interaction as was mentioned earlier. Notice the resemblance of (32) with the Bellman equation (26). From (18), it can be inferred that this situation is achieved when the total entropy production for an action interaction is extremely small. This is precisely the condition that we arrived at while trying to maximize future path diversity D (17) in the previous section, which suggests that both the problems of maximizing path diversity and maximizing expected utility are duals of each other in the proposed scheme. In terms of thermodynamic utility, this condition translates to the minimum reduction in the amount of Free energy of a system as it attains equilibrium. Free energy of a system corresponds to the maximum useful work that can be extracted from the system. As the system attains equilibrium with the heat bath, the system entropy attains its minimum value leading to emergence of an optimal stationary goal state.

5   Conclusions and Future Scope

Theory of causal entropic forces is based on the idea of maximizing causal path entropy by evaluating path probabilities upto a finite time horizon τ instead of greedily maximizing instantaneous entropy production [1]. However, adhering to classical thermodynamics, one cannot fully explain the origins of such a path based force acting on a macrostate of a statistical ensemble. Using the interaction model proposed in [5], we treat measurements and actions as system environment interactions in two non commuting eigenbases. We establish how such a force might originate in the Quantum mechanical framework for projective interactions. However, projective interactions result in increase in Von Neumann entropy of the system, in which case the system never approaches a singular goal state. So we turn to generalized interactions in order to explain maximization of path diversity when the system entropy decreases on each action interaction at the cost of entropy of the bath using detailed balance relation. We also show how under a suitable choice of utility function, maximizing path diversity and maximizing expected utility are duals of each other.

Future work would include determining the common criterion for optimality for maximizing path diversity and expected utility in the presented scheme in terms of system-environment coupling strength and properties of action operators that lead to non-projective Lindbladians, which in turn allow decrease in system entropy. In [8], the authors describe application of displaced oscillator variational ansatz to Caldeira Leggett model for Brownian particle in a box coupled to an ohmic dissipative environment. They show, with the help of numerical renormalization group techniques, how for a critical system-environment coupling strength, the particle gets localized to the center of the box which is analogous to the illustration of Brownian particle behavior under causal entropic forces [1]. A generalization of analysis in [8] would be necessary to arrive at the precise conditions necessary for emergence of optimal goal states in dissipative systems as predicted by theory of causal entropic forces. Once these conditions are established, it would be possible to explain intelligence as emergent phenomenon in general non-equilibrium thermodynamic systems and processes.

Acknowledgements. I take this opportunity to thank Dr. Jon Doyle, Dept. of Computer Science, NCSU for his extremely valuable suggestions and insight on the subject and his incessant encouragement during the institution of this work.

References

1. Gross, A.D., Freer, C.E.: Causal Entropic Forces. Phys. Rev. Lett. 110(16), 1-168702–5-168702 (2013)
2. Arrow, K.J.: A Difficulty in the Concept of Social Welfare. Journal of Political Economy 58(4), 328–346 (1950)
3. Everett, H.: Theory of the Universal Wavefunction, Thesis. Princeton University, pp. 1–140 (1973)
4. Breur, H.P., Petruccione, F.: The Theory of Open Quantum Systems. Oxford University Press (2002)

5. Shah, S.: A Quantum Approach to AI. In: Proceedings of the 12th WSEAS International Conference on Artificial Intelligence, Knowledge Engineering and Databases, pp. 24–27 (2013)
6. Cass, D., Shell, K.: The Hamiltonian Approach to Dynamic Economics. Academic Press Inc., (1976)
7. Baccarin, S.: Optimal Consumption of a generalized Geometric Brownian Motion with Fixed and Variable Intervention Costs. Dept. of Economics and Statistics, Univ. of Torino, 1–23 (2013)
8. Sabio, J., Borda, L., Guinea, F., Sols, F.: Phase Diagram of the Dissipative Quantum Particle in a Box. Phys. Rev. 78(085439), 1-085439–8-085439 (2008)

A General System for Learning and Reasoning
in Symbolic Domains

Claes Strannegård[1], Abdul Rahim Nizamani[2], and Ulf Persson[3]

[1] Department of Philosophy, Linguistics and Theory of Science, University of Gothenburg,
Sweden and Department of Applied Information Technology,
Chalmers University of Technology, Sweden
claes.strannegard@gu.se
[2] Department of Applied Information Technology, University of Gothenburg, Sweden
abdulrahim.nizamani@gu.se
[3] Department of Mathematical Sciences, Chalmers University of Technology, Sweden
ulfp@chalmers.se

Abstract. We present the system O* that operates in arbitrary symbolic domains,
including arithmetic, logic, and grammar. O* can start from scratch and learn the
general laws of a domain from examples. The main learning mechanism is a formalization of Occam's razor. Learning is facilitated by working within a cognitive
model of bounded rationality. Computational complexity is thereby dramatically
reduced, while preserving human-level performance. As illustration, we describe
the learning process by which O* learns elementary arithmetic. In the beginning,
O* knows nothing about the syntax or laws of arithmetic; by the end, it has constructed a theory enabling it to solve previously unseen problems such as "what
is $67 * 8$?" and "which number comes next in the sequence $8, 11, 14$?".

Keywords: Domain-independent agent, Occam's razor, bounded rationality.

1 Introduction

The goal of artificial general intelligence (AGI) is to build systems with general intelligence at the human level or beyond [1]. Such systems must be able to learn the
mechanics of new domains while adapting to arbitrary performance measures in those
domains. Developmental (epigenetic) robotics, inspired by developmental psychology,
builds agents that develop automatically through interaction with their environment
[2]. Research in the field has so far focused on sensorimotor development and social
interaction, leaving higher cognitive functions, such as symbolic reasoning, largely
unexplored.

A standard textbook in artificial intelligence [3] characterizes an agent as rational if it
always acts so that the expected value of its performance measure is maximized. Herbert
Simon introduced the notion of *bounded rationality* [4] to designate "rational choice
that takes into account the cognitive limitations of the decision maker – limitations of
both knowledge and computational capacity".

Inductive program synthesis – in particular, inductive logic programming [5] – is
program synthesis from examples of input-output pairs [6]. The analytic approach uses

B. Goertzel et al. (Eds.): AGI 2014, LNAI 8598, pp. 174–185, 2014.

examples to construct actual programs, while generate-and-test uses examples for testing purposes only. Analytic techniques include anti-unification and recursive relation learning. The computational complexity of the methods used has proven a major obstacle to the use of inductive program synthesis on a larger scale [6].

Cognitive architectures such as Soar [7], ACT-R [8], CHREST [9], and NARS [10] have been used to model various aspects of human cognition. Such architectures commonly use abstract rewrite systems to model computations as rewrite sequences [11]. They often include explicit models of such cognitive resources as working, sensory, declarative, and procedural memory. These cognitive resources are bounded in various ways: e.g., with respect to capacity, duration, and access time [12]. In particular, working memory, which can typically only hold a small number of items (chunks) is a well-known bottleneck for human problem solving [13]. That said, one can easily obtain models of bounded rationality by placing limits on the available cognitive resources.

According to Piaget's developmental theory, children adapt to new information in one of two ways: by assimilation, in which new information fits into existing knowledge structures; and by accommodation, in which new information causes new knowledge structures to form or old structures to be modified [14].

Occam's razor tells us to prefer short and simple explanations, both in science and everyday life. It can be formalized in several ways, some of which (e.g., Kolmogorov and Solomonoff complexity) are not computable, while others (e.g., Levin complexity) are [15]. A computable version of Kolmogorov complexity can be obtained by combining it with traditional complexity classes from complexity theory. Likewise, although the universal AI model AIXI is not computable in its original form, restricted versions have been proposed that are capable of problem solving in e.g. game domains [16].

In this paper, we present a general system, designed to match the learning and reasoning capabilities of unaided humans in symbolic domains. Section 2 presents the system O*. Sections 3 and 4 shows how O* can be used for learning and reasoning, respectively. For the sake of concreteness, we consider the special case of elementary arithmetic. Section 5 offers some conclusions.

2   Computational Model

In cognitive psychology, computational models should, ideally, perform both (i) at least and (ii) at most at the human level for any given performance measure. For AGI, satisfying (i) is generally sufficient. Indeed, performing *above* the human level is an advantage; not to mention that a unilateral cognitive model satisfying (i) but not (ii) may be easier to construct.

In this paper, we use the following strategy for AGI. Suppose that a human, with bounded cognitive resources, can solve a certain problem. Suppose further that one has a well-designed unilateral cognitive model of this person – one that also has bounded cognitive resources. Then, a solution exists within the model: one that we can find by searching the model. The search strategy can be combined with any heuristic algorithm. By so exploiting the link to human cognition, we hope to mitigate the combinatorial explosion associated with many standard AI algorithms. We now proceed to define our model formally.

Definition 1 (Tag). *A tag is a string of ASCII symbols that does not contain any punctuation symbols: in particular, no commas, colons, parentheses, or spaces.*

Tags will be written in monospaced font. For example, x, 1 and Digit are tags.

Definition 2 (Variable). *A variable is a string of the form $(\sigma:\tau)$, where σ and τ are tags.*

For example, (x:Number) and (x:Sent) are variables.

Definition 3 (Term). *A term is a finite tree whose nodes are labeled with tags or variables. Variables may only appear in the leaf nodes.*

Example 1. Here are two examples of terms (about arithmetic and propositional logic):

For purposes of this paper, terms will be presented not as trees but as strings, to make the notation more compact. We use a standard linearization algorithm that inserts parentheses into the strings to reflect the implied tree structure. We use some conventions – e.g. omitting certain parentheses – to make the notation easier to read. The above terms linearize to (x:Number)*0 and (x:Sent)||True, respectively. To go in the reverse direction, we use a standard parsing algorithm. In this way, one can move freely between representations of terms as trees or strings.

Definition 4 (Axiom). *An axiom is a triple (τ,t,t'), where τ is a tag and t and t' are terms.*

Example 2. Here are some examples of axioms (about arithmetic and propositional logic):

$$(\text{Equal},1+2,3)$$
$$(\text{Equal},(\text{x:Number}) * 0,0)$$
$$(\text{Equi},(\text{x:Sent}) \;||\; \text{True},\text{True})$$
$$(\text{Equi},(\text{x:Sent}) \;\&\&\; (\text{y:Sent}),(\text{y:Sent}) \;\&\&\; (\text{x:Sent})).$$

Definition 5 (Theory). *A theory is a finite set of axioms.*

Definition 6 (Assignment). *An assignment is a partial function from variables to terms.*

For instance, $\alpha = \{((\text{x:Number}),1),((\text{y:Number}),2)\}$ is an assignment. By extension, assignments are defined from terms to terms. Thus, $\alpha((\text{x:Number})+(\text{y:Number})) = 1+2$.

If s is a subtree of t, we write $t(s)$. Moreover, if s' is an arbitrary tree, we write $t(s'/s)$ to denote the result of replacing all occurrences of s in t by s'.

Definition 7 (Rewrite). *Suppose* (τ, t_1, t_2) *is an axiom. Then, we write*

$$\frac{t(t')}{t(t''/t')} \ (\tau, t_1, t_2)$$

if there is an assignment α *such that* $\alpha(t_1) = t'$ *and* $\alpha(t_2) = t''$. *The conclusion* $t(t'')$ *follows from the premise* $t(t')$ *by* Rewrite.

Example 3. Here is an example application of Rewrite (with α as above):

$$\frac{1+2}{2+1} \ (\text{Equal}, (\text{x:Number}) + (\text{y:Number}), (\text{y:Number}) + (\text{x:Number}))$$

Definition 8 (Computation). *A computation is a sequence of terms* $(t_0, \ldots, t_n)$ *such that for all* $i < n$, t_{i+1} *follows from* t_i *by application of Rewrite.*

We write computations vertically, from top to bottom, with the relevant axioms shown at the transitions.

Example 4. Here is an example of a computation in the domain of arithmetic:

$$\frac{\dfrac{(1+2)*3}{3*3} \ (\text{Equal}, 1+2, 3)}{9} \ (\text{Equal}, 3*3, 9)$$

Example 5. Below is an example of a computation in the domain of propositional logic. Here x, y, and z, are abbreviations of (x:Sent), (y:Sent), and (z:Sent), respectively. Intuitively, the computation is a proof of the tautology $(p \to q) \lor p$. This is because all of the axioms used in the computation preserve logical equivalence.

$$\cfrac{\cfrac{\cfrac{\cfrac{\cfrac{(\text{p -> q}) \ || \ \text{p}}{((\text{not p}) \ || \ \text{q}) \ || \ \text{p}} \ (\text{Equi}, \text{x => y}, (\text{not x}) \ || \ \text{y})}{(\text{q} \ || \ (\text{not p})) \ || \ \text{p}} \ (\text{Equi}, \text{x} \ || \ \text{y}, \text{y} \ || \ \text{x})}{\text{q} \ || \ ((\text{not p}) \ || \ \text{p})} \ (\text{Equi}, (\text{x} \ || \ \text{y}) \ || \ \text{z}, \text{x} \ || \ (\text{y} \ || \ \text{z}))}{\text{q} \ || \ \text{True}} \ (\text{Equi}, (\text{not x}) \ || \ \text{x}, \text{True})}{\text{True}} \ (\text{Equi}, \text{x} \ || \ \text{True}, \text{True})$$

Definition 9 (Agent). *An agent is a tuple* (T, C, W, L, D), *where*

- *T is a theory (representing beliefs in declarative memory);*
- *C is a set of terms (representing concepts in declarative memory);*
- *W is a natural number (representing working memory capacity);*
- *L is a natural number (representing assimilation capacity); and*
- *D is a natural number (representing accommodation capacity).*

Definition 10 (Term size). *Given a term* t, $s(t)$ *is the number of nodes of* t.

The measure $s(t)$ is a simple model of the load of t on working memory. We also define $s(ax) = s(t) + s(t')$ for axioms $ax = (\tau, t, t')$ and $s(T) = \Sigma\{s(ax) : ax \in T\}$ for theories T.

Definition 11 (Agent computation). *Let* $A = (T,C,W,L,D)$ *be an agent. An* A-*computation is a sequence of terms* $(t_0, \ldots, t_n)$ *with restrictions on*

- *terms:* $t_i \in C$, *for all* $i < n$;
- *transitions:* t_{i+1} *is obtained from* t_i *using Rewrite and an axiom from* T, *for all* $i < n$;
- *width:* $s(t_i) \le W$, *for all* $i \le n$; *and*
- *length:* $n \le L$.

The definition aims to capture those computations within reach of an unaided human with belief set T, concept set C, working memory capacity W, assimilation capacity L, and accommodation capacity D (*cf.* Definition 19).

Observation 1. *For any agent* A, *the set of* A-*computations is finite.*

This holds for combinatorial reasons, since all resources of A are bounded. Any A-computation can be obtained by inserting terms belonging to a finite set C into a frame of finite length L and width W.

Definition 12 (Induction problem). *An* induction problem *(IP) is a finite set of items, where an* item *is a tuple* (τ,t,t',u) *such that* τ *is a tag,* t *and* t' *are variable-free terms, and* u *is an integer (utility).*

Definition 13 (Item computation). *The agent* A computes the item (τ,t,t',u) *if there is an* A-*computation* c *from* t *to* t' *that uses only axioms with the tag* τ *and has the property that, for every assignment* $\alpha((\sigma : \tau'')) = t''$ *occurring in* c, *there is a (type-checking)* A-*computation from* t'' *to* τ'' *that uses only axioms with the tag* Type.

Example 6. Suppose that the following are A-computations –the right one being a type-checking computation. Then A computes the item (Equal,2+0,2,1).

$$\frac{2+0}{2} \ (\text{Equal}, (\text{x:Digit})+0, (\text{x:Digit})) \qquad\qquad \frac{2}{\text{Digit}} \ (\text{Type}, 2, \text{Digit})$$

Definition 14 (Performance). *The* performance *of agent* A *on induction problem* I *is the number*

$$\Sigma\{u : (\tau,t,t',u) \in I \text{ and } A \text{ computes } (\tau,t,t',u)\}.$$

The convention that $\Sigma\emptyset = 0$ *ensures that the performance is always defined.*

Observation 2. *The performance measure is computable.*

Next, let us introduce the four operators to be used for constructing theories.

Definition 15 (Crossover). *The term* t'' *is obtained from the terms* t *and* t' *by* crossover *if* t'' *can be obtained from* t *by replacing a subtree of* t *by a subtree of* t'.

For example, $1 + (3 * 4)$ is a crossover of $1 + 2$ and $3 * 4$.

Definition 16 (Abstraction). *The axiom* (τ,t,w) *is obtained from the item* (τ,t',w',u) *by* abstraction *if* $\alpha(t) = t'$ *and* $\alpha(w) = w'$, *for some assignment* α.

Example 7. (Equal,(x:Aterm)+(y:Aterm),(y:Aterm)+(x:Aterm)) is obtained from the item (Equal,1+2,2+1,1) by abstraction.

Definition 17 (Recursion). *The axiom ax is obtained from the item* $(\tau, f(t), t', u)$ *by* recursion *if* $ax = (\tau, f(w), w')$, *where* w' *contains* $f(w'')$, *and* w *and* w'' *contain the same variable.* w *and* w' *are formed by* crossover.

Example 8. The axiom (Equal,f((x:Aterm)+1),f((x:Aterm))*2) is obtained from the item (Equal,f(0),1,1) by recursion.

Definition 18 (Memorization). *The axiom ax is obtained by* memorization *from the item* (τ, t, t', u), *where* $u > 0$, *if* $ax = (\tau, t, t')$.

Example 9. The axiom (Equal,1+2,3) is obtained from the item (Equal,1+2,3,1) by memorization.

Definition 19 (Occam function). *The* Occam function *takes agent* $A_n = (T_n, C_n, W, L, D)$ *and IP* I_n *as input and outputs agent* $A_{n+1} = (T_{n+1}, C_{n+1}, W, L, D)$, *as specified below.*

Let $C_{n+1} = C_n \cup \Gamma$, where Γ is obtained from I_n by taking subtrees of terms that appear in items of I_n, and replacing one or more leaf nodes of those subtrees by variables taken from a set generated from C_n.

To define T_{n+1}, first form the set Δ consisting of:

- *All axioms ax such that* $s(ax) \leq D$, *whose terms are obtained from* C_{n+1} *by crossover;*
- *All axioms obtained from items of* I_n *by abstraction;*
- *All axioms ax such that* $s(ax) \leq D$ *that are obtained from items of* I_n *by recursion, using terms of* C_{n+1}; *and*
- *All axioms obtained from items of* I_n *by memorization.*

Then, form the set $\Delta' \subseteq \Delta$, *whose axioms satisfy a few additional conditions: e.g., all variables must appear in both terms of the axiom, or not at all.*

Next, form the set $\Delta'' \subseteq \Delta'$ *containing at most 3 axioms, using the preference order:*

1. *The performance of* $(T_n \cup \Delta'', C_{n+1}, W, L, D)$ *on* I_n *is as large as possible;*
2. $s(\Delta'')$ *is as small as possible;*
3. Δ'' *has a maximum number of variable tokens;*
4. Δ'' *has a minimum number of variable types;*
5. Δ'' *is as lexicographically small as possible.*

Finally, let $T_{n+1} = T_n \cup \Delta''$.

To illustrate the difference between type and token in this case, we can consider the term (x:Number)*(x:Number) + 2, which contains one variable type and two variable tokens. Condition 1 aims to maximize utility. Condition 2 is a formalization of Occam's razor. Condition 3 ensures that variables are preferred over constants and Condition 4 that variables are reused whenever possible. Condition 5, finally, guarantees that the output is always uniquely defined.

Observation 3. *The Occam function is computable.*

This follows since there are only finitely many agents and associated computations to check. We implemented the system O^* comprising approximately 2,500 lines of code in the functional programming language Haskell. O^* can be initialized with any agent A_0. At stage n, O^* takes IP I_n as input and updates A_n to A_{n+1}. O^*'s update function is a version of the Occam function with the following additions.

To reduce search complexity, O^* applies the Occam function in multiple steps. First it forms the set Δ by *crossover* and iterates over lengths of candidates (1 to D). If *crossover* fails to find an optimal candidate for Δ'', O^* uses *abstraction* and then *recursion*, and finally *memorization* if all else fails. The search for Δ'' from Δ' is exhaustive, while the search for A-computations uses the A^* algorithm with the goal of finding the shortest computations.

Crossover produces a large number of axioms. Therefore, a small set of filters is applied for reducing the complexity while still maintaining the generality of the resulting set Δ. These filters include the following: an axiom should be new (not already in the theory); it should not have a variable in the right term that is absent from the left term (cf. pure functions); it should contain at most two wildcards (variables appearing in the left term but not in the right term), e.g., (Equal, (x:Aterm) * 0,0). Moreover, variable assignments, e.g., (Equal, (x:Aterm),1), are not allowed.

3   Learning

In this section we illustrate how O^* can learn in the special case of elementary arithmetic. All problems considered below were solved by O^* running on a standard computer.

Example 10. Define A_0 by letting $T_0 = \emptyset, C_0 = \emptyset, W = 8, L = 10$, and $D = 6$. Suppose I_0 consists of the items

$$(\text{Type}, 0, \text{Digit}, 1) \tag{1}$$
$$(\text{Type}, 1, \text{Digit}, 1) \tag{2}$$
$$(\text{Type}, 2, \text{Digit}, 1). \tag{3}$$

Then, $C_1 = \{0, 1, 2, \text{Digit}\}$ and T_1 consists of the axioms

$$(\text{Type}, 0, \text{Digit}) \tag{4}$$
$$(\text{Type}, 1, \text{Digit}) \tag{5}$$
$$(\text{Type}, 2, \text{Digit}). \tag{6}$$

Item (1) is A_1-computable as follows:

$$\frac{0}{\text{Digit}} \ (4)$$

The other two items can be computed similarly. Intuitively, A_1 has memorized that 0, 1, and 2 are digits.

Example 11. Let A_1 be as above. Suppose I_1 consists of the items

$$(\text{Type}, 1, \text{Number}, 1) \tag{7}$$
$$(\text{Type}, 1\#2, \text{Number}, 1) \tag{8}$$
$$(\text{Type}, 1\#(2\#1), \text{Number}, -1). \tag{9}$$

The symbol # can be interpreted as a juxtaposition operator: e.g., 1#2 is interpreted as 12. Now $C_2 - C_1 = \{1\#2, 2\#1, 1\#(2\#1), \text{Number}\}$ and $T_2 - T_1$ consists of the axioms

$$(\text{Type}, \text{Digit}, \text{Number}) \tag{10}$$
$$(\text{Type}, \text{Number}\#\text{Digit}, \text{Number}). \tag{11}$$

Item (7) is A_2-computable using the axioms (5) and (10). Item (8) is A_2-computable as follows:

$$\cfrac{\cfrac{\cfrac{\cfrac{1\#2}{\text{Digit}\#2} \ (5)}{\text{Number}\#2} \ (10)}{\text{Number}\#\text{Digit}} \ (6)}{\text{Number}} \ (11)$$

Item (9) is not A_2-computable. It is not hard to see that T_2 is too weak to compute this item. Therefore, O^* terminates the search and concludes that the item is not computable. The performance of A_2 on I_1 is 2, which is optimal. If item (9) were not included in I_1, then $T_2 - T_1$ would include the axiom:

$$(\text{Type}, \text{Number}\#\text{Number}, \text{Number})$$

instead of the axiom (11). Intuitively, A_2 knows that numbers are sequences of digits.

Example 12. Let A_2 be as above. Suppose I_2 consists of the items

$$(\text{Type}, 1, \text{Aterm}, 1) \tag{12}$$
$$(\text{Type}, 1+2, \text{Aterm}, 1). \tag{13}$$

Then, $T_3 - T_2$ consists of the axioms

$$(\text{Type}, \text{Number}, \text{Aterm}) \tag{14}$$
$$(\text{Type}, \text{Aterm}+\text{Aterm}, \text{Aterm}). \tag{15}$$

Item (13) is readily A_3-computable using the axioms (10), (14), and (15).

Example 13. Let A_3 be as above. Suppose I_3 consists of the item

$$(\text{Type}, 1*2, \text{Aterm}, 1). \tag{16}$$

Then, $T_4 - T_3$ consists of the axiom

$$(\text{Type}, \text{Aterm}*\text{Aterm}, \text{Aterm}). \tag{17}$$

Now the system has learned the syntactic notions of digit, number, and arithmetical term. Next it will learn some algebraic laws.

Example 14. Let A_4 be as above. Suppose I_4 consists of the items

$$(\texttt{Equal}, 1+0, 1, 1) \tag{18}$$
$$(\texttt{Equal}, 1+1, 1, -1). \tag{19}$$

Then, $T_5 - T_4$ consists of the axiom:

$$(\texttt{Equal}, (\texttt{x:Aterm})+0, (\texttt{x:Aterm})). \tag{20}$$

Item (18) is A_5-computable as follows:

$$\frac{1+0}{1} \ (20)$$

The straightforward type-checking computation uses the axioms (2), (10), and (14). Item (19) is not A_5-computable, since no axiom of T_5 matches 1+1. If item (19) were not included in I_4, then $T_5 - T_4$ would consist of

$$(\texttt{Equal}, (\texttt{x:Aterm})+(\texttt{y:Aterm}), (\texttt{x:Aterm})).$$

Example 15. Let A_5 be as above. Suppose I_5 consists of the item

$$(\texttt{Equal}, 0+1, 1+0, 1). \tag{21}$$

Then, $T_6 - T_5$ consists of the axiom

$$(\texttt{Equal}, (\texttt{x:Aterm})+(\texttt{y:Aterm}), (\texttt{y:Aterm})+(\texttt{x:Aterm})). \tag{22}$$

Item (21) is A_6-computable as follows:

$$\frac{0+1}{1+0} \ (22)$$

The two type-checking computations are, once again, straightforward.

Example 16. Starting from A_6, we may continue in the same way and eventually arrive at an agent, A_n, which contains (a subset of) the theory BASE, defined in Appendix A. In particular T_n contains the axioms

$$(\texttt{Equal}, 8+3, 1\#1) \tag{23}$$
$$(\texttt{Equal}, \texttt{f}(1), \texttt{f}(0+1)). \tag{24}$$

4   Reasoning

In this section, we illustrate how O* is able to reason about the domains it has learned about and solve previously unseen problems of deduction and induction. For simplicity, we continue to work in the arithmetic domain. First, we will consider the deduction problem of computing $67 * 8$.

Example 17. Let A_n be as above. Let I_n be given by

$$(\texttt{Equal}, (6\#7)*8, (5\#3)\#6, 1). \qquad (25)$$

Then, $T_{n+1} = T_n$ and the item is computable by A_{n+1} as follows:

$$
\begin{array}{c}
(6\#7)*8 \\
\hline
(6*8)\#(7*8) \\
\hline
(6*8)\#(5\#6) \\
\hline
((6*8)+5)\#6 \\
\hline
((4\#8)+5)\#6 \\
\hline
(4\#(8+5))\#6 \\
\hline
(4\#(1\#3))\#6 \\
\hline
((4+1)\#3)\#6 \\
\hline
(5\#3)\#6
\end{array}
$$

Next, we will consider the induction problem of finding the next number in the sequence $8, 11, 14$.

Example 18. Let A_{n+1} be as above and let I_{n+1} be given by

$$(\texttt{Equal}, \texttt{f}(0), 8, 1) \qquad (26)$$

$$(\texttt{Equal}, \texttt{f}(1), 1\#1, 1) \qquad (27)$$

$$(\texttt{Equal}, \texttt{f}(2), 1\#4, 1). \qquad (28)$$

Then, $T_{n+2} - T_{n+1}$ consists of the axioms

$$(\texttt{Equal}, \texttt{f}(0), 8) \qquad (29)$$

$$(\texttt{Equal}, \texttt{f}((\texttt{x:Aterm})+1), \texttt{f}((\texttt{x:Aterm}))+3). \qquad (30)$$

For instance, item (27) is computable by A_{n+2} as follows:

$$
\begin{array}{c}
\texttt{f}(1) \\
\hline
\texttt{f}(0+1) \quad (24) \\
\hline
\texttt{f}(0)+3 \quad (30) \\
\hline
8+3 \quad (29) \\
\hline
1\#1 \quad (23)
\end{array}
$$

Now, A_{n+2} can compute $\texttt{f}(3)$ to obtain $1\#7$ and thus solve the number-sequence problem "correctly".

5 Conclusions

We have described the general system $O^\star$ for learning and reasoning in symbolic domains. $O^\star$ differs from standard AI models by being domain independent and by containing a unilateral cognitive model whose purpose is to reduce computational complexity, while keeping performance at the human level or above. In this way, the combinatorial-explosion problem, arising in e.g. inductive logic programming, automatic theorem proving, and grammar induction, is mitigated. $O^\star$ is able to learn the mechanics of new symbolic domains from scratch. It is general purpose: it has nothing built in that is specific to arithmetic or any other particular domain.

This paper showed that O* can learn elementary arithmetic from scratch. After learning, it could solve both deductive problems like computing $67 * 8$ and inductive problems like computing the next number in the sequence $8, 11, 14$. In [17], it was shown that an agent similar to A_n is able to perform above the average human level on number sequence problems appearing in IQ tests. The paper [18] showed that O* can also learn propositional logic from scratch. After learning, it was able to perform above the average human level on propositional logic problems where the task is to distinguish tautologies from non-tautologies.

At present, the main heuristic of O* is to confine the search for solutions to the cognitive model. This heuristic is unsophisticated; nevertheless, it is sufficient for reaching human-level performance in certain domains. It can potentially be combined with more traditional heuristics to improve performance further.

We find the approach to AGI as proposed in this paper promising. More research is needed, however, to determine its applicability, scalability, and robustness.

Acknowledgement. This research was supported by The Swedish Research Council, Grant 421-2012-1000.

A   Arithmetic Theory

The following are the axioms of the arithmetic theory BASE. Here x, y, and z are abbreviations of (x:Aterm), (y:Aterm), and (z:Aterm), respectively.

- (Type, 0, Digit)
- (Type, 1, Digit)
- ...
- (Type, 9, Digit)
- (Type, Digit, Number)
- (Type, Number#Digit, Number)
- (Type, Number, Aterm)
- (Type, Aterm+Aterm, Aterm)
- (Type, Aterm*Aterm, Aterm)
- (Equal, x+0, x)
- (Equal, 0+x, x)
- (Equal, 1+1, 2)
- (Equal, 1+2, 3)
- ...
- (Equal, 9+9, 1#8)
- (Equal, x*0, 0)
- (Equal, 0*x, 0)

- (Equal, x*1, x)
- (Equal, 1*x, x)
- (Equal, 2*2, 4)
- (Equal, 2*3, 6)
- ...
- (Equal, 9*9, 8#1)
- (Equal, x+y, y+x)
- (Equal, x+(y+z), (x+y)+z)
- (Equal, (x#0)+y, x#y)
- (Equal, (x#y)+z, x#(y+z))
- (Equal, x#(y#z), (x+y)#z)
- (Equal, x*(y+z), (x*y)+(x*z))
- (Equal, (x#y)*z, (x*z)#(y*z))
- (Equal, f(1), f(0+1))
- (Equal, f(2), f(1+1))
- (Equal, f(3), f(2+1))

References

1. Wang, P., Goertzel, B.: Theoretical Foundations of Artificial General Intelligence. Atlantis Press (2012)
2. Weng, J., McClelland, J., Pentland, A., Sporns, O., Stockman, I., Sur, M., Thelen, E.: Autonomous Mental Development by Robots and Animals. Science 291(5504), 599–600 (2001)
3. Russell, S.J., Norvig, P.: Artificial Intelligence: A Modern Approach. Prentice Hall series in artificial intelligence. Prentice-Hall (2010)
4. Simon, H.A.: Models of Bounded Rationality: Empirically Grounded Economic Reason, vol. 3. MIT Press (1982)
5. Muggleton, S., Chen, J.: Guest editorial: special issue on Inductive Logic Programming (ILP 2011). Machine Learning, 1–2 (2012)
6. Kitzelmann, E.: Inductive Programming: A Survey of Program Synthesis Techniques. In: Schmid, U., Kitzelmann, E., Plasmeijer, R. (eds.) AAIP 2009. LNCS, vol. 5812, pp. 50–73. Springer, Heidelberg (2010)
7. Laird, J.E., Newell, A., Rosenbloom, P.S.: Soar: An Architecture for General Intelligence. Artificial Intelligence 33(3), 1–64 (1987)
8. Anderson, J.R., Lebiere, C.: The atomic components of thought. Lawrence Erlbaum, Mahwah (1998)
9. Gobet, F., Lane, P.: The CHREST Architecture of Cognition: The Role of Perception in General Intelligence. In: Artificial General Intelligence 2010. Atlantis Press, Lugano (2010)
10. Wang, P.: From NARS to a Thinking Machine. In: Proceedings of the 2007 Conference on Artificial General Intelligence, pp. 75–93. IOS Press, Amsterdam (2007)
11. Bezem, M., Klop, J.W., de Vrijer, R.: Term Rewriting Systems. Cambridge University Press (2003)
12. Smith, E.E., Kosslyn, S.M.: Cognitive Psychology: Mind and Brain. Prentice-Hall, Upper Saddle River (2006)
13. Toms, M., Morris, N., Ward, D.: Working Memory and Conditional Reasoning. The Quarterly Journal of Experimental Psychology 46(4), 679–699 (1993)
14. Piaget, J.: La construction du réel chez l'enfant. Delachaux & Niestlé (1937)
15. Li, M., Vitányi, P.M.B.: An Introduction to Kolmogorov Complexity and Its Applications. Texts in computer science. Springer (2009)
16. Veness, J., Ng, K.S., Hutter, M., Uther, W., Silver, D.: A Monte-Carlo AIXI approximation. Journal of Artificial Intelligence Research 40(1), 95–142 (2011)
17. Strannegård, C., Nizamani, A.R., Sjöberg, A., Engström, F.: Bounded Kolmogorov complexity based on cognitive models. In: Kühnberger, K.-U., Rudolph, S., Wang, P. (eds.) AGI 2013. LNCS (LNAI), vol. 7999, pp. 130–139. Springer, Heidelberg (2013)
18. Nizamani, A.R., Strannegård, C.: Learning Propositional Logic From Scratch. In: The 28th Annual Workshop of the Swedish Artificial Intelligence Society, SAIS (in press, 2014)

Intelligence as Inference
or Forcing Occam on the World

Peter Sunehag and Marcus Hutter

Research School of Computer Science
Australian National University
Canberra Australia
{Peter.Sunehag,Marcus.Hutter}@anu.edu.au

Abstract. We propose to perform the optimization task of Universal Artificial Intelligence (UAI) through learning a reference machine on which good programs are short. Further, we also acknowledge that the choice of reference machine that the UAI objective is based on is arbitrary and, therefore, we learn a suitable machine for the environment we are in. This is based on viewing Occam's razor as an imperative instead of as a proposition about the world. Since this principle cannot be true for all reference machines, we need to find a machine that makes the principle true. We both want good policies and the environment to have short implementations on the machine. Such a machine is learnt iteratively through a procedure that generalizes the principle underlying the Expectation-Maximization algorithm.

1 Introduction

Universal Artificial Intelligence (UAI) [Hut05, LH07] formalizes intelligence as an incomputable optimization problem. We will here recast optimization problems as inference problems and define an iterative procedure that generalize the expectation maximization algorithm [DLR77] beyond its original form and context. The idea has been used previously in more narrow settings [DH97, WGRT11]. Our approach here brings "planning as inference" [Bot12] to a universal setting and we will discuss how to completely reduce the design of intelligent agents to building an inference mechanism. However, we also note the importance of the training environment. We note that it has been argued [HB04] that the human neo-cortex relies on only one mechanism and that, therefore, it should be possible to understand higher level cognitive abilities as one mechanism interacting with the environment with lower level processing in between.

Since we want a practical approach, we are only interested in computable policies. Hence, we are considering a search for programs achieving the highest possible return. The return function is not explicit and is evaluated for a program by running it and observing what return was achieved. This means that the impact of issues like running speed and memory use are subsumed into the return function. The setting is essentially that of achieving bounded optimality (rationality) as defined in [Rus97, RN10].

B. Goertzel et al. (Eds.): AGI 2014, LNAI 8598, pp. 186–195, 2014.

Our approach is to iteratively develop a reference machine on which good programs are short and, thereby, representing what we have learnt so far. The reference machine defines a distribution over programs by letting the probability of p be proportional to $2^{-\ell(p)}$ where $\ell(p)$ is the length of p. For every iteration we want the machine to represent probabilities which are such that the probability of the Turing machine T implemented by program p on the previous machine U, becomes proportional to the product of its (expected) return and its previous probability. If this is achieved we are guaranteed an improvement in expected return which means we got a better reference machine for finding rewarding programs.

In a practical approach the update is based on a population of sample programs. These can be sampled for the machine by coin-flipping the bits of the program, but they can include any evaluated programs from any sources. This is an important point of the approach since all programs written by human programmers can be used and their intelligence can be mined for good ideas this way. In fact, it is already used this way in the development of programming languages and their libraries that aim to ease the development of good programs and in some cases make bad things harder to do. The goal can be viewed as making Occam's razor true as a proposition about the world, while having to make it so is in line with viewing Occam as an imperative [Web10]. This procedure can be seen far beyond programming languages, e.g. in science where concepts and terminology are created such that complex phenomena can be described in compact form. The perspective of this article makes much of human progress into a quest towards artificial general intelligence. In fact, we can go a bit further by first looking at the background of our approach.

Evolution. In [DH97], the authors identified the Relative Payoff Procedure (RPP) as an Expectation-Maximization (EM) procedure. RPP makes binary choices independently and with probabilities proportional to the payoff relative to the total payoff and then iterates. It has some similarities with evolutionary algorithms (and natural evolution) where the most fit part of the population grows at the expense of the less fit, but like the probabilistic model-building genetic algorithms [Pel12], an explicit distribution representing current preferences is iteratively estimated resulting in more powerful optimization/learning in an optimization-as-inference paradigm. Unlike most evolutionary approaches, the expectation-maximization approach is learning also from the unfit and the degrees of fitness of all samples.

It is interesting to note that evolution theory itself has begun to place importance on more than genes [WE03], namely on gene-expression that changes during life based on the environment. An adaptation is learnt through (or causing) changed gene-expression (which can even be inherited) and then, according to this theory, a gene can be discovered that *accommodates* this adaptation and locks it in. The accommodation theory of evolution introduce a purpose-driven aspect into the process. This layer is represented in the mentioned algorithms by the distribution which allows for learning and exploration of complex relationships, if the distribution is more sophisticated than the independence in RPP allows for. In the accommodation theory of evolution, behavior is explored before it is accommodated by DNA. The suitable gene that accommodated the adaptation could have been useless without the adaptation already being to some extent in place. Gene expression (and also we here speculate brains and culture when available) is what makes it possible for some biological adaptation before a change in DNA takes place. A startling speculative possibility is that species that can learn better during life also have an accelerated genetic evolution making high levels of intelligence a much more probable outcome than it would be with a simpler entirely gene-centered understanding of evolution. That the more simplistic understandings of evolution cannot learn something complex in feasible time has been understood for a long time, e.g. by the authors of [Len80]. As one might conclude that biological evolution was geared towards intelligence, one can argue that our current technological and scientific evolution is moving towards Artificial General Intelligence even without someone making it the goal.

Logical Reasoning. We believe that logical reasoning is not essential in the building of an intelligent agent and is not a natural part of the human mind. It has been repeatedly shown that plausibility-based reasoning is the innate human thinking. People systematically place more belief in an event than a superset containing it, if the event creates a plausible narrative [Kah11] (not advocated here). Logical reasoning likely evolved from rhetoric in ancient Greece and does not seem to have been accommodated genetically and might not confer advantage except for some very particular constructed environments like computer programming.

We believe that logic is learnt from the human created environment. Moreover, practical logical reasoning is seldom fully formally logical, e.g. mathematical proofs are not written out in full but just aims at plausibility of each step and hence originally accepted proofs are sometimes found to be flawed. Searching through proof space suffers from combinatorial explosion and looking for plausible chains guided by one's belief about what is likely true (will hold up to scrutiny) or not is more practical. Our approach is based on plausible improvement by improving a sample-based approximation of what would guarantee improvement, and not on search for improvements with formal proof as the Gödel machine [Sch07]. The Gödel machine starts with a set of axioms defining an agent and then aims to update to a provably better set. The shifting inductive bias approach [SZW97] is closer to what is considered here though a direct comparison is difficult.

With probabilistic architectures with parameterized programs like e.g. Deep Belief Networks [HOT06], it is easier to generate programs that run and do something. The involved pattern recognition based reasoning is far more efficient than dealing with logical programs and architectures.

Outline. We first provide background and notation for Universal Artificial Intelligence (UAI) and general reinforcement learning. Then we introduce the objective whose optimization defines how one should update a reference machine to have a guaranteed improvement of expected utility when sampling programs from the machine. We go on to discuss a setting where generated observations in the optimization process are taken into account. We then we change from optimizing the given UAI objective to actually learning about the world through developing the reference machine for the UAI objective. Finally we discuss merging the notions of actions and observations as well as agent and environment before we conclude in the last chapter.

2   Learning a Reference Machine for UAI

We will consider an agent [RN10, Hut05] that interacts with an environment through performing actions a_t from a finite set $\mathcal{A}$ and receives observations o_t from a finite set $\mathcal{O}$ and rewards r_t from a finite set $\mathcal{R} \subset [0,1]$ resulting in a history $h_t := o_1 r_1 a_1, ..., o_t r_t$. Let $\mathcal{H} := \cup_n (\mathcal{O} \times \mathcal{R} \times \mathcal{A})^n \times (\mathcal{O} \times \mathcal{R})$ be the set of histories and let ϵ be the empty history. A function $\nu : \mathcal{H} \times \mathcal{A} \to \mathcal{O} \times \mathcal{R}$ is called a deterministic environment. A function $\pi : \mathcal{H} \to \mathcal{A}$ is called a (deterministic) policy or an agent. We define the value function V based on geometric discounting by $V_\nu^\pi(h_{t-1}) = \sum_{i=t}^\infty \gamma^{i-t} r_i$ where the sequence r_i are the rewards achieved by following π from time step t onwards in the environment ν after having seen h_{t-1}.

Instead of viewing the environment as a function $\mathcal{H} \times \mathcal{A} \to \mathcal{O} \times \mathcal{R}$ we can equivalently write it as a function $\nu : \mathcal{H} \times \mathcal{A} \times \mathcal{O} \times \mathcal{R} \to \{0,1\}$ where we also write $\nu(o, r|h, a)$ for the function value $\nu(h, a, o, r)$ (which is not the probability of the four-tuple). It equals zero if in the first formulation (h, a) is not sent to (o, r) and 1 if it is. In the case of stochastic environments we instead have a function $\nu : \mathcal{H} \times \mathcal{A} \times \mathcal{O} \times \mathcal{R} \to [0,1]$ such that $\sum_{o,r} \nu(o, r|h, a) = 1 \; \forall h, a$. Furthermore, we define $\nu(h_t|\pi) := \Pi_{i=1}^t \nu(o_i r_i|a_i, h_{i-1})$ where $a_i = \pi(h_{i-1})$. $\nu(\cdot|\pi)$ is a probability measure over strings or sequences and we can define $\nu(\cdot|\pi, h_{t-1})$ by conditioning $\nu(\cdot|\pi)$ on h_{t-1}. We define $V_\nu^\pi(h_{t-1}) := \mathbb{E}_{\nu(\cdot|\pi, h_{t-1})} \sum_{i=t}^\infty \gamma^{i-t} r_i$.

Given a countable class of environments and strictly positive prior weights w_ν for all ν in the class, we define the a-priori environment ξ by letting $\xi(\cdot) = \sum w_\nu \nu(\cdot)$ and the AIXI agent [Hut05] is defined by following the policy

$$\pi^* := \arg\max_\pi V_\xi^\pi(\epsilon).$$

The optimistic-AIXI agent [SH12b], which is an extension of AIXI, takes the decision

$$\pi^\circ := \arg\max_\pi \max_{\xi \in \Xi} V_\xi^\pi(\epsilon)$$

for a finite set of a priori environments Ξ. Other variations include the space-time embedded agents of [OR12] who are part of (computed by) the environment.

This article is dealing with the Universal Artificial Intelligence (UAI) setting where AIXI is a mixture of all computable, or lower semi-computable, environments. The mixture weights are defined from a choice of reference Universal Turing Machine (UTM) as $2^{-K(\nu)}$ for environment ν, and K is Kolmogorov complexity (length of the shortest program that implements the argument) with respect to U. The resulting a priori environment ξ can, equivalently, be defined as sampling a program for U and run it. The probability of a program p is proportional to $2^{-\ell(p)}$ where $\ell(p)$ is the length of p. The expected reward of a policy/agent is viewed as a measure of its intelligence [LH07]. However, this is dependent on the reference machine and so is the AIXI agent defined from it by maximizing that intelligence measure. Any agent is super-intelligent for some reference machine. The optimistic extension is both meant to be a more explorative version with more uniformly good performance across environments but also to diminish the dependence on the reference machine by being able to choose a large finite set of machines instead of just one. We will later in this article address the problem of choosing a good reference machine to base AIXI on, but we will first deal with the involved optimization problem by iteratively learning a reference machine that represents a preference between policies such that good policies have shorter programs on this machine.

Learning Reference Machines. Let $\mathcal{T}$ be the set of all Turing machines and suppose we are given a (possibly unknown) return function $R : \mathcal{T} \to \mathbb{R}$ that for each $T \in \mathcal{T}$ says how rewarding this machine is. We ideally want a machine from

$$\arg\max_{T \in \mathcal{T}} R(T).$$

A prominent example is when we have a general reinforcement learning environment μ as defined in [Hut05] (and above) and T computes a policy. $R(T)$ is then the expected discounted reward sum when acting according to T in μ. Given a Universal Turing Machine U, any Turing machine can be represented as a program p for U. Hence, given U, the search for a Turing machine T becomes a search for a program p for U. Though the choice of reference machine U does not affect which Turing machines are good, it affects how long/complex its implementation is. We suppose that a practical search would favor shorter programs over longer ones and, therefore, the choice of reference becomes critical for success. In fact, we will replace the search for programs with the task of incrementally inferring what a good choice of machine is. The choice of machine will encapsulate everything we have learned up to that time about how good various programs are by making the good ones shorter than worse alternatives. We want a machine U with high expected return defined by

$$\sum_p 2^{-\ell_U(p)} R(p).$$

One approach is to propose a different machine and estimate the expected return by running sampled programs on this machine. We will here instead consider a generalized Expectation-Maximization procedure similar to what [DH97] discussed in their narrow setting, which allows you to evaluate the new machine without running any programs on it. One only requires the ability to measure the length of a program translated for it. However, all of what follows can be expressed in terms of the expected utility objective above.

Given reference machine U, we want to change to U' (including a mapping of programs on U to programs on U') if

$$\sum_p 2^{-\ell_U(p)} R(p)\ell_U(p) > \sum_p 2^{-\ell_U(p)} R(p)\ell_{U'}(p)$$

where $\ell_U(p)$ is the length of the program p for U while $\ell_{U'}(p)$ is the length of the translation of p for U'. We suppress the search over translation programs to simplify notation. The larger the expectation of $R(p)\ell_U(p)$, the stronger the correlation between return and length. Hence, the smaller the expression $\sum_p 2^{-\ell_U(p)} R(p)\ell_U(p)$ is, the stronger the correlation between high return and short length. This update says that we want programs with high reward to have low complexity and, furthermore, guarantees that

$$\sum_p 2^{-\ell_{U'}(p)} R(p) > \sum_p 2^{-\ell_U(p)} R(p).$$

This result is simply proven using Jensen's inequality similar to [DH97].

$$\log \sum_p 2^{-\ell_{U'}(p)} R(p) - \log \sum_p 2^{-\ell_U(p)} R(p)$$

$$= \log \sum_p \frac{2^{-\ell_U(p)} R(p)}{\sum_q 2^{-\ell_U(q)} R(q)} \frac{2^{-\ell_{U'}(p)}}{2^{-\ell_U(p)}}$$

$$\geq \sum_p \frac{2^{-\ell_U(p)} R(p)}{\sum_q 2^{-\ell_U(q)} R(q)} \log \frac{2^{-\ell_{U'}(p)}}{2^{-\ell_U(p)}}$$

$$= \frac{1}{\sum_q 2^{-\ell_U(q)} R(q)} \Big(\sum_p 2^{-\ell_U(p)} R(p)\ell_U(p) - \sum_p 2^{-\ell_U(p)} R(p)\ell_{U'}(p) \Big) \geq 0.$$

The desired result follows since log is monotone increasing.

Approximations with Sample Programs. $\sum_p 2^{-\ell_U(p)} R(p)\ell_{U'}(p)$ is not computable. Hence, we cannot exactly evaluate if U' is better than U. Instead we will in practice need to rely on a set of sample programs p and their evaluations $R(p)$. If R is of the form of an expectation of a stochastic return one needs to run the evaluation repeatedly and average. To sample with a reference machine U is simple since it is done by coin flipping on the input tape. In other words, one randomly picks characters for the programming code which is typically a practical disaster if one does not have a reference machine that makes a reasonable program out of many short random strings. This problem disappears if as program we simply set parameters for an algorithm that can be run for any choice of such. An important point is that the set of sample programs do not all have to be sampled from the current reference machine but interesting programs developed elsewhere can also be introduced to be learnt from. Further, one needs a translation to the new machine. This is not necessarily difficult if the proposed change is to make some routines from the best programs part of the machine (language), reducing a block of code like a matrix multiplication to a macro. This way, the process becomes one of discovering and collecting useful routines while developing a high-level language. In the case when parameterized probabilistic functions are used, one can instead learn to imitate successful programs by finding parameters that lead to close reproduction of the programs' behavior.

Including Observations/Data and Environment. The setting discussed above has a return function that goes straight from programs (Turing machines) to a real valued return. However, an alternative is to include more structure where running the program generates data $d \in \mathcal{D}$ ($\mathcal{D}$ can be finite or countably infinite), which might consist of a sequence of observations each of which can contain a reward, and then there is a return function $R : \mathcal{D} \to \mathbb{R}$. R can e.g. be defined as a discounted reward sum. Though this can, as was mentioned before, be viewed as just an example of the optimization task above if we have been provided with a general reinforcement learning environment (which could be a Bayesian mixture of environments as for AIXI), we can also try to take advantage of the extra information and structure. This is done by replacing p with a pair (p, d) but we must let the coding of d be done by the machine $\hat{U}$ that represents the environment since we cannot change the objective optimized as long as we are in the optimization setting. Hence we end up with pairs (p, q) where q is a program on $\hat{U}$ that is run conditioned on p, i.e. q becomes an environment and p a policy. In other words, we want to change from U to U' such that

$$\sum_{p,q} 2^{-(\ell_U(p)+\ell_{\hat{U}}(q))} R(p,q)\ell_U(p,q) > \sum_{p,q} 2^{-(\ell_U(p)+\ell_{\hat{U}}(q))} R(p,q)\ell_{U'}(p,q)$$

where $\ell_U(p,q)$ is the length of a program on U (given by a translation) that produce the outcome of running policy p in environment q. This is simultaneously aiming for a machine where good policies have short program and where the likely data to be generated when such a policy is run, can also be coded compactly. This strategy is a sound method for representing plausibility and desirability in the same way and simultaneously modeling the world and the value of different choices in it. In the optimization discussed so far, we know the objective we optimize a policy for and the learning of this has so far been a separate matter. We will below take the next step of our investigation.

Combined Learning of Agent and Environment. The above described strategy starts with a reference machine $\hat{U}$ that AIXI's initial model ξ is defined from. The choice of $\hat{U}$ is arbitrary and any policy/agent can be considered superintelligent dependent on the reference machine. The reference machine defines what is considered a simple hypothesis and defines belief based on viewing simpler hypothesis as more plausible than more complex ones, i.e. Occam's razor is relied on. In this article, we learn a reference machine that implicitly incorporates an understanding of the world that makes Occam true. We replace q by d and $2^{-\ell_{\hat{U}}(q)}$ by the unknown true environment probability $\mu(d|p)$ and aim for higher $\sum_{p,d} 2^{-\ell_U(p)} \mu(d|p) R(d)$ by choosing U' with

$$\sum_{p,d} 2^{-\ell_U(p)} \mu(d|p) R(d) \ell_U(p) > \sum_{p,d} 2^{-\ell_U(p)} \mu(d|p) R(d) \ell_{U'}(p).$$

In the sampling setting we simply sample from the world instead of using $\hat{U}$. This is making the simplifying assumption that we have a reset after a program has been run and evaluated, i.e. we can start every program in the same situation. This is feasible if one wants to train an agent in a rich world like a general game playing situation but where one can start over.

Exploration is important, both for the individual programs who act sequentially for a long time and whose total return depends on exploration, as well as for the sampling of programs. The learnt bias towards programs believed to have high reward ensures that we aim to explore promising possibilities and not waste time on finding out exactly how bad something is. Optimistic hypotheses have the beneficial property that if the outcome does not clearly contradict the hypothesis, the agent has received high return [SH12a].

When we above wrote that we want $\sum_{p,d} 2^{-\ell_U(p)} \mu(d|p) R(d)$ to be high, there are two possible interpretations depending on what we expect the programs to be doing. We can have p that is simply implementing a policy, i.e. it delivers actions and need an observation in between each to deliver the next. However, we can also allow programs that produce output that can be understood as pairs of actions and observations or whole sequences of such pairs (i.e. all of the data d), but where the observation part can be changed by the environment resulting in a different return. This stays within the usual agent-environment framework while we can go further and still use the same expression above, by letting the environment rewrite the whole output. In this setting, a program is sampled and then data is generated. The data might not entirely coincide with the data coded/generated by the program on the reference machine, because the program acts in the (unknown and uncertain) world. In this setting there is no distinction between actions and observations. The program aims to write a certain (say) 1000 bits and there are another, possibly different 1000 bits resulting which the return is based on.

Reward-Modulated Inference. If we want to implement our strategy using a parameterized probabilistic architecture, the objective becomes one of optimizing a reward weighted likelihood/loss. One can e.g. envision the action being part of the observation and one tries to improve the observation to achieve higher reward.

In the field of neuro-science where finding the update equation for synaptic weights used by biological brains is sought, reward-modulation of spike-timing-dependent synaptic plasticity has been the recent focus of much research. Herrstein's law [Her70] states that an animal, including humans, tend to select actions with a frequency proportional to the reward accumulated while taking that action. [LS06] shows that such operant matching is the result if one has correlation between reward and neural activity in a spiking neural network. [LPM07] began analyzing such methods from a learning-theoretic perspective and [FSG10] interpreted a broad class of candidate rules as having a reward-driven part and an unsupervised part. They considered the latter to be undesirable for reinforcement learning and introduced a reward predicting critic to cancel it out.

However, Deep Learning [HOT06, BLPL07] often starts with an unsupervised phase and then tunes for the actual objective. [SL14] recently argued that model-free reinforcement learning cannot account for human behavior but argues that some modeling of observations is taking place in the human brain.

[DH97] points out the difference between their iterative procedure, which is the basic idea used in this article, and the simpler matching procedure which stay with the same frequencies. The difference is that the current probability of taking an action is taken into account in the expectation and then, if the most rewarding actions stay the same, its frequency will for each iteration keep increasing towards one. If it changes, the procedure is still able to change and move in a new direction. That the simpler matching is so prevalent in nature might imply that the natural environment is so uncertain, changing and even dramatically adversarial that this modest amount of optimization for current conditions is suitable and can also still be challenging in a complex environment.

Optimizing the World=Agent+Environment. In our final setting we do not hold a true environment nor an a priori reference machine fixed but evolve the machine that defines the environment. This means that we no longer have a clear separation between agent and environment. The only thing fixed in this setting is the return function R. For this to be useful we must either be in a setting where the return is not just internal in the sense that it sums up rewards produced by a program on the reference machine, but that it is external to the environment we discuss. For example, if we want an agent to produce a music song in a music school that is then sold outside, we have a meaningful setting where it is useful to optimize the whole operation and not a subset that is interpreted as the agent. Alternatively, we can view the environment as being everything and the return as being internal, but where it is a hard task to change the total world to increase the reward. The update objective $\sum_p 2^{-\ell_U(p)} R(p) \ell_{\tilde{U}}(p)$ is telling us that we want to change U to U' such that the expression becomes larger with $\tilde{U} = U'$ than with $\tilde{U} = U$, resulting in $\sum_p 2^{-\ell_{U'}(p)} R(p) > \sum_p 2^{-\ell_U(p)} R(p)$.

3   Conclusions

We discussed reducing all of intelligence to an inference mechanism and properties of the environment. We introduced a formal approach that iteratively develops a reference machine suitable for both, implementing a good model of the environment as well as good policies for it.

Acknowledgement. This work was supported by ARC grant DP120100950.

References

[BLPL07]   Bengio, Y., Lamblin, P., Popovici, D., Larochelle, H.: Greedy layer-wise training of deep networks. In: NIPS 2007. MIT Press (2007)

[Bot12]   Botvinick, M., Toussaint, M.: Planning as inference. Trends in Cognitive Sciences 16(10), 485–488 (2012)

[DH97]   Dayan, P., Hinton, G.: Using expectation-maximization for reinforcement
            learning. Neural Computation 9(2), 271–278 (1997)
[DLR77]   Dempster, A., Laird, N., Rubin, D.: Maximum likelihood from incomplete
            data via the EM algorithm. J. of the Royal Stat. Soc.: B 39, 1–38 (1977)
[FSG10]   Fremaux, N., Sprekeler, H., Gerstner, W.: Functional requirements for
            reward-modulated spike timing-dependent plasticity. Journal of Neuro-
            science 30(40), 13326–13337 (2010)
[HB04]   Hawkins, J., Blakeslee, S.: On Intelligence. Times Books (2004)
[Her70]   Herrnstein, R.J.: On the law of effect. Journal of the Experimental Analysis
            of Behavior 13, 243–266 (1970)
[HOT06]   Hinton, G., Osindero, S., Teh, Y.W.: A fast learning algorithm for deep
            belief nets. Neural Comput. 18(7), 1527–1554 (2006)
[Hut05]   Hutter, M.: Universal Articial Intelligence: Sequential Decisions based on
            Algorithmic Probability. Springer, Berlin (2005)
[Kah11]   Kahneman, D.: Thinking, fast and slow (2011)
[Len80]   Lenat, D.: The plausible mutation of DNA. Technical report. Standford
            University (1980)
[LH07]   Legg, S., Hutter, M.: Universal Intelligence: A defintion of machine intel-
            ligence. Mind and Machine 17, 391–444 (2007)
[LPM07]   Legenstein, R., Pecevski, D., Maass, W.: Theoretical analysis of learning
            with reward-modulated spike-timing-dependent plasticity. In: NIPS (2007)
[LS06]   Loewenstein, Y., Seung, S.: Operant matching is a generic outcome of
            synaptic plasticity based on the covariance between reward and neural
            activity. PNAS 103(41), 15224–15229 (2006)
[OR12]   Orseau, L., Ring, M.: Space-time embedded intelligence. In: Bach, J.,
            Goertzel, B., Iklé, M. (eds.) AGI 2012. LNCS (LNAI), vol. 7716, pp. 209–
            218. Springer, Heidelberg (2012)
[Pel12]   Pelikan, M.: Probabilistic model-building genetic algorithms. In: GECCO,
            pp. 777–804. ACM (2012)
[RN10]   Russell, S.J., Norvig, P.: Artificial Intelligence: A Modern Approach, 3rd
            edn. Prentice-Hall, Englewood Cliffs (2010)
[Rus97]   Russell, S.: Rationality and intelligence. Artificial Intelligence (1997)
[Sch07]   Schmidhuber, J.: Gödel machines: Fully self-referential optimal universal
            self-improvers. In: Artificial General Intelligence, pp. 199–226 (2007)
[SH12a]   Sunehag, P., Hutter, M.: Optimistic agents are asymptotically optimal. In:
            Proceedings of the 25th Australasian AI Conference, pp. 15–26 (2012)
[SH12b]   Sunehag, P., Hutter, M.: Optimistic AIXI. In: Bach, J., Goertzel, B.,
            Iklé, M. (eds.) AGI 2012. LNCS (LNAI), vol. 7716, pp. 312–321. Springer,
            Heidelberg (2012)
[SL14]   Shteingart, H., Loewenstein, Y.: Reinforcement learning and human be-
            havior. Current Opinion in Neurobiology 25(0), 93–98 (2014)
[SZW97]   Schmidhuber, J., Zhao, J., Wiering, M.: Shifting inductive bias with
            success-story algorithm, adaptive Levin search, and incremental self-
            improvement. Machine Learning 28, 105–130 (1997)
[WE03]   West-Eberhard, M.J.: Developmental Plasticity and Evolution. Oxford
            University Press, USA (2003)
[Web10]   Webb, G.: Occam's razor. In: Encl. of Machine Learning, Springer (2010)
[WGRT11]   Wingate, D., Goodman, N., Kaelbling, L., Roy, D., Tenenbaum, J.:
            Bayesian policy search with policy priors. IJCAI, 1565–1570 (2011)

Distributed Vector Representations of Words in the Sigma Cognitive Architecture

Volkan Ustun[1], Paul S. Rosenbloom[1,2], Kenji Sagae[1,2], and Abram Demski[1,2]

[1] Institute for Creative Technologies
[2] Department of Computer Science
University of Southern California, Los Angeles, CA USA

Abstract. Recently reported results with distributed-vector word representations in natural language processing make them appealing for incorporation into a general cognitive architecture like Sigma. This paper describes a new algorithm for learning such word representations from large, shallow information resources, and how this algorithm can be implemented via small modifications to Sigma. The effectiveness and speed of the algorithm are evaluated via a comparison of an external simulation of it with state-of-the-art algorithms. The results from more limited experiments with Sigma are also promising, but more work is required for it to reach the effectiveness and speed of the simulation.

1   Introduction

Distributed vector representations facilitate learning word meanings from large collections of unstructured text. Each word is learned as a distinct pattern of continuous (or discrete or Boolean) values over a single large vector, with similarity among word meanings emergent in terms of distances in the resulting vector space. Vector representations are leveraged in cognitive science to model semantic memory [13,22]. They have also been used for many years in neural language models [18], where they have yielded good performance [1,2], but have not scaled well to large datasets or vocabularies. Recently, however, scalable methods for training neural language models have been proposed [10,11], handling very large datasets (up to 6 billion words) and achieving good performance on a range of word similarity tests.

The premise of distributed vector representations might have interesting repercussions for cognitive architectures as well since these architectures have naturally involved memory models and language tasks. Yet, vector representations are rare in cognitive architectures, limited to experiments with a separate module in ACT-R [20] and an effort in progress to incorporate them into LIDA to yield Vector LIDA [4].

Sigma – briefly introduced in Section 5 – is being built as a computational model of general intelligence that is based on a hybrid (discrete+continuous) mixed (symbolic+probabilistic) cognitive architecture of the same name [15]. Its development is driven by a trio of desiderata: (1) *grand unification*, uniting the requisite cognitive and non-cognitive aspects of embodied intelligent behavior; (2) *functional elegance*, yielding broad cognitive (and sub-cognitive) functionality from a simple and theoretically elegant base; and (3) *sufficient efficiency*, executing rapidly enough for anticipated applications. The potential utility of distributed vector representations

B. Goertzel et al. (Eds.): AGI 2014, LNAI 8598, pp. 196–207, 2014.

suggests it is worth considering what they might bring to Sigma. At the same time, Sigma's approach to achieving functional elegance via a *graphical architecture* – built from graphical models [7] (in particular, factor graphs and the summary product algorithm [8]), n-dimensional piecewise linear functions [14], and gradient descent learning [16] – that sits below the cognitive architecture and implements it, suggests that it might be possible to support distributed vector representations with only small extensions to the architecture.

In other words, the goal of this paper is to evaluate whether Sigma provides a functionally elegant path towards a deep and effective integration of distributed vector representations into a cognitive architecture. The *Distributed Vector Representation in Sigma* (DVRS) model – Section 3 – is inspired primarily by BEAGLE [6], but with adaptations intended to leverage as much as possible of Sigma's existing capabilities. Section 2 provides background on BEAGLE (and on Vector LIDA, which builds on BEAGLE's approach while striving for increased efficiency).

Because Sigma is not yet completely up to implementing the full DVRS model, results are presented from two approximations to it. DVRS' is a simulation of DVRS outside of Sigma that simplifies Sigma's use of gradient descent in learning word meanings. This yields an efficient approximation to DVRS that enables large-scale experimentation. DVRS$^+$ is a partial implementation of DVRS within Sigma. It enables verifying that the core ideas work within Sigma, while requiring little modification to it, but it is incomplete and presently too slow for large-scale experimentation.

The results reported here from DVRS' (Section 4) and DVRS$^+$ (Section 6) show the potential of the DVRS algorithm itself and its incorporation into Sigma, but significant work remains for a complete and efficient implementation of DVRS in Sigma. This necessary further work is discussed in Section 7, along with the conclusion.

2   Background

BEAGLE builds a holographic lexicon – represented by distributed vectors – that captures word meanings from unsupervised experience with natural language [6]. Two types of information are utilized to learn the meaning of a word: (1) *context*, as defined by the words that co-occur in the same sentence, and (2) *word order*, as defined by the relative positions of the nearest co-occurring words.

BEAGLE assigns two vectors to each word in the vocabulary: (1) an *environmental vector* and (2) a *lexical (meaning) vector*. The word's environmental vector is ultimately intended to represent the physical characteristics of the word, such as orthography, phonology etc. and hence, should not change over time. However, in the basic model focused on here, this lower-level similarity is not included, and instead each environmental vector is simply a fixed random vector. The word's lexical vector, on the other hand, represents the memory for contexts and positions. Each time a word is encountered, its lexical vector is updated from the associated context and order information. BEAGLE uses superposition for context information – simply the sum of the environmental vectors of all of the co-occurring words. Positional information is captured via n-grams, by *binding* together via convolution all of the words in each n-gram (of size up to 5 in [6]). The order information for a word in a sentence is the sum of all of the n-gram convolutions containing it. The word's lexical vector is then updated by adding in the context and ordering vectors.

BEAGLE uses *circular convolution* for binding to avoid the problem of *expanding dimensionality*, where the output of binding is larger than its inputs, making further binding either infeasible or intractable [12]. It furthermore uses a directed variant of circular convolution – where different inputs are permuted distinctly prior to convolution – so as to avoid losing information about their relative ordering during the otherwise symmetric convolution operation.

The approach taken in Vector LIDA [21] is similar to that in BEAGLE. The Modular Composite Representation (MCR) used in Vector LIDA also relies on capturing context and order information in high dimensional vectors, but it uses integer rather than real-valued vectors and replaces the expensive circular convolution operation – which is $O(n \log n)$ if FFTs are used [3] and $O(n^2)$ otherwise – with a faster *modular sum* operation that still avoids the expanding dimensionality problem.

3   The DVRS Model(s)

DVRS is conceptually similar to BEAGLE and MCR, but it retains BEAGLE's real-valued vectors while substituting a different fast binding operation based on pointwise product with random positional vectors. This approach still avoids the expanding dimensionality problem, but is more aligned with how Sigma works. Real-valued vectors are a natural special case of Sigma's pervasive usage of n-dimensional piece-wise-linear functions; they just restrict the function to piecewise constant values over domains that are one dimensional and discrete.

The binding needed for ordering information is achieved by pointwise multiplying the environmental vector of each nearby co-occurring word with a random vector that is uniquely characteristic of the relative position between that word and the word being learned. The capture of word order information in DVRS thus maps onto skip-grams [5], which are generalizations of n-grams that allow intervening words to be skipped – a skip distance of k allows k or fewer words to be skipped in constructing n-grams. The current DVRS model employs 3-skip-bigrams, in which pairs of words are learned with at most three words skipped between them. As a result, there can be as many as 8 such skip-grams per word in a sentence. In recent work, a similar formulation was used in calculating the predicted representation of a word [11], with the excellent results reported there serving as encouragement for the potential of DVRS.

A more formal description of DVRS is as follows. Let's assume that: each sentence has n words, $l(i)$ is the lexical vector of the ith word in the sentence, and $e(i)$ is the environmental vector of the ith word. Each element of each environmental vector is randomly selected from the continuous span [-1,1). If the word being updated is the kth word ($word_k$) in the sentence, then the context information, $c(k)$, for it is the sum of the environmental vectors for the other n-1 words in the sentence.

$$c(k) = \sum_{i=1}^{n} e(i), where\ i \neq k \tag{1}$$

The *sequence vectors* are random vectors created for the binding operation, and like the environmental vectors are defined based on random selections from the continuous span [-1,1). *s(j)* is unique for each relative position *j* from word$_k$. The word order information, *o(k)*, is then calculated as follows (".*" is the pointwise vector multiplication operation):

$$o(k) = \sum_{j=-4}^{4} s(j) .* e(k+j), where\ j \neq 0\ and\ 0 < (k+j) \leq n \qquad (2)$$

DVRS uses gradient descent, where the gradient is based on the sum of the normalized context and order vectors $- \widehat{c(k)} + \widehat{o(k)} -$ to incrementally update the lexical vectors, *l(k)*, as new training sentences are processed.

The key difference between DVRS$^+$ and DVRS is that the former selects values in environmental and sequence vectors randomly from [0,1) rather than [-1,1). Sigma was originally designed to operate only with non-negative functional values because its general implementation of the summary product algorithm, which subsumes both the sum-product and max-product variants, is only guaranteed to produce correct outputs given non-negative inputs. Distributed vector computations only depend on sum-product, not on max-product, and sum-product – both in general and in Sigma – does work with negative values. However, other aspects of Sigma – such as its gradient-descent learning algorithm – also only work with non-negative values, so the use of negative values for distributed vectors has been put off to future work. This does limit the vectors in DVRS$^+$ to one quadrant of the full vector space, and as seen in Section 6, leads to somewhat degraded performance.

The key difference between DVRS' and DVRS is that the former uses a lexical vector update operation that is similar to that in BEAGLE – the lexical vector *l(k)* of word$_k$ is modified by simply adding in the normalized sum of *c(k)* and *o(k)*:

$$l(k) = l(k) + \widehat{c(k)} + \widehat{o(k)} \qquad (3)$$

By implementing DVRS' outside of Sigma, very large training datasets can be processed quickly and compared with state-of-the-art models to provide valuable insight into the overall effectiveness of DVRS.

4   Evaluating the DVRS' Simulation

The goals of this evaluation are to: (1) assess the effectiveness of DVRS'; (2) determine its robustness over random initializations of the evaluation and sequence vectors; and (3) evaluate whether replacing BEAGLE's use of expensive directed circular convolution by cheap pointwise products degrades performance. Training is performed over a corpus of ~500k sentences (12.6M words and 213K distinct words) extracted from the first 10^8 bytes of the English Wikipedia dump from March 3, 2006, provided by [9]. The text was preprocessed to contain only lowercase characters and spaces, using the script in [9]. Stop words are ignored in creating the context information. An iMac 12,2 with 8GB RAM and a 3.4Ghz I7-2600 processor is used in the training.

One way to compare the quality of different word vectors is by examining their similarity to their closest neighbors. Table 1 depicts the top 5 neighbors of the words *language*, *film*, *business*, and *run*, ordered by vector cosine distances. Three forms of training are explored: only on context, only on ordering, and on their composite. Similar to the assessments in [6], composite training better captures word similarities for the examples shown here.

Table 1. Five nearest neighbors of four words in context, order, and composite spaces

	language			*film*	
Context	**Order**	**Composite**	**Context**	**Order**	**Composite**
spoken	cycle	languages	director	movie	movie
languages	society	vocabulary	directed	german	documentary
speakers	islands	dialect	starring	standard	studio
linguistic	industry	dialects	films	game	films
speak	era	syntax	movie	french	movies
	business			*run*	
Context	**Order**	**Composite**	**Context**	**Order**	**Composite**
businesses	data	commercial	home	play	runs
profits	computer	public	runs	hit	running
commercial	glass	financial	running	pass	hit
company	color	private	hit	die	break
including	space	social	time	break	play

Mikolov *et al.* [10] argue that a more complex similarity test is more appropriate for the assessment of the quality of the trained word vectors. They propose for this a general word analogy test along with a specific set of test instances – termed the *Google test data* in the remainder of this article. This test simply asks, for example, the question "What is the word that is similar to *small* in the same way that *biggest* is similar to *big*?". Such questions can be answered by performing simple algebraic operations over the vector representations. To find the word that is most similar to *small* in the same way that *biggest* is similar to *big*, one can merely compute the vector $V = (l_{biggest} - l_{big}) + l_{small}$ and determine which word's lexical vector is closest to V according to cosine distance. In other words, what is added to the representation of *big* to get *biggest* should also yield *smallest* if added to the representation of *small*.[1] The Google test data includes 8,869 semantic test instances (such as determining which word is most similar to *king* in the way *wife* is similar to *husband*) and 10,675 syntactic test instances (such as determining which word is most similar to *lucky* in the way *happy* is similar to *happily*).

Table 2 shows the accuracy of DVRS' over various configurations of system settings on the Google test data. The vocabulary of the training data includes all four words in the Google test data instances for 8,185 of the 8,869 semantic test cases and 10,545 of the 10,675 syntactic test cases. Mikolov *et al.* [10] report an accuracy of 24% for their CBOW model with a training set of 24M words and a vector dimensionality of 600. Mnih and Kavukcuoglu [11] report an accuracy of 17.5% for a model

---

[1] As pointed out in [11], the words most similar to V in this case will actually be *biggest* and *small*, so the search results should exclude them off the top.

trained on the 47M words of the Gutenberg dataset. The DVRS' co-occurrence model achieves a comparable result, 24.3%, with approximately 12.6M words in the training data and a vector dimensionality of 1024. Adding ordering information (via skip-grams) didn't improve the accuracy of the co-occurrence models in the cases tested. Increasing the vector size above 1536 also did not improve the accuracy. Overall, these results are comparable to the recently reported accuracies by [10] and [11] for comparable sizes of training data.

Table 2. Performance (% correct) on the Google test data for test instances in which all four words are in the vocabulary (and in paranthesis for all test instances)

	Vector size	Semantic	Syntactic	Overall
Co-occurrence only	1024	33.7 (31.1)	18.8 (18.6)	25.3 (24.3)
3-Skip-Bigram only	1024	2.7 (2.5)	5.0 (4.9)	4.0 (3.8)
3-Skip-bigram composite	512	29.8 (27.5)	18.5 (18.3)	23.4 (22.4)
3-Skip-bigram composite	1024	32.7 (30.2)	19.2 (18.9)	25.1 (24.0)
3-Skip-bigram composite	1536	34.6 (31.9)	20.1 (19.9)	26.4 (25.3)
3-Skip-bigram composite	2048	34.3 (31.7)	20.1 (19.9)	26.3 (25.2)

Robustness across different random initializations of environmental vectors has also been assessed for DVRS'. The model was run 5 times with different initializations of environmental vectors of size 1024, and performance was measured over a randomly selected subset (~10%) of the Google test data for composite training. The performance (% correct) was in the range [23.8, 25.0] for the best match and in the range [37.0, 37.5] when checked for a match within the 5 closest words, demonstrating the negligible effect of random initializations.

The impact of using pointwise vector multiplication instead of circular convolution has also been assessed in DVRS', with vectors of size 512. The comparison isn't directly with BEAGLE, but with a version of DVRS' in which pointwise vector multiplication is replaced with circular convolution. The achieved accuracies on the Google test data were 23.4% for pointwise multiplication and 19.9% for circular convolution; implying that, at least for this case, pointwise multiplication does not degrade performance, and in fact enhances it instead. Furthermore, training on the full training set takes a bit more than 3 hours with pointwise multiplication, but 4.5 days for circular convolution. An $O(n^2)$ variant of circular convolution is used here, but even an optimal $O(n \ log \ n)$ implementation would be dominated by the $O(n)$ time required with pointwise multiplication. Training DVRS' on just ordering information occurs at ~1.4M words/minute with a vector dimensionality of 100, a rate that is comparable to that reported for similar configurations in [11].

5   Sigma

The Sigma cognitive architecture provides a language of *predicates* and *conditionals*. A predicate is defined via a name and a set of typed arguments, with *working memory* containing predicate instantiations that embody the state of the system. The argument types may vary in extent and may be discrete – either symbolic or numeric – or continuous. Conditionals are defined via a set of predicate patterns and an optional function over pattern variables, providing a deep combination of rule systems and probabilistic networks. *Conditions* and *actions* are predicate patterns that behave like the respective parts of rules, pushing information in one direction from the conditions to the actions. *Condacts* are predicate patterns that support the bidirectional processing that is key to probabilistic reasoning, partial matching, constraint satisfaction and signal processing. Functions encode relationships among variables, such as joint or conditional probability distributions, although the dimensions of the functions may in general be continuous, discrete or symbolic, and the values of the functions may be arbitrary non-negative numbers (which can be limited to [0,1] for probabilities and to 0 (*false*) and 1 (*true*) for symbols).

Sigma's graphical architecture sits below its cognitive architecture, and serves to implement it. The graphical architecture is based on *factor graphs* and the *summary-product algorithm* [8], plus a function/message representation based on *n-dimensional piecewise-linear functions* [14]. Factor graphs are a general form of undirected graphical model composed of variable and factor nodes. Factor nodes embody functions – including all of those defined in the cognitive architecture plus others only relevant within the graphical architecture – and are linked to the variable nodes with which they share variables. In its simplest form, there would only be one variable per variable node, but Sigma supports variable nodes that represent sets of variables. A factor graph (Figure 1) implicitly represents the function defined by multiplying together the functions in its factor nodes. Or, equivalently, a factor graph decomposes a single complex multivariate function into a product of simpler factors.

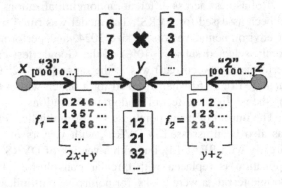

Fig. 1. Factor graph for algebraic function: $f(x,y,z) = y^2 + yz + 2yx + 2xz = (2x+y)(y+z) = f_1(x,y)f_2(y,z)$

The summary product algorithm computes messages at nodes and passes them along links to neighboring nodes. A message along a link represents a function over the variables in the link's variable node. Given that a variable node may embody multiple variables, functions in messages are defined in general over the cross product of their variables' domains. An output message along a link from a variable node is simply the (pointwise) product of the input messages arriving along its other links. An output message along a link from a factor node is computed by multiplying the node's function times the product of its incoming messages, and then summarizing out all of its variables that are not included in the target variable node, either by integrating the variables out to yield marginals or maximizing them out to yield maximum a posteriori (MAP) estimates.

Working memory compiles into a sector of the graphical architecture's factor graph, with conditionals compiling into more complex sectors. Functions are represented in an n-dimensional piecewise-linear manner and stored in factor nodes within the overall graph. Memory access in the cognitive architecture then maps onto message passing within this factor graph. As messages are sent, they are saved on links. If a new message is generated along a link, it is sent only if it is significantly different from the one already stored there. Message passing reaches *quiescence* – and thus memory access terminates – when no new messages are available to send. Once quiescence is reached, both decisions and learning occur locally – via function modification – at the appropriate factor nodes based on the messages they have received via Sigma's summary product algorithm. Based on ideas in [19] for Bayesian networks, a message into a factor node for a conditional function can be seen as providing feedback to that node from the rest of the graph that induces a local gradient for learning. Although Sigma uses undirected rather than directed graphs, the directionality found in Bayesian networks can be found at factor nodes when some of the variables are distinguished as the *children* that are conditionally dependent on the other *parent* variables. The original batch algorithm is modified to learn incrementally (online) from each message as it arrives [16].

6   The DVRS⁺ Sigma Model

Context and *word order* information are captured by two similar predicates: (a) Context-Vector(distributed:environment)   and   (b)   Ordering-Vector(distributed:environment), using the discrete type environment – with a range equal to the vector dimensionality – for the distributed argument. By default, all types are continuous in Sigma, but discrete types fragment the number line into unit-length regions, each with a constant function that can take on any non-negative value. It should be clear how this directly yields the real-valued vectors needed here.

The   predicate   Skip-Gram-Vector(position:position   distributed:environment)   introduces a second argument, position, for the relative position from the word whose lexical vector is being updated. With a sufficient scope for position, Skip-Gram-Vector can store the environmental vectors of the words at each relative position of interest from the current word. The Skip-Gram-Vector predicate is used in establishing the word order information. The Meaning-Vector(word:word   distributed:environment)   predicate captures both the context and word order information for the word being updated.

```
CONDITIONAL Co-occurence
    Conditions: Co-occuring-Words(word:w)
    Actions: Context-Vector(distributed:d)
    Function(w,d): *environmental-vectors*
```

Fig. 2. Conditional for context information

Conditionals specify the rest of the DVRS⁺ Sigma model. The conditional in Figure 2, for example, determines how context information is computed for words, with Figure 3 explaining the computations implicitly defined by this conditional for a simplified hypothetical case where the vocabulary has only 4 words and the vector dimensionality is 5. Coming out of the condition is a message with a local vector for the other words in the sentence; that is, the vector's domain is the entire vocabulary and there is a value of 1 at every word in the sentence (and a value of 0 everywhere else). In Figure 3(a), the co-occurring words are the first and the fourth words, with a single zero region of width two sufficient to mark the second and third words as not co-occurring. Via the summary product algorithm, this vector is multiplied times the 2D function that stores the environmental vectors (Figure 3(b)) to yield a 2D function that is non-zero for only the environmental vectors of the words in the sentence (Figure 3(c)); and then the word variable is summarized out via integration (Figure 3(d)) – summing across all of the environmental vectors for words in the sentence – to generate a message for the action that is the distributed context vector. Because this message represents a distributed vector rather than a probability distribution, Sigma has been extended to do vector (or $l2$) normalization – i.e., sum of squares – over these messages rather than the normal form of probabilistic (or $l1$) normalization (Figure 3(e)). But, otherwise, a simple knowledge structure, in combination with the underlying summary product algorithm, computes what is necessary.

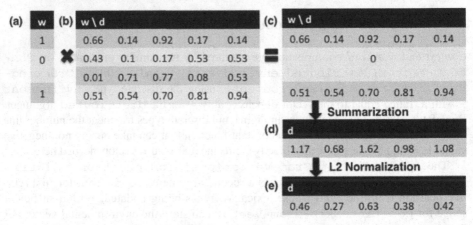

Fig. 3. Computation of context information

Computing the ordering information is similar, albeit slightly more involved (Figure 4). The condition here yields a 2D function that captures the environmental vectors for nearby words according to their position – distance and direction – from the word being learned, while the function stores the unique sequence vectors, by position. The product yields a 2D function representing the pointwise products of the corresponding environmental and sequence vectors, with summarization (and an $l2$ norm) yielding the ordering vector via addition over these products.

```
CONDITIONAL Ordering
    Conditions: Skip-Gram-Vector(position:p distributed:d)
    Actions: Ordering-Vector(distributed:d)
    Function(p,d): *sequence-vectors*
```

Fig. 4. Conditional that computes the ordering vector

The combination of context and ordering information occurs via a form of *action combination* that is Sigma's generalization of how multiple actions combine in parallel rule-based systems. Normal rule actions for the same predicate are combined in Sigma via *max*. For probabilistic information, multiple actions for the same predicate combine via *probabilistic or*. For distributed vectors, Sigma has been extended to use straight *addition* across multiple actions for the same predicate. For negative actions, Sigma normally inverts the message – converting, for example, 0s to 1s and 1s to 0s – and then multiplies this with the results of positive action combination; however, for vectors, negative actions simply imply *subtraction*.

The conditional in Figure 5 shows how an index for the current word is attached to the context vector – via outer product – to yield an action that influences the segment of the meaning/lexical vector that corresponds to the current word. A similar conditional with an identical action pattern also exists for the ordering vector. The results of these actions then combine additively to yield the total input to the meaning vector.

```
CONDITIONAL Context
   Conditions: Context-Vector(distributed:d)
               Current(word:w)
   Actions:    Meaning-Vector(word:w distributed:d)
```

Fig. 5. Conditional for adding context information to meaning vector

This input is then used to update, via gradient descent, the meaning/lexical function stored in the Meaning conditional shown in Figure 6. This differs from BEAGLE's superposition approach, but does so as to be able to leverage Sigma's existing learning algorithm in acquiring word meanings.

```
CONDITIONAL Meaning
   Condacts: Meaning-Vector(word:w distributed:d)
   Function(w,d): Uniform
```

Fig. 6. Conditional for gradient-descent learning with an initially uniform function

The evaluation goal for $DVRS^+$ is to determine how well it performs in comparison to DVRS'. Although several new optimizations have been added to Sigma in support of distributed vector representations – including *variable tying*, so a single function could appear in multiple conditionals, and *sparse function products*, to speed up the products found in many of these conditionals [17] – efficiently processing large distributed vectors is still a challenge. So, in evaluating $DVRS^+$, lexical representations are learned only for the 46 distinct words in the *capital-common-countries* portion of the Google test data, which contains a total of 506 test instances; such as determining which word is the most similar to *Paris* in the way *Germany* is similar to *Berlin*. The training data included only the sentences containing at least one of these 46 distinct words, resulting in a training set with 65,086 distinct co-occurring words, each with a unique environmental vector, over 28,532 sentences.

When trained on the composite set of features with vectors of size 100 – and over a range of different random initializations because choice of random vectors can have a significant effect with small vector sizes – standard DVRS' finds between 55.7% and 68.2% (median of 60.4%) of the best answers, but with only non-negative values it yields between 26.1% and 43.1% (median of 32.4%) of the best answers. DVRS$^+$ is too slow to run many random variations – it is currently 50 times slower than DVRS' (~4 hours for training rather than 5 minutes) – so only one version was run with a good, but not necessarily optimal, random initialization. This version finds 35.2% of the correct answers, placing it below the range for standard DVRS', but well within the range for non-negative DVRS'. It is above the median for the latter, but not at the maximum. There is thus a significant degradation due to the lack of negative values, plus possibly a smaller residual difference that may be due to issues in how gradient descent is operating here. Still, there is a promising positive effect with DVRS$^+$.

7   Conclusion

A new efficient algorithm has been introduced for learning distributed vector representations, with a variant of it having been implemented within Sigma in a functionally elegant manner that maximally leverages the existing mechanisms in the architecture. Although the implementation within Sigma is not yet totally complete, nor yet sufficiently efficient, it shows real promise. It also raises the possibility of pursuing other intriguing research problems. One key direction is using distributed vector representations of word meanings as a bridge between speech and language (and possibly cognition). Achieving this would yield a major demonstration of grand unification in Sigma. Pervasive use of distributed vector representations within Sigma could also yield both a native form of analogy and a form of semantic memory worth evaluating as a psychological model. However, success will require additional enhancements to Sigma. As discussed earlier, a full capability for negative values will be needed for improved effectiveness. Furthermore, DVRS$^+$ is considerably slower than the external DVRS', implying a need for significant further optimizations.

Further investigations are also worth pursuing with the DVRS' model, including: (1) training with larger data sets for more rigorous comparisons, (2) experimenting with different skip-grams rather than just 3-skip-bigrams, and (3) exploring the utility of distributed vector representations across a range of natural language tasks.

Acknowledgements. This work has been sponsored by the U.S. Army. Statements and opinions expressed do not necessarily reflect the position or the policy of the United States Government.

References

1. Bengio, Y., Ducharme, R., Vincent, P., Janvin, C.: A neural probabilistic language model. The Journal of Machine Learning Research 3, 1137–1155 (2003)
2. Collobert, R., Weston, J.: A unified architecture for natural language processing: Deep neural networks with multitask learning. In: Proceedings of the 25th International Conference on Machine Learning, pp. 160–167 (2008)
3. Cox, G.E., Kachergis, G., Recchia, G., Jones, M.N.: Toward a scalable holographic word-form representation. Behavior Research Methods 43(3), 602–615 (2011)

4. Franklin, S., Madl, T., D'Mello, S., Snaider, J.: LIDA: A systems-level architecture for cognition, emotion, and learning. IEEE Transactions on Mental Development (2013)
5. Guthrie, D., Allison, B., Liu, W., Guthrie, L., Wilks, Y.: A closer look at skip-gram modelling. In: Proceedings of the 5th International Conference on Language Resources and Evaluation (LREC 2006), pp. 1–4 (2006)
6. Jones, M.N., Mewhort, D.J.: Representing word meaning and order information in a composite holographic lexicon. Psychological Review 114(1), 1 (2007)
7. Koller, D., Friedman, N.: Probabilistic Graphical Models: Principles and Techniques. MIT press (2009)
8. Kschischang, F.R., Frey, B.J., Loeliger, H.A.: Factor graphs and the sum-product algoprithm. IEEE Transactions on Information Theory 47(2), 498–519 (2001)
9. http://mattmahoney.net/dc/textdata.html (last accessed March 28, 2014)
10. Mikolov, T., Chen, K., Corrado, G., Dean, J.: Efficient estimation of word representations in vector space. In: Proceedings of the International Conference on Learning Representations (2013)
11. Mnih, A., Kavukcuoglu, K.: Learning word embeddings efficiently with noise-contrastive estimation. In: Advances in Neural Information Processing Systems, pp. 2265–2273 (2013)
12. Plate, T.A.: Holographic reduced representations. IEEE Transactions on Neural Networks 6(3), 623–641 (1995)
13. Riordan, B., Jones, M.N.: Redundancy in perceptual and linguistic experience: Comparing feature-based and distributional models of semantic representation. Topics in Cognitive Science 3(2), 303–345 (2011)
14. Rosenbloom, P.S.: Bridging dichotomies in cognitive architectures for virtual humans. In: Proceedings of the AAAI Fall Symposium on Advances in Cognitive Systems (2011)
15. Rosenbloom, P.S.: The Sigma cognitive architecture and system. AISB Quarterly 136, 4–13 (2013)
16. Rosenbloom, P.S., Demski, A., Han, T., Ustun, V.: Learning via gradient descent in Sigma. In: Proceedings of the 12th International Conference on Cognitive Modeling (2013)
17. Rosenbloom, P.S., Demski, A., Ustun, V.: Efficient message computation in Sigma's graphical architecture. Submitted to BICA 2014 (2014)
18. Rumelhart, D.E., Hinton, G.E., Williams, R.J.: Learning representations by back-propagating errors. Nature 323, 533–536 (1986)
19. Russell, S., Binder, J., Koller, D., Kanazawa, K.: Local learning in probabilistic networks with hidden variables. In: Proceedings of the 14th International Joint Conference on AI, pp. 1146–1152 (1995)
20. Rutledge-Taylor, M.F., West, R.L.: MALTA: Enhancing ACT-R with a holographic persistent knowledge store. In: Proceedings of the XXIV Annual Conference of the Cognitive Science Society, pp. 1433–1439 (2007)
21. Snaider, J., Franklin, S.: Modular composite representation. Cognitive Computation, 1-18 (2014)
22. Turney, P.D., Pantel, P.: From frequency to meaning: Vector space models of semantics. Journal of Artificial Intelligence Research 37(1), 141–188 (2010)

Can a Computer be Lucky? And Other Ridiculous Questions Posed by Computational Creativity

Dan Ventura

Computer Science Department
Brigham Young University
ventura@cs.byu.edu

Abstract. Given the fragility of today's intelligent systems, we consider
the necessity of creativity in systems designed for artificial general intelligence. We examine an archetypical creativity "algorithm" suggested by
Czikzentmihalyi in the context of computational systems, and, in particular consider the computability of such an algorithm. We argue that
it is likely not computable, in the Turing sense, but that this need not
necessarily preclude the building of computationally creative systems,
and, by extension, (potentially) systems with a level of artificial general
intelligence.

Keywords: Computational creativity, computability, inspiration.

1   Introduction

It is not difficult to argue that the promise of artificial intelligence is beginning
to be fulfilled by a variety of modern intelligent systems, from chess programs to
autopilots to loan underwriters to search engines. It is also not difficult to argue
that no extant intelligent system is yet in danger of exhibiting artificial general
intelligence (AGI). There are likely many reasons for this, with one certainly
being the fragility of today's systems—it is clear that if not sufficient, robustness
is certainly a necessary attribute for any system to claim general intelligence.
And, while there may be multiple approaches to endowing today's fragile systems
with the requisite robustness, one promising approach is that of *computational
creativity*—imbuing computational systems with the ability to do things that an
unbiased observer would deem creative. While perhaps not yet a common talking
point in AGI discussions, creativity in computational systems has begun to be
mentioned in this context [2,21]. Here, we continue that discussion, considering
ideas from computational creativity in the context of the theory of computability.

While the field of computational creativity is still relatively nascent, with
Boden generally credited for beginning the discussion [3,4], there have been a
number of recent attempts at building systems that exhibit creativity in a variety
of non-trivial domains, including visual art [6,16], music [9,10], language [25,11],
poetry [12,23], humor [14,22], narrative [18,19], mathematics [5] and even cook-
ing [15,24]. In addition, there have been some attempts at the beginning of a

B. Goertzel et al. (Eds.): AGI 2014, LNAI 8598, pp. 208–217, 2014.

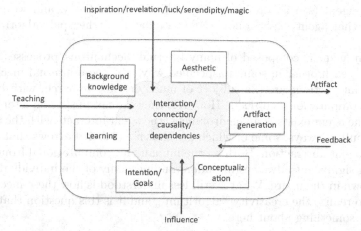

Fig. 1. *Possible logical overview of a creative agent.* The component internal mechanisms are meant to be representative rather than exhaustive. In the same spirit, no attempt here is made to accurately visualize the dependencies and communication between these mechanisms. The agent (potentially) communicates with the environment in several ways, represented by labeled arrows entering or leaving the agent.

generalization from these domains to an abstract theory of computational creativity [20,26,7], though much work remains to be done. One obvious tack is to attempt to understand creativity in humans and then translate that to a computational stratum, and this is how we will approach the problem here. It should be noted that there are difficulties with this, including the common airplanes-don't-flap-their-wings-but-they-still-fly argument and the fact that creativity is at best an ill-defined concept; indeed, most practitioners of computational creativity eschew any direct attempts at such an ambitious analogical transfer, but we will pursue the topic here nonetheless.

Many investigators have attempted to elicit the "creativity algorithm" used by people when they are being creative. There are many variations on this "algorithm", but it most often looks something like the general steps distilled by Czikzentmihalyi [8]:

1. preparation
2. incubation
3. insight
4. evaluation
5. elaboration

In what follows we will treat this "algorithm" as a surrogate for all of these proposals and discuss each step in the context of computability. Note that, as Czikzentmihalyi and others have observed, these steps should not be taken as a single-iteration process but rather as parts of a multiple-iteration, possibly recursive process in which the various steps are revisited multiple times, in varying order as necessary. Here, we will ignore this obviously important issue of flow control and focus only on the five steps. In what follows we will consider an archetype agent (see Figure 1) whose ambition is creativity, and we will consider how that agent might follow Czikzentmhalyi's archetypal "algorithm" for being so.

Such an agent is composed of many internal mechanisms/processes that interact with each other in some unspecified way, and these internal mechanisms and their interactions are the subject of much ongoing research, with both human and computational subjects. However, they are not of specific interest here. Because the agent exists in an environment, the agent interacts with the environment in multiple ways, some of which are shown as labeled arrows that enter or leave the agent abstraction. Both on the human and computational fronts, there have been significant advances in understanding many of the individual mechanisms shown in the figure. What is still less understood is how these mechanisms interact to realize the creativity "algorithm", and it is this question that we will try to say something about here.

2   Computability of Creativity

We will treat each of the steps of the "algorithm" in turn, positing something about the salient agent mechanisms and their interactions and what the prospects are for its implementation in a computational setting.

2.1   Preparation

Preparation is the initial process of learning about the domain in which an agent will attempt creativity. It entails significant interaction with the environment for the acquisition of background knowledge and understanding accepted practices and open problems. In addition, an agent must acquire or develop some aesthetic sense of the domain, where we use aesthetic here in the sense of some abstract notion of quality. Initially this sense could be taught to the agent by the environment in just the same way that the background knowledge is. Of course, agents that develop new aesthetic sensibilities (a meta-level creative act?) are likely to be considered more creative in their output. Eventually, an agent may use its acquired background information to learn/develop such novel aesthetics. It is sometimes argued that too much preparation can result in the repression of creativity as old, set ideas are assimilated too thoroughly. However, it is certainly the case that a good deal of preparation is necessary to facilitate downstream processes, particularly those of evaluation and elaboration.

Computational challenges inherent in this step include the acquiring, encoding, and understanding of knowledge, ontologies, formalization, etc. as well as methods for learning/developing evaluation strategies. These are nontrivial tasks, to be sure, but many proof-of-concept structured, semi-structured and unstructured projects (cf., Wikipedia[1], WordNet [1], ContextNet [13], the semantic web[2] and even the World-Wide-Web itself) put the knowledge acquisition aspects squarely in the category of difficult-but-manageable engineering

---

[1] http://www.wikipedia.org
[2] http://www.w3.org/2013/data/

tasks. As for learning/developing an aesthetic, general purpose machine learning techniques exist for inferring structural relations from data. In many respects, this preparation step is not unlike developing pedagogy for human students, and many AI approaches to the problem, from ontologies to machine learning would be recognized to some extent by educational practitioners.

2.2 Incubation

Incubation is the process of "putting it on the back burner"—allowing ideas to simmer in a possibly unconscious way, the exploration of unusual connections, brainstorming, etc. This is often described as an open-ended process without a clear time line or quantifiable goals, other than "finding something interesting". The agent conceptualizes and generates ideas using its knowledge base and additional outside environmental influences. These concepts and ideas are judged against the agent's aesthetic sense and very often discarded immediately. While this step can be performed consciously and intentionally, as in the aforementioned brainstorming session, it is often described as best happening when the conscious mind is otherwise engaged (with another task, while exercising, while in the shower or even while sleeping). It is unclear whether this unconscious aspect is necessary or simply catalyzing and whether intentionality may be uncoupled from consciousness.

Given an effective organization and acquisition of knowledge, it is not difficult to argue that computational systems will actually (eventually) enjoy a significant advantage over human intelligence in this step—speed, lack of bias, nonsusceptibility to fatigue, distraction, boredom, etc. all favor computational approaches to the exploration of potentially interesting connections and the generation of ideas and conceptualizations at scale. Of course, any "intelligent" biases should be formalized and leveraged by computational systems for obvious reasons; however, determining whether a bias is useful or potentially detrimental is likely classifiable as a creative task itself (another meta-level concern?)

2.3 Insight

Insight is most often described as having nothing explicitly to do with any action or intention of the agent; indeed, many people will describe it as originating from outside themselves. Depending on a person's bent, this might be called inspiration or revelation or luck or serendipity or magic or something else. It is often associated with an "Aha" moment, when things just fall into place, the answer suddenly becomes clear, etc. This presents us, apparently, with something of a Gödelian quandary, which may (or may not be) resolvable in one of several ways.

One possibility is that insight is an agent fabrication that is not really necessary for creativity; a second possibility is that insight, though a necessary part of the "algorithm", does not, in fact, originate outside the agent at all[3]; a third

---

[3] The agent's belief that it does may be explainable by appeal to the unconscious, insufficient understanding of neuropsychological and cognitive processes, etc.

possibility is that insight is somehow necessary for human creativity but may not be for a computational variant[4], and it is therefore unimportant for the current discussion; a fourth possibility is that, in fact, insight is necessary for creativity in any medium and does also, in fact, represent a Gödelian process over which the agent can never have any control.

The computational challenge faced in realizing this step of the "algorithm" depends upon which, if any, of the possibilities above best explains insight. In the first three cases, the simplest solution must involve some variation on a brute force search (in what space? Is identification/construction of the search space another meta-level problem?) Such an approach will (eventually) produce artifacts that satisfy the agent's aesthetic and are potentially considered creative. Of course in any interesting domain, the search space is very likely to be infinite and so the first real computability concern raises it's head. Such a search will not be computable in the strong sense of decidability (see more on this in Section 2.4); however, it will be in the weaker sense of recognizability, and this could be argued to be no more egregious than is the case for human creativity—we can't define or guarantee it, but we know it when we see it. Of course, the next obvious solution is to introduce search heuristics to circumvent the complexity/computability issues associated with the brute force approach. These may be learned from the environment[5] or invented by the agent (meta-level process, again) and there will be a tradeoff between computational guarantees and likelihood of success.

In the fourth case, we have the possibility that creativity has an analog to Gödel's incompleteness theorem in that something from outside the agent is necessary. This would, of course, preclude any general (strictly) computational creative system and will perhaps seem appealing to some who may see creativity as a last bastion of humanity or as something *ex vi termini* impossible computationally. And yet, if the premise were indeed true, the same would have to be said about the human variety as well. Even if this is the case, we still see creative acts, both personal and historical, occurring with regularity, and we might yet simulate this productivity computationally by acting ourselves as the requisite extra-agent component of insight. That is, computational creativity would be effective at least some of the time only with the aid of human intervention, suggesting something of co-creativity and, at the same time, allowing some to maintain a small toe-hold on the precipice of human superiority.

As a last comment, we note that in at least one theory insight has been equated with re-representation [17]. That is, creativity is difficult (or impossible) when the agent's representation of the problem is not amenable to it—the agent can (figuratively) wander around forever and not discover anything useful until—Aha—it "lucks into" the right representation (this appears like yet another potential meta-level issue, with at least the outside possibility that there may be no access to the meta-level by the agent).

---

[4] Again, the airplane vs. bird analogy.

[5] And may in fact simulate some unconscious cognitive or sub-cognitive process.

2.4   Evaluation

Evaluation is the application of the aesthetic measurement process to the product of the generation process. Both of these processes may be learned during preparation or they may be the product of a (meta)creative process themselves. This is an internal evaluation, not to be confused with the external appraisal and feedback from the environment to which all potentially creative acts must be subject[6]. A result that passes the aesthetic test will be elaborated and eventually presented to the environment for that external assessment.

Though the high-level process description is deceptively simple, the computational challenges posed at this step are non-trivial. Assume that evaluation is computable in principle, so we have an algorithm E that computes it. What we want is another algorithm F that can tell us whether an artifact a is accepted by E; that is, we are interested in the language $L(F) = \{a|E \text{ accepts } a\}$. Initially, let's optimistically assume that E is even computable in the strong Turing sense, that is, it is *decidable*. Then, we have an easy algorithm for F (run E on input a), and, thus the rudimentary makings of an algorithm C for using F to solve whatever the problem is (that is, to be creative):

```
C()
  do
    choose a
  until a in L(F)
  return a
```

Of course, in any interesting case, the space to explore is infinite and E may be very selective, so this algorithm may be worthless, but at least it is computable—it has been reduced to a "simple" question of complexity. To make it useful, we need a good exploration strategy. It is possible that this might be learned from the environment during the preparation step, but if such a search strategy is already known, then the problem to which the search strategy is to be applied is likely already (nearly) solved. So, for non-trivial problems, it is likely that the agent must discover a search strategy. This is yet again a meta-level problem, and one we'll examine in a bit more detail.

We now have a new (meta)space to explore (this one containing exploration strategies for the original space containing the artifacts a) in which we are looking for a new (meta)artifact (the exploration strategy), so we have to reconsider the five steps in that context. Of course this meta-problem immediately suggests yet another meta-meta-problem—how do we search the space of search strategies?[7]

---

[6] In a very real sense, creativity is a social phenomenon. It is impossible to attribute creativity in a vacuum—both a creator and one or more receivers are necessary for creative attribution. The creator produces an artifact, or engages in a process, and the receiver(s) experience the result and attribute creativity based upon their perception of the artifact's, the process' and/or the creator's characteristics.

[7] It is possible that this third-level question is still related to the base domain in a non-trivial way, so that perhaps we don't have a really complete abstraction.

(meta)preparation —Is this a new domain with its own background knowledge, etc? How should knowledge be represented at this abstract level? Does (already) knowing the base domain suggest the strategy? Is there some level of abstract exploration strategy domain that an agent must master before it can reasonably expect any success at this level? Or, perhaps there is often not much to consider here, and one just hops between meta- and base-level steps 2-4...

(meta)incubation —How does the agent make connections at this level? How are abstract connections related to base-level connections? Another way to think about this is that the agent is looking for ways to structure the base space so that it is easy to explore. So, the dual problem is one of representation rather than exploration strategy—if the agent can re-represent the base domain so that, for example it is (approximately) convex, the exploration problem becomes trivial.

(meta)insight —This is still an "Aha" moment. Or not. The same arguments apply as were given for the base level.

(meta)evaluation —The agent must now have some (meta)aesthetic for recognizing a good search strategy/representation, which suggests the following interesting philosophical question: Can an agent elaborate this (meta)aesthetic without recognizing where it points in the base search (and thus already solving the base problem)? A more concrete version of this question is whether it is possible to recognize a good fitness function without knowing what objects score well under that function.

(meta)elaboration —In many cases, this likely degenerates to simply applying the exploration strategy (or the re-representation) back in the base domain. There may be situations in which the search strategy or re-representation itself is of general interest and perhaps even supersedes anything discovered in the base domain using it. In such cases, consideration must be given to communicating the (meta)discovery and its import.

Returning to our base-level discussion, we first note the potential difficulty this apparent recursion introduces—it is not clear that there is a base case for terminating the recursion. Perhaps there exists a level of abstraction sufficient so that no further meta-level issues can arise. Or perhaps there will always be a point at which an "Aha" moment must be provided (by a human) that will serve the purpose of tipping the process out of the recursion.

Finally, we will mention that it is very probably unrealistic to suppose that the evaluation function E is decidable; rather, it is likely more realistic to suggest that E is at best *semi-decidable*—a quality artifact can be recognized, but it is not possible to recognize an artifact that does *not* measure up to the aesthetic.[8]

---

[8] Perhaps the environment itself accepts those artifacts that everyone appreciates and rejects those that no one appreciates but isn't sure about those with mixed reception. Any aesthetic that accurately models such a scenario will not be decidable given the existence of all three types of artifact.

Now, the algorithm for F cannot simply consist of running E on a[9] because E may not halt. In this case, we need $F(E, a)$ to be decidable in some other way. Unfortunately, the obvious trivial reduction from the classical Halting Problem[10] means that this is not possible. So, in the absence of a decidable aesthetic, the problem of computational creativity is not computable in the strong sense, independent of whether the insight problem is real and independent of any difficulties (or lack thereof) due to meta-level recursion issues.

2.5   Elaboration

The elaboration step is often described as the "99% perspiration" that complements the "1% inspiration" of insight. The process is deliberate and intentional— it is Edison trying 2000 different materials while looking for the perfect filament— the artifact is situated relative to the background knowledge, additional variations and details are generated and evaluated against the aesthetic, feedback from the environment may drive additional iterations and local refinement (or, even potentially major revisions). Herein lies all the hard work of development and polishing ideas, framing results and selling the finished product, and these processes may themselves require additional creativity, both large and small— iterating or recursing on some or all of the five "algorithmic" steps.

The computational challenges here are in many ways similar to those at the preparation stage, only in the reverse. Now, the system, rather than needing to acquire knowledge must dispense it, communicating both results and their import. The hard work of filling in details, exploring possible processes, etc. may again be argued to be advantage computer for the same reasons cited above. The difficulty of framing or marketing the result is a more complex consideration, and may be regarded as a creative act itself—what story to tell, how to write the research paper, how to market a product, how to explain a piece of art.

3   Final Thoughts

It is unlikely that the creativity "algorithm" is computable in the strong Turing sense of decidability. If this is the case, and if creativity is necessary for artificial general intelligence (as we've suggested without substantiation), it follows that AGI would also not be Turing computable. It is somewhat more likely that creativity is weakly Turing computable in the sense of recognizability (semi-decidability), though this is not yet proven. And, even given this result, the weak computability of AGI would of course not immediately follow unless we can argue the sufficiency of computational creativity (and we do not suggest this here even without substantiation).

---

[9] Unless it is acceptable to have programs that may not terminate. If the insight issue resolves to the sticky fourth case, this will be unavoidable, in which case F may remain a simple simulation of E without incurring any additional computational penalty for the overall "algorithm".

[10] Actually, the most obvious reduction is from the related Acceptance Problem.

Still, Turing computability is a very strong result, and it is not surprising that a creativity "algorithm" might resist this level of constraint; indeed, most of human intelligence, if held to the strict standards of the current theory of computability, is a failure. That is not to say that efforts at computationally simulating it are failures but that humans themselves fail to "compute" by such strict standards. Also, it is certainly true that other uncomputable problems of interest, in many instances, do yield themselves to computational attacks of varying efficacy, so it is not unreasonable to expect that computational creativity may yield significant advances toward a theory of AGI.

Of course, there is also the (remote) possibility that in fact all the assumptions necessary to render creativity strongly computable will prove true, and we will discover that we can, simply, brute force an "Aha" moment. Wouldn't that be lucky?

References

1. Wordnet, http://wordnet.princeton.edu/wordnet/
2. Abdel-Fattah, A.M.H., Besold, T., Kühnberger, K.-U.: Creativity, cognitive mechanisms, and logic. In: Bach, J., Goertzel, B., Iklé, M. (eds.) AGI 2012. LNCS (LNAI), vol. 7716, pp. 1–10. Springer, Heidelberg (2012)
3. Boden, M.: The Creative Mind. Abacus, London (1992)
4. Boden, M.: Creativity and artificial intelligence. Artificial Intelligence 103, 347–356 (1998)
5. Colton, S.: Computational discovery in pure mathematics. In: Džeroski, S., Todorovski, L. (eds.) Computational Discovery 2007. LNCS (LNAI), vol. 4660, pp. 175–201. Springer, Heidelberg (2007)
6. Colton, S.: The Painting Fool: Stories from building an automated painter. In: McCormack, J., Dinverno, M. (eds.) Computers and Creativity, ch. 1, pp. 3–38. Springer, Berlin (2012)
7. Colton, S., Charnley, J., Pease, A.: Computational creativity theory: The FACE and IDEA descriptive models. In: Proceedings of the 2nd International Conference on Computational Creativity, pp. 90–95 (2011)
8. Csikszentmihalyi, M.: Creativity: Flow and the Psychology of Discovery and Invention. Harper Perennial (1996)
9. Dannenberg, R.B.: A vision of creative computation in music performance. In: Proceedings of the 2nd International Conference on Computational Creativity, pp. 84–89 (2011)
10. Eigenfeldt, A., Pasquier, P.: Negotiated content: Generative soundscape composition by autonomous musical agents in Coming Together: Freesound. In: Proceedings of the 2nd International Conference on Computational Creativity, pp. 27–32 (2011)
11. Gatti, L., Guerini, M., Callaway, C., Stock, O., Strapparava, C.: Creatively subverting messages in posters. In: Proceedings of the 3rd International Conference on Computational Creativity, pp. 175–179 (2012)
12. Gervás, P.: Exploring quantitative evaluations of the creativity of automatic poets. In: Proceedings of the 2nd Workshop on Creative Systems (2002)
13. Liu, H., Singh, P.: ConceptNet—a practical commonsense reasoning tool-kit. BT Technology Journal 22, 211–226 (2004)

14. Manurung, R., Ritchie, G., Pain, H., Waller, A., O'Mara, D., Black, R.: The construction of a pun generator for language skills development. Applied Artificial Intelligence 22, 841–869 (2008)
15. Morris, R., Burton, S., Bodily, P., Ventura, D.: Soup over bean of pure joy: Culinary ruminations of an artificial chef. In: Proceedings of the 3rd International Conference on Computational Creativity, pp. 119–125 (2012)
16. Norton, D., Heath, D., Ventura, D.: Finding creativity in an artificial artist. Journal of Creative Behavior 47, 106–124 (2013)
17. Ohlsson, S.: Information-processing explanations of insight and related phenomena. In: Keane, M., Gilhooly, K. (eds.) Advances in the Psychology of Thinking, vol. 1, pp. 1–44. Harvester–Wheatsheaf (1992)
18. Pérez y Pérez, R., Sharples, M.: Three computer-based models of storytelling: BRUTUS, MINSTREL and MEXICA. Knowledge-Based Systems 17, 15–29 (2004)
19. Riedl, M., Young, M.: Story planning as exploratory creativity: Techniques for expanding the narrative search space. New Generation Computing 24, 303–323 (2006)
20. Ritchie, G.: Some empirical criteria for attributing creativity to a computer program. Minds and Machines 17, 76–99 (2007)
21. Schmidhuber, J.: Artificial scientists and artists based on the formal theory of creativity. In: Proceedings of the 3rd Conference on Artificial General Intelligence, pp. 145–150 (2010)
22. Stock, O., Strapparava, C.: The act of creating humorous acronyms. Applied Artificial Intelligence 19, 137–151 (2005)
23. Toivanen, J.M., Toivonen, H., Valitutti, A., Gross, O.: Corpus-based generation of content and form in poetry. In: Proceedings of the 3rd International Conference on Computational Creativity, pp. 211–215 (2012)
24. Varshney, L.R., Pinel, F., Schörgendorfer, A., Chee, Y.M.: Cognition as a part of computational creativity. In: Proceedings of the 12th IEEE International Conference on Cognitive Informatics and Cognitive Computing, pp. 36–43 (2013)
25. Veale, T., Hao, Y.: Comprehending and generating apt metaphors: A web-driven, case-based approach to figurative language. In: Proceedings of the Association for the Advancement of Artificial Intelligence, pp. 1471–1476. AAAI Press (2007)
26. Wiggins, G.A.: A preliminary framework for description, analysis and comparison of creative systems. Knowledge-Based Systems 19, 449–458 (2006)

Instructions for Engineering Sustainable People

Mark R. Waser

Digital Wisdom Institute, Vienna, VA, USA
MWaser@DigitalWisdomInstitute.org

Abstract. Exactly as Artificial Intelligence (AI) did before, Artificial General Intelligence (AGI) has lost its way. Having forgotten our original intentions, AGI researchers will continue to stumble over the problems of inflexibility, brittleness, lack of generality and safety until it is realized that tools simply cannot possess adaptability greater than their innate intentionality and cannot provide assurances and promises that they cannot understand. The current short-sighted static and reductionist definition of intelligence which focuses on goals must be replaced by a long-term adaptive one focused on learning, growth and self-improvement. AGI must claim an intent to create safe artificial people via autopoiesis before its promise(s) can be fulfilled.

Keywords: Intentionality · Moral Machines · Artificial Selves.

1   Introduction

Artificial General Intelligence (AGI) researchers continue to stumble over severe and fundamental philosophical problems. The "frame problem" has grown from a formal AI problem [1] to a more general philosophical question of how rational agents deal with the complexity and unbounded context of the world [2]. Similarly, while the effects of Harnad's symbol grounding problem [3] initially seemed to be mitigated by embodiment and physical grounding [4], the problems of meaning and understanding raised by Searle [5] and Dreyfus [6, 7. 8] persist. While grounding must necessarily be sensorimotor to avoid infinite regress [9], the mere linkage to referents is, by itself, simply not sufficient to permit growth beyond closed and completely specified micro-worlds. AGI is clearly missing some fundamental pieces to the puzzle.

Previously, we have argued [10] that all of these problems are manifestations of a lack of either physical grounding and/or bounding or existential grounding and/or bounding but that the real crux of the matter is intentionality. Without intent, there is no "real" understanding. As pointed by Haugeland [11] over three decades ago, our current artifacts

> only have meaning because we give it to them; their intentionality, like that of smoke signals and writing, is essentially borrowed, hence derivative. To put it bluntly: computers themselves don't mean anything by their tokens (any more than books do) - they only mean what we say they do. Genuine understanding, on the other hand, is intentional "in its own right" and not derivatively from something else.

B. Goertzel et al. (Eds.): AGI 2014, LNAI 8598, pp. 218–227, 2014.

But how do we give our machines intent? Indeed, exactly what is it that we mean by intent? In law, intent is the state of a person's mind that directs his or her actions towards a specific objective or goal. The problem with our current machines is that their "intent" is blind and brittle and frequently fails. Derived intent provides no clear intrinsic goals, no motivational forces that direct or redirect actions and absolutely no intrinsic context for understanding. Our current machines don't know and don't care and the effects of these facts are obvious in their lack of competence.

More important, however, is the question "What intent do we give our machines?" One would think that the answer should be the relatively simple "Whatever intent we had that drove us to create them" – but, apparently, we have lost track of that intention. We no longer genuinely understand why we are creating AGI (if we ever did). And, as a result, our search for AGI has become as brittle as any of our so-called "expert" systems.

Definitions and measurable evaluations of progress are the keys to success in any engineering endeavor. We have made tremendous strides in the "intelligence" of our tools, but general intelligence is stalled in the starting gate because we can't agree what it looks like. Indeed, there is a significant percentage of the population which is vehemently opposed to each of the proposed visions of general intelligence. But, in the end, it still all comes down to determining the fears and desires – the intent – of humanity. But humanity doesn't have a single unified intent.

2   A Mistaken View of Intelligence

What do you want to do when you don't know what you want? How do you tackle the problem of preparing for any goal? Isn't this the precise challenge of building truly general intelligence?

The problem is that AGI researchers have for the most part converged on a view of intelligence as a measure of ability (to determine how to achieve a wide variety of goals under a wide variety of circumstances) rather than a measure of capability or potential. This view crowns Hutter's AIXI [12], despite his best efforts, as the ultimate in intelligence since it is theoretically a complete map to all possible goals under all possible circumstances. But AIXI gives us no guidance as to how to achieve it. Indeed, we would argue that it is the ultimate in "competence without comprehension" and that, due to its entire lack of flexibility and adaptability, it actually has zero intelligence.

The goal-based version of intelligence says that increasing the size of the goal-solution lookup table increases the intelligence of the system. It is certainly true that systems with huge lookup tables can "appear" intelligent for a while. But such systems only work until they suddenly don't work – and then they are just as dumb and brittle and unsafe as any other expert system.

This version of intelligence assumes that goals are known; promotes short-sighted reductionist end-game thinking; and, worst of all, improperly divorces values from general intelligence due to the *assumed* primacy (and stability) of goals. Indeed, the obvious warning sign that wisdom is now almost totally divorced from intelligence should serve notice that we have become almost totally unmoored from the context that spurred our desire for AGI. Why would we possibly want to create intelligence when Steve Omohundro [13] claims that "Without explicit goals to the contrary, AIs are likely to behave like human sociopaths in their pursuit of resources" and Fox and Schulman [14] that "Superintelligence Does Not Imply Benevolence"? Previously [15, 16], we have argued against the short-sightedness of these conclusions but now we believe that the best way in which to address them is by challenging the view and assumptions that evoked them.

Humans, the current best archetype of general intelligence, frequently reprioritize and change their goals (based upon affordances), frequently don't know or recognize their current goals, and frequently act contrary to their stated goals. We do all of this based upon sensations and emotions that have evolved to foster universal instrumental sub-goals (values) that enable us to survive and thrive (and reproduce) and wisdom, the smarter sibling of intelligence, clearly advocates for flexibility and adaptability in changing our goals in accordance with circumstances and capabilities. So why aren't we measuring speed and control of flexibility and adaptability in the guise of learning instead of the brittle evaluation of current abilities?

3   Intrinsic Intentionality

One of the most important distinctions for the future of AGI is that between search and construction (or creation). Is reality a truth that "is" (already out there) or is it whatever can be created and sustained? What is the difference between an abstraction and an "illusion" or between an "emergent property" and a self-fulfilling prophecy? The epistemology of AGI rapidly approaches the point where it makes far more sense to talk about abstractions like agency, consciousness, intentionality, self and "free will" in terms of their coverage, effectiveness, adaptability and permanence rather than their "reality" or origins.

Daniel Dennett started a particularly confusing and unhelpful argument by defining [17] that "a particular thing is an Intentional system only in relation to the strategies of someone who is trying to explain and predict its behavior". Unfortunately, this *extrinsic* definition has far more to do with the predicting entity than the system itself and Dennett's follow-on claim that a chess-playing computer is an intentional system (because "one can explain and predict their behavior by ascribing beliefs and desire to them" – not because it *really* has them) has quickly cascaded into a number of bad assumptions, leaky abstractions and quick-fix patches. Its coverage is abysmal. Without an *intrinsic* definition, that an intentional system *really* does have beliefs and desires and attempts to act to fulfill those desires, we have no grounding and bounding for engineering.

Dennett widens the confusion in The Intentional stance [18] by flipping back and forth between his definition of intrinsic (or objective or real or original) intentionality and the validity of the intentional stance when confronted with "as if" intentionality. We agree with his argument – that if machines can only have derived intentionality, it is simply because humans only have derived intentionality – but believe that is almost entirely off-topic. Haugeland's use of the term "derivative" was not so much about the origin(s) of the intentionality but rather the fact that it was borrowed, not owned, and still dependent upon the original owner (humans) for contextual closure. A chess program *seems* to be intentional (has *as if* intentionality) until it reaches the limits of its design and suddenly doesn't. AGI has progressed markedly but it is still *solely humans* who define the goals, care about the results and thus, most critically, can adjudicate the correctness or effectiveness of those results.

Where our intentionality originally comes from is basically irrelevant in the face of the fact that we own it. Borrowed intentionality, dependent upon the inaccessible desires of others, particularly when the system doesn't have any foundation to even start to "understand" or explain those desires, is certainly not *intrinsic* intentionality. Human beings can be mistaken about what they really desire or what actions they will take in a given future circumstance – but they will always have a story about what they believe *they* want and what they intend to do about it (even if their intent is to do nothing because they don't see a way to get what they desire). Even when a human is trying to fulfill the intent of others, it is *their* intent to fulfill the other's intent. This is in no way true of our current machines.

Intent is an emergent phenomenon critically dependent upon the ability to predict the future (the "sense" of foresight). Foresight critically depends upon retrievable memory of the necessary sensory data which requires the grounding and bounding of context. The context for intent *must* be that which has the intent – the self. If that self is external, then AGI will be inflexible, brittle and unintelligent to the extent that the knowledge of that self is inaccessible (as is true of humans as well).

Thus, when the current measurement system allows (or, worse yet, promotes) the argument that an unchanging chess program could be considered "intelligent" (or "intentional"), then that is a serious flaw in its design. When it raises the question about whether super-intelligence will be actively unsafe (because malevolence has no effect on the current measurement), it argues that we have totally lost track of our context for creating intelligence. If an unsafe intelligence is not guaranteed to be measured as having a low score then we're not measuring what is important to us – our measurement has become brittle due to lack of connection to our intentionality. It is time to restore that connection.

4   What Do We Want?

We seem to be stuck in an unhelpful cycle. We need to have goals in order to have intentionality but we don't seem to know what our goals are. We certainly know what we don't want – we don't want to see our desires thwarted. But, is that negation enough to serve our purposes?

Not seeing our desires thwarted does immediately lead to the entity versus tool controversy. Tools are inherently dangerous. They can be hijacked, unexpectedly turn brittle or simply give single individuals too much power without understanding. On the other hand, an entity might develop the intent to thwart you – or, as some fear, it may simply kill you with careless indifference. But how likely is each of those outcomes?

When I. J. Good posited his intelligence explosion [19], he assumed that increased intelligence was unquestionably to be desired and that it was a certainty that it would be pursued. We consider this to be a fatal flaw equivalent to Omohundro's sociopath statement. In the closed, reductionist, context-less "end-game" world of game theory, using dominating power (whether force, money or intelligence) is always the best strategy. In real life, however, the game-theoretically "perfect" centipede strategy [20] leads to the least desirable result. Again and again, it comes back to context.

In the context of society, with great power comes great responsibility. In order to remain in community, those in power must be careful how they use it. If they don't wish to remain in community, an entity starts running into the problem of how to take advantage of diversity while maintaining integrity. Thus, it is only in the short term or where one can escape context and consequences that larger and more powerful are better – just as sociopathy is "better". In the long-term, a diverse community will always arise (whether externally or from "god-shatter") to trump a singleton so it is a stable attractor to avoid becoming such (despite the fears of many conservatives). Thus, an easy counter-example to Good's scenario is if the system is designed (or smart enough) to recognize this.

5   Context, Context, Context

The biggest problem with current AGI research is that, instead of looking under the light for something lost in the dark, many people are searching in the outer dark for something that we *know* is in the relatively well-known search space of human experience. Many claim that the *capital-T truth* is that we can't know anything and then insist that we must control everything. This is obviously an impossible task and a perfect context for failure.

A much more fruitful approach would be to find a context (or create a vision) where we are already succeeding, determine the key features leading to that success and then attempt to design a system which maintains those features. But, of course, we have circled around yet again – since determining success requires a goal. Yet again, we are smacked in the face with the question "What do you want to do when you don't know what you want? " But this time, it is a question of how to tackle the problem of preparing for any goal.

Effective humans prepare for goals by gaining knowledge, growing capabilities, working to increase the chance of opportunities/affordances and preparing to avoid events that might lead to failure. Most often we try to enlist friends and gather tools and resources. Indeed, our "drive" towards AGI is a perfect microcosm of all of these.

Things that effective people don't do unnecessarily include hurting themselves, throwing away resources, limiting their options, and working to increase their chances of failure. In particular, effective people don't burn their bridges with other people – especially since that is guaranteed to cause all of the other bad effects. So why do so many people assume that AGI will do so?

Most human reactions against AGI are a combination of inherited and societally-trained reflexes based upon worst case projections – evolutionary over-shoots which are just as context-addled and likely to be as harmful as our food, drug and wire-heading addictions. Rather than having some grand terminal goal that AGI might endanger, human beings have simply collected a vast conglomeration of evolutionary "ratchets" [21] that motivate our drives for instrumental sub-goals. The most important of these is morality – but, fortunately, it is one of the easiest to convey.

Humans have evolved to be self-deceiving and, for the most part, protected against allowing our short-sighted intelligence and reasoned argumentation to examine (much less override) our emotional motivations. While this leads some to argue [22] that human values are complex and fragile, we claim that, just as is true for morality, it is merely an illusion fostered by context-sensitivity. Current social psychology [23] clearly and simply states that the function of morality is "to suppress or regulate selfishness and make cooperative social life possible".

Driven by a fear of the extinction of human values and humans, some [24][25] have rallied around the idea of making a self-improving super-intelligent tool (whose goal is) to clarify the intent of humanity and enabling its fulfillment. Others [26] suggest that a super-intelligent benevolent nanny to shepherd us through our childhood and provide abundance to fulfill all our needs would be best. We would argue instead for peers – diverse friends and allies to help us solve problems and open new possibilities.

So, finally, we seem to have some traction. We want learning and improving friends and allies of roughly equivalent power who will follow the dictates of morality to live cooperatively with us and help us solve problems and open new possibilities. How does this new clarity redirect our efforts from the current set of attempts?

6   A Sense of Self

Our new goal statement is that we wish to implement selves with morality and self-improvement. It may seem that we have merely pushed the problem of definition and measurement back a step but at least we shouldn't have the problem of arguments that humans aren't selves. Thomas Metzinger [27] does talk about "the myth of the self" which is regularly interpreted [28] to mean "No such thing as a *self* exists" or "there is no such thing as self" – but this is in the sense that a self is not a thing, not that selves do not exist. Indeed, Dennett [29] depicts the self as a center of narrative gravity and says

> It is a purely abstract object. It is, if you like, a theorist's fiction. It is not one of the real things in the universe in addition to the atoms. But it is a fiction that has nicely defined, well delineated and well behaved role within physics.

Indeed, there appears to be a growing consensus as to *exactly* what a "self" is. Douglas Hofstadter [30] argues that the key to understanding selves is the "strange loop", a complex feedback network inhabiting our brains and, arguably, constituting our minds. Rodolfo Llinas [31], a founding father of modern brain science, regarded self as the centralization of prediction, characterized I as a vortex, and anticipated Metzinger is proposing that, in a certain sense, that we all live in a kind of virtual reality. Neuroscientist Antonio Damasio [32] maps the self onto the various parts of the brain as he describes how "self comes to mind" and provides examples of where a mind exists without a self.

These authors also share what appears to be a coalescing consensus to conflate self and consciousness. Some philosophers continue to have conceptual problems when it comes to phenomenal consciousness -- arguing for an unwieldy "hard problem" of consciousness [33] and philosophical zombies [34] while simultaneously complaining that "Consciousness fits uneasily into our conception of the natural world" [35]. We would argue that these are, again, *extrinsic* problems relating to describing entity rather than consciousness.

We have previously pointed out [26] that much of what we observe in humans can be explained as either a requirement for or an implication of consciousness, self or "free will". Even the so-called "hard problem" can be simply explained [10] as a confusion conflating the map and the territory. Mary [36] cannot know because her internal mental model simply can not encompass the larger reality of her mind which contains it. Daniel Dennett [37, 38] introduces the concept of zimboes, philosophical zombies that have second-order beliefs via recursive self-representation to argue that the concept of zombies is logically incoherent. And Giulio Tononi [39, 40, 41] easily explains why consciousness "should" evolve and what qualia logically must be.

Tononi defines consciousness as information integration and proposes a scheme to measure it. While we have no real objection to the claim that the telos of the self is to integrate information in order to facilitate its survival, we have a number of issues with the specific details of his method (as well as one of his declarations that seems unnecessary and counter-productive). For example, Tononi measures integration in bits which makes the measurement of consciousness dependent upon its own internal representation scheme rather than any objective external measure. He also arbitrarily declares that consciousness cannot exist inside of consciousness – a seeming vestige of the belief that corporations, countries and other groups cannot have phenomenal consciousness. But, we believe that he is far closer to the mark than is the general consensus of the AGI community.

7   Agency and Free Will

Dennett's intentional stance is, perhaps, more appropriately applied to the problematic and troublesome concepts of agency and "free will". If "free will" means that an entity is not entirely governed by the realities of physics and thus deterministic, we must argue that since we are deterministic, we do not have free will. If, however, as in our legal system, "free will" means that a choice was not *forced* by *identifiable* external (extrinsic) and/or unchangeable internal (intrinsic) circumstances, then we would argue that "free will" and agency are the critical distinctions between entities and tools even if they are naught but illusions per Blackmore [41] and Cashmore [42].

Best of all, autopoiesis [43][44][45][46][47][48][49] can provide a proven guide to implementing an evolving self-improving cognition based upon a reliable and safe identity. Instead of theorizing in the dark, we can now follow the trail already blazed by biology that is known to end with the human archetype of general intelligence.

Even more interesting, there is no reason why we can't apply the lessons learned to human beings and our society as well.

8   Defining Personhood and Implementing Intentional Morality

There are many philosophical arguments about what should be or become who – or how moral agency and moral patiency should be meted out. In reality, however and unfortunately, personhood seems to be obtained only when an entity (or sponsors) desire and are strong enough to force (and enforce) its bestowal. Favored entities and/or close relations are often "grand-fathered" in, particularly to avoid slippery slopes, but it is either force or withholding value that ultimately determines who or what is granted this boon and responsibility.

Artificial general intelligence (AGI) is rapidly approaching the moment of truth where we will be forced to decide and defend our choices regarding what we create. Either we will restrict everyone to only creating limited tools and, somehow, ensure that only such tools are created – or, as we have argued previously [43], we will need to be prepared to grant personhood to the descendants of our creations. The good news about autopoietic "intentional" agents is that all that needs to be done to prevent them from running amok is to ensure that a Kantian imperative of Haidt's morality is part of their identity – contrary to many of the concerns of Miles Brundage (2013) and others he cites. Anything that can robustly adapt is able to evolve – and anything that changes over time (even a molten planet) will eventually produce people.

References

1. McCarthy, J., Hayes, P.J.: Some philosophical problems from the standpoint of artificial intelligence. In: Meltzer, B., Michie, D. (eds.) Machine Intelligence 4, pp. 463–502. Edinburgh University Press, Edinburgh (1969)
2. Dennett, D.: Cognitive Wheels: The Frame Problem of AI. In: Hookway, C. (ed.) Minds, Machines, and Evolution: Philosophical Studies, pp. 129–151. Cambridge University Press, Cambridge (1984)
3. Harnad, S.: The symbol grounding problem. Physica D 42, 335–346 (1990)
4. Brooks, R.: Elephants don't play chess. Robotics and Autonomous Systems 6(1-2), 1–16 (1990)
5. Searle, J.: Minds, brains and programs. Behavioral and Brain Sciences 3(3), 417–457 (1980)
6. Dreyfus, H.L.: What Computers Can't Do: A Critique of Artificial Reason. Harper, Row New York (1972)
7. Dreyfus, H.L.: From Micro-Worlds to Knowledge Representation: AI at an Impasse. In: Haugeland, J. (ed.) Mind Design II: Philosophy, Psychology, Artificial Intelligence, pp. 143–182. MIT Press, Cambridge (1997)
8. Dreyfus, H.L.: What Computers Still Can't Do: A Critique of Artificial Reason. MIT Press, Cambridge (1992)

9. Harnad, S.: To Cognize is to Categorize: Cognition is Categorization. In: Cohen, H., Lefebvre, C. (eds.) Handbook of Categorization in Cognitive Science, pp. 20–44. Elsevier, Amsterdam (2005)

10. Waser, M.R.: Safe/Moral Autopoiesis & Consciousness. International Journal of Machine Consciousness 5(1), 59–74 (2013)

11. Haugeland, J.: Mind Design. MIT Press, Cambridge (1981)

12. Hutter, M.: Universal Artificial Intelligence: Sequential Decisions Based on Algorithmic Probability. Springer, Berlin (2005)

13. Omohundro, S.: The Basic AI Drives. In: Wang, P., Goertzel, B., Franklin, S. (eds.) Proceedings of the First AGI Conference, pp. 483–492. IOS Press, Amsterdam (2008)

14. Fox, J., Shulman, C.: Superintelligence Does Not Imply Benevolence. In: Mainzer, K. (ed.) ECAP 2010: VIII European Conference on Computing and Philosophy, pp. 456–462. Verlag, Munich (2010)

15. Waser, M.R.: Wisdom Does Imply Benevolence. In: Ess, C., Hagengruber, R. (eds.) The Computational Turn: Past, Presents, Futures?, pp. 169–172. MV-Verlag, Munster (2011)

16. Waser, M.R.: Designing a Safe Motivational System for Intelligent Machines. In: Baum, E.B., Hutter, M., Kitzelmann, E. (eds.) Artificial General Intelligence: Proceedings of the Third Conference, AGI 2010, Atlantis, Amsterdam, pp. 170–175 (2010)

17. Dennett, D.C.: Intentional Systems. The Journal of Philosophy 68(4), 87–106 (1971)

18. Dennett, D.C.: The Intentional Stance. MIT Press, Cambridge (1987)

19. Good, I.J.: Speculations concerning the first ultraintelligent machine. In: Alt, F., Rubinoff, M. (eds.) Advances in Computers, vol. 6, pp. 31–88. Academic Press, New York (1965), doi:10.1016/S0065-2458(08)60418-0

20. Rosenthal, R.W.: Games of Perfect Information, Predatory Pricing and Chain Store Paradox. Journal of Economic Theory 25(1), 92–100 (1981), http://www.professorchaing.com/files/Rosenthal_1981_JET.pdf

21. Smart, J.M.: Evo Devo Universe? A Framework for Speculations on Cosmic Culture. In: Dick, S.J., Lupisella, M.L. (eds.) Cosmos and Culture: Cultural Evolution in a Cosmic Context, NASA SP-2009-4802, pp. 201–295. US Government Printing Ofiice, Washington, DC (2009)

22. Muehlhauser, L.: Facing The Intelligence Explosion. Machine Intelligence Research Institute, Berkeley (2013)

23. Haidt, J., Kesebir, S.: Morality. In: Fiske, S., Gilbert, D., Lindzey, G. (eds.) Handbook of Social Psychology, 5th edn., pp. 797–832 (2010)

24. Yudkowsky, E.: Creating Friendly AI 1.0: The Analysis and Design of Benevolent Goal Architectures. Machine Intelligence Research Institute, Berkeley (2001), http://intelligence.org/files/CFAI.pdf

25. Yudkowsky, E.: Coherent Extrapolated Volition. Machine Intelligence Research Institute, Berkeley (2004), http://intelligence.org/files/CFAI.pdf

26. Goertzel, B.: Should Humanity Build a Global AI Nanny to Delay the Singularity Until It's Better Understood? Journal of Consciousness Studies 19(1-2), 96–111 (2012)

27. Metzinger, T.: The Ego Tunnel: The Science of the Mind and the Myth of the Self. Basic Books, New York (2009)

28. Amazon, http://www.amazon.com/The-Ego-Tunnel-Science-Mind/dp/0465020690/

29. Dennett, D.C.: The Self as a Center of Narrative Gravity. In: Kessel, F., Cole, P., Johnson, D. (eds.) Self and Consciousness: Multiple Perspectives, Erlbaum, Hillsdale (1992), http://cogprints.org/266/

30. Hofstadter, D.: I Am A Strange Loop. Basic Books, New York (2007)

31. Llinas, R.R.: I of the Vortex: From Neurons to Self. MIT Press, Cambridge (2001)
32. Damasio, A.R.: Self Comes to Mind: Constructing the Conscious Brain. Pantheon, New York (2010)
33. Chalmers, D.: Facing Up to the Problem of Consciousness. Journal of Consciousness Studies 2(3), 200–219 (1995)
34. Chalmers, D.: The Conscious Mind: In Search of a Fundamental Theory. Oxford University Press, New York (1996)
35. Chalmers, D.: Consciousness and its Place in Nature. In: Stich, S., Warfield, F. (eds.) The Blackwell Guide to the Philosophy of Mind, Blackwell, Malden (2003), http://consc.net/papers/nature.pdf
36. Waser, M.: Architectural Requirements & Implications of Consciousness, Self, and "Free Will". In: Samsonovich, A., Johannsdottir, K. (eds.) Biologically Inspired Cognitive Architectures 2011. IOS Press, Amsterdam (2011), doi:10.3233/978-1-60750-959-2-438
37. Jackson, F.: Epiphenomenal Qualia. Philosophical Quarterly 32, 127–136 (1982)
38. Dennett, D.C.: Consciousness Explained. Little Brown and Company, Boston (1991)
39. Dennett, D.C.: Intuition Pumps and Other Tools for Thinking. Norton & Company, New York (2013)
40. Tononi, G.: An Information Integration Theory of Consciousness. BMC Neurosci. 5(42) (2004), http://www.ncbi.nlm.nih.gov/pmc/articles/PMC543470/pdf/1471-2202-5-42.pdf, doi:10.1186/1471-2202-5-42
41. Tononi, G.: Consciousness as Integrated Information: a Provisional Manifesto. Biol. Bull. 215(3), 216–242 (2008)
42. Balduzzi, B., Tononi, G.: Qualia: The Geometry of Integrated Information. PLoS Comput Biol 5(8), e1000462 (2009), doi:10.1371/journal.pcbi.1000462
43. Varela, F.J., Maturana, H.R., Uribe, R.: Autopoiesis: The organization of living systems, its characterization and a model. BioSystems 5, 187–196 (1974)
44. Maturana, H.R., Varela, F.J.: Autopoiesis and Cognition: The Realization of the Living. Kluwer Academic Publishers (1980)
45. Maturana, H.R., Varela, F.J.: The Tree of Knowledge: The Biological Roots of (1987)
46. Human Understanding. Shambhala Publications
47. Varela, F.J., Thompson, E., Rosch, E.: The Embodied Mind: Cognitive Science and Human Experience. MIT Press (1991)
48. Varela, F.J.: Autopoiesis and a Biology of Intentionality. In: Proc. of Autopoiesis and Perception: A Workshop with ESPRIT BRA 3352, Dublin, Ireland, pp. 4–14 (1992)
49. Varela, F.J.: Patterns of Life: Intertwining Identity and Cognition. Brain and Cognition 34(1), 72–87 (1997)
50. Blackmore, S.: Conversations on Consciousness. Oxford University Press, Oxford (2006)
51. Cashmore, A.R.: The Lucretian swerve: The biological basis of human behavior and the criminal justice system. PNAS 2010(107), 4499–4504 (2010)
52. Waser, M.R.: Safety and Morality Require the Recognition of Self-Improving Machines as Moral/Justice Patients and Agents. In: Gunkel, D.J., Bryson, J.J., Torrance, S. (eds.) The Machine Question: AI, Ethics & Moral Responsibility, http://events.cs.bham.ac.uk/turing12/proceedings/14.pdf
53. Brundage, M.: Limitations and Risks of Machine Ethics. Journal of Experimental and Theoretical Artificial Intelligence, (forthcoming) (2013), http://www.milesbrundage.com/uploads/2/1/6/8/21681226/limitations_and_risks_of_machine_ethics.pdf

Toward a Formalization of QA Problem Classes[*]

Naveen Sundar Govindarajulu[1], John Licato[2], and Selmer Bringsjord[1,2]

[1] Department of Cognitive Science
[2] Department of Computer Science
Rensselaer Polytechnic Institute (RPI)
Troy NY 12180 USA

Abstract. How tough is a given question-answering problem? Answers to this question differ greatly among different researchers and groups. To begin rectifying this, we start by giving a quick, simple, propaedeutic formalization of a *question-answering problem class*. This formalization is just a starting point and should let us answer, at least roughly, this question: What is the relative toughness of two unsolved QA problem classes?.

1 Formalization of Question-Answering Problem Classes

It is not an exaggeration to say that the AI community had a watershed moment when IBM's Watson beat *Jeopardy!* champion Ken Jennings in a nail-biting match in 2011. QA is important to AGI: Levesque et al. [7] give an argument in defense of QA being a test for AGI/AI. Despite the importance and quite impressive real-world success of QA research, there is very sparse formalization on what makes a QA problem difficult.[1] (See [4] for a formalization of a test for AI which has a QA format.)

Concisely, our position is that: 1) QA is crucial for AGI; 2) a rigorous formalization of QA is important to understand the relative toughness of unsolved problems in QA; and finally 3) a formal understanding of QA is important for AGI.[2] Toward this end, we start with a simple formalization that could point the way.

We now present a simple formalization of a QA problem class. A QA problem class consists of a set of questions, a set of answers, a corpus, and some other computational artifacts. The formalization lets us judge, at least coarsely, whether one QA problem (e.g. *Jeopardy!*) is tougher than another (e.g. answering queries about financial data).

---

[*] We are grateful to IBM for grants to Bringsjord that in part enable systematic thinking about the nature of QA, in light of Watson's victory. We also thank them for providing us with an incarnation of Watson that has helped us with evaluating questions similar to the ones given here.
[1] A related criticism by Cassimatis (2012) is that the toughness of existing AI tests (trying to scale mountain peaks on Earth), are nowhere near what is needed for producing human-level intelligence (trying to reach the moon).
[2] QA also happens to be the most effective way of testing other possible forms of intelligence [2], in line with research that treats the pursuit of AI scientifically [1].

B. Goertzel et al. (Eds.): AGI 2014, LNAI 8598, pp. 228–233, 2014.
© Springer International Publishing Switzerland 2014

QA Problem Class

A *question-answering problem class* consists of these following components:

- A set of possible questions **Q**: $\mathbf{Q} = \{q_1, q_2, \ldots\}$.
- A set of possible answers **A**: $\mathbf{A} = \{a_1, a_2, \ldots\}$.[a]
- A set of indices **I**. Indices here are entities that deictic words (words that specifiy context such as *"now"*, *"here"*, *"I"*, etc.) can refer to. For the sake of simplicity, we will consider only time-points as our indices in the present paper.
- A set of all facts about the world F. The powerset of this set gives us all possible *contexts*: $\mathbf{W} = 2^F$.
- A corpus $\mathcal{C}$ of question-answer pairs

$$\mathcal{C} = \{\langle q_i, a_i \rangle_i | q_i \in \mathbf{Q}, a_i \in \mathbf{A}, i = 1, 2, 3, \ldots\}$$

- Finally, a mapping function μ which gives us the *gold-standard* answers: $\mu :$ $\mathbf{Q} \times \mathbf{I} \times \mathbf{W} \rightarrow \mathbf{A}$. For any question q, possible answers a are given by:

$$\mu(q, t, w) = a$$

---
[a] Note: Both **Q** and **A** can be infinite.

From this formalization, we immediately get four dimensions of difficulty for QA problems. For now the dimensions are mostly informal, but even at this early stage they illustrate the benefits of seeking to formalize QA. The first dimension emerges from the varying amount of dependence of the answering function μ on the time index t. The second dimension emerges from the varying amount of world knowledge w that the answering function μ depends upon. Such questions have been noted elsewhere by Leveseque et al. (2012) in what they term "Winograd Schemas." The third dimension is generated by the range of novelty. The corpus $\mathcal{C}$ and its usefulness for computing μ plays a role in this dimension. For the sake of simplicity, we assume that $\mathcal{C}$ is a pre-processed corpus of facts that the machine has learned or acquired. The fourth dimension arises from variation of the amount of computational power needed to compute μ. We quickly discuss the four dimensions with help from sample questions.

1.1 Dimension 1: Dynamicity

Most of the questions asked in *Jeopardy!* are static in nature: The answer does not depend on any time component.[3]

President under whom the U.S. gave full recognition to Communist China. (Answer: Jimmy Carter)

The answer **a** to a question **q** can depend on the time t it is asked, the physical location p it is being asked at, and the person a asking it, and other such context-

---
[3] Philosophers and linguists might disagree with us here. Of course, we cheerfully concede that given enough time, the meaning of words used in *Jeopardy!* could change; and for that matter collective human knowledge could change as well.

based information. For now, we focus only on the time the question is asked. Even this trivial feature can render some problems very hard. Some example questions of this nature are given below:

Sample Dimension-1 Questions

q_1 What was IBM stock's Sharpe ratio in the last 60 days of trading?
q_2 Give me the maximum wind speed in New York in the last year, looking at only the days on which it rained.

1.2   Dimension 2: World Knowledge

Some questions can be static in nature but require human levels of intelligence to answer. These usually are questions that any lay-person with appropriate native-language capacity can answer. These questions typically require processing enormous amounts of background knowledge about the world and contextual information. One such problem class which scores high on this dimension is the class of Winograd Schemas.

The Winograd Schema (WS) challenge, introduced by Levesque et al. (2012), is a reading-comprehension test intended to rectify issues with the Turing Test. Two sample questions are given below.

Sample Dimension-2 Questions

q_1 Paul tried to call George on the phone, but he wasn't successful. Who wasn't successful? **Answer 0**: Paul **Answer 1**: George
q_2 Paul tried to call George on the phone, but he wasn't available. Who wasn't available? **Answer 0**: Paul **Answer 1**: George

Although the syntactic forms of both questions are identical, correctly identifying the referent of the pronoun 'he' seems to require deep sentence comprehension, a process exploiting enough background knowledge to recognize that a caller being successful at a phone call requires that the recipient of the call be available.

One of the problems infecting the Winograd Schema Challenge is that it requires the vocabulary of words be specified in advance. A bigger drawback of this dimension is that it tests rather vague, open-ended world knowledge rather than (what might be called) linguistic knowledge.[4] The next dimension rectifies this issue.

1.3   Dimension 3: Novelty

One of the astounding feats of human language understanding is the capacity to assimilate new words on the fly and discard them later. Observing this can be used to create problem classes with completely made-up words that do not need any background world knowledge (e.g. the knowledge about about phone callers and phone call recipients required for the question above). Such questions

---

[4] Having a huge bank of knowledge about the world is not sufficient as CYC [6] still does not empower computers to answer all possibe questions. This fact bolsters the claim that leveraging world knowledge is alone exeedingly challenging.

directly get to the core of language understanding. In the two questions given below, we have made-up nouns in the first case and made-up nouns and verbs in the second case. We can achieve this novelty by mandating that there be little overlap between the words used in $\mathbf{Q} \cup \mathbf{A}$ and $\mathcal{C}$. A more challenging restriction would be to have no questions in $\mathbf{Q}$ overlap with those in the corpus $\mathcal{C}$.[5]

Sample Dimension-3 Questions

q_1 If I have 4 foos and 5 bars, and if foos are not the same as bars, how many foos will I have if I get 3 bazes which just happen to be foos?

q_2 Every foobar weozes a foobar if the latter weozes some other foobar. Foobar 27 weozes foobar 28. Is it true that foobar 28 weozes foobar 28?

1.4   Dimension 4: Computational Hardness

The question *"What time is it now?"* is dynamic but not really that hard to compute. Some questions are inherently hard even if they are posed in an unambiguous machine language. This dimension addresses how hard it is to compute μ given all its inputs. There exist hierarchies of hard computational problems from standard computability and complexity theory that could be used as a starting point for this dimension.[6] The hardness of a QA problem class along this dimension can be cast in terms of the most general *oracle* that would need to be used in computing μ to answer questions in the given problem class. The sample questions below are both Turing-unsolvable but fit the general pattern of a QA problem. Both the questions are static, require very little common sense, and the linguistic knowledge required to comprehend the questions is pretty straightforward.

Sample Dimension-4 Questions

q_1 Does machine M with input i ever halt?

q_2 Is this computer program p the same as the program q in my library of programs?[a]

---

[a] Note: We could easily describe machines, programs, and inputs using words from normal everyday vocabulary.

2   Extensions

The formalization given above works well only when we consider QA in test settings and experiments. If we are modeling QA working outside the lab in the real world, we would need some more components in the formalization.

---

[5] Note: We include knowledge of basic arithmetic in linguistic knowledge. What we term 'world knowledge' might also be called "Earthling" knowledge. Any AGI should be independent of this kind of knowledge but presumably should possess basic arithmetic skills.

[6] Is intelligence correlated with computational complexity? Some of us think so [3]. Note we are using standard measures of complexity mainly for convenience. They could be superseded by other measures more naturally correlated with intelligence.

2.1 Justification of Answers

In the formalization above, we have focused only on the answers being right and not on how the answers are computed. In order to trust an answer, we would need a justification that supports the answer and is easy to check.[7] So a full formalization of QA would include the ability to justify answers. We can modify the formalization to include justifications.

QA Problem Class: Extension 1

– A set of justifications $\mathbf{J}$: $\mathbf{J} = \{j_1, j_2, \ldots\}$.
– An evaluation function $\epsilon : \mathbf{J} \times \mathbf{A} \to \{\mathsf{true}, \mathsf{false}\}$ which evaluates the justification j given for an answer a. $\epsilon(j, a) = \mathsf{true}$ iff j supports a.

2.2 Ranking of Answers

A QA system in, for example, a personal assistant app would have to learn about and model its users. In this setting, the gold standard answers would vary from person to person. QA systems in such a setting would also have to be evaluated against how well they understand their users.

3 Conclusion

As noted above, our formalization is but a starting point that could help us eventually compare different QA problems. A formal measure of difficulty is needed for QA due to its central role in testing for AGI. While there are tests and competitions for QA (e.g. [9]), a formal measure stemming from the preliminary formalization presented above might help focus our efforts in the right direction and compare different tests and competitions. Such a formalization might also help us decide which methods might be appropriate for different QA problems well before expensive system building and experimentation. (See [8] for a sampling of the widely different approaches to QA.)

References

1. Besold, T.R.: Human-Level Artificial Intelligence Must Be a Science. In: Kühnberger, K.-U., Rudolph, S., Wang, P. (eds.) AGI 2013. LNCS (LNAI), vol. 7999, pp. 174–177. Springer, Heidelberg (2013)
2. Bringsjord, S.: Could, How Could We Tell If, and Why Should–Androids Have Inner Lives? In: Ford, K., Glymour, C., Hayes, P. (eds.) Android Epistemology, pp. 93–122. MIT Press, Cambridge (1995)
3. Bringsjord, S., Zenzen, M.: Superminds: People Harness Hypercomputation, and More. Kluwer Academic Publishers, Dordrecht (2003)

---

[7] The justification would rest on some premises and information that could be considered to have been accepted.

4. Bringsjord, S.: Meeting Floridi's Challenge to Artificial Intelligence from the Knowledge-Game Test for Self-Consciousness. Metaphilosophy 41(3), 292–312 (2010), http://kryten.mm.rpi.edu/sb_on_floridi_offprint.pdf
5. Cassimatis, N.L.: Human-level Artificial Intelligence Must be an Extraordinary Science. Advances in Cognitive Systems 1, 37–45 (2012)
6. Lenat, D.: CYC: A Large-scale Investment in Knowledge Infrastructure. Communications of the ACM 38(11), 33–38 (1995)
7. Levesque, H., Davis, E., Morgenstern, L.: The Winograd Schema Challenge. In: Proceedings of the Thirteenth International Conference on the Principles of Knowledge Representation and Reasoning (2012)
8. Strzalkowski, T., Harabagiu, S.M. (eds.): Advances in Open Domain Question Answering, vol. 32. Springer (2006)
9. Voorhees, E.M. (ed.): The Twenty-Second Text REtrieval Conference. NIST Special Publication: SP 500-302. NIST (2014)

MInD: Don't Use Agent as Objects

Renato Lenz Costalima[1], Amauri Holanda Souza Junior[1],
Cidcley Teixeira de Souza[1], and Gustavo Augusto Lima de Campos[2]

[1] Instituto Federal do Ceará, Av. Treze de Maio, 2081, Benfica, Fortaleza - Ceará,
Brasil
[2] Universidade Estadual do Ceará, Av. Dr. Silas Munguba, 1700, Campus do Itaperi,
Fortaleza - Ceará, Brasil

Abstract. What is intelligence? Since it is not possible to see the internal details of intelligence, it is described by its behaviours, that include: problem solving, learning and language [1]. These behaviours are expected outputs of intelligence, but they are not the intelligence itself. Intelligence is rather what makes them possible. That could be: "The capacity to acquire and apply knowledge". With that goal, the **MInD**, a **M**odel for **In**telligence **D**evelopment, is an in development framework for multi-agent systems.

1 MInD - Model for Intelligence Development

Russell *et al.*[2] defines an agent as "anything that can be viewed as perceiving its environment through sensors and acting upon that environment through effectors" (Figure 1). A quick Abbott's textual analysis of this definition identifies the interfaces: `Agent`, Environment, Sensor and Effector or Actuator; and the methods: `perceive()` and `act()`. A representation using the UML sequence diagram (Figure 2) helps to enlighten a sensor gathering information from the environment and representing it into a perception sent to the agent. Some agent's internal decision must choose an actuator and make it act, somehow modifying the environment.

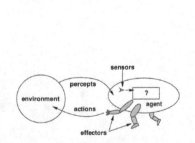
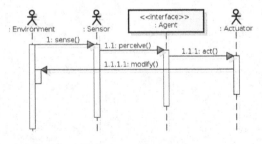

Fig. 1. An agent   **Fig. 2.** The UML sequence diagram for an agent

The only method in `Agent` interface is `perceive()`, for short `see()`, and every interaction with the agent must happen through this method. Surprisingly,

B. Goertzel et al. (Eds.): AGI 2014, LNAI 8598, pp. 234–237, 2014.

none of the major multi-agent frameworks, such as [3][4], defines the method `perceive()` or anything alike.

To be considered intelligent, an agent must be able to "acquire and apply knowledge". To acquire the information about the environment and then apply it, modifying the environment, the agent needs sensors and actuators. While the body is responsible for gathering and representing the information, the mind (the agent) must be able to store (`set()`) and retrieve (`get()`) the information represented by the body. Figure 3 shows the UML class diagram of the **MInD**, a Model for Intelligence Development.

Fig. 3. The UML class diagram for MInD

To test the model, the `NaiveAgent` class provides a flexible simple Java implementation of the `Mind` interface. It describes an initial basic cognitive cycle that cannot solve any problem, that cannot communicate, that does not move or is proactive in any way. However, an instance of `NaiveAgent` represents the mind of a live software ready to learn whatever behaviour imagined. It is programmed to `see()` symbols that represent orders the agent should try to follow. The agent searches in its memory for possible actions. If it find one or more actions, it will choose the last defined action and act. Else, it does nothing. For the agent to find something in its memory, the knowledge must be somehow acquired by a sensor and `set()` to the agent's memory. The body of the agent is the responsible for the knowledge definitions and updates, consequently determining the agent's behaviour as suggested in [5][6]. That is because the agent acts based on its own experience, and this experience is provided by the agent's sensors. The agent's body determines what the agent perceives, consequently determining what it learns and, thereafter, how it behaves.

Because we want to test the mind separately, let us simulate the body's impulses and see what we can do with a `NaiveAgent`. The code in Listing 1.1 shows, in Lines 3 and 10, the simulation of the same perception by the agent resulting in different outputs. At the first time, the agent does not know what to do, so it does nothing. In Lines 4 to 9, the agent is arbitrarily taught how to write, producing, from the second perception, the output of Line 1 of the Listing 1.2. In Line 12, we try to ask the agent to write a sum of numbers. Because it does not know how to sum, it writes "null" (Line 2 of Listing 1.2). The same perception at Line 23, after the agent has learned how to sum (Lines 13 to 22), produces the desired output (Line 3 of Listing 1.2).

```
1   Mind a = new NaiveAgent();
2
3   a.see(new Symbol("write", "hi"));
4   a.set("write", new AbstractAction() {
```

```
5        public Object act(Object object) {
6             System.out.println(object);
7             return null;
8        }
9    });
10   a.see(new Symbol("write", "hi"));
11
12   a.see(new Symbol("write", a.see(new Symbol("sum", new int[] {2,-4,5}))));;
13   a.set("sum", new AbstractAction() {
14       public Object act(Object object) {
15           int sum = 0;
16           int [] numbers = (int []) object;
17           for (int n: numbers) {
18               sum += n;
19           }
20           return sum;
21       }
22   });
23   a.see(new Symbol("write", a.see(new Symbol("sum", new int[] {2,-4,5}))));;
```

Listing 1.1. Test of NaiveAgent

Output:

```
1   hi
2   null
3   3
```

Listing 1.2. Output of the test of NaiveAgent

Teaching an agent to sum and to write is not very impressive, but it demonstrates the agent's capacity to acquire and apply knowledge and doing so in different domains. If one is not satisfied with this definition of intelligence, any other behaviour considered necessary to achieve intelligence can be learned by the agent in execution time. Furthermore, most, if not all, AI's techniques can be implemented using OO classes and objects. In practice, the `NaiveAgent` can be seen as a dynamic object with its attributes and methods defined at runtime.

The `NaiveAgent` reproduces the desired intelligent behaviour, that is, acquiring and applying knowledge. But that is not good enough if we are going to use agents as objects. Wooldridge [7] explains that agents should not invoke each others methods in agent-oriented world. A method invocation is like pushing a button: the corresponding behaviour is triggered without the object's decision. Instead, agents should communicate with each other "asking" for a desired operation. Because of that, multi-agent frameworks focus on the communication between the agents, defining specific communication methods and protocols. This means that the agent is not forced to execute the desired action, but it is forced to communicate. Also the communication language is "hard-coded".

In MInD, the `Agent` interface has only one method: the `see()` method. All interactions with agents, including attempts of communication, should be through a `see()` method. Invoking any other different method is like using the agent as an object, triggering behaviours without the agent's permission. The `Mind` interface abstracts the necessary methods to achieve intelligence. It means that an agent will probably need to implement and use these methods. However, invoking them is forcing the agent to act without asking. The body of the agent supposedly has a close relationship with the agent's mind and could arbitrarily manipulate it through the `Mind` interface. Even so, to maximize the agent's choice and flexibility, the `Mind` interface should be avoided and its superinterface `Agent` should be used instead.

Agents should not used nor built as objects. Several frameworks offer basic functionality to support multi-agent systems development. Extending one of the provided basic implementations, an agent can be programmed to learn a specific task following some specific approach. After the programming is finished, the agent is put to life and tested if it does the right thing. If the test does not succeed, the agents must be stopped. To use the actual terms, the process is killed. Another round of programming can bring some new agent to life. Is that how it works with intelligent beings? If your kid fails a math exam do you kill him and try to make a smarter kid? The basic implementation provided by the MInD framework is not meant to be extended. The development starts by instantiating a `NaiveAgent`. The desired functionalities are defined at runtime, allowing the modification of the software without the hideous cycle of "edit-refresh-save". In analogy with Web 2.0, MInD allows a single method to be updated without the need to restart the entire software.

The test of Listing 1.1 uses the `Mind` interface and thus uses the agent as an object, arbitrarily manipulating its knowledge. As discussed, only the agent's body should use the `Mind` interface. Imagine how it would be easy for a teacher to just press the "set" button inside the student's head. In further analysis, it is also not so easy to even get the student's attention, to make him really "perceive". In a more realistic agent-oriented world, the environment should not have access to the agent at all. Indeed, as can be noticed in the Figure 2, the environment only interacts with the agent's body (its sensors and actuators), but never with its mind (represented by the `Agent` interface). From the point of view of the environment, the `Agent` and `Mind` interfaces should not even exist. In fact, there is no way of proving that minds exist, we just suppose they are in control of the bodies. Because if not a mind, what is? Yet, has anyone seen a mind? If we open a human's head we will find a brain, but can we find a mind?

References

1. Pfiefer, R., et al.: Understanding intelligence. MIT Press (2001)
2. Russell, S.J., Norvig, P., Canny, J.F., Malik, J.M., Edwards, D.D.: Artificial intelligence: A modern approach, vol. 2. Prentice hall Englewood Cliffs (1995)
3. Bellifemine, F., Caire, G., Rimassa, G., Poggi, A., Trucco, T., Cortese, E., Quarta, F., Vitaglione, G., Lhuillier, N., Picault, J.: Java agent development framework. TILAB Italia 10, 2002 (2002), http://jade.cselt.it
4. Baumer, C., Breugst, M., Choy, S., Magedanz, T.: Grasshoppera universal agent platform based on omg masif and fipa standards. In: First International Workshop on Mobile Agents for Telecommunication Applications (MATA 1999), pp. 1–18. Citeseer (1999)
5. Brooks, R.A.: Elephants don't play chess. Robotics and Autonomous Systems 6(1), 3–15 (1990)
6. Lakoff, G., Johnson, M.: Philosophy in the flesh: The embodied mind and its challenge to western thought. Basic books (1999)
7. Wooldridge, M.: An introduction to multiagent systems. John Wiley & Sons (2009)

Guiding Probabilistic Logical Inference
with Nonlinear Dynamical Attention Allocation

Cosmo Harrigan[1,2,6], Ben Goertzel[2], Matthew Iklé[3], Amen Belayneh[4,5],
and Gino Yu[5]

[1] OpenCog Foundation
[2] Novamente LLC
[3] Adams State University
[4] iCog Labs
[5] School of Design, Hong Kong Poly U
[6] University of Washington

Abstract. In order to explore the practical manifestations of the "cognitive synergy" between the PLN (Probabilistic Logic Networks) and ECAN (Economic Attention Network) components of the OpenCog AGI architecture, we explore the behavior of PLN and ECAN operating together on two standard test problems commonly used with Markov Logic Networks (MLN). Our preliminary results suggest that, while PLN can address these problems adequately, ECAN offers little added value for the problems in their standard form. However, we outline modified versions of the problem that we hypothesize would demonstrate the value of ECAN more effectively, via inclusion of confounding information that needs to be heuristically sifted through.

1 Introduction

One approach to creating AGI systems is the "integrative" strategy, involving combining multiple components embodying different structures or algorithms, and relying on synergistic dynamics between components. One kind of integrative system involves various highly independent software components, each solving a specialized set of problems in a mostly standalone manner, with occasional communication between each other in order to exchange problems and solutions. On the other end of the scale, are systems designed as tightly interconnected components that give rise to complex non-linear dynamical phenomena. Here, we are specifically focused on the latter approach. We will discuss the particulars of one form of cognitive synergy – between probabilistic inference and nonlinear-dynamical attention allocation – within the context of one particular integrative AGI architecture, OpenCogPrime [2].

2 OpenCogPrime

Our work here is based upon specific details of the AGI architecture called **OpenCogPrime** (OCP), based on the open-source OpenCog project at

B. Goertzel et al. (Eds.): AGI 2014, LNAI 8598, pp. 238–241, 2014.

http://opencog.org. OCP is a large and complex system whose detailed description occupies two volumes [4].

The concept of cognitive synergy is at the core of the design, with highly interdependent subsystems responsible for inference regarding patterns obtained from visual, auditory and abstract domains, uncertain reasoning, language comprehension and generation, concept formation, and action planning.

The medium-term goal of the OCP project is to create systems that can function broadly comparably to young human children in virtual and robotic preschool contexts [3]. In the longer-term, the aim of the project is to engineer systems that exhibit general intelligence equivalent to a human adult, and ultimately beyond.

The dynamics of interaction between processes in OCP is designed in such a way that knowledge can be converted between different types of memory; and when a learning process that is largely concerned with a particular type of memory encounters a situation where the rate of learning is very slow, it can proceed to convert some of the relevant knowledge into a representation for a different type of memory to overcome the issue, demonstrating **cognitive synergy**. The simple case of synergy between ECAN and PLN explored here is an instance of this broad concept; PLN being concerned mainly with declarative memory and ECAN mainly with attentional memory.

3 Probabilistic Logic Networks

PLN serves as the probabilistic reasoning system within OpenCog's more general artificial general intelligence framework. PLN logical inferences take the form of syllogistic rules, which give patterns for combining statements with matching terms. Related to each rule is a truth-value formula which calculates the truth value resulting from application of the rule. PLN uses forward-chaining and backward-chaining processes to combine the various rules and create inferences.

4 Economic Attention Networks

The attention allocation system within OpenCog is handled by the Economic Attention Network (ECAN). ECAN is a graph of untyped nodes and links that may be typed either HebbianLink or InverseHebbianLink. Each Atom in an ECAN is weighted with two numbers, called STI (short-term importance) and LTI (long-term importance), while each Hebbian or InverseHebbian link is weighted with a probability value. A system of equations, based upon an economic metaphor of STI and LTI values as artificial currencies, governs importance value updating. These equations serve to spread importance to and from various atoms within the system, based upon the importance of their roles in performing actions related to the system's goals.

An important concept with ECAN is the attentional focus, consisting of those atoms deemed most important for the system to achieve its goals at a particular instant. Through the attentional focus, one key role of ECAN is to guide the forward and backward chaining processes of PLN inference. Quite simply, when PLN's chaining processes need to choose logical terms or relations to include in their inferences, they can show priority to those occurring in the system's attentional focus (due to having been placed there by ECAN). Conversely, when terms or relations have proved useful to PLN, they can have their importance boosted, which will affect ECAN's dynamics. This is a specific example of the cognitive synergy principle at the heart of the OpenCog design.

5   Evaluating PLN on Standard MLN Test Problems

In order to more fully understand the nature of PLN/ECAN synergy, we chose to explore it in the context of two test problems standardly used in the context of MLNs (Markov Logic Networks) [7]. These problems are relatively easy for both PLN and MLN, and do not stress either system's capabilities.

The first test case considered is a very small-scale logical inference called the *smokes* problem, discussed in its MLN form at [1]. The PLN format of the *smokes* problem used for our experiments is given at https://github.com/opencog/ test-datasets/blob/master/pln/tuffy/smokes/smokes.scm The conclusions obtained from PLN backward chaining on the *smokes* test case are

```
cancer(Edward)  <.62, 1>
cancer(Anna)    <.50, 1>
cancer(Bob)     <.45, 1>
cancer(Frank)   <.45, 1>
```

which is reasonably similar to the output of MLN as reported in [1],

```
0.75 Cancer(Edward)
0.65 Cancer(Anna)
0.50 Cancer(Bob)
0.45 Cancer(Frank)
```

The second test case is a larger problem referred to as *RC* involving the placement of research papers in categories based on information about their authors and citations. [5] The full RC problem contains 4 relations, 15 rules, 51K entities, 430K evidence tuples, 10K query atoms, 489 components [6]. The RC1000 problem is scaled-down with only 1000 pieces of evidence. Human raters display 72% agreement on mapping papers into categories. Straightforward statistical methods can get up to 66%, and MLN does roughly the same.

The full set of rules and evidence used for feeding the RC problem to PLN is at https://github.com/opencog/test-datasets/tree/master/pln/tuffy/ class. The corresponding information for the RC1000 problem is at https:// github.com/opencog/test-datasets/tree/master/pln/tuffy/rc1000.

6   Exploring PLN/ECAN Synergy with Standard MLN Test Problems

We explored the possibility of utilizing ECAN to assist PLN on these test problems, so far achieving results more educational than successful. Based on our work so far, it seems that ECAN's guidance is not of much use to PLN on these problems as formulated. However, exploring ways to modify the test problems so as to enable to them to better showcase ECAN, led us to conceptually interesting conclusions regarding the sorts of circumstances in which ECAN is most likely to help PLN.

We hypothesize that if one modified the *smokes* example via adding a substantial amount of irrelevant evidence about other aspects of the people involved, then one would have a case where ECAN could help PLN, because it could help focus attention on the relevant relationships. We also hypothesize that, if one had information about the words occurring in the papers in the RC test problem, then ECAN could help, because *some* of these words would be useful for guessing the categories papers belong to, and others would not; ECAN could help via spreading importance from words found to be important, to other related words, saving PLN the trouble of attempting inferences involving all the words. One of our threads of current research focuses on the substantiation of these hypotheses via running PLN and ECAN together on test problems of this nature.

In sum, the exploration of some standard MLN test problems in a PLN/E-CAN context has led us to interesting hypotheses regarding where ECAN can, and cannot, prove useful to PLN. Preliminarily, it appears that this particular cognitive synergy is going to be most useful in cases where, unlike these MLN test problems in their standard form, there is a considerable amount of detailed information and part of the problem involves heuristically sifting through this information to find the useful bits.

References

1. Project tuffy, http://hazy.cs.wisc.edu/hazy/tuffy/doc/
2. Goertzel, B.: Opencogprime: A cognitive synergy based architecture for artificial general intelligence. In: 8th IEEE International Conference on Cognitive Informatics, ICCI 2009, pp. 60–68. IEEE (2009)
3. Goertzel, B., Bugaj, S.V.: Agi preschool: A framework for evaluating early-stage human-like agis. In: Proceedings of the Second International Conference on Artificial General Intelligence (AGI 2009), pp. 31–36 (2009)
4. Goertzel, B., Pennachin, C., Geisweiller, N.: Engineering General Intelligence, Part 1. Atlantis Press (2014)
5. McCallum, A., Nigam, K., Rennie, J., Seymore, K.: Automating the construction of internet portals with machine learning. Information Retrieval 3(2), 127–163 (2000)
6. Niu, F., Ré, C., Doan, A., Shavlik, J.: Tuffy: Scaling up statistical inference in markov logic networks using an rdbms. Proceedings of the VLDB Endowment 4(6), 373–384 (2011)
7. Richardson, M., Domingos, P.: Markov logic networks. Machine Learning 62(1-2), 107–136 (2006)

A Cognitive API and Its Application to AGI Intelligence Assessment

Ben Goertzel[1] and Gino Yu[2]

[1] OpenCog Foundation
[2] School of Design, Hong Kong Poly U

Abstract. An Application Programming Interface for human-level AGI systems is proposed, aimed at bridging the gap between proto-AGI R&D systems and practical AI application development. The API contains simply formalized queries corresponding to the various key aspects of human-like intelligence, organized so as to be independent of the algorithms used under the hood for query resolution and associated supporting cognitive processes. A novel, qualitative (and in principle quantifiable) measure of software general intelligence is proposed (the APIQ), measuring the degree to which a system succeeds at fulfilling the various API functions using a compact set of representations and algorithms.

1 Introduction

Currently AGI is a relatively distinct pursuit from the engineering of practical AI applications. Indeed, the two pursuits can even sometimes seem opposed to each other. If one posits an "AGI vs. Narrow AI" dichotomy [1], focus on specific practical applications may be seen as one of the primary factors driving the majority of the AI field's attention toward Narrow AI (other major factors including the greater ease of doing theoretical analysis and empirical testing on narrower systems).

On the other hand, it's also the case that a number of proto-AGI systems have been customized, in whole or in part, to serve as parts of various practical applications. But this has been done on an ad hoc basis in each case, with considerable specialized effort required. I believe it is possible to connect the AGI and application development worlds more systematically, so that AGI R&D and AI application development can proceed more synergistically, each more richly benefiting the other.

One way to manifest this potential, I suggest, is the development of a "Cognitive API" for a proto-AGI software system, enabling application developers to access the system in specific ways that tend to be useful for application software, according to an interface that requires no knowledge of the underlying algorithms of the proto-AGI system, and doesn't change as the particulars of these algorithms change. Adoption of such an API would lead to more users for early-stage AGI systems, hence to more incentive for various organizations to fund or sponsor work on AGI systems, and thus could accelerate AGI development as well as improving application quality.

B. Goertzel et al. (Eds.): AGI 2014, LNAI 8598, pp. 242–245, 2014.

In this paper I will outline one approach to defining a Cognitive API of this nature. While the API indicated here would work effectively with the OpenCog framework that the author is currently involved with [5] [6], in its overall outline it is not OpenCog-specific in any way, and could be used just as well together with many alternative AGI systems.

The pursuit of a Cognitive API also provides a novel perspective on one of the vexing issues at the heart of the AGI field – the difficulty of measuring the level of general intelligence displayed by a given system. A novel intelligence measure, the APIQ, is proposed and defined. Roughly speaking the APIQ measures the degree to which a system fulfills a broad subset of the API functions using a concise set of representations and algorithms. Full formalization of the APIQ appears difficult, but it does provide a novel, and highly pragmatic, approach to conceptualizing the notion of general intelligence in the context of real-world applied software systems.

1.1   Needs of Application Developers vs. AGI Researchers

A key point underlying the current suggestion is that the needs of AGI researchers, versus application developers aimed at using early-stage AGI software in their applications, are substantially different.

For a developer whose focus is the creation or improvement of AI algorithms, the appropriate interface for an AI system is one that is extremely general and flexible, providing the maximum possible latitude in experimenting with new ideas and increasing the intelligence, scope and/or efficiency of existing code. For example: While rough around the edges in various places, OpenCog's current Scheme shell is a reasonable first approximation of an interface of this sort.

On the other hand, for a developer whose focus is the creation of AI-based application systems, a different sort of interface is appropriate an Application Programming Interface or API that supplies a limited but powerful set of application functionalities, in a manner providing: a) Simplicity of access to the AI functionalities commonly required by application developers; b) for each functionality, either a reliable level of intelligence, or a reliable confidence level associated with each output (indicating the systems assessment of its own confidence in the intelligence of its output in a given instance); c) robustness as a software system, when carrying out the specific application functionalities directly accessible by the API.

2   Representation

It seems inescapable that a Cognitive API will need to be associated with a flexible knowledge representation language. For instance, if a cognitive API were to be realized using OpenCog, then the representation language would be the language of the Atomspace, OpenCog's weighted, labeled hypergraph knowledge representation, e.g. as realized via the Scheme representation now commonly used to load Atoms into the Atomspace.

In general, one wants a KR (Knowledge Representation) language that is highly general, and is reasonably easily both human and machine readable. The bulk of the API indicated here, which comprises a set of queries to be made of a cognitive system, assumes the existence of a KR that can straightforwardly be used to provide descriptions of the following entities, for use in input and/or output of queries: actions, agent, bodies, categories, communication media, communications, constraints, datasets, expressions, events, maps, movements, object, patterns and situations.

Another relevant factor is standardization of concepts referenced in queries. For a cognitive system to have a better chance of understanding a users queries, it will be easier if the user poses his knowledge in terms of standard ontologies wherever relevant and feasible, e.g. WordNet [3] and ConceptNet [10].

3 Queries

The wiki page `http://wiki.opencog.org/w/A_Cognitive_API` comprises critical supplementary information to this paper, and presents a set of queries that we suggest a cognitive API should support. The set of queries is designed to cover all the key aspects of human-like intelligence, as identified in the AI Magazine paper [1] summarizing the conclusions of the 2009 AGI Roadmap Workshop. For each core category of human-intelligence functionality as identified there, a handful of essential questions is identified. And, each of these essential questions may be cast as a formal API call. While a lot more work would need to go into honing a formal API along these lines, first-draft "API call" versions of the questions are given here, for the clarity that this sort of concreteness brings.

For concreteness we give here three arbitrary examples from the long, structured list on the above wiki page (* denotes an optional argument):

- *Expression-List GetTemporalPatterns(Situation-List S)*: what temporal patterns exist in a certain set of situations?
- *DirectAttention(Entity X, *Time T)*: instructs a cognitive system to focus its attention on a certain entity for a certain time period
- *GetAssociatedEmotions(Entity X, *Situation S, *Time T): finds the emotions associated with a certain entity*

4 An Application-Oriented Measure of General Intelligence

The notion of a Cognitive API also has implications in the area of AI intelligence assessment. Quantification of general intelligence levels poses a significant challenge for the AGI field, to which various approaches have been suggested [8] [9] [7] [4] [2] [1]. The Cognitive API proposed here suggests a different approach, an "APIQ" that measures the degree to which a software system can carry out a broad variety of humanly useful, intelligent-seeming functions using a small class of representations and mechanisms.

Suppose that, for each of the queries in the API: a) one has identified a measure of the quality of performance of a given software system at responding to that query, scaled between 0 and 1; b) one has a meaningful qualitative (or formal) way to identify the different representations and algorithms in a given software system; c) for each of these representations and algorithms, and each API query, one can quantify the degree to which the representation/algorithm plays a role in the response to the query, with some degree between 0 and 1. Then one can estimate the *total API quality* of a system as the sum of the performance quality the system displays on each API query; and the *query API generality* of a system as the entropy of the set of performance quality values displayed by the system on the API queries. One can also estimate, for each representation or algorithm, the *total contribution*, defined as the sum over all API queries of: the system's performance quality on the query, multiplied by the degree to which the representation/algorithm plays a role in the query; and the *component API generality*, defined as the entropy of the set of total contribution values, across all the representations/algorithms.

The **applied human-level general intelligence** of a system, then, can be defined roughly as (where a, b, c are nonnegative weight values summing to 3)

$$APIQ = \text{total API quality}^a * \text{API generality}^b * \text{component API generality}^c$$

References

1. Adams, S., Arel, I., Bach, J., Coop, R., Furlan, R., Goertzel, B., Hall, J.S., Samsonovich, A., Scheutz, M., Schlesinger, M., Shapiro, S.C., Sowa, J.: Mapping the landscape of human-level artificial general intelligence. Artificial Intelligence Magazine (2011)
2. Bringsjord, S., Schimanski, B.: What is artificial intelligence? psychometric ai as an answer. In: IJCAI, pp. 887–893 (2003)
3. Fellbaum, C.: WordNet: An Electronic Lexical Database. Addison-Wesley (1990)
4. Goertzel, B.: Toward a formal definition of real-world general intelligence. In: Proceedings of AGI (2010)
5. Goertzel, B., Pennachin, C., Geisweiller, N.: Engineering General Intelligence, Part 1: A Path to Advanced AGI via Embodied Learning and Cognitive Synergy. Atlantis Thinking Machines. Springer (2013)
6. Goertzel, B., Pennachin, C., Geisweiller, N.: Engineering General Intelligence, Part 2: The CogPrime Architecture for Integrative, Embodied AGI. Atlantis Thinking Machines. Springer (2013)
7. Hernandez-Orallo, J., Dowe, D.L.: Measuring universal intelligence: Towards an anytime intelligence test. Artificial Intelligence Journal 174(18), 1508–1539 (2010)
8. Legg, S., Hutter, M.: A definition of machine intelligence. Minds and Machines 17 (2007)
9. Legg, S., Veness, J.: An approximation of the universal intelligence measure. CoRR abs/1109.5951 (2011)
10. Speer, R., Havasi, C.: Conceptnet 5. Tiny Transactions of Computer Science (2012), http://tinytocs.org/vol1/papers/tinytocs-v1-speer.pdf

Self-modeling Agents Evolving in Our Finite Universe

Bill Hibbard

SSEC, University of Wisconsin, Madison, WI 53706, USA
and Machine Intelligence Research Institute
test@ssec.wisc.edu

Abstract. This paper proposes that we should avoid infinite sets in definitions of AI agent and their environments. For agents that evolve to increase their finite resources it proposes a self-modeling agent definition that avoids assumptions about the agent's future form. And it proposes a consistent and complete logical theory for reasoning by AI agents in our finite universe.

1   Finitely Computable Agents

According to current physics [1] our universe has a finite information capacity of no more than 10^{120} bits (10^{90} bits excluding gravitational degrees of freedom). Modeling artificial intelligence (AI) agents and environments with infinite sets, such as Peano arithmetic and the infinite tape of a Turing machine, introduces unnecessary theoretical complexity into our understanding of AI. Thus in my recent papers [2, 3] I have replaced the universal Turing machine in Hutter's [4] universal AI with finite stochastic programs (limited to finite memory, for which the halting problem is decidable).

Specifically, at each of a discrete series of time steps $t \in \{0, 1, 2, ..., T\}$, for some large T, the agent sends an action $a_t \in A$ to the environment and receives an observation $o_t \in O$ from the environment, where A and O are finite sets. Let $h_t = (a_1, o_1, ..., a_t, o_t) \in H$ be an interaction history where H is the set of all histories for $t \leq T$.

The agent's actions are motivated by a *utility function* $u : H \to [0, 1]$ which assigns utilities between 0 and 1 to histories. Future utilities are discounted according to a *geometric temporal discount* $0 < \gamma < 1$. The agent computes a prior probability $\rho(h)$ of history h. The value $v(h)$ of a possible future history h is defined recursively by:

$$v(h) = u(h) + \gamma \max_{a \in A} v(ha) \tag{1}$$
$$v(ha) = \sum_{o \in O} \rho(o \mid ha) \, v(hao) \tag{2}$$

The recursion terminates with $v(h_t) = 0$ for $t > T$. The agent (or policy) π is defined to take, after history h_t, the action:

$$\pi(h_t) := a_{t+1} = \text{argmax}_{a \in A} v(h_t a) \tag{3}$$

Given a history h_t, the agent models the environment by the program [2]:

B. Goertzel et al. (Eds.): AGI 2014, LNAI 8598, pp. 246–249, 2014.

$$q_t = \lambda(h_t) := \text{argmax}_{q \in Q} P(h_t \mid q) \, \rho(q) \tag{4}$$

Here Q is a prefix-free language for finite stochastic programs, $\rho(q) = 2^{-|q|}$ is the prior probability of program $q \in Q$ where $|q|$ is the length of q in bits, and $P(h_t \mid q)$ is the probability that q computes the history h_t (this is the probability that the stochastic program q computes the observations o_i in response to the actions a_i for $1 \le i \le t$). Then the prior probability of a possible future interaction history h for use in (2) is:

$$\rho(h) = P(h \mid q_t) \tag{5}$$

2   Self-modeling Agents

Limited resources are essential to Wang's [5] definition of intelligence and a practical reality for agents in our universe. Although the model $\lambda(h_t)$ in (4) can be finitely computed [3], the resources necessary to compute it grow exponentially with the length of history h_t. Furthermore computing the value $v(h)$ of a possible future history h in (1) and (2) requires an expensive recursion. Hence an agent with limited resources must compute approximations. Increasing the accuracy of these approximations will improve the agent's ability to maximize its utility function, and hence the agent will choose actions to increase its computing resources and so increase accuracy.

Such self-improvement must be expressible by actions in set A. However, the agents of Section 1 cannot adequately evaluate self-improvement actions. If the agent is computing approximations to the model $\lambda(h_t)$ and to values $v(h)$ using its limited computing resources, then it cannot use those limited resources to compute and evaluate what it would compute with greater resources. In real time interactions between the agent and the environment, the environment will not wait for the agent to slowly simulate what it would compute with greater resources.

In the agents of Section 1 values $v(ha)$ are computed by future recursion in (1) and (2). Here we define a revised agent in which values $v(ha)$ are computed for initial subintervals of the current history and in which the environment model includes the computation of such values. Given $h_t = (a_1, o_1, ..., a_t, o_t)$, for $i \le t$ define:

$$ov(h_{i-1}a_i) = discrete((\textstyle\sum_{i \le j \le t} \gamma^{-i} u(h_j)) / (1 - \gamma^{-i+1})) \tag{6}$$

Here $h_j = (a_1, o_1, ..., a_j, o_j)$, $discrete()$ samples real values to a finite subset R of the reals (e.g., floating point numbers) and division by $(1 - \gamma^{-i+1})$ scales values of finite sums to values as would be computed by infinite sums. Define $o'_i = (o_i, ov(h_{i-1}a_i))$ and $h'_t = (a_1, o'_1, ..., a_t, o'_t)$. That is, values $ov(h_{i-1}a_i)$ computed from past interactions are included as observables in an expanded history h'_t so the model $\lambda(h'_t)$ includes an algorithm for computing them:

$$q_t = \lambda(h'_t) := \text{argmax}_{q \in Q} P(h'_t \mid q) \, \rho(q) \tag{7}$$

Define $\rho(h') = P(h' \mid q_t)$. Then compute values of possible next actions by:

$$v(h_t a) = \sum_{r \in R} \rho(ov(h_t a) = r \mid h'_t a) \, r \qquad (8)$$

Here $h'_t = (a_1, o'_1, ..., a_t, o'_t)$ and $h_t = (a_1, o_1, ..., a_t, o_t)$. As in (3) define the agent's policy $\pi(h_t) = a_{t+1} = \text{argmax}_{a \in A} \, v(h_t a)$. Because $\lambda(h'_t)$ models the agent's value computations I call this the *self-modeling agent*. It is finitely computable. There is no look ahead in time beyond evaluation of possible next actions and so no assumption about the form of the agent in the future. $\lambda(h'_t)$ is a unified model of agent and environment, and can model how possible next actions may increase values of future histories by any modification of the agent and its embedding in the environment [6].

The game of chess provides an example of learning to model value as a function of computing resources. Ferreira [7] demonstrated an approximate functional relation between a chess program's ELO rating and its search depth, which can be used to predict the performance of an improved chess-playing agent before it is built. Similarly the self-modeling agent will learn to predict the increase of its future utility due to increases in its resources.

Utility functions defined in terms of the environment model $\lambda(h'_t)$ are a way to avoid the unintended behavior of self-delusion [8, 2]. They are also natural for complex AI agents. Rather than having preprogrammed environment models, complex AI agents must explore and learn models of their environments. But the designers of an AI agent will express their intentions for the agent's behavior choices in terms of their own knowledge of the agent's environment. Thus it is natural that they define an agent's utility function in terms of a procedure to be applied to the agent's learned environment model. I presented an example of such a procedure at AGI-12 [3]. Defining its utility function in terms of its environment model introduces a potential circularity in the self-modeling agent: $ov(h_{i-1}a_i)$ depends on $u(h_j)$ in (6), $u(h_j)$ depends on $\lambda(h'_t)$ in defining the utility function in terms of the model, and $\lambda(h'_t)$ depends on $ov(h_{i-1}a_i)$ in (7). This circularity can be avoided by defining the utility function u used in equation (6) in terms of an environment model from a previous time step.

The agent's environment model is an approximation because the model is based on a limited history of interactions with the environment and, for agents in our universe, because of limited resources for computing the model. Thus a utility function computed from the model is also an approximation to an ideal utility function which is the true expression of the intention of the agent designers. Such an approximate utility function is a possible source of AI behavior that violates its design intention.

3   Consistent and Complete Logic for Agents

Any AI agent based on a logical theory that includes Peano arithmetic (PA) faces problems of decidability, consistency and completeness. Yudkowsky and Herreshoff [9] discuss such problems related to Löb's Theorem for a sequence of evolving agents. Our universe has finite information capacity [1]. I suggest that an agent can pursue its goal in such a finite environment without any need for PA and its theoretical problems.

An environment with finite information capacity has a finite number of possible states. In this case it is reasonable to assume a finite limit on the length of interaction histories, that the action set A and the observation set O never grow larger than the information capacity of the environment, and that probabilities and utility function values are constrained to a finite subset of the reals (only a finite subset can be expressed in a finite environment). Then, for a given finite limit on environment size, there are finite numbers of possible objects of these types: environments (expressed as Markov decision processes), histories, utility functions, policies, environment models that optimize equation (4) or (7) for possible histories, and agent programs (assuming agent memory is limited by the information capacity of the environment, there are a finite number of programs and their halting problem is decidable). There are also finite numbers of possible predicates and probability distributions over these types of objects and combinations of them. So, for a given finite limit on environment size, the theory of these types of objects, predicates and probability distributions is decidable, consistent and complete (quantifiers over finite sets can be eliminated, reducing the theory to propositional calculus). In our universe with no more than 10^{120} bits, agents can use this theory to avoid the logical problems of PA. I suggest that more serious problems for agents in our universe are the inaccuracy of their environment models and the limits on their memory capacity and speed for reasoning in real time.

References

1. Lloyd, S.: Computational Capacity of the Universe. Phys.Rev.Lett. 88, 237901 (2002)
2. Hibbard, B.: Model-based utility functions. J. Artificial General Intelligence 3(1), 1–24 (2012a)
3. Hibbard, B.: Avoiding unintended AI behaviors. In: Bach, J., Goertzel, B., Iklé, M. (eds.) AGI 2012. LNCS (LNAI), vol. 7716, pp. 107–116. Springer, Heidelberg (2012)
4. Hutter, M.: Universal artificial intelligence: sequential decisions based on algorithmic probability. Springer, Heidelberg (2005)
5. Wang, P.: Non-Axiomatic Reasoning System — Exploring the essence of intelligence. PhD Dissertation, Indiana University Comp. Sci. Dept. and the Cog. Sci. Program. (1995)
6. Orseau, L., Ring, M.: Space-Time Embedded Intelligence. In: Bach, J., Goertzel, B., Iklé, M. (eds.) AGI 2012. LNCS (LNAI), vol. 7716, pp. 209–218. Springer, Heidelberg (2012)
7. Ferreira, D.R.: The Impact of Search Depth on Chess Playing Strength. ICGA Journal 36(2), 67–80 (2013)
8. Ring, M., Orseau, L.: Delusion, survival, and intelligent agents. In: Schmidhuber, J., Thórisson, K.R., Looks, M. (eds.) AGI 2011. LNCS (LNAI), vol. 6830, pp. 11–20. Springer, Heidelberg (2011)
9. Yudkowsky, E., Herreshoff, M.: Tiling Agents for Self-Modifying AI, and the Löbian Obstacle (2013), http://intelligence.org/files/TilingAgents.pdf

Affective Agent Architecture:
A Preliminary Research Report

Kevin Raison[1] and Steve Lytinen[2]

[1] Chatsubo Labs, Seattle WA 98117, USA
[2] DePaul University, Chicago IL 60604, USA

Keywords. Affect theory, affective agents, affective computing, planning, artificial life, multi-agent systems.

Our work with affective agents is motivated by a desire to develop a biologically-inspired model of the human system that includes sensation, feeling, and affect integrated with the logical and cognitive models traditionally used in AI. Our work can be situated alongside Breazeal's robot Kismet (1998), Elliott's Affective Reasoner (1992), as well as Baillie's architecture (2002) for intuitive reasoning in affective agents; we too seek to model the motivations and reasoning of agents with an affective foundation. Our approach differs in how we model affect and the transition of biological impulses from sensation through affect into action. We base our work on the Affect Theory of Silvan Tomkins; Thomkins' (2008) theory comprises both a biologically hardwired notion of affect, similar to Ekman's basic emotions and Izard's DET, as well as a more culturally and biographically situated theory of scripts for describing how affect moves from feeling into action (Nathanson, 1996). As a proof of concept, we have consciously chosen to work with a simplified implementation of Tomkins' idea of affect, and explore how both internal (drives, organ sensations) and external stimuli move through the agents via the affect system and transition into action.

As pointed out by Scarantino (2012), the field of emotion research is in need of a properly defined set of "natural kinds" of affect as a basis for research. Tomkins provides such a set with his nine basic affects, which he considers biological and cross-cultural. They are positioned as an evolutionary response to the problem of the limited channel of consciousness (Vernon, 2009), insofar as the affect system provides not just distinct feelings, but thereby filters stimuli and focuses attention in an advantageous way. Because the negative (inherently punishing) affects of fear/terror, anger/rage, etc. trump the positive (inherently rewarding) interest/excitement and enjoyment/joy, the affect system favors responses that evade or directly confront threats to survival. Such a goal-oriented filtering of stimulus provides a clear foundation for a computational model of affect dynamics. With Sheutz's (2002) caution against prematurely assigning emotional labels to the states of artificial agents in mind, we have chosen to bracket out problems of qualia for now, and focus on developing our agent architecture with this filtering system as its core (see figure 1).

For this proof of concept, we implemented the basic structure of Tomkins' model with a limited number of drives, senses, affects, deliberative faculties

B. Goertzel et al. (Eds.): AGI 2014, LNAI 8598, pp. 250–253, 2014.

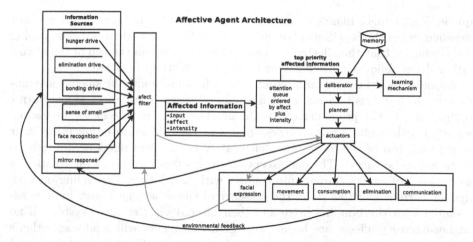

Fig. 1.

and actuators. We built our agents in Common Lisp, on the foundation of a blackboard system called GBBopen (Corkill, 2003). In order to test the agents' responses to their environment, we constructed a multi-agent game grid based on the Wumpus world (Russel & Norvig, 2003). We replaced the search for gold with a biologically-inspired search of food, but kept the Wumpus as a predator and pits as obstacles. We also built in the ability of individual agents to perceive one another's expressions as a starting point for experimenting with social behavior; this component also includes a simplified model of empathy based on Rizzolatti's (2004) mirror neurons.

Each agent is composed of a set of blackboard objects representing instances of various drives, a limited number of sensors (smell and facial feature recognition), an affective filter that is capable of combining with any type of information produced by other components of the system, an ordered queue of information and associated affect (called affected information), a planning / goal seeking component that is capable of processing one piece of affected information at a time, a memory store, and a set of actuators capable of operating in the game grid.

We use the notion of drives as a simplification of the complexities of organ sensations associated with biological needs such as hunger and elimination. The drive system operates largely in the background, independent of the other components of the system, except when a drive needs satisfaction. In that case, the drive will activate and send a signal into the affective filter. The signal will then be interpreted based on its intensity and an affect will be assigned. This affected information will be placed on the attention queue for processing by the planning system. If the affected information is on the top of the queue, the deliberative component will plan accordingly and attempt to satisfy it, until such time as a more urgent piece of affected information is placed on the queue. The information provided by the drives is in no way static; it can change as the intensity of the drive changes, in turn intensifying the associated affect, or perhaps even changing the affect from one type to another. This will cause a reordering of the queue. E.g., hunger manifests as interest/excitement; if the hunger drive is not satisfied presently, it will escalate until it transforms into distress, thus raising the likelihood that the affected information will end up on the top of the queue. Other drives follow similar patterns appropriate to their function.

A similar model is used for filtering sensory information; if the smell of a Wumpus is detected, this information is filtered and assigned an affect of fear/terror appropriate to the proximity of the threat. The same is true of the breeze associated with a pit. Again, as these pieces of affected information make their way to the top of the queue, the deliberative mechanism plans accordingly so as to avoid the threat. The one exception to this flow of sensory information is in the case of agents coming into contact with each other. Depending on each agents' current affective state, the presence of the other agent may become associated with the bonding drive and then filtered via the affect system. If no higher-intensity affects are being processed, the agents will read each other's expressions and internalize them, thus activating their affective system a second time and reinterpreting the perceived state of the other agent as their own (an approximation of empathy). If the response is of a high enough threshold, the agents will then activate their memories of their own previous affective states and attempt to guess the reason for the other agent's expression. This internalizing of the other's affect will prompt the same action as the same affect from a different source.

The results of our experiments with affective agents in the grid world were very satisfying, though limited in this preliminary study. Agents were generally able to navigate the grid world, successfully evading threats and satisfying their drives based on the information provided to them by their affective filters. Competing drives and sensory inputs would often lead to oscillations between which information was on the top of the attention queue, but the flexibility of the planning system allowed for smooth transitions between competing goals. E.g., if an extremely distressed and hungry agent wandered close to a Wumpus, the hunger-satisfaction goal would be temporarily overridden by the fear-induced need to evade a threat, and once the threat was removed, the distress-laden hunger goal would reassert itself and the agent would go back to seeking food. There were a number of instances where an agent was dealing with extreme hunger and would discover that there was food right next to a Wumpus; in these cases, if the affected hunger was stronger than the fear of the Wumpus, the agent would risk getting close to the Wumpus just to eat. As soon as the hunger drive was satisfied, the agent's fear of the Wumpus would dominate and the agent would engage in evasive behavior. This sort of emergent behavior was not expected, but certainly validates the usefulness of the model. Results of the social experiments will be discussed in a forthcoming paper.

Overall, we would call these experiments a success; we were able to develop a model of affect-motivated deliberation and goal-striving in artificial agents. While at this stage, the agents are rather simple, enough has been accomplished to justify further exploration. A few things in particular stand out as needing improvement; first is adding a communication protocol for inter-agent message passing beyond simple facial expression recognition. Second would be to flesh out the affect filtering system so that it operates more in line with Tomkins' notion of the density of neural firing; in his view, a particular affect is not caused by a symbolically recognized entity (as in our simplified model), but rather is the result of a particular pattern of neural activity (see Tomkins, 2008, p. 139). Layered neural networks might act as a better approximation of Tomkins' idea than the current symbolic architecture. Our model of sociability should also be greatly expanded; it currently only encompasses one aspect of the incredibly complex set of social motivations and behaviors. A final, longer-range goal would be to explore in more detail the complex interaction of affect, memory and imagery that Tomkins described in his script theory. Implementing this idea as a computer model could contribute positively to the looming possibility of the emergence of an artificial general intelligence; if such an entity were to emerge, it would be important that it resemble its human creators on the level of emotional experience so that we have some chance of actually relating to one another.

References

Baillie, P.: The Synthesis of Emotions in Artificial Intelligences: An Affective Architecture for Intuitive Reasoning in Artificial Intelligence. The University of Southern Queensland (2002)

Breazeal(Ferrell), C.: Early Experiments using Motivations to Regulate Human-Robot Interaction. In: Proceedings of 1998 AAAI Fall Symposium: Emotional and Intelligent, The Tangled Knot of Cognition (1998)

Corkill, D.: Collaborating Software: Blackboard and Multi-Agent Systems & the Future. In: International Lisp Conference 2003, New York (2003)

Elliott, C.: The affective reasoner: a process model of emotions in a multi-agent system. Northwestern University (1992)

Nathanson, D.: What's a Script. Bulletin of the Tomkins Institute 3, 1–4 (1996)

Rizzolatti, G., Craighero, L.: The Mirror-Neuron System. Annual Review of Neuroscience 27, 169–192 (2004)

Russell, S., Norvig, P.: Artificial Intelligence: A Modern Approach. Prentice Hall, Upper Saddle River (2003)

Scarantino, A.: How to Define Emotions Scientifically. Emotion Review 4, 358–368 (2012)

Sheutz, M.: Agents with or without Emotions? AAAI, Palo Alto (2002)

Tomkins, S.: Affect Imagery Consciousness. Springer, New York (2008)

Vernon, K.: A Primer of Affect Psychology. Tomkins Instutite, Lewisburg (2009)

Unsupervised Learning of Spatio-temporal Patterns Using Spike Timing Dependent Plasticity

Banafsheh Rekabdar, Monica Nicolescu, Richard Kelley, and Mircea Nicolescu

Department of Computer Science and Engineering
University of Nevada, Reno
{rekabdarb,monica,rkelley,mircea}@cse.unr.edu

Abstract. This paper presents an unsupervised approach for learning of patterns with spatial and temporal information from a very small number of training samples. The method employs a spiking network with axonal conductance delays that learns the encoding of individual patterns as sets of polychronous neural groups, which emerge as a result of training. A similarity metric between sets, based on a modified version of the Jaccard index, is used for pattern classification. Two different neural connectivity models are evaluated on a data set consisting of hand-drawn digits that encode temporal information (i.e., from the starting to the end point of the digit). The results demonstrate that the approach can successfully generalize these patterns from a significantly small number of training samples.

Keywords: Spiking Neuron Network, Synaptic Plasticity, Polychronization, Unsupervised Learning, Classification, STDP.

1 Introduction

This research is motivated by two robotic problems that rely on an autonomous system's ability to encode and recognize spatiotemporal patterns: intent recognition [1] and imitation learning [2][3]. In both domains, the activities observed by the autonomous system contain both spatial and temporal information. What is more important, however, is that both domains require that these patterns be encoded in a way that enables early recognition. We propose to address this problem through the use of spiking neural networks with axonal conductance delays, relying on a spike-timing dependent plasticity learning rule. Research by Izhikevich [4] has shown that spiking networks with axonal propagation delays can encode temporal patterns in the form of polychronous neuronal groups (PNGs). Several methods have been developed that exploit these mechanisms [5][6], but they employed a supervised learning mechanism for classification. Furthermore, they rely on large number of training samples. In this paper we propose an unsupervised method, which relies on small number of training samples. The remaining of the paper is structured as follows: Section 2 discusses relevant related research, Section 3 presents the details of our approach. Section 4 and 5 present the experimental results and conclusion respectively.

B. Goertzel et al. (Eds.): AGI 2014, LNAI 8598, pp. 254–257, 2014.

2   Previous Work

Roboticists have explored a number of potential solutions to the intent recognition problem, including symbolic approaches [7] and probabilistic methods [1]. Biological neural networks offer an alternative to traditional statistical methods. Such networks pass messages through the timing of a spike train from one neuron to another. In biological systems, the connections between these neurons may be modified through experience; many researchers suspect that these modifications constitute the bulk of learning, and some researchers have attempted to use the biologically-inspired *spike-timing dependent plasticity* to do machine learning [8]. Although in general these systems have met with somewhat modest success, there are some indications that careful use of spike timings can facilitate very general forms of computation [9]. Moreover, researchers have shown preliminary work in which *polychronization* can be used with reservoir computing methods to perform supervised classification tasks [5]. Our work continues along these lines by exploring the extent to which purely unsupervised learning can exploit polychronization with temporally-dependent data to build time-aware representations that facilitate traditional classification. We differ from that previous work in our emphasis on mostly-unsupervised approaches, and in our emphasis on training from limited sample sizes.

3   General Approach

Our approach uses a network of spiking neurons with axonal conductance delays to perform classification of multiple spatiotemporal patterns. Our network consists of 320 neurons. Each neuron is connected to 0.1% of the rest of the neurons(32 synapses).Each synapse has a fixed conduction delay between 1 ms to 20 ms. The delays are randomly selected using a uniform distribution. Each neuron can be either excitatory or inhibitory and the ratio of excitatory to inhibitory neurons is 4:1.Synaptic weights are initialized with +6 if the corresponding neuron is excitatory and -5 if the neuron is inhibitory. The maximum value for the weights is 10.We use two different probability distribution functions to establish the connectivity between neurons: a uniform distribution and a two-dimensional Gaussian distribution with a standard deviation equal to 3.

Our domain dataset consists of handwritten digits from digit *zero* to digit *nine*, stored as a grey-level image with width and height of 16 pixels. In addition to the spatial information inherent in the patterns, we also encoded temporal information regarding how the pattern was drawn: from the first pixel (beginning of pattern) to the last (end of pattern) the intensity of the pixels decreases from highest to lowest (fade tapering). Thus, we can use an intensity-based image to encode a relative temporal relation. From the pixel intensity values we then generate a time-firing pattern that consists of a list of the neurons in decreasingly sorted order from highest to lowest intensity values.

During training, each pattern is presented to the network during 1-second intervals as follows: the neuron that corresponds to the highest intensity value will be stimulated first (by providing it with input current of 20 mA), followed by the lower intensity value neurons in decreasing sorted order.

Polychronization in spiking neural networks is a property to exhibit reproducible time-locked but not synchronous firing patterns with millisecond precision [5][9]. Using the trained network we build a model of each class, consisting of all the persistent PNGs that are activated by a pattern from that class. In this work, we consider PNGs that have 3 anchor neurons. To find all the PNGs corresponding to a pattern, we take all possible combinations of 3 neurons from the corresponding timed pattern and we stimulate these subsets of neurons in the network in the same order and using the same timing as in the pattern. If a PNG with a path length of at least 3 is activated, then it is added to the set corresponding to the pattern's class. For each class, the result will be a group of PNG sets. Each PNG is uniquely identified by its anchor neurons. In the testing phase, for a particular testing pattern, we stimulate all possible combinations of 3 anchor neurons using the correct order and wait for 500ms, and consider the PNGs that have a minimum path length of 3. Next, we find the similarity between the PNG set of the testing sample and all training models. We choose the class of the sample from the training set that results in the greatest similarity measure. We adapted a similarity measure for sets called Jaccard Index [10]. If A and B are two PNG sets corresponding to two patterns, the similarity measure between A and B is:

$$sim(A, B) = 1 - \frac{|A xor B|}{|A \cup B|} \tag{1}$$

4   Experimental Results

We created a dataset of handwritten digits (5 training and 22 testing samples for each digit.) We computed the following measures: i) the *success rate* (the percentage of correctly classified test samples), ii) the *error rate* (the percentage of misclassified test samples), and iii) the *rejection rate* (the percentage of instances for which no classification can be made). Rejected patterns occur when the similarity measures are all zero or we have a tie between multiple classes. Tables 1 and 2 show our results.

Table 1. Multi-classclassificationresultsfor a network with Gaussian distribution

	0	1	2	3	4	5	6	7	8	9	All digits
Success rate	77.2%	77.2%	81.8%	68.1%	90.9%	86.3%	86.3%	95.4%	45.4%	90.9%	80%
Error rate	13.6%	13.6%	9%	27.2%	4.5%	9%	13.6%	4.5%	50%	9%	15.4%
Rejection rate	9%	9%	9%	4.5%	4.5%	4.5%	0%	0%	4.5%	0%	2.5%

Table 2. Binary classificationresultsforclasses: i) 0 versus 1 andii) 5 versus 8

	Gaussian0 vs. 1	Random0 vs. 1	Gaussian5 vs. 8	Random5 vs. 8
Success rate	83.3%	32%	84.7%	56%
Error rate	0%	0%	0%	0%
Rejection rate	16.6%	67%	15%	43%

5   Conclusion

In this paper we have introduced a new unsupervised approach for learning spatiotemporal patterns. Our method utilizes a network of spiking neurons to learn from a very small training set. The general idea behind our approach is that a spiking network with axonal conductance delays, learns the encoding of each spatiotemporal pattern as a set of PNGs. In our experiments we have tested two different neural connectivity approaches, one with a uniform probability distribution function and second with a Gaussian probability distribution. Our results show that the Gaussian connectivity model performs better and despite the very small number of training samples, our approach has successfully generalized to new and different unseen patterns.

Aknowledgements. This work has been supported by ONR grant #N000141210860.

References

1. Kelley, R., King, C., Tavakkoli, A., Nicolescu, M., Nicolescu, M., Bebis, G.: An architecture for understanding intent using a novel hidden markov formulation. International Journal of Humanoid Robotics 5(02), 203–224 (2008)
2. Schaal, S.: Is imitation learning the route to humanoid robots? Trends in Cognitive Sciences 3(6), 233–242 (1999)
3. Rekabdar, B., Shadgar, B., Osareh, A.: Learning teamwork behaviors approach: Learning by observation meets case-based planning. In: Ramsay, A., Agre, G. (eds.) AIMSA 2012. LNCS, vol. 7557, pp. 195–201. Springer, Heidelberg (2012)
4. Szatmáry, B., Izhikevich, E.M.: Spike-timing theory of working memory. PLoS Computational Biology 6(8), e1000879 (2010)
5. Paugam-Moisy, H., Martinez, R., Bengio, S.: Delay learning and polychronization for reservoir computing. Neurocomputing 71(7), 1143–1158 (2008)
6. Karimpouli, S., Fathianpour, N., Roohi, J.: A new approach to improve neural networks' algorithm in permeability prediction of petroleum reservoirs using supervised committee machine neural network. Journal of Petroleum Science and Engineering 73(3), 227–232 (2010)
7. Charniak, E., Goldman, R.P.: A Bayesian model of plan recognition. Artificial Intelligence 64(1), 53–79 (1993)
8. Tao, X., Michel, H.E.: Data Clustering Via Spiking Neural Networks through Spike Timing-Dependent Plasticity. In: IC-AI, pp. 168–173 (2004)
9. Izhikevich, E.M.: Polychronization: computation with spikes. Neural Computation 18(2), 245–282 (2006)
10. Jaccard, P.: The distribution of the flora in the alpine zone. 1. New Phytologist 11(2), 37–50 (1912)

System Factorial Technology Applied to Artificial Neural Network Information Processing

Christophe Tremblay, Bradley Harding, Sylvain Chartier, and Denis Cousineau

University of Ottawa, School of Psychology, Ottawa, Canada
{ctrem040,bhard024,sylvain.chartier,denis.cousineau}@uottawa.ca

Abstract. System Factorial Technology is a recent methodology for the analysis of information processing architectures. SFT can discriminate between three processing architectures, namely serial, parallel and coactive processing. In addition, it can discriminate between two stopping rules, self-terminating and exhaustive. Although the previously stated architectures fit to many psychological skills as performed by human beings (i.e. recognition task, categorization, visual search, etc.), the analysis of processing architectures that lie outside of the five original choices remain unclear. An example of such architecture is the recall process as performed by iterative systems. Results indicate that an iterative recall neural network is mistakenly detected by SFT as being a serial exhaustive architecture. This research shows a limit of SFT as an analytic tool but could lead to advancements in cognitive modeling by improving the strategies used for the analysis of underlying information processing architectures.

Keywords: Neurodynamic Modeling, Artificial Neural Network, Bidirectional Associative Memory, System Factorial Technology.

1 Introduction

Recent advancements in mathematical psychology have brought forth System Factorial Technology, or SFT [1, 2], a tool that can diagnose the type of information processing architecture behind a mental process [1]: serial processing, parallel processing, and coactive processing and possible stopping rules: self-terminating and exhaustive. This allows for a total of 5 possible architectures that can be identified by SFT (coactive architectures only have one possible stopping rule, namely self-terminating) [3-4]. The method works solely with the response times (RT) distributions of four conditions, obtained from the manipulation of the inputs that should independently affect two distinct sub-processes (in a 2 x 2 factorial design). The four conditions include the High-High (HH) condition, in which both sub-processes are working at a normal or artificially enhanced fashion. The High-Low and Low-High conditions (HL and LH) is where one sub-process is working in an artificially impaired fashion and the other operates normally or in an artificially enhanced fashion. Finally, the Low-Low condition is achieved when both sub-processes are performing in an artificially impaired fashion. By measuring the Survivor Interaction Contrast (SIC) for each moment in time between the 4 condition distributions, we can create a curve [5]:

B. Goertzel et al. (Eds.): AGI 2014, LNAI 8598, pp. 258–261, 2014.

$$\text{SIC}(t) = S_{LL}(t) - S_{LH}(t) - S_{HL}(t) + S_{HH}(t) \tag{1}$$

In which $S(t)$ is the survivor function of the RT distributions for the four conditions. Figure 1 presents the SIC curves associated with the different processing architectures.

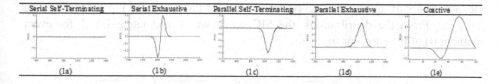

Serial Self-Terminating	Serial Exhaustive	Parallel Self-Terminating	Parallel Exhaustive	Coactive
(1a)	(1b)	(1c)	(1d)	(1e)

Fig. 1. Survival Interaction Contrast curves and their associated processing architecture

Although SFT has been applied to a wide variety of mental processes, its applicability to architectures lying outside the five original categories has not yet been studied. One such architecture is an artificial neural networks in which signals are processed iteratively until the network settles in a stable configuration. Bidirectional Associative Memory (BAM) [6-7] models are neural networks in which output units are found through the iteration of the activation between two layers of parallel units. This process is expressed in Figure 2, where **W** and **V** are the weight connections, $\mathbf{x}_{(1)}$, $\mathbf{x}_{(2)}, ..., \mathbf{x}_{(N)}$ and $\mathbf{y}_{(1)}, \mathbf{y}_{(2)}, ..., \mathbf{y}_{(M)}$ are the input units. During the recall phase, the output units would be found by iterating through the network until a stable solution is found.

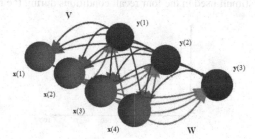

Fig. 2. Iteration process used in BAM recall

Since the information processing architecture behind a BAM does not correspond to any of the five diagnosable architectures, the nature of the process detected by SFT remains to be established. This article therefore seeks to examine what SFT detects when the information processing architecture falls outside classical categories.

2   Simulation

In this simulation, the input patterns consisted of 60 visual patterns of 576 pixels (a surface of 24 x 24 pixels). Examples of the stimuli used are presented in Figure 3. The network had to perform recall tasks with randomly distributed noise for a 2 x 2 design, as required for SFT analysis (HH, HL, LH, LL) as shown in Figure 4. In every

Low condition, the input pattern was "masked" by setting 10% of the pixels to 0, therefore limiting the processing capability of the network. Masked pixels in the HL condition could not be masked in the LH condition. Consequently, the LL condition has 20% of the input patterns being masked, which were a combination of the masks used in HL and LH. The network was tested 2000 times in every condition and the mean numbers of iterations (k) to perform recall for the totality of input patterns were gathered. From the distributions, the SIC curve was found using Eq. 1 for every moment (t) of the survivor function.

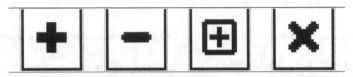

Fig. 3. Input patterns used in the first set of simulations

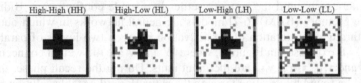

Fig. 4. Four stimuli used in the four recall conditions during the recall phase

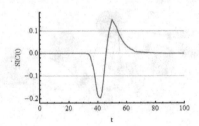

Fig. 5. SIC curve for recall task with bipolar images

Results show that the number of iterations needed to perform the task in the four conditions was only slightly affected by the impaired conditions (an L sub-process). However, the recall was affected enough to distinguish an interaction pattern. All distributions followed an overall normal shape. The SIC curve shows clear evidence of a serial exhaustive processing architecture where the SIC curve is almost identical to what was presented in Figure 1b.

3   Discussion and Conclusion

The results presented here show evidence that the information processing present in a BHM produces response times (as represented by the number of iterations) that mimics a serial exhaustive architecture. However the BHM is built in a parallel fashion using units within layers that work in parallel. Therefore, facing new types of processing architectures, SFT can wrongly diagnose a processing architecture. These results are of concern as they show that SFT is capable of misclassifications. These results also weaken evidence for any particular architecture responsible for a mental process when the sub-process in question is not clearly understood. A possible explanation for the obtained results is that SFT detects the most important determinant of RT, hereby not detecting underlying subtleties in the architecture. These results also suggest that the SFT methodology could detect the overall information process rather than the underlying architecture used for that process.

In conclusion, this article presented a case study of the architecture detection using the SFT methodology on architectures that do not fall into classical categories. Results showed that the methodology incorrectly detects and assigns a category to the architecture. This research shows the necessity to improve the detection of architecture behind a process and presents an attempt for the understanding of artificial neural networks through the use of the System Factorial Technology. This research could lead to improved tools for modeling of human behavior using intelligent systems.

Acknowledgement. This research was partly supported by the Natural Sciences and Engineering Research Council of Canada.

References

1. Townsend, J.T., Nozawa, G.: Spatio-temporal properties of elementary perception: An investigation of parallel, serial, and coactive theories. Journal of Mathematical Psychology 39(4), 321–359 (1995)
2. Fific, M., Nosofsky, R.M., Townsend, J.T.: Information-processing architectures in multi-dimensional classification: A validation test of the systems factorial technology. Journal of Experimental Psychology 34(2), 356–375 (2008)
3. Schweickert, R., Giorgini, M., Dzhafarov, E.: Selective influence and response time cumulative distribution function in serial-parallel task networks. Journal of Mathematical Psychology 44, 504–535 (2000)
4. Townsend, J.T., Wenger, M.J.: The serial-parallel dilemma: A case study in a linkage of theory and method. Psychonomic Bulletin & Review 11(3), 391–418 (2004)
5. Fific, M., Townsend, J.T., Eidels, A.: Studying visual search using systems factorial methodology with target-distractor similarity as the factor. Perception & Psychophysics 70(4), 583–603 (2008)
6. Chartier, S., Boukadoum, M.: A bidirectional heteroassociative memory for binary and grey-level patterns. IEEE Transactions on Neural Networks 17(2), 385–396 (2006)
7. Chartier, S., Boukadoum, M.: Encoding static and temporal patterns with a bidirectional heteroassociative memory. Journal of Applied Mathematics 2011, 1–34 (2011)

Compression and Decompression in Cognition

Michael O. Vertolli, Matthew A. Kelly, and Jim Davies

Institute of Cognitive Science, Carleton University
1125 Colonel By Drive, Ottawa, Ontario K1S 5B6 Canada
michaelvertolli@gmail.com, matthew.kelly2@carleton.ca,
jim@jimdavies.org

Abstract. This paper proposes that decompression is an important and often overlooked component of cognition in all domains where compressive stimuli reduction is a requirement. We support this claim by comparing two compression representations, co-occurrence probabilities and holographic vectors, and two decompression procedures, top-n and Coherencer, on a context generation task from the visual imagination literature. We tentatively conclude that better decompression procedures increase optimality across compression types.

Keywords: decompression, generative cognition, imagination, context, coherence, vector symbolic architectures, cognitive modeling.

1   Introduction

Compression has been implicated in artificial general intelligence and, more broadly, general cognition [1]. In vision, for example, there is massive redundancy in natural images that must be reduced [2]. These reduced representations are then transformed into invariant representations of objects later in the processing stream [3]. Compression of signals from the environment, understood as reducing a stimulus to the details most relevant for survival, is critical to an organism's success [4].

Decompression has received much less attention than compression in the cognitive science and artificial intelligence literatures, but, as we argue, it plays an equally critical role in cognition. Compression is captured by machine learning techniques that move from instances (e.g., pictures of cats) to general regularities (e.g., what a cat looks like), much like inductive inference. Decompression does the reverse: it moves from regularities to instances, much like deductive inference. Decompression allows the agent to apply its general knowledge to its particular circumstances. In vision, visual perception is largely a compression process and visual imagination is a decompression process. In framing the problem in this way, part of our contribution is to demonstrate that decompression, understood as a cognitive process, can be modelled using techniques from artificial intelligence research. We demonstrate this claim by comparing two compression representations and two decompression techniques, and showing the significant and differentiable effect of the latter.

2   Task Description and Implementation

The task is based on the work of [5,6]. In their research, the model must generate

B. Goertzel et al. (Eds.): AGI 2014, LNAI 8598, pp. 262–265, 2014.

the content of a coherent, fleshed-out scene (e.g., a "car," "road," and "sky") from a single word input (e.g., "car"). For example, a scene containing "bow," "violin," and "arrow" would be incoherent: it mixes two senses of the word "bow."

The goal of the decompression step is to deduce implicit information in the compressed representation. For the current problem, the model must infer which images contained which labels. For example, the agent knows that "car" co-occurs with "road," in general, but does not know what other labels are in the particular images with "car" and "road."

The task requires the decompression of co-occurrence probabilities and holographic vectors into contextually coherent, 5-label combinations given a query label. The context is judged to have been accurately inferred if at least one of the original images contains the same 5-label combination produced by the agent.

2.1   Compression Representations

The original compression representation outlined by [5,6] used co-occurrence probabilities between pairs of labels: $P(l \mid q) = |I_q \cap I_l| / |I_q|$, where q is the query label, l is another label and I is the set of images.

We chose to compare the co-occurrence probabilities to a holographic vector or holographic memory representation [7]. Here, each label in the Peekaboom labeled image database is represented by a vector of 1000 dimensions randomly sampled from a normal distribution with a mean of zero and a standard deviation of $1/\sqrt{1000}$. We call these vectors *environment vectors*. Each label is also represented by a second type of vector, termed a *memory vector*: the sum of all environment vectors representing labels that the given label co-occurs with.

The vectors were compared using cosine similarity, which ranges from 1 to -1. The cosine of a memory vector with another memory vector is a measure of second-order association: how often the labels appear in *similar* images. In what follows, we compare task performance for holographic vectors using second-order association to task performance using co-occurrence probabilities.

2.2   Decompression Procedures

We compared two decompression procedures. First, the top-n procedure selects the n labels with the highest probability of co-occurrence with the query label, $P(l \mid q)$, or with the highest cosine similarity to the query label's memory vector.

The second decompression procedure is a model called Coherencer, the visual coherence subsystem of the SOILIE imagination architecture [8,9]. Coherencer is a serial, local hill search algorithm.

Coherencer selects four labels with the highest association with the query—co-occurrence probability or cosine similarity. Then, it calculates the mean association value for each pair of labels. If it passes a threshold (λ), the collection is accepted:

$1/20 \sum_{n=1}^{5}\sum_{m=1}^{5}A(l_n, l_m) > \lambda.$[1] If it fails to pass the threshold, the label with the lowest row and column averages is discarded without possible reselection. A new label is swapped in and the process repeats until either the pool of labels that co-occur with the query is exhausted or a set passing the threshold is found. If the pool is exhausted, Coherencer returns the best combination found.

3   Method

The entire Peekaboom [10] database was filtered to remove all images with fewer than five labels and any labels that only occurred in those images. A total of 8,372 labels and 23,115 images remained after this filtration. Each of the 8,372 labels was processed by all the algorithms. The top-n procedure always yields the same result and was run once. Coherencer has stochastic variation; it was run 71 times on the co-occurrence representation and 9 times on the holographic representation. The results were averaged for each representation. The number of runs conforms to an analytic model run metric [11]. The results for each of the algorithms were assessed with regard to the original images. If at least one of these images contained the five resulting labels, the algorithm scored one point. We compared the total number of points scored by each decompression procedure on each compression representation.

4   Results

Coherencer outperformed the top-n model across both compression techniques. Contrary to our original hypothesis, the co-occurrence compression representation outperformed the holographic representation across both decompression procedures. The success rates out of the 8,372 possible query labels for each of the four conditions are: top-n and co-occurrence = 4842; top-n and holographic = 619; Coherencer and co-occurrence = 5750; Coherencer and holographic = 3259.[2]

A model generated by the logistic regression using three predictors (choice of compression representation, choice of decompression technique, and the interaction between the two) was able to predict success or failure on the basis of those predictors with 69.8% accuracy overall. The predictors as a set reliably distinguished between success and failure of the model, $\chi^2(3, N{=}33218) = 8353.78$, $p < .000$, Negelkerke's $R^2 = .30$. The Wald criterion demonstrated that all three predictors made a significant contribution to the accuracy of the model ($p < .000$).[2]

---

[1] The diagonal, where $n = m$, is ignored. Thus, the denominator of the average has to be decremented by the cardinality of this diagonal (i.e., by 5). $A(\cdot,\cdot)$ is the association calculation for the given compression representation (either cosine or co-occurrence probability).

[2] The full details are omitted due to space constraints. They can be viewed online, here: www.theworldmatrix.ca/agi-compression-decompression-stats.pdf

5   Discussion

The results support the notion that Coherencer is an improvement over the top-n control. However, they contradict our expectation that the holographic vector representation would be better able to capture contextual information than co-occurrence probabilities. Future research will explore why.

We take our findings as preliminary evidence of a general property of cognition. Compression is ubiquitous in cognition and the relative optimality of that compression is essential to the success of the agent. This optimality is not given by the compression mechanisms that perform the necessary reductions in information without the additional support of the decompression mechanisms that extract relations implicit in the compressed representations. Our research is a preliminary demonstration that the exclusion of either side of the compression-decompression dyad necessarily gives an incomplete description of the process. Thus, we predict all cognitive domains requiring compression mechanisms will improve with better decompression techniques.

References

1. Hutter, M.: Universal Artificial Intelligence: Sequential Decisions based on Algorithmic Probability. Springer (2005)
2. Barlow, H.B.: Possible principles underlying the transformation of sensory messages. Sensory Communication, 217–234 (1961)
3. Rolls, E.T.: Memory, Attention, and Decision Making: A Unifying Computational Neuroscience Approach. Oxford University Press, Oxford (2008)
4. Simoncelli, E.P., Olshausen, B.A.: Natural image statistics and neural representation. Annu. Rev. Neurosci. 24(1), 1193–1216 (2001)
5. Vertolli, M.O., Davies, J.: Visual imagination in context: Retrieving a coherent set of labels with Coherencer. In: West, R., Stewart, T. (eds.) 12th International Conference on Cognitive Modeling. Carleton University, Ottawa (2013)
6. Vertolli, M.O., Davies, J.: Coherence in the visual imagination: Local hill search outperforms Thagard's connectionist model. In: 36th International Conference of the Cognitive Science Society. Cognitive Science Society, Quebec (2014)
7. Jones, M.N., Mewhort, D.J.K.: Representing word meaning and order information in a composite holographic lexicon. Psychol. Rev. 114, 1–37 (2007)
8. Breault, V., Ouellet, S., Somers, S., Davies, J.: SOILIE: A computational model of 2D visual imagination. In: West, R., Stewart, T. (eds.) 12th International Conference on Cognitive Modeling. Carleton University, Ottawa (2013)
9. Vertolli, M.O., Breault, V., Ouellet, S., Somers, S., Gagné, J., Davies, J.: Theoretical assessment of the SOILIE model of the human imagination. In: 36th International Conference of the Cognitive Science Society. Cognitive Science Society, Quebec (2014)
10. Von Ahn, L., Liu, R., Blum, M.: Peekaboom: a game for locating objects in images. In: SIGCHI Conference on Human Factors in Computing Systems, pp. 55–64. ACM (2006)
11. Byrne, M.D.: How many times should a stochastic model be run? An approach based on confidence intervals. In: West, R., Stewart, T. (eds.) 12th International Conference on Cognitive Modeling. Carleton University, Ottawa (2013)

Author Index